THE COMPLETE BOOK OF HOME BAKING

By the same author

THE COMPLETE BOOK OF DESSERTS

The Complete Book of Home Baking

BY ANN SERANNE

FABER AND FABER, 24 RUSSELL SQUARE, LONDON

First published in 1970
by Faber and Faber Limited
24 Russell Square London WC1
Printed in Great Britain by
Latimer Trend & Co. Ltd Whitstable
All rights reserved

SBN : 571 09112 1

Copyright © 1950 by Doubleday & Company Inc

Grateful acknowledgment is made to the Wheat Flour Institute, Chicago, for the following pictures: Steps in molding yeast bread, Cushions, Bowknots, Kolacky, Bubble Loaf, Apple Coffeecake, Crumble Coffeecake, Honey Twist, Stollen.

Grateful acknowledgment is made to the General Foods Corporation for these pictures: Butterscotch Biscuits, Biscuit Bunnies, Apple Dumplings, One-egg Cakes, Ribbon Cake, Angel Food, Cherry Jelly Roll, Squares of Angel Food, Sweetheart Cake, Woolly Lamb, Petits Fours, Cupcakes, Sweetheart Petits Fours, Fig-filled Cookies, Brownies, Holiday Cake, Flower Cake, Strawberry Shortcake, Cookies, Fruitcake, Deep-dish Peach Pie, Fresh Cherry Pie, Old-time Tarts, Open Peach Pie, Chocolate Cream Pie and Tarts.

WITH THANKS TO KATY AND JACK

"GIVE US THIS DAY OUR DAILY BREAD"

The art of baking, as we know baking today in its many forms, is so synonymous with the baking of bread down through the centuries and throughout the countries of the world that it is difficult to dissociate them in one's mind.

Any combination of flour and liquid which makes a batter or a dough and is subsequently baked in the oven or atop the stove is technically bread, and bread is many things to many men.

Bread means the crunch of smooth golden crust as the knife cuts through a warm loaf and a small boy reaching for the butter and the jam; it means hot spicy gingerbread and cinnamon buns and the fragrance of a sunny kitchen; it means fruit-filled coffeecakes, delicate pastries, crisp cookies – in fact everything that is comfortable, homelike, and full of flavor.

America has borrowed profusely from other countries. Regional foods such as Boston brown bread, Southern corn bread, pone, and hoecakes contribute only the slightest thread to the warp and woof of our baking formulae and techniques.

Sweet breads came to us from Greece, Portugal, and Spain; poppy-seed crescents from Czechoslovakia; crumpets, fruitcakes, and tea rings from England; oat and potato cakes from Scotland; kuchens, stollens, and pumpernickel from Germany; gingerbread from Holland; wheatcakes from India; blinis, blintzes, and sour rye from Russia; strudels from Austria and Hungary; gâteaux, petits fours, croissants, brioches, and babas from France. All these and many more add up to one word – BREAD. What other single syllable in the English language can say so much?

Bread also means wheat. And it was the Egyptians who first grew wheat in vast quantities along the magically fertile banks of the Nile. The walls of Egyptian tombs brought to life the history of a civilization which the corrosion of four thousand years failed to destroy. Arduous hours of carving in stone show the Egyptian farmer sowing seeds in the black, moist, alluvial soil, harvesting the sun-ripened stalks; binding the bulging sheaves and threshing the golden grain – grain that was ground into wheat, moistened with water, and baked in cone-shaped ovens. Only the baking differed from that of prehistoric man, who cooked his mash of bruised grain and water on flat stones heated in the glowing embers of his fire.

But one day occidental man discovered the miracle of fermentation – a miracle which raised the Egyptians above all other peoples of the ancient world. No other food before or since has had such an influence on men and nations. Civilization itself was nourished and grew to manhood on bread.

To Americans bread means raised bread – bread made light and tender by the leavening action of yeast, by baking powder, by soda and sour cream, by air whipped into egg whites or folded between layers of rich dough. Let us deal first with yeast breads.

A.S.

vi	PREFACE
xiii	PUBLISHER'S NOTE
xiv	CONVERSION TABLES

1	**1. YEAST BREADS**
10	PLAIN AND VARIETY BREADS
20	SWEET ROLLS AND BREADS, TEA RINGS, KUCHENS, AND STOLLEN
56	YEAST EGG BREADS, BRIOCHES, AND BABAS
65	YEAST DOUGHNUTS AND PANCAKES
72	**2. QUICK BREADS**
73	BAKING POWDER BISCUITS, DUMPLINGS, AND COBBLERS
83	MUFFINS
88	BAKING POWDER BREADS AND COFFEECAKES
98	CORN BREADS
105	DOUGHNUTS
110	FRITTERS

115	PANCAKES
124	WAFFLES

3. CAKES

129	
131	BUTTER CAKES
145	ANGEL FOOD, SPONGE, AND CHIFFON CAKES
155	DESSERTS FROM GÉNOISE OR SPONGECAKE
159	FRUITCAKES
170	CHEESE CAKES
174	JIFFY EASY-MIX CAKES
179	TORTES
188	LITTLE CAKES AND PETITS FOURS
194	CAKE DECORATING

4. COOKIES

204	
206	BASIC COOKIES
210	SUGAR COOKIES
216	CHOCOLATE COOKIES
221	OATMEAL COOKIES
224	GINGER AND SPICE COOKIES
230	FRUIT AND NUT COOKIES
239	MACAROONS AND KISSES
242	COOKIES FROM OTHER LANDS
249	CHRISTMAS AND OTHER HOLIDAY COOKIES

5. PIES, PASTRIES, AND PUDDINGS

252	
259	TWO-CRUST PIES
266	ONE-CRUST PIES
275	FRUIT-FILLED TORTES
279	CREAM AND CUSTARD PIES
288	MERINGUE PIES
290	CHIFFON PIES
297	DEEP-DISH PIES
300	INDIVIDUAL PIES, TARTS, AND TURNOVERS
309	A FEW BAKED PUDDINGS

313	**6. FINE PASTRIES**
313	PÂTE A CHOUX
315	PÂTE FEUILLETÉE
321	HUNGARIAN PUFF PASTRY
323	SWEDISH OR DANISH PASTRY
329	STRUDELS
337	**7. FROSTINGS, FILLINGS, SAUCES**
337	DECORATIVE FROSTINGS
338	UNCOOKED BUTTER FROSTINGS
340	FONDANT FROSTINGS
342	CREAMY COOKED FROSTINGS
346	MERINGUE FROSTINGS
348	FILLINGS
353	SAUCES
356	**APPENDIX**
356	BAKED PRODUCTS IN YOUR HOME FREEZER
361	RULES FOR SUCCESSFUL BAKING
362	EQUIPMENT
363	INDEX

ILLUSTRATIONS

following page 76

Yeast Breads

STEPS IN KNEADING YEAST DOUGH
RAISING AND PUNCHING DOWN YEAST DOUGH
STEPS IN MOLDING YEAST BREAD
PARKER HOUSE ROLLS
PAN ROLLS
CLOVERLEAF ROLLS
CRESCENTS
BUTTERFLIES
CUSHIONS
FAN TANS
CLOVERLEAF, FAN TAN, AND CRUSTY ROLLS
TRIPLE DECKERS
CROSSETTES
TWO-IN-ONE TWISTS
BOWKNOTS
CINNAMON PINWHEELS
CINNAMON TWISTS
KOLACKY
SWEDISH TEA RING
BUBBLE LOAF
APPLE COFFEECAKE
CRUMBLE COFFEECAKE
HONEY TWIST

following page 172

OLD-FASHIONED DESSERT BREAD
FROSTED FRUIT LOAF
STOLLEN

Quick Breads
APPLE DUMPLINGS
BUTTERSCOTCH BISCUITS
BISCUIT BUNNIES

Cakes
VARIATIONS OF ONE-EGG CAKE
VARIATIONS OF ONE-EGG CAKE
ANGEL FOOD
RIBBON CAKE
CHERRY JELLY ROLL
SQUARES OF ANGEL FOOD
SWEETHEART CAKE
WOOLLY LAMB
PETITS FOURS
CUPCAKES
SWEETHEART PETITS FOURS

following page 268
HOLIDAY CAKE
FLOWER CAKE
STRAWBERRY SHORTCAKE
FRUITCAKES

Cookies
BROWNIES
FIG-FILLED COOKIES
REFRIGERATOR, DROPPED, AND ROLLED COOKIES
CHOCOLATE AND VANILLA PINWHEELS

Pies and Pastries
DEEP-DISH PEACH PIE
FRESH CHERRY PIE
OPEN PEACH PIE
OLD-TIME TARTS
CHOCOLATE CREAM PIE AND TARTS

PUBLISHER'S NOTE

No attempt has been made to adapt this edition for the English (or rather non-American) cook as it is felt that although some of the terms used may not be those to which she is accustomed, their meaning is generally clear. The notes and tables that follow will enable her to use the recipes without difficulty. The measures used throughout the book are standard American cup measures and it is now possible to buy these for a few shillings; at the time of going to press they are obtainable from Harrods Ltd., Knightsbridge, London, S.W.1 and many other stores throughout the country. Use of such measures is strongly recommended for the sake of simplicity and accuracy; but the measuring tables can, of course, be used as an alternative guide.

AMERICAN COOKING TERMS	ENGLISH EQUIVALENTS
American cheese	Cheddar
Baking soda	Bicarbonate of Soda
Biscuit	Scone
Brownies	Dark coloured biscuits
Brown sugar	Soft moist sugar *not* demerara
Confectioners' sugar	Icing sugar
Cornstarch	Cornflour
Drawn butter	Melted butter
Farina	Semolina
Farola	Fine semolina
Graham flour	100% wholemeal flour
Graham crackers	Digestive biscuits
Grits	Hulled and coarsely ground corn or other meal
Gumbo	Okra
Heavy cream	Double cream
Kisses	Small meringues
Light cream	Single cream
Marguerite	Salty biscuit, covered with icing and nuts
Molasses	Black treacle
Muffins—*see below*	
Pancakes	Flapjacks or griddle scones
Pecans	Walnuts
Pie	Open tart
Raisin	Sultana
Shortening	Butter or margarine
Soft shortening	Trex or Spry *not* lard
Spoon bread	Type of soufflé, made with cornmeal
Sultana	Raisin
Zwieback crumbs	Rusk crumbs

Muffins: American muffins bear no resemblance to English muffins and there is, in fact, no English equivalent. Small dariole moulds can be used instead of muffin tins, which are unobtainable in this country.

ANGLO-AMERICAN COOKING TERMS

FATS

Butter and margarine: these may be used interchangeably. If lard or other cooking fats are used instead, reduce the amount by about one-eighth and add extra salt, e.g. instead of 4 oz butter, use 3½ oz cooking fat and an extra ¼ teaspoon of salt.

Soft shortening: use only the homogenized cooking fats such as 'Trex', 'Spry', etc. Never substitute ordinary lard when 'soft shortening' is specified.

Oils: do not use olive oil, unless this is especially asked for, but some other vegetable oil, such as peanut oil.

FLOUR

Many American cake recipes ask for a special cake flour, e.g. 'all-purpose', 'enriched'. In this case use the best quality plain white flour available and only three and a half ounces for every four ounces specified.

Graham flour: 100 per cent wholewheat flour.

RAISING AGENTS

When following an American recipe it is advisable to take one of the following precautions:

either use 1½ times the amount of baking powder specified in the recipe;

or sprinkle the specified amount over the mixture before the last few strokes of mixing, then bake immediately.

SUGARS

Use caster sugar when white sugar is specified.

Confectioners' sugar: icing sugar.

Molasses: use black treacle.

Maple syrup: this can occasionally be bought in this country. Unless it is particularly required for its distinctive flavour golden syrup can be used.

Brown sugar: soft moist brown sugar, *not* demerara.

Golden syrup can usually be substituted for corn syrup, sorghum, etc.

CHOCOLATE

Usually unsweetened chocolate is required in U.S. recipes.

1 square of chocolate: 1 oz = ¾ oz cocoa + ¼ oz fat.

MISCELLANEOUS

Yeast: When asked for one cake of compressed yeast use two-thirds of an ounce of fresh yeast or the equivalent of this in dried yeast.
Gelatine: 1 envelope = ⅓ oz ordinary gelatine.

MIXING

Methods of mixing are fairly standardized although the Americans make more use of the quick-mix methods than is usual in Britain. It is also quite possible to meet Americans who have never made a cake by hand but always with a mixer. Thus a recipe that asks for "two minutes' beating" means an electrical mixer is used for this length of time. When beating by hand, 150 strokes are the equivalent of one minute of beating in a mixer.

SIZES OF TINS OR PANS

These are standardized in America. Those in common use have the following measurements:
Bread tin: 9 ins. by 5 ins. by 3 ins. deep.
Square pan: 9 ins. by 9 ins. by 2 ins. deep.
Oblong pan: 13 ins. by 9 ins. by 2 ins. deep.
Round layer pan: 8 ins. by 1¼ ins. deep or 9 ins. by 2 ins. deep.

AMERICAN CAN SIZES

8 oz.: 1 cup
No. 1: 2 cups or 16 oz.

Picnic: 1¼ cups or 10 oz.
No. 2: 2½ cups or 20 oz.

OVEN TEMPERATURES

Oven	°F	°C	Gas Mark
Very cool	250 – 275	121 – 135	¼ – ½
Cool	300	149	1 – 2
Warm	325	163	3
Moderate	350	177	4
Fairly hot	375 – 400	191 – 204	5 – 6
Hot	425	218	7
Very hot	450 – 475	232 – 246	8 – 9

N.B. To convert Centigrade temperatures to Fahrenheit, multiply by 9, divide by 5 and then add 32. Conversely, to turn Fahrenheit temperature into Centigrade, subtract 32, multiply by 5 and divide by 9.

THE METRIC SYSTEM

Comparative ounce/gram weights.
(All weights to nearest whole figure.)

0·035 oz.	=1 gram	8¾ oz.	=250 grams
1 oz.	=28 grams	9 oz.	=255 ,,
2 oz.	=57 ,,	10 oz.	=284 ,,
3 oz.	=85 ,,	11 oz.	=312 ,,
3½ oz.	=100 ,,	12 oz.	=340 ,,
4 oz.	=113 ,,	13 oz.	=369 ,,
5 oz.	=142 ,,	14 oz.	=397 ,,
6 oz.	=170 ,,	15 oz.	=425 ,,
7 oz.	=198 ,,	16 oz.	=454 ,,
8 oz.	=227 ,,		(0·454 kilograms)
		17½ oz.	=500 ,,

N.B. 1 kilogram = 2·2 lb.

Comparative British Imperial pint/litre capacity.

½ pint	=0·28 litre	½ litre	=0·88 pint
¾ pint	=0·43 ,,		(generous ¾ pint)
1 pint	=0·57 ,,	¾ litre	=1·32 pints
1¼ pints	=0·71 ,,	1 litre	=1·76 ,,
1½ pints	=0·85 ,,	1¼ litres	=2·20 ,,
1¾ pints	=0·99 ,,	1½ litres	=2·64 ,,
2 pints	=1·14 litres	1¾ litres	=3·08 ,,
2½ pints	=1·42 ,,	2 litres	=3·52 ,,
3 pints	=1·70 ,,	2½ litres	=4·40 ,,
3½ pints	=1·99 ,,	3 litres	=5·28 ,,
		3½ litres	=6·16 ,,

N.B. 1 gallon (8 pints) = 4·55 litres.

1 litre = 0·22 gallon
10 litres = 2·2 gallons

1 decilitre = 3½ fl. oz.
5·6 decilitres = 20 fl. oz. (1 pint)
1·8 centilitres = 1 tablespoonful
0·6 centilitres = 1 teaspoonful

AMERICAN MEASURES

American pint = 16 fl. oz.
American standard cup = 8 fl. oz. (American ½ pint)
American tablespoonful = ·50 fl. oz. (15·0 ccs)
American teaspoonful = ·16 fl. oz. (5·0 ccs)
N.B. There are approx. 25 British tablespoonfuls of water in an American pint.

COMPARATIVE MEASURES

American cup (8 fl. oz. capacity)	Weight in ounces Approximate	Weight in grams Approximate
Butter, margarine, lard	8	227
Suet, shredded	4	120
Cheddar cheese, grated	4	113
Cream, double	8	236
Milk, condensed	11	306
Milk, evaporated	9	255
Bread-crumbs—fresh	1	28
Bread-crumbs—dry	4	113
Rice	6½	182
Flour—plain, self-raising	4	113
Currants	5	142
Raisins—seedless	6	164
Raisins—stoned	5	142
Dates, stoned, and chopped peel	6	178
Cherries, glacé	7	198
Almonds, whole and blanched	6	152
Walnuts, halved	4	100
Sugar—granulated, caster	7	198
Sugar—icing	4½	128
Syrups and honey	11½	328

THE COMPLETE BOOK OF HOME BAKING

1. Yeast Breads

Yeast bread, that ancient and universal food, is the largest single item in the daily diet of families in many parts of the world. It is eaten at almost every meal and for between-meal snacks.

The availability, variety, perfection, and economy of commercial breads in America today has made the baking of bread in individual households almost a lost art.

A woman's skill as a homemaker was once judged by the lightness, flavor, and aroma of the bread she baked. That day has passed forever. Modern woman is unlikely to return *en masse* to "bread day," but for an occasional treat a home-baked loaf hot from the oven will be the more appreciated because of its rarity and will satisfy the longing of those who can recall the pleasurable memory of the fragrant loaves that Grandmother took from the big, comfortable stove in her cozy kitchen.

Perhaps today's housewife will see the value of making a quantity of refrigerator dough, removing each day only the amount necessary for fresh, hot dinner rolls, for a Sunday breakfast fruit-filled coffeecake, or for an afternoon tea ring. The variety of sweet rolls, buns, cakes, and kuchens that can be made from a single basic recipe is endless.

If one does not want to bother about the mysteries of yeast, yeast doughs, and yeast batters, these same results can be achieved from a package of one of the many hot roll mixes within reach on the grocery shelf today.

YEAST

More than a thousand years before the birth of Christ the Egyptians and Babylonians attributed the art of fermentation to the wisdom and grace of the god Osiris. Bread as well as wine and cheese—"blessed symbols of peace and plenty"—would never have been discovered or produced in quantity for the nurture of mankind, had it not been for the phenomena of the living yeast cell.

Yeast is a minute fungus which grows by sending off buds to form new plants, and by forming spores which may also become new plants. It transforms a dough into the delicate, porous substance we call bread and gives to the bread its characteristic fragrance and flavor.

As the yeast grows it gives off carbon dioxide gas, which expands the elastic cell walls of the gluten in the flour and thereby makes the dough "rise." It also gives off alcohol which may develop into acetic acid, causing the dough to become sour if the growth is allowed to continue too long. The alcohol is driven off by the heat of the baking.

Leavened bread was made for many years by mixing a portion of leftover yeast dough with a new batch. Even today, in some parts of the country, there still exists the friendly custom of borrowing a cup of "sour dough" from a neighbor.

If the supply of homemade yeast or yeast starter ran out, salt-rising bread was made instead, the fermentation being started from the "wild yeast" in the air. This bread has a distinctive flavor and texture and is greatly admired by those who have developed a taste for it.

Fortunately for the modern homemaker, yeast in either compressed or dry form is readily available.

Yeast must be fresh and active.

Compressed yeast is very perishable and should not be kept longer than a week in the refrigerator. The plants are alive and active and start to grow immediately on contact with food, warmth, moisture, and air. When fresh, it is a tan-gray in color, moist and practically odorless. It should break with a clean edge. If it is dry, sour-smelling, or streaked with dark gray, it must not be used.

Dry yeast will keep for several weeks on the pantry shelf, since the plants are asleep and will not become active until revived in water. It remains in good condition even longer if kept in a cool place. Dry yeast must be dissolved in ¼ cup or more of lukewarm water before it is used.

The contents of one package of dry yeast, when dissolved according to the directions on the package, may be used in place of one yeast cake.

AMOUNT OF YEAST   From 1 to 2 per cent of the weight of the flour is usually the amount of yeast necessary to make a dough rise. This means 1 to 2 cakes (or envelopes) of yeast for every 6 to 8 cups of flour. Quick-rising, refrigerator, or very rich doughs require more yeast. The standard amount for these doughs is often doubled, and sometimes tripled.

Under favorable conditions of moisture, heat, and food, yeast multiplies rapidly.

MOISTURE   Moisture may be supplied by water, milk, potato water, or a mixture of any or all of these. Many varieties of bread and rolls, such as French or Vienna breads and hard rolls, are made with water. Breads made with milk are more nourishing and flavorful and are inclined to stay moist longer. Potato water adds an attractive flavor and also helps keep the loaf moist.

Milk or potato water should first be scalded and then cooled to lukewarm. This scalding makes the dough easier to handle and destroys certain bacteria which might cause the dough to sour. It also improves the texture and flavor of the bread.

HEAT   Yeast is destroyed by very high or very low temperatures. The temperature at which yeast ferments and the dough develops most satisfactorily is between 75° and 85° F. This means that the room in which you work, the temperature of the flour, and the temperature of the liquid should all be about 80° F., making a sum total of 240° F. Naturally the only sure way to know the temperature of these three factors is to use a small, inexpensive thermometer.

In the average home kitchen it is quite likely, unless the flour is stored in a storage room, that the temperature of the kitchen and the temperature of the flour will be the same. Some people warm the flour in the warming oven, but the best way to adjust the temperature of the dough is to vary the temperature of the liquid.

TO MAKE A DOUGH THAT IS 80° F.

If the temperature of the room is	80°	70°	90°
and the temperature of the flour is	80°	70°	90°
the temperature of the liquid should be	80°	100°	60°
TOTAL	240°	240°	240°

If no thermometer is available, the best way to judge the temperature of the liquid is to place a drop on the inside of the wrist. If there is no sensation of either warmth or coolness, it is between 80° and 85° F., or lukewarm.

When it is necessary to adjust the temperature of the dough by any severe change in the temperature of the liquid (over 85° F. or below 75° F.), it is important to remember to add the softened yeast to the liquid *only after* the temperature of the liquid has been reduced or increased by the addition of some of the flour.

FOOD *Flour* is the chief ingredient in all breads. It is the gluten in wheat flour that enables the batter or dough to hold the leavening gas produced by the fermentation of the yeast.

There are two basic kinds of wheat flour: soft wheat flour, which feels as smooth as satin, and hard wheat flour, which feels somewhat granular. They both make good bread, but of different qualities. Soft wheat flour makes a finer-grained bread. Hard wheat flour makes a more porous bread of greater volume. Hard wheat flour also requires more liquid than soft wheat flour to make a pliable dough.

Commerical bakers use a bread flour especially milled for their use from hard wheat because they require a strong gluten dough that will hold up under severe mechanical manipulation. Most homemakers, however, will find that an all-purpose flour will fulfill their baking requirements very satisfactorily.

Sugar is quick food for yeast and adds flavor to the bread. It is also partly responsible for the golden color of the crust. If the dough does not contain enough sugar the yeast will use it all in making carbon dioxide and alcohol, and the bread will bake without browning. On the other hand, doughs containing a large amount of sugar must be baked in a moderate oven or they may brown too quickly.

One tablespoon sugar for every 2 cups flour is the standard amount used for plain bread. Sweet bread and rolls contain larger amounts. Too much sugar, however, retards the activity of the yeast, and therefore a longer rising period is necessary, or a greater quantity of yeast is used.

Shortening lubricates the gluten meshwork of the dough so that it can expand smoothly and easily. It also makes the bread rich and tender, improves the flavor, increases the volume and keeping qualities, and aids in the browning. Vegetable shortening, margarine, lard, and oils are frequently used in place of butter.

One teaspoon of shortening for every 2 cups flour is the minimum amount used for plain bread and rolls.

Salt gives flavor to bread and plays a part in conditioning the gluten so that the dough expands smoothly. It also tends to stabilize the fermentation process.

One teaspoon salt for each 2 cups flour is the usual proportion.

Eggs added to bread doughs make rolls and fancy breads of delicate structure with a flaky crust. They are responsible for the rich flavor and color of the ever-popular French egg bread, or brioche.

METHODS OF MIXING AND RAISING DOUGH

There are two traditional methods for making yeast breads.

THE PLAIN DOUGH OR SHORT METHOD The dough is completed in one mixing. All the ingredients are combined to make a soft dough which is kneaded to satin smoothness and set to rise in a warm place (75°–85° F.) until doubled in bulk. It is then punched down and divided into loaves or formed into rolls. These again must be allowed to rise before baking.

THE SPONGE OR LONG METHOD The liquid and yeast are combined with just enough flour to make a thin batter. This batter is covered and placed in a warm place for several hours or overnight to become porous and bubbly and "like a sponge." Then the sugar, salt, shortening, and enough flour are added to make a dough that can be kneaded. The kneaded dough is allowed to rise until doubled in bulk. It is then punched down, shaped, and again allowed to double in bulk before it is baked.

This method has the advantage of using less yeast and the disadvantage of requiring attention over a longer period of time. The longer fermentation gives a slightly different flavor in the baked product but tends to weaken the gluten structure. In general, when using the sponge method it is advisable to use hard wheat flour.

STEPS IN MAKING YEAST BREAD

MIXING Both dry and compressed yeast should be softened in a little lukewarm water (80°–85° F.) and allowed to stand for 10 minutes before using, to allow the yeast cells to separate, swell, and become active. They can then begin their work as soon as they are added to the dough.

There are various methods of mixing a dough. The liquid, salt, sugar, and shortening may be added to the flour, or the flour may be added to the liquid which has been combined with the sugar, salt, and shortening. The exact amount of flour can never be given, as different flours in different climates absorb different amounts of moisture. Flour can be beaten into the liquid until the dough is stiff enough to be turned out on a floured board. More flour can then be worked into the dough with the hands until it becomes the proper consistency for kneading.

KNEADING Kneading thoroughly mixes the flour and liquid, and makes the dough more elastic, thus holding safely the gas bubbles manufactured by the yeast in the gluten network. A poorly mixed dough will break down and allow the escape of the bubbles.

Fold the dough over toward you on itself and press down and away from you with the heels of both hands. Give the dough a quarter turn and repeat the process until the dough feels smooth, satiny, and elastic. From 5 to 10 minutes kneading is generally required to make a good dough. Doughs made from hard wheat flour require more kneading than those made from all-purpose or soft wheat flour.

Flour should be used sparingly during kneading. If too much flour is worked in, the dough will become stiff. The resulting bread will be coarse-textured and tough.

BEATING Not all yeast doughs need kneading. Many soft doughs used for a variety of small breads, rolls, coffeecakes, and sweet breads may be thoroughly mixed by beating.

RAISING When the dough has been kneaded, shape it into a smooth ball and place it in a warm, lightly greased bowl. Brush the surface of the dough lightly with melted shortening so that it can stretch as the dough rises. Cover the bowl lightly with a clean towel. Do not cover tightly, as the yeast needs air as well as moisture, warmth, and food in order to grow. Place the bowl in a warm place (80°–85° F.) away from drafts until it has doubled in bulk.

This is a general rule which applies nicely for most all-purpose flours. For soft wheat flour the rule should be until almost doubled in bulk. With some hard wheat flours, the dough should be allowed to increase in volume as much as two and a half or even three times.

To test a sufficiently risen dough, press two fingers deeply into the dough, and withdraw them quickly. If the dough has risen enough, a deep depression will remain; if the depression disappears quickly, the dough should be allowed to rise more.

Rising time depends greatly on the temperature of the dough, the atmospheric conditions, the amount of yeast in the dough, the richness of the dough, and the kind of flour used. In general, doughs made with 1 yeast cake and 2 cups liquid will double in bulk in 3 hours. Each subsequent rising requires less time. The rising time may be hastened by increasing the quantity of yeast, but care must be taken not to overdo it, or the bread will have a very "yeasty" flavor which is objectionable to many palates. Two yeast cakes to each 2 cups liquid will speed up rising time without giving it too potent a yeast flavor.

Rising time may be hastened by greater heat (90° F.) or by placing the bowl containing the dough over hot water. The longer process of fermentation, however, and the slow rising is preferable for tastier, better-flavored, and better-textured bread. If the fermentation is too fast there is not enough time for the necessary changes, which are largely responsible for the delicious flavor of homemade breads, to take place.

Frequently recipes call for a double rising of the dough before it is shaped into loaves or rolls. Actually it may be allowed to rise several times without detrimental effect. It must, however, be punched down as soon as it reaches its full rise, as risen dough sours very easily if allowed to stand too long, and the bread made from overraised dough will have large holes throughout.

PUNCHING DOWN This is done by pushing the fist into the center of the dough and folding the edges toward the center. A dough made from soft or all-purpose wheat flour may be immediately shaped into loaves or rolls. In general, doughs made from hard wheat flour should be allowed to rise a second time, but a second rising will not be harmful to any dough, regardless of the kind of flour used.

For a second rising, turn the dough in the bowl so that the smooth side of the ball is up, cover again, set in a warm place, and allow it to rise again until doubled. This time a gentle finger test which leaves a slight indentation tells you when the dough is sufficiently risen to bake. The punching down breaks up the large gas pockets and makes available to the yeast plants a new supply of oxygen.

SHAPING INTO LOAVES When the dough is ready for shaping into loaves, punch it down and cut it into as many parts as there are to be loaves. Form each part into a smooth ball, cover lightly with a clean towel, and allow to rest for 10 minutes. This brief resting period makes the dough more responsive to manipulation.

To mold a loaf, first flatten a ball of dough with the palms of the hands into a flat oblong. Fold the dough in half lengthwise and flatten again. Next stretch it to elongate it until it is about three times as long as the bread pan in which it is to be baked. Bring the ends to the center, overlapping, and press firmly together. Fold lengthwise in thirds and seal the edges by pressing them down firmly until they remain in place. Roll dough over and place the molded loaf in a greased bread pan, sealed edge down, brush the surface lightly with melted fat, cover pan lightly with a clean cloth, and set in a warm place (80°–85° F.) to rise until it has doubled in bulk, or until rising is complete.

BAKING The oven should be preheated to the correct temperature before the bread is put in to bake.

Baking stops the fermentation of the yeast, evaporates the alcohol which develops during fermentation, and changes some of the starch into dextrins.

Bread and plain rolls should be placed in a hot oven. During the first 10 minutes of baking, the leavening gas expands rapidly and the gluten cells stretch to accommodate it. Then the heat gradually sets the gluten cells. Since the heat of the oven first reaches that part of the loaf which extends above the pan, this portion rises and expands more quickly than the part protected by the pan.

If the bread has not risen sufficiently before baking, the baked bread will be smaller in volume than that of a completely raised dough. If the bread has risen too much, the gluten strands are already so thinly stretched that they break when the heat of the oven expands the gas, the gas escapes, and the bread falls.

Pans should be placed in the center of the oven and not touching the sides of the oven or each other, to allow for circulation of heat and even baking.

BAKING TEMPERATURES

Bread—for deep brown crust—	425°–400° F. throughout baking period
for light crust—	425° F. for 15 minutes 350° for remainder of baking time
Plain Rolls	425° F. throughout baking period
Sweet Rolls	375°–350° F. throughout baking period

Baking times depend upon the size of the loaves as well as the temperature. A regulation-size loaf usually requires from 50 minutes to 1 hour, and rolls from 15 to 25 minutes. Breads are baked when they shrink slightly from the sides of the pan and have a hollow sound when lightly thumped.

The characteristic crisp and glazed crust of French or Vienna bread and rolls is the result of baking at a high temperature in special ovens that are supplied with moist steam. The steam forms a coating of moisture on the surface, which gives the dough time to expand and to develop its crust. Unfortunately this kind of professional baking cannot be duplicated in the home. Somewhat similar results may be obtained by placing a flat pan of boiling water in the hot oven just before the bread is put in.

To increase crustiness, brush top of loaves with slightly beaten egg white 10 minutes before baking time is complete. On the other hand, if you wish a soft crust, brush the top of loaves with melted butter 10 minutes before baking is complete.

COOLING Bread and rolls should be removed from the pans as soon as they are taken from the oven and placed on wire cooling racks or across the edges of the baking pans, so the cool air can reach them on all sides. This prevents moisture from condensing and spoiling the crispness of the crust and the lightness of the inner bread.

For a shiny, tender crust, brush the loaves with warm water while still hot and cover them with a clean towel for a few minutes to allow them to steam slightly.

STORING BREAD

When thoroughly cooled, bread and rolls may be stored

in a clean breadbox or tin. Sterilize your breadbox at least once a week by washing it in hot sudsy water, scalding it with boiling water, and drying it well—if possible, in the sunshine. Wrapping individual loaves in wax paper preserves the freshness for a longer time. Highly spiced, fruit, or nut breads should be tightly wrapped in wax paper to prevent the flavors from penetrating plain loaves. Remove stale bread from the box, as it will take the moisture away from fresh loaves.

Keeping bread in the refrigerator in plastic refrigerator bags retains the fresh quality for the longest possible time.

TO FRESHEN BREAD AND ROLLS

Sprinkle with water and warm in a moderate oven or place in a dampened brown paper bag and place in a moderate oven until the bag is dry.

WHAT CONSTITUTES A GOOD LOAF OF BREAD?

Some insist on a thick, crisp crust, others want a crust that is soft and delicate. Some prefer a loose, open-textured inner bread, while still others like it fine-grained.

Let us settle for the standards set by the Wheat Flour Institute of Chicago—a wise and noble arbiter of all problems in home baking. I quote the words of Mrs. Clara Gebhard Snyder, director of the Institute:

"A good loaf is symmetrical in shape, good in volume and rich golden-brown in color. The entire loaf is brown, although the top may be somewhat deeper in color than the sides and bottom.

"The crumb is silky in appearance, uniformly creamy white in color, and reasonably fine and even in grain.

"Good bread *tastes* good. It has a somewhat bland flavor, yet at the same time the delicious, indescribable flavor of wheat."

BASIC RECIPE FOR PLAIN BREAD DOUGH AND METHOD IN DETAIL

There are a thousand and one recipes for plain bread dough. Almost every good "old-fashioned" housewife has her favorite which has been handed down in her family through the generations. It is always successful, and she swears by it as the only recipe. But just in case your great-grandmother did not pass her bread recipe along, here is a modern recipe, easy and as foolproof for the home kitchen as any in existence.

INGREDIENTS FOR 4 LOAVES
>2 cakes or packages yeast
>2 cups lukewarm water
>2 cups milk
>4 tablespoons sugar
>4 teaspoons salt
>4 tablespoons shortening
>12 cups sifted all-purpose flour

FOR 2 LOAVES, divide ingredients in half
FOR 6 LOAVES, add one half the recipe, except for yeast (2 is sufficient)
FOR 8 LOAVES, use twice the recipe, except for yeast (2 is sufficient as yeast works faster in larger doughs)
1 loaf = 1 dozen rolls or 1 coffee ring

METHOD
1. Soften the yeast in ½ cup of the lukewarm water.
2. Scald the milk and pour it into a large mixing bowl. Add sugar, salt, shortening, and the rest of the warm water (1½ cups). Cool to lukewarm (80°–85° F.).
3. Add 2 cups of the flour, stirring well, and then add the softened yeast. Add 4 more cups of the flour and beat with a wooden spoon until almost smooth and very elastic. The batter should sheet from the spoon.
4. Add the remaining flour to make a dough that is light but does not stick to the hands. More or less flour than is called for in the ingredients may be necessary to arrive at the exact dough, as flours vary a great deal in moisture and gluten content.
5. Turn out on a lightly floured board, cover, and allow to rest for 10 minutes. Then knead until the dough is smooth and elastic.
6. Shape the dough into a ball and place it in a lightly greased bowl. Brush the surface of the dough lightly with melted shortening, cover, and allow it to rise in a warm place (80°–85° F.) until doubled in bulk (about 2 hours).
7. Punch down, cover, and allow it to rise again until doubled in bulk (about 1 hour). If preferred, shape the dough into loaves after the first rising.
8. Divide the dough into 4 equal portions. Shape each part into a smooth ball, cover, and allow to rest for 10 minutes.
9. Shape each part into loaves. Place them in greased bread pans,

3½ ×7½ ×2¾ inches. The dough should fill the pans two thirds full. Cover with a damp cloth and allow the loaves to rise until doubled in bulk (about 1½ hours). The sides of the raised dough should reach the top of the pan, and the center should be well rounded above it.
10. Bake in a moderately hot oven (400° F.) for 50 minutes.

For greater detail in making bread, read the first part of this chapter.

BASIC RECIPE FOR PLAIN BREAD DOUGH—SPONGE METHOD

INGREDIENTS FOR 2 LOAVES

THE SPONGE
1 cake or package yeast
1 cup lukewarm water
1 tablespoon sugar
2 cups enriched flour

Soften the yeast in the lukewarm water. Add the sugar and then add the flour to form a thick batter, beating until smooth. Cover and allow to rise in a warm place (80°–85° F.) until very bubbly (about 1 hour).

THE DOUGH
1 cup milk
2 tablespoons sugar
2 teaspoons salt
2 tablespoons shortening
4 cups enriched flour

METHOD
1. Stir down the risen sponge.
2. Scald the milk, add sugar, salt, and shortening, and cool to lukewarm. Add to the sponge.
3. Add enough additional flour to make a soft dough, but one which does not stick to the hands. Turn out on lightly floured board and knead for 10 minutes, or until smooth and satiny.
4. Shape into ball and place in lightly greased bowl. Brush the surface of the dough lightly with melted shortening, cover, and allow to rise in a warm place (80°–85° F.) until doubled in bulk (about 2 hours).
5. Punch down, cover, and allow to rise again until doubled in bulk (about 1 hour).
6. Cut dough in half and shape each half into a ball. Cover and

allow to rest for 10 minutes.
7. Shape into loaves, place in greased bread pans, and allow to rise until doubled in bulk (about 1½ hours).
8. Bake in a hot oven (400° F.) for 50 minutes.

For greater detail in the making of bread, read the first part of this chapter.

Plain bread rolls, such as Parker House or cloverleaf, may be made with a plain bread dough. More frequently, however, these are made from a sweet dough. The method for forming these different rolls will be found in the section of this chapter devoted to rolls and sweet breads.

TO MAKE SWEET DOUGH OR COFFEE RINGS FROM PLAIN BREAD DOUGH

After the first rising, work into the dough with the hands
    2 eggs, well beaten
    ¼ cup melted shortening
    ½ cup sugar
    ¾ to 1 cup sifted all-purpose flour
or enough flour to make a dough that no longer sticks to your hands or to the mixing bowl. Then knead and allow it to rise at proper temperature until doubled in bulk (1½ hours). Punch down, divide into rolls, coffeecakes, or rings, and allow to rise again before baking.

FOR A COMBINATION OF PLAIN BREAD AND SWEET ROLLS

Make a quantity of dough sufficient for 4 loaves of bread. After the first rising, divide dough in half. Proceed with one half as for bread, shaping it into 2 loaves. To the other half add one half the ingredients listed above and follow the directions for a sweet dough. Makes 2 dozen sweet rolls or 1 dozen sweet rolls and 1 coffeecake.

VIENNA BREAD

Make Plain Bread Dough according to directions and shape it into long thin loaves. With kitchen scissors make gashes on top of the loaves about 3 inches apart and 1½ inches deep. Place the loaves several inches apart on a greased baking sheet and let them rise until they are doubled in bulk. Brush the tops with slightly beaten egg white and bake at 425° F. for 50 minutes. Remove them from the oven, brush the tops again with egg white, and sprinkle with salt and poppy or sesame seeds. Return the loaves to the oven for 10 minutes longer, or until the seeds are brown.

BUTTER BRAIDS

Divide enough Plain Bread Dough to make 1 large loaf into 6 ropes and make 2 braids, one a little smaller than the other. Place the smaller braid on top of the larger braid, tapering both at the ends. Brush the top with beaten egg, sprinkle with poppy seeds, let rise, and bake according to directions for plain bread.

BREAD STICKS

Roll out Plain Bread Dough ½ inch thick and cut it into strips ½ inch wide. Roll the cut pieces into long, pencillike strips and place on a greased baking sheet. Cover and allow the sticks to rise in a warm place until doubled in bulk. Brush with beaten egg, sprinkle with poppy seeds, if desired, and bake for 10 minutes at 425° F.

CRUSTY PLAIN WATER ROLLS OR BREAD (VIENNA TYPE)

INGREDIENTS FOR 2 DOZEN ROLLS

1 cake or package yeast
1 cup lukewarm water
1 tablespoon sugar
1 teaspoon salt
2 tablespoons melted shortening
2 egg whites, beaten
4 cups enriched flour

Soften the yeast in ¼ cup of the lukewarm water. To the rest of the water add the sugar, salt, and shortening. Add 1 cup of the flour and beat well. Add the softened yeast and the egg whites and mix thoroughly. Add sufficient flour to make a soft dough. Turn the dough out on a lightly floured board and knead until it is smooth and elastic (about 8 minutes). Shape into a smooth ball and place in a lightly greased bowl. Brush the surface lightly with melted shortening, cover, and allow it to rise in a warm place until doubled in bulk (about 2 hours). Punch down, cover, and allow to rise again until doubled in bulk (about 1 hour). Punch down and divide into small portions for rolls, or in half for 2 loaves.

Let rest for 10 minutes. Shape into round rolls and place 2 inches apart on a greased baking sheet; or shape into loaves and place in greased bread pans. Cover and allow to rise in a warm place until doubled in bulk (about 1½ hours). Bake rolls at 450° F. for 20 minutes. Bake loaves at 375° F. for 50 minutes. Place a large flat pan filled with boiling water in the bottom of the oven a few minutes before putting in the rolls or bread. Ten minutes before the baking time is complete, brush the tops with lightly beaten egg white.

BREAD VARIATIONS FROM BASIC RECIPES

After all the flour is mixed in, add the special ingredients and mix thoroughly. Then knead and proceed as for plain bread. You may wish to divide the dough into loaves and make different breads from each loaf.

NUT BREAD To each loaf add 1 cup coarsely chopped nuts.
DATE BREAD To each loaf add 1 cup cut-up dates.
RAISIN BREAD To each loaf add 1 cup raisins.
FRUIT AND NUT BREAD To each loaf add 1 cup chopped, dried fruit and ½ cup chopped nuts. Frost the warm baked loaf with confectioners' sugar which has been mixed to a paste with boiling water.
CRACKED WHEAT BREAD To each loaf add 2 tablespoons honey and 1 cup cracked wheat.
WHOLE WHEAT BREAD To each loaf add 4 tablespoons molasses and ¾ cup graham (whole wheat) flour.
RYE MOLASSES BREAD To each loaf add 2 tablespoons molasses, 2 tablespoons dark corn syrup, and ¾ cup rye flour. Bake at 400° F. for 40 minutes. One cup raisins may also be added, as well as ½ cup chopped nuts.

For the following specialty breads, make the indicated changes in the ingredients of the basic recipes.

BRAN BREAD Substitute 4 cups bran for 4 cups of the wheat flour. Additional wheat flour may be necessary to bring the dough to the correct consistency for kneading.
HONEY BREAD Use ¼ cup honey in place of the sugar.
BUTTERMILK BREAD Use ½ buttermilk or sour milk and ½ water for the liquid. Add 1 teaspoon soda to the first addition of flour.

SALT RISING BREAD

Salt rising bread has a disagreeable odor while it is rising and baking. This odor is diffused in the baking. It is never as light as other breads, but is close-grained and has a distinctive flavor. It dries out quickly, but it makes excellent toast.

INGREDIENTS FOR 2 LOAVES
 1 cup whole milk
 2 tablespoons sugar
 1½ teaspoons salt
 ⅓ cup white corn meal
 1 cup lukewarm water
 4¼ cups sifted all-purpose flour
 2 tablespoons melted shortening

Scald the milk, remove from the fire, and stir in 1 tablespoon of the sugar, the salt, and the corn meal. Mix thoroughly and place the mixture in a large fruit jar or pitcher. Cover the container and place it in a pan of water which is hot to the hand (120° F.). Allow it to stand in a warm place for 7 or 8 hours, or overnight, or until it has fermented.

Make a soft sponge by adding to the fermented mixture the water, 2 cups of the flour and the remaining sugar. Beat thoroughly, using an electric mixer if available. Place the sponge in the hot-water bath (120° F.) and allow it to rise until it is very light and full of bubbles. Turn the sponge into a large, warm mixing bowl and gradually stir in the remaining flour, or enough to make a fairly stiff dough which does not stick to the hands and can be kneaded. Knead for 10 minutes. Divide the dough in half, shape into loaves, and place in generously greased bread pans. Brush the loaves with melted shortening, cover the loaves with a light, clean towel, and allow them to rise in a warm place until the dough is twice its original size. Bake at 400° F. for 10 minutes, reduce oven temperature to 350° F., and bake for another 30 minutes.

SOUR DOUGH FRENCH BREAD

For some reason or other American homemakers have suddenly become interested in the making of sour dough French bread. It would be impossible to write a book on baking without including in it the method for this particular bread, even though it is the general opinion that it should be left to commerical bakers. The extreme refinement of the flour in America today makes it practically impossible for a housewife in her own kitchen to achieve a suitable starter, or to duplicate the final results produced in the bakery. If you still wish to attempt it, after this discouragement, go to your local baker and buy from him the hardest bread flour that he has, or better still, coax away from him a pound of sour dough French bread starter.

INGREDIENTS FOR 2 SMALL LOAVES

STARTER
1 cake or package yeast
2½ cups lukewarm water
1 tablespoon sugar
1 tablespoon salt
2 cups sifted enriched bread flour

Crumble the yeast in ½ cup lukewarm water and let stand for 10 minutes. Stir. Add remaining water, sugar, salt, and flour. Mix well. Allow to stand in a covered bowl for 3 days at room temperature (78°–80° F.). The container should be large enough to permit the starter to increase in height about 4 times without going over the top. Stir down daily. When ready to make the bread, measure into a bowl 1 cup starter. To the remaining starter add 1 cup lukewarm water, ½ cup flour, and 1 teaspoon sugar. Cover and allow it to stand until ready to make bread again.

DOUGH
1 cup starter
½ cup milk
2 tablespoons sugar
2 tablespoons shortening
2–3 cups sifted enriched bread flour

Scald the milk. Add the sugar and shortening and stir. Cool this mixture to lukewarm and add to the starter. Stir in the flour, adding more if necessary to make a medium dough. Turn out on a lightly floured board and knead for about 10 minutes. Place the dough in a greased bowl, brush the top lightly with melted shortening, cover, and allow it to rise in a warm place (80°–85° F.), free from drafts, until doubled in bulk (about 1½ hours). Punch down. Allow it to rise again until doubled in bulk (about 35 minutes). Punch down and allow to rest for about 10 minutes. Shape into loaves, place in small greased bread pans, cover with a clean towel, and allow the loaves to rise until doubled in bulk (about 1 hour). Bake in a moderate oven (400° F.) for about 30–40 minutes.

If a hard crust is desired, brush the tops of the loaves with a mixture of 1 slightly beaten egg white and 1 tablespoon water. Cover the pans with a damp cloth and allow to rise as directed. Place a large flat pan of boiling water in the preheated oven a few minutes before putting in the loaves. After 10 minutes in the oven, brush again with the egg-white mixture. After 20 minutes' baking, brush again.

SOUR DOUGH RYE BREAD

Make starter as above. Use rye flour in place of the enriched bread flour for the dough and add 1 tablespoon caraway seeds. Proceed as directed for Sour Dough French Bread. Bake at 375° F. for about 1 hour.

SWEDISH RYE BREAD

INGREDIENTS FOR TWO LOAVES

2 cups milk
1 teaspoon salt
3 tablespoons brown sugar
2 cakes or packages yeast
3 cups all-purpose flour
3 cups rye flour
1 tablespoon caraway seeds

Scald the milk, add salt and brown sugar, and cool to lukewarm (80°–85° F.). Add the yeast and dissolve thoroughly. Stir in the wheat flour and beat thoroughly. Then stir in the rye flour and a little more all-purpose flour, if necessary, to make a dough that does not stick to the hands. Turn out on a lightly floured board and knead until smooth and elastic. Place in a greased bowl, cover, and allow to rise in a warm place until doubled in bulk. Punch down, knead the caraway seeds into the dough, shape into loaves, place in greased pans, brush tops with melted butter, and allow to rise until doubled in bulk. Bake at 375° F. for 50 minutes.

SALLY LUNN BREAD

1 cup milk
½ cup butter
2 tablespoons sugar
2 eggs, slightly beaten
1 cake or package yeast
½ cup lukewarm water
4 cups sifted all-purpose flour
1 teaspoon salt

Scald the milk, add the butter and sugar, and let the mixture cool to lukewarm, then stir in the eggs. Dissolve the yeast in the lukewarm water and let it stand for 5 minutes. Sift the flour and salt into a mixing bowl and add the dissolved yeast. Stir in the milk mixture and beat the dough thoroughly. Cover with a clean towel and allow the dough to rise, in a warm place, until doubled in bulk. Toss the dough on a lightly floured board and knead until it is smooth, elastic, and not sticky to the hands. Shape the dough into 2 small loaves, place them in greased loaf pans, and brush the tops with melted butter. Place them in a warm place and allow them to rise until doubled in bulk. Bake in a moderate oven (350° F.) for about 40 minutes, or until the crust is golden brown. Serve hot, with butter and jam.

GARLIC BREAD

Cream ¼ pound butter with 1 clove garlic which has been mashed to a pulp. Slice a loaf of French bread almost to the bottom crust, leaving the slices still attached. Spread each slice with garlic butter. Brush the top with a little melted butter and place in a 400° F. oven for about 10 minutes, or until heated through and brown on top. Serve immediately.

HERB BREAD

Cream ¼ pound butter with 4 tablespoons chopped parsley and 2 tablespoons chopped chives. Slice a loaf of French bread as directed for Garlic Bread, spread each slice with the herb butter, and place in a 400° F. oven for about 10 minutes, or until heated through and brown on top. Serve very hot.

Other herb combinations are thyme-parsley, sage-savory-parsley, and tarragon-chives.

100 PER CENT WHOLE WHEAT BREAD

INGREDIENTS FOR 2 LOAVES

½ cup brown sugar
⅔ cup lukewarm water
2 cakes or packages yeast
2 teaspoons salt
2 cups milk, scalded
6½ cups unsifted whole wheat flour
2 tablespoons melted shortening

Stir 1 teaspoon of the sugar into the water, add the yeast, stir until it is thoroughly dissolved, and allow to stand for 10 minutes. Add the rest of the brown sugar and the salt to the hot milk and cool to lukewarm (80°–85° F.). Add the yeast mixture to the lukewarm milk mixture, stir in 3 cups of the flour and the melted shortening. Mix thoroughly. Add the remaining flour gradually, until you have a dough which does not stick to your hands. Turn onto a lightly floured board (use all-purpose flour for kneading and shaping) and knead for 10 minutes. Place in a greased bowl, grease top of dough lightly, cover with a clean cloth, and allow it to rise in a warm place until doubled in bulk. Place on a floured board again and divide in half. Allow the dough to rest for 10 minutes and then shape it into loaves. Grease the top of the loaves, place them in greased bread pans, cover, and allow to rise in a warm place until light and the rounded tops come well above the sides of the pans (about 1 hour). Bake at 400° F. for 10 minutes. Reduce oven temperature to 375° and bake for 40 minutes longer.

SWEET ROLLS AND BREADS

From one basic recipe a great variety of sweet breads and rolls in different forms may be made by simply changing the flavoring; by adding nuts, fruit, or spices. Dainty, light-as-a-feather, tasty sweet rolls are easy to make and determine the success of a meal probably more than any other single food.

Here are a few everyday rules:
1. Larger amounts of sugar and fat in sweet bread dough retard the action of the yeast, so larger amounts of yeast are necessary.
2. The dough should be kept softer than for plain bread—just as soft as can be handled without sticking.
3. The dough should be handled as lightly as possible when being shaped for the pans. The pastry board should be lightly dusted with flour; excess flour and too much kneading should be avoided, as they tend to yield a tough product.
4. The dough should never be allowed to become crusted over during the rising period. Keep it covered well at all times, but not smothered.
5. To have a light, fluffy texture, allow the dough to rise each time to fully double in bulk. Allow the rolls to rise in the pans until more than doubled.
6. In general, rolls with little sugar should be baked quickly in a hot oven (425° F.), and the temperature should be reduced after 5 minutes to 400° F. Sweeter rolls and coffeecakes require a moderate oven so that they do not brown too much before being fully

baked. Use an initial temperature of 375° F., reducing after 5 minutes to 350° F.

Crusty rolls should be baked rather slowly in a moderate oven (about 350° F.).

GLAZING AND DECORATING

Dainty decorative touches on sweet rolls add charm and please the sweet tooth.

GLAZING Most rolls, unless they are to be frosted on top, are glazed with milk, plain or sweetened with a little sugar; unbeaten egg white mixed with 2 tablespoons cold water; or slightly whipped egg yolk mixed with a little milk. Brush the tops of the rolls with glaze just before baking and again before taking them from the oven.

FROSTING A simple frosting for sweet rolls and coffeecake is made by adding a few tablespoons of hot milk or boiling water to 1 cup of confectioners' sugar and mixing it to a spreading consistency. Flavor with vanilla or almond extract or lemon. The frosting should not be too thick and should be applied while the rolls or cakes are still warm, but not hot.

GARNISHES Garnish sweet rolls with nuts, shredded coconut, candied fruit, candied fruit peel, or poppy seeds.

FILLINGS Depressions are sometimes made in the top of unbaked rolls, and these are then filled with a teaspoon of jam, jelly, marmalade, or candied fruit.

BASIC SWEET DOUGH

INGREDIENTS FOR 3 DOZEN ROLLS, 3 COFFEECAKES, OR 3 MEDUM-SIZED LOAVES

2 cakes or packages yeast
¼ cup lukewarm water
1 cup milk
½ cup sugar
1 teaspoon salt
½ cup shortening (part butter)
5 cups all-purpose flour
2 eggs, beaten

METHOD

Soften the yeast in the lukewarm water. Scald the milk, add the sugar, salt, and shortening, and cool to lukewarm (80°–85° F.). Add part of the flour to make a thick batter and mix well. Add the softened yeast and the eggs and beat thoroughly. Add enough additional flour to make a dough which is soft but does not stick to the hands. Turn out on a lightly floured board and knead until smooth and satiny. Place in a greased bowl, cover, and allow to rise in a warm place until doubled in bulk (about 1½ hours). Punch down and allow to rest for 10 minutes. Then shape into rolls, tea rings, or coffeecakes. Allow to rise until doubled (about 1 hour). Bake at 350° F. for 30 minutes for coffeecakes, 20–25 minutes for rolls.

BASIC WHOLE WHEAT SWEET DOUGH Substitute whole wheat flour for half the white flour.

REFRIGERATOR DOUGHS

Almost any yeast dough may be refrigerated, but some respond better to this treatment than others. Sweet doughs made with milk will keep about 4 days. Those made with water will keep an entire week. Bread doughs, which contain little sugar, can be kept only 3 days.

The low temperature of the refrigerator retards the activity of the yeast. When the dough is removed and allowed to become warm the yeast resumes its activity and the dough begins to rise again. However, unless the dough contains plenty of sugar and fat to feed the yeast plants during their retarded period the action may be partially or completely destroyed. The right temperature at which to store refrigerator doughs is between 45° and 50° F. A cool spot in your cellar may provide the perfect place. Test it with a thermometer. Damp cold is really better than the cold of the refrigerator, as it prevents the dough from drying out.

HOW TO STORE REFRIGERATOR DOUGH The surface of the dough should be brushed with melted shortening immediately after the dough is mixed. Cover and store it in the refrigerator, or other suitable place, for 2 hours, or until needed. When ready to use, punch down the dough and cut off as much as is needed for rolls or coffeecake and return the remainder of the dough to the refrigerator for further storage.

The dough may be allowed to come to room temperature before shaping, but since this takes several hours it is easier to shape the dough immediately. Even then it will take longer to rise, so be sure you allow plenty of time and permit the dough to fully double in bulk. The time will vary with the temperature of the dough and the room. In general, it will take rolls 2 hours and molded loaves of bread 4-5 hours to double in bulk.

BASIC REFRIGERATOR DOUGH

INGREDIENTS FOR 3 DOZEN ROLLS

    2 cakes or packages yeast
    ½ cup lukewarm water
    1½ cups milk
    ½ cup sugar
    2 teaspoons salt
    ½ cup shortening
    2 eggs, beaten
    5½ cups all-purpose flour

Soften the yeast in the lukewarm water. Scald the milk and add to it the sugar, salt, and shortening. Cool to lukewarm. Add 2 cups flour and mix thoroughly. Add the softened yeast and the eggs and beat well. Add enough additional flour to make a dough that is soft but not sticky. Turn out on lightly floured board and knead for 5 minutes, or until smooth and elastic. Grease the surface, wrap and place in the refrigerator, or place in a lightly greased bowl, cover and put in warm place to double in bulk. Punch down. Shape the desired amount of dough into rolls and allow to rise until doubled (about 1 hour). Form the remaining dough into a ball, brush the surface lightly with melted shortening, cover, and place in refrigerator. When more hot fresh rolls are wanted, remove the amount of dough needed from the refrigerator and mold immediately into desired shapes, or, if preferred, let the dough stand in a warm room for an hour before shaping. Place the shaped rolls on greased pans, allow to rise until doubled and bake at 400° F. for 20 minutes.

POTATO DOUGH (LENDS ITSELF WELL TO REFRIGERATION)

INGREDIENTS FOR 4 DOZEN ROLLS OR 4 COFFEECAKES

    1 cake or package yeast
    1½ cups lukewarm water
    ⅔ cup sugar
    1½ teaspoons salt
    ⅔ cup butter or a mixture of butter and other shortening
    2 eggs, well beaten
    1 cup lukewarm unseasoned mashed potatoes
    7-8 cups sifted all-purpose flour

Soften the yeast in ½ cup of the lukewarm water. To the remaining water add the sugar, salt, shortening, and 2 cups of the flour. Mix thoroughly. Add the softened yeast, the eggs, and the lukewarm mashed potatoes and beat well. Add enough additional flour to make a dough that is soft but not sticky. Turn out on a lightly floured board and knead for 5 minutes, or until smooth and elastic. To bake immediately, remove quantity of dough desired and follow the directions for raising, shaping, and baking. Round up the remainder, brush the surface lightly with melted shortening, cover, and store in the refrigerator until ready to use.

RICH POTATO DOUGH—SPONGE METHOD

INGREDIENTS FOR 4 DOZEN ROLLS

1 cake or package yeast
1 cup lukewarm water
1 cup unseasoned mashed potatoes
1 cup sugar
4 eggs, beaten
1 cup softened butter
1 teaspoon salt
6–7 cups all-purpose flour

Dissolve the yeast in the lukewarm water. Add the mashed potatoes and the sugar and let the mixture stand, covered lightly with a towel, in a warm place overnight.

Next day add the eggs, butter, and salt. Sift in the flour and mix with a spoon until it becomes difficult to stir. Then, with your hands, mix in more flour until you have a soft light dough. Roll out on a floured board about ½ inch thick and cut out small rounds with a floured cooky cutter. Place the rounds 1 inch apart on a buttered baking sheet, cover with a towel, and let stand in a warm place until they have doubled in bulk (about 2 hours). Bake in a hot oven (400° F.) for 10 minutes. Do not overbake. The dough or the cut-out rounds may be kept in the refrigerator or in a cool place for several days before baking, but then you must allow a longer time for them to rise (about 3 hours).

If you wish to refrigerate the shaped rolls, brush the tops with melted shortening, cover the baking sheet on which the rolls are placed with a towel and store in a cool place.

BASIC BEATEN BATTER

Beaten batters require no kneading, but whether or not this is an advantage is a moot point, since the batter requires thorough beating. It does, however, require less time both in the making and in the rising period. Beaten batters cannot be shaped into rolls. They can be spooned into muffin cups to make puff buns or can be used with various toppings to make delicious coffeecakes.

INGREDIENTS FOR 2 COFFEECAKES OR 2½ DOZEN ROLLS

    1 cake or package yeast
    ¼ cup lukewarm water
    1 cup milk
    ¼ cup sugar
    1 teaspoon salt
    ½ cup shortening (part butter)
    2 eggs, beaten
    3¼ cups all-purpose flour

Soften the yeast in lukewarm water. Scald the milk and add to it the sugar, salt, and shortening. Cool to lukewarm. Add 1 cup of the flour and beat thoroughly. Add the softened yeast and eggs. Again beat well. Add remaining flour to make a thick batter and beat thoroughly until smooth. Cover and let rise until doubled in bulk (about 1 hour).

TEA PUFFS Make ½ Basic Beaten Batter recipe and when it is light and doubled in bulk stir it down. Drop by spoonfuls into greased muffin pans. Mix together ½ cup sliced almonds, ¼ cup sugar, and ½ teaspoon cinnamon, and sprinkle this mixture over the top of the muffins. Let rise in a warm place until doubled (about 45 minutes). Bake at 375° F. for 25 minutes. Makes 16 muffins.

ROLLS IN VARIED SHAPES

PAN ROLLS (SOFT SIDES) Place balls of sweet dough almost touching in buttered deep-sided square or round pans. Cover them with a towel and let them rise in a warm place, free from draft, until doubled in bulk. Bake in a hot oven (425° F.) about 15 minutes.

PARKER HOUSE ROLLS Roll sweet dough out ¼ inch thick. Spread with very soft butter and cut in rounds with a 3-inch cooky cutter. Make a light cut in the dough with the back of a knife across each round and slightly off center. Fold so that the smaller half overlaps the lower half. Press edges together tightly at ends of crease to keep them from springing open. Place quite close together on greased baking sheet or pan. Cover with a towel and let them rise until doubled in bulk. Bake in a hot oven (425° F.) about 15 minutes.

CLOVERLEAF ROLLS Form sweet dough into round balls the size of walnuts and place 3 balls in each greased muffin cup, or dip each ball in melted butter before placing in cups. Two larger balls may be used instead of three, and one large ball in the middle surrounded by little balls the size of marbles makes a nice variation. Use medium-sized cups for first two and large-sized cups for latter. Cover and let rise until doubled in bulk. Bake in a hot oven (425° F.) about 15 minutes.

DINNER ROLLS Form sweet dough into cylindrical shapes with tapered ends and place on lightly greased baking sheet, 1 inch apart. Let rise and bake in a hot oven (425° F.) about 15 minutes.

CRESCENTS Roll sweet dough into a circle about 10 inches in diameter and ¼ inch thick and cut into 8 pie-shaped pieces. Stretch the wide end of the triangle a little and roll the dough toward the small end. Shape into a crescent and place on greased baking sheet, 1 inch apart. Cover with a towel and let rise in a warm place, free from draft, until doubled in bulk. Bake in a hot oven (425° F.) for about 15 minutes.

BUTTERFLIES Roll sweet dough into rectangle ¼ inch thick and 6 inches wide. Brush with melted butter and roll up like a jelly roll. With a sharp knife cut into 2-inch pieces and place on greased baking sheet, 2 inches apart. Press firmly across the center of each piece with the dull edge of the knife. Cover with a towel and let rise in a warm place, free from draft, until doubled in bulk. Bake in a hot oven (425° F.) for about 15 minutes.

FAN TANS Roll sweet dough into a very thin rectangle. Brush with melted butter and cut into strips about 1 inch wide. Pile 7 strips one on top of the other. Cut pieces 1½ inches wide and place on end in greased muffin pans. Cover with a towel and let rise in a warm place, free from draft, until doubled in bulk. Bake in a hot oven (425° F.) for about 15 minutes.

LUCKY CLOVERS Break off pieces of sweet dough and form into round smooth balls. Place the balls in greased muffin pans and with kitchen scissors cut each ball in half and then into quarters, cutting almost through to the bottom of the rolls. Brush lightly with melted butter. Cover with a towel and let them rise in a warm place, free from draft, until doubled in bulk. Bake in a hot oven (425° F.) for about 15 minutes.

LONG JOHNS Roll out sweet dough ½ inch thick and cut into strips 6 inches long and ½ inch wide. Roll each strip into a long stick, roll in melted butter, and place on a greased baking sheet about 1 inch apart. Cover with a towel and let them rise in a warm place, free from draft, until doubled in bulk. Bake in a hot oven (425° F.) for about 15 minutes.

CUSHIONS Roll sweet dough into a square ½ inch thick and with a sharp knife cut into 2-inch squares. Place on greased baking sheet, 1 inch apart. After they have doubled in bulk, make a diagonal cut across each roll. Cover with a towel and let rise in a warm place, free from draft, until doubled in bulk. Bake in a hot oven (425° F.) for about 15 minutes. After baking, and while still warm, brush with Confectioners' Sugar Icing and fill cut with jelly or marmalade.

TRIPLE DECKERS Roll sweet dough into an oblong ¼ inch in thickness. Brush the surface lightly with melted butter and fold the ends in lengthwise toward the center to form 3 layers. Cut crosswise with a sharp knife into 1½-inch strips and seal the ends firmly. Place on greased baking sheet about 1 inch apart, cover with a towel, and let them rise in a warm place, free from draft, until doubled in bulk. Bake in a hot oven (425° F.) about 15 minutes.

CROSSETTES Roll sweet dough into an oblong ¼ inch in thickness. Brush the surface with melted butter and cut it into 4 inch squares. Cut the squares in half to make triangles. Fold the base of the triangle to within ½ inch of the top. Fold the point of the triangle over and seal firmly. Place the crossettes on a greased baking sheet about 1 inch apart, cover with a towel and let them rise in a warm place, free from drafts, until doubled in bulk. Bake in a hot oven (425° F.) about 15 minutes.

TWISTED ROLLS

Roll sweet dough into long oblong shape about ¼ inch thick. Spread with melted butter and fold half the dough over the other half. Trim edges and cut into strips ½ inch wide and 6 inches long. Use strips to make twists.

BOWKNOTS Tie strips into knots and press down lightly on greased baking sheet. Cover with a towel and let rise in a warm place, free from draft, until doubled in bulk. Bake in a hot oven (425° F.) about 15 minutes.

SNAILS Hold one end of the twisted strip down on baking sheet and wind strip around and around. Tuck end firmly underneath. Cover with a towel and let rise in a warm place until doubled in bulk. Bake in a hot oven (425° F.) about 15 minutes.

FIGURE 8 Twist strip and bring up one end to meet the other, stretching a little if necessary, to form a figure 8. Double twists may be made the same way. Cover with a towel and let rise in a warm place until doubled in bulk. Bake in a hot oven (425° F.) about 15 minutes.

ROSETTES Follow directions for Bowknots. After tying, bring one end through center and the other over the side. Cover with a towel and let rise in a warm place until doubled in bulk. Bake in a hot oven (425° F.) about 15 minutes.

TWO-IN-ONE TWISTS Roll sweet dough into an oblong ¼ inch in thickness. Brush the surface lightly with melted butter and fold in half lengthwise. Cut crosswise with a sharp knife into strips ¾ inch wide. Take hold of each end of a strip, twist in opposite directions and seal the ends firmly. Place the twists on a greased baking sheet about 2 inches apart, cover with a towel and let them rise in a warm place, free from draft, until doubled in bulk. Bake in a hot oven (425° F.) about 15 minutes.

RAISIN NUT BUNS

To ½ recipe of Basic Sweet Dough add 1 cup raisins and ½ cup chopped nuts when kneading. Allow the dough to rise until light and doubled in bulk, and then turn out on lightly floured board. Divide into pieces about the size of a golf ball and form into smooth balls. Place the balls close together in greased cake pans. Brush the tops with melted butter and allow to rise until doubled in bulk. Bake at 375° F. for 20 minutes. Before removing them from the oven, glaze the tops with ¼ cup milk sweetened with 1 tablespoon sugar. Makes 1½ dozen buns.

COCONUT BUNS

½ recipe Basic Sweet Dough
14-ounce can moist coconut
2 teaspoons vanilla
1 cup confectioners' sugar
2 tablespoons hot milk

Make the Basic Sweet Dough, adding two thirds of the coconut and

1 teaspoon of the vanilla to the dough. Allow to rise according to directions until doubled in bulk. Punch down and turn out on a lightly floured board, roll out ¼ inch thick, and cut into 2-inch rounds. Place 2 inches apart on greased baking sheet, cover with a clean towel, and allow to rise until doubled in bulk (about 1 hour). Bake in a moderate oven (375° F.) for 12–15 minutes. Place on cake rack and while hot frost with an icing made by mixing the confectioners' sugar with the hot milk and the remaining teaspoon vanilla. Sprinkle with the remaining coconut. Makes 2 dozen buns.

POPPY SEED CRESCENTS

Make a sweet dough, roll out, and cut according to the directions for Crescents. Spread the base of the triangles with Poppy Seed Filling, roll and shape into crescents. Place on greased baking sheet, brush with beaten egg yolk, and sprinkle with sugar. Cover with a clean cloth and allow to rise in a warm place until doubled in bulk. Bake at 375° F. for 20–25 minutes.

POPPY SEED FILLING   Combine 1 cup sugar and 2 cups water and boil for 10 minutes. Add 1 cup ground poppy seeds, 1 teaspoon cinnamon, and 1 teaspoon grated lemon rind. Cool before using.

YEAST CORN MUFFINS

 1 cup milk
 ¼ cup sugar
 1 teaspoon salt
 1 cup corn meal
 ¼ cup butter or shortening
 2 eggs, well beaten
 1 cake or package yeast
 ¼ cup warm water
 2 cups all-purpose flour

Scald milk and add to it the sugar, salt, corn meal, and butter. Cool to lukewarm, then add the eggs and the yeast, which has been dissolved in the warm water. Add flour, using more, if necessary, to make a soft dough that does not stick to the hands. Knead on floured board. Cover and allow to rise until doubled in bulk. Punch down. Knead and roll out 1 inch thick. Cut into rolls and place in deep pan, not touching. Cover and allow to rise until more than doubled in size. Bake in hot oven (425° F.) for 15–20 minutes. Makes 2 dozen muffins.

ORANGE ROLLS

Substitute ¼ cup orange juice for the same amount of liquid in Basic Sweet Dough and add 2 tablespoons grated orange peel. Form rolls of any desired shape, allow to rise, and bake according to directions for sweet rolls. While still warm, spread with Orange Topping.

ORANGE TOPPING Combine to a smooth paste of spreading consistency 2 tablespoons orange juice, 1 teaspoon grated orange peel, and 1 cup confectioners' sugar.

HONEY FINGERS

Place Twisted Rolls in a buttered pan, the bottom of which is covered with a ½-inch layer of honey and sprinkled thickly with chopped nuts. Allow to rise and bake as for Twisted Rolls and remove them from the pan immediately after taking them from the oven.

HONEY SNAILS

Place Snails on baking sheet and brush with a mixture of ¼ cup softened butter, ⅔ cup confectioners' sugar, 1 egg white, and 2 tablespoons honey. Allow to rise until doubled in bulk (about 1 hour) and bake at 350° F. for 20 minutes.

CINNAMON TWISTS

1 recipe Sweet Dough
1½ cups sugar
4 teaspoons cinnamon

When sweet dough is doubled in bulk, punch down and turn it out on a lightly floured board. Divide the dough in half. Roll out each half into a square ⅛ inch thick and brush the surface with melted butter. Sprinkle the center third of each oblong with 4 tablespoons of the sugar-cinnamon mixture. Fold one third of the dough over the center third. Sprinkle with 4 tablespoons of the sugar-cinnamon mixture and fold the remaining third of dough over the two layers. Cut with a sharp knife crosswise into strips about 1 inch wide. Take hold of each strip and twist in opposite directions. Seal the ends firmly. Place the twists on greased baking sheets about 1½ inches apart and sprinkle the tops with the remaining sugar and cinnamon. Cover with a towel, let rise in a warm place, free from drafts, until doubled in bulk and bake in a hot oven (425° F.) about 20 minutes.

PINWHEELS

Any of the sweet doughs may be filled with a large variety of fruits and nuts, sugar and spice, jam, marmalade, chutney, or honey—even peanut butter—according to taste or ingredients on hand. The method is always the same:

METHOD

When the sweet dough is light and doubled in bulk, punch it down and allow it to rest for 10 minutes. Roll it out into a rectangle ¼ inch thick and 6 inches wide. Brush the surface with melted butter, sprinkle generously with filling, and roll up lengthwise like a jelly roll, sealing the edge. Cut into slices and place cut side down on a greased pan or in greased muffin cups. Allow to rise in a warm place until doubled in bulk (about 1 hour) and bake at 350° F. for 25 minutes. One half the recipe for Basic Sweet Dough will make 1½ dozen rolls.

CINNAMON PINWHEELS Mix together ½ cup sugar and 2 teaspoons cinnamon and reserve about 2 tablespoons of this mixture. Sprinkle the rest, with ½ cup raisins, over the buttered surface and roll. Cut into 1-inch slices and place cut side down on a greased deep layer cake pan. Brush top with milk and sprinkle with the remaining sugar-cinnamon mixture. Allow to rise and bake at 350° F. for 25 minutes.

BUTTERSCOTCH PECAN ROLLS In the bottom of muffin cups put ½ teaspoon butter, 1 teaspoon brown sugar, ½ teaspoon water, and a few pecan halves. When a sweet dough is light and doubled in bulk (any basic sweet dough recipe may be used), punch down. Allow to rest for 10 minutes and roll into a long, narrow sheet ½ inch thick and 8 inches wide. Brush with melted butter, sprinkle with ½ cup brown sugar, and roll up like a jelly roll, sealing the edge. Cut into 1-inch slices. Place slices, cut side down, in prepared muffin tins. Allow to rise until doubled in bulk (about 45 minutes) and bake at 350° F. for 25 minutes. Allow rolls to stand for 1 minute after taking from oven, before removing them from the tins.

STICKY ORANGE ROLLS Put 1 teaspoon honey in the bottom of well-buttered muffin tins. Roll out Basic Sweet Dough into a large rectangle and spread with a mixture of 2 tablespoons softened butter, 2 tablespoons sugar, and 2 teaspoons grated orange rind. Roll and cut into slices 1½ inches thick. Place cut side down in prepared muffin tins and allow to rise until doubled in bulk. Bake at 375° F. for 20 minutes. Allow to stand for 1 minute after taking from oven before removing the rolls from the muffin tins.

FRUIT AND NUT PINWHEELS Roll Basic Sweet Dough into a sheet and brush with melted butter. Cover the surface thickly with currants, raisins, cut citron, nuts, brown sugar, and cinnamon. Roll and cut into 1-inch pieces and stand the rolls closely together in a high-sided pan which has been heavily buttered and then covered with a ¼-inch layer of honey or corn syrup. Allow to rise in a warm place until doubled in bulk and bake at 375° F. for about 25 minutes. Allow the rolls to stand in the pan for a few minutes before removing them.

TWO EXCELLENT FILLING COMBINATIONS ARE:

NO. 1
½ cup chopped nuts
½ cup chopped dates
Grated rind of 1 lemon
¼ cup chopped candied fruit
¼ cup sugar
½ teaspoon nutmeg

NO. 2
½ cup ground, cooked prunes or apricots
½ cup seedless raisins
2 tablespoons chopped citron
3 tablespoons chopped fruit peel
¼ cup chopped nuts
Brown sugar
Cinnamon

COCONUT CURLS Roll out a sweet dough into a rectangle and brush the surface with melted butter, then sprinkle with ½ cup brown sugar and 1 cup coconut. Roll and cut into 1-inch slices. Grease muffin tins with butter and sprinkle the bottoms with brown sugar and coconut. Place a slice, cut side down, in each cup. Allow to rise until doubled in bulk and bake at 375° F. for 20–25 minutes. Allow to cool in tins for 1 minute before removing them.

SURPRISE ROLLS

Like Pinwheels, Surprise Rolls lend themselves to a great variety of fillings.

Divide Basic Sweet Dough in half and roll each half into a thin sheet about ¼ inch thick. Place a fruit filling (see fillings for Kolacky and Pinwheels) or a thick layer of jam, marmalade, or chutney on top of one sheet, which has been brushed with melted butter, and cover with the second sheet of dough. Cut into rounds with a cooky cutter—make them small and dainty for tea—and place 1 inch apart on a greased cooky sheet to rise.

Small muffin tins lend themselves to Surprise Rolls. In this case the dough does not have to be rolled out. Place a small round of dough in the bottom of a greased muffin cup. On top of this place your filling, always a little dot of butter, some sugar, and a little spice, and place another small round of dough on top. Allow to rise and bake at 350° F. for 20–25 minutes, depending on the size of the rolls.

Try making Surprise Rolls in muffin cups with one of the following in between. If you use a refrigerator sweet dough you can make a new "surprise" each day.

1. A fresh orange or grapefruit section sprinkled with brown sugar.
2. A date, pitted and stuffed with a nut and sprinkled with sugar and a dash of nutmeg.
3. A slice of marshmallow.
4. Chopped pecans, butter, brown sugar, and cinnamon.
5. Ground almonds mixed to a paste with a little heavy cream, which has been sweetened with brown sugar and flavored with cinnamon.
6. Half a cooked apricot, honey, and a pinch of ground cloves.

KOLACKY

½ recipe Basic Sweet Dough
2 tablespoons melted butter
Filling (see below)
Confectioners' sugar

When Basic Sweet Dough is light and doubled in bulk, punch down and allow to rest for 10 minutes. Divide dough into pieces the size of walnuts and form each part into a ball. Place the balls 2 inches apart on a greased baking sheet and allow them to rise in a warm place for about 15 minutes. Press down the center of each roll with the thumb to make a hollow, leaving a raised rim about ¼ inch thick around the outside. Brush hollows with melted butter and fill with marmalade, jam, or chutney or with about 2 tablespoons of any of the following fillings. Allow to rise until doubled in bulk (about 45 minutes) and bake at 350° F. for 20 minutes. When cool, sprinkle generously with confectioners' sugar. Makes 24 Kolacky.

PRUNE OR APRICOT FILLING Combine 1 cup chopped cooked prunes or apricots with 2 tablespoons prune or apricot juice, ¼ cup sugar, 1 tablespoon lemon juice, ½ teaspoon cinnamon, and ¼ teaspoon ground cloves. Mix well.

APPLE FILLING Peel and slice 2 large apples and cook with 2 tablespoons water and 2 tablespoons red cinnamon candy until the slices are tender but not mushy.

APRICOT PRUNE FILLING Wash and boil together ¼ pound each dried prunes and dried apricots until they are tender. Pit the prunes, then chop the fruits finely together. Sweeten to taste and mix with ¼ cup chopped nut meats and 1 teaspoon grated orange or lemon rind.

DATE AND BUTTER FILLING Cook 1 cup washed, pitted dates with 2 tablespoons sugar, 2 tablespoons water, a pinch salt, and 2 tablespoons butter, stirring constantly to prevent scorching, until thick. Flavor with 1 teaspoon vanilla.

DATE AND NUT FILLING Pit and cook 1 cup dates with ¼ cup water and ½ teaspoon grated orange rind for 15 minutes. Remove from fire and beat in 1 tablespoon brown sugar, then stir in ¼ cup chopped nuts.

FIG AND NUT FILLING Substitute figs for dates in the preceding recipe and flavor with ¼ teaspoon almond extract.

POPPY SEED FILLING Cook 1 cup ground poppy seeds in ¼ cup milk, 2 tablespoons corn syrup, and 1 tablespoon sugar for about 5 minutes. Stir in 1 teaspoon butter and ¼ teaspoon ground cinnamon.

MUNKER, *Danish Ebleskiver*

2¼ cups milk
¼ cup butter
2 cups flour
Pinch salt
1 tablespoon sugar
3 eggs
1 cake or envelope yeast
1 teaspoon sugar
¼ teaspoon ground cardamom
Cooked apples

Heat 2 cups of the milk with the butter until the butter is melted. Sift the flour into a bowl, add half the butter-milk mixture, and beat thoroughly for 15 minutes. Stir in the salt, the tablespoon of sugar, and the unbeaten eggs, one at a time. Dissolve the yeast in the ¼ cup milk with the 1 teaspoon sugar and add to the rest of the milk, making sure that the milk is not hotter than lukewarm. Add the yeast mixture and the cardamom to the batter, stir well, cover, and let rise in a warm place for ½ to 1 hour.

Heat the Munk iron, put a little butter in each hole, and when the butter is hot, put 1 tablespoon of the batter in each hole. When the cakes have cooked for a moment put a small piece of cooked apple in the center of each Munker. A little jam or marmalade may be used instead of the apple if desired. Turn the cakes with a fork while they are still soft in the middle and fry until they are a golden brown on both sides. Roll the cooked cakes in sugar and serve them warm.

PLUM BUNS

½ recipe Basic Sweet Dough
18 cooked prunes, pitted
4 tablespoons sugar
2 teaspoons cinnamon
Confectioners' Sugar Icing

When Basic Sweet Dough is light and doubled in bulk, punch down and allow to rest for 10 minutes. Divide into pieces the size of an egg and shape each part into a ball. Flatten each ball into a circle and in the center of each place a prune. Mix together the cinnamon and sugar and sprinkle a generous ½ teaspoon over each prune. Bring the edges of the circle together over the prune and seal firmly. Place the rolls sealed side down on a greased baking sheet, 2 inches apart, and allow to rise in a warm place until doubled in bulk (about 1 hour). Bake at 350° F. for 25 minutes. Makes 18 buns.

HUNGARIAN FILLED BUNS

1 cake or package yeast
2 tablespoons lukewarm water
½ cup butter
3 cups all-purpose flour
6 tablespoons sour cream
3 egg yolks, beaten
2 tablespoons sugar
½ teaspoon salt
Lukewarm milk

Soften the yeast in the lukewarm water. Cut the butter into the flour with 2 knives or a pastry blender. Add the sour cream and egg yolks and mix well. Add the sugar, salt, and the softened yeast, and enough milk to make a dough that is soft but not sticky. Allow to rise in a warm place until doubled in bulk. Punch down and allow to rest for 10 minutes. Roll out thinly, spread lightly with softened butter, fold the sides over the center and the ends to the center, envelope fashion. Roll thinly and fold again. Repeat this procedure twice more. The dough is now ready to be cut into rolls; rolled and cut into pinwheels or made into filled squares; or triangles of dough may be filled and rolled to form horns and crescents. Brush the rolls with beaten egg white and sprinkle with anise or poppy seed. Allow to rise again until doubled in bulk and bake at 350° F. for 20 minutes. Makes 2 dozen rolls.

    CHEESE FILLING Press 2 cups cottage cheese through a sieve and mix to a paste with 3 beaten eggs, 1 tablespoon sugar, the grated rind of 1 lemon, ½ cup raisins, and ¼ teaspoon nutmeg.

    PRUNE FILLING Mix together into a stiff paste 2 cups chopped, cooked prunes, the grated rind of 1 lemon, 2 tablespoons sugar, and ½ teaspoon cinnamon.

    RAISIN FILLING Boil together 1 cup sugar and 1 cup water. Add 1 cup chopped raisins, 1 cup chopped nuts, 1 teaspoon cinnamon, and the grated rind of 1 lemon. Cook for about 8 minutes, stirring until thick.

LEMON DROPS

½ recipe Basic Sweet Dough
2 tablespoons melted butter
Lemon Sugar

When Basic Sweet Dough is light and doubled in bulk, divide into 2 equal parts, punch down, and allow to rest for 10 minutes. Roll each part into a long roll about ¾ inch thick. Cut into pieces ½ inch long and shape into balls. Dip balls in melted butter and then into Lemon Sugar and place 5 balls into each cup of a greased muffin tin. Place in a warm spot and allow to rise until doubled in bulk (about 45 minutes). Bake at 350° F. for 25 minutes. Makes about 18 rolls.

    LEMON SUGAR Combine well ½ cup sugar with 2 tablespoons grated lemon rind.

HOT CROSS BUNS FROM SWEET DOUGH

To ½ recipe for Basic Sweet Dough add:
1 teaspoon cinnamon
½ teaspoon allspice
1 cup currants

When dough is light and doubled in bulk, punch it down and allow it to rest for 10 minutes. Divide into 18 parts and shape each part into a ball. Place ½ inch apart on a greased baking sheet and allow to rise in a warm place until doubled in bulk (about 1 hour). Bake at 350° F. for 20 minutes. Remove at once from the pans and make a cross of Confectioners' Sugar Icing on each roll. Makes 18 rolls.

BUTTERMILK ROLLS

1 cake or package yeast
¼ cup lukewarm water
1½ cups buttermilk
2 tablespoons shortening
½ teaspoon soda
2 tablespoons sugar
1½ teaspoons salt
4 cups all-purpose flour

Soften the yeast in the lukewarm water. Scald the buttermilk and add to it the shortening, soda, sugar, salt, and 2 cups of the flour. Beat for several minutes, then add enough additional flour to make a light but not sticky dough. Turn out on lightly floured board and knead for 8 minutes. Place in a greased bowl, grease the surface of the dough, cover, and allow it to rise in warm place until doubled in bulk (about 1½ hours). Punch down and roll out on a lightly floured board. Cut into rounds and place in a high-sided, greased pan, close together but not touching. Allow to rise until doubled in bulk (45 minutes) and bake at 350° F. for 20-25 minutes.

OLD ENGLISH HOT CROSS BUNS

1 cake or package yeast
¼ cup lukewarm water
1 cup sugar
½ cup softened butter
3 large eggs, separated
2¼ cups milk, scalded and cooled to lukewarm
1½ teaspoons salt
1 teaspoon nutmeg
8 cups all-purpose flour
Confectioners' Sugar Icing

Soften the yeast in the lukewarm water. In the evening cream together the sugar and butter until light and fluffy. Stir in the egg yolks, which have been well beaten, and then the lukewarm milk. Add the softened yeast and then half the flour, which has been sifted with the salt and nutmeg, and beat well. Stir in the remaining flour and the egg whites, which have been stiffly beaten, and blend well. Place in a lightly greased bowl, grease the top of the dough, cover, and allow to stand in a warm place overnight.

In the morning place the dough on a lightly floured board and knead well, adding a little more flour, if necessary, to make a dough that is very light but not sticky. Roll dough out ½ inch thick and cut into 3-inch rounds. Place the rounds on lightly greased cooky sheets, brush the tops with melted butter, cover with a clean cloth, and allow to rise until doubled in bulk (about 1½ hours). With kitchen scissors or a knife cut a deep cross on each bun and bake at 375° F. for 20-25 minutes. Remove from oven and glaze with vanilla-flavored Confectioners' Sugar Icing.

SAFFRON BUNS

1½ cakes or packages yeast
¼ cup lukewarm water
1 teaspoon sugar
1 cup shortening (part butter)
½ cup sugar
1½ teaspoons salt
1 teaspoon grated nutmeg
1 cup scalded milk
½ teaspoon saffron infusion*
8 cups sifted all-purpose flour
¾ cup currants
½ cup shredded citron

Soften the yeast in the lukewarm water, add 1 teaspoon sugar and allow to stand in a warm place for about 15 minutes.

Cream the butter and the sugar in a large bowl. Add to it the salt, nutmeg, and milk, and stir until the shortening is mixed. Cool to lukewarm. Add the yeast mixture, the saffron infusion, and the flour, blending until well mixed and adding more flour, if necessary, to make a soft but not sticky dough. Mix in the currants and citron, which has been dredged with a little flour, turn out on a lightly floured board, and knead for 10 minutes. Place in a lightly greased bowl. Brush the top with melted shortening, cover, and allow to rise in a warm place until doubled in bulk (about 2 hours). Punch down, shape into buns, place on baking sheet, brush the tops with a little beaten egg or milk, and allow to rise until doubled in bulk

*Pour 1 tablespoon boiling water on a pinch of saffron and allow to steep for 5 minutes.

(about 1 hour). Bake at 400° F. for 10 minutes. Reduce oven temperature to 350° F. and bake for another 10–15 minutes, according to the size of the buns. Glaze the tops with a thin Confectioners' Sugar Icing. Makes about 30 small buns.

SCHNECKEN, *Sour Cream Dough Snails*

    1 cake or package yeast
    ¼ cup lukewarm water
    ½ cup shortening (part butter)
    2½ cups all-purpose flour
    2 eggs, beaten
    ½ cup sugar
    1 teaspoon salt
    1 cup sour cream
    Sugar, cinnamon, chopped nuts, and raisins

Soften the yeast in the lukewarm water. Cut the shortening into the flour, add the yeast, eggs, sugar, salt, and sour cream. Beat very thoroughly and place in a greased bowl. Cover and place in the refrigerator overnight. The next day remove from the refrigerator to a warm place and allow to rise until doubled in bulk. Punch down, place on a lightly floured board, and knead, adding more flour to make a dough that is not sticky. Roll out into a thin sheet. Sprinkle the surface thickly with sugar, cinnamon, chopped nuts, and raisins and roll up like a jelly roll. Cut in ½-inch pieces and place on a greased baking sheet. Allow to rise in a warm place until doubled in bulk and bake at 350° F. for about 30 minutes.

FILLED HORNS, *Pozsonyi Patko*

    1 cake or package yeast
    1 cup milk, scalded and cooled to lukewarm
    1 cup butter
    4 cups all-purpose flour
    2 egg yolks, beaten
    1 teaspoon salt
    1 tablespoon sugar
    1 cup sour cream

Dissolve the yeast in the milk and allow to stand for 15 minutes. Cut the butter into the flour with 2 knives or a pastry blender, add egg yolks, salt, sugar, softened yeast, and the sour cream. Work quickly into a smooth dough, handling as little as possible, and allow it to rest in a warm place for 2 hours. Toss it on a lightly floured board and roll out to ¼ inch in thickness, cut into 3-inch squares, and place 1 teaspoon of the filling in the center of each square. Roll into horns, place on baking sheet, 1 inch apart, and allow to rise in a warm place for 45 minutes. Brush with beaten egg yolk several times during the rising period. Bake at 350° F. until golden-brown, or about 20 minutes.

FILLING   Combine 2 cups ground walnuts or poppy seeds with ¾ cup sugar, 1 teaspoon cinnamon or vanilla, and the grated rind of 1 lemon.

SOUR CREAM TWISTS

Make the same dough as for Schnecken, omitting the sugar. Remove the dough from the refrigerator and roll out into a thin sheet on a lightly sugared breadboard. Divide ½ cup sugar into 3 parts and sprinkle one part over the dough. Fold dough into thirds and roll thin. Again sprinkle with sugar and fold into thirds. Roll out and sprinkle with sugar and fold into thirds. This has now been done 3 times, and all the sugar has been used. Now roll the dough into a rectangle and cut strips of dough 1 inch wide and 4 inches long. Twist each strip and arrange on an ungreased cooky sheet. Allow to rise until the dough has doubled in bulk (about 45 minutes) and bake at 350° F. for 15 minutes.

BUTTER HORNS

1 cake or package yeast
2 tablespoons lukewarm water
¾ cup light cream
¾ cup butter
4 egg yolks, beaten
¾ teaspoon salt
3–3½ cups all-purpose flour

Dissolve the yeast in the lukewarm water and allow to stand for 5 minutes. Scald the cream and add the butter. Cool to lukewarm. Add the yeast mixture and the rest of the ingredients in order. Put the dough in a wet napkin and tie at the top. Place it in a bowl and cover with water at room temperature. Allow to stand until the dough floats (about 2 hours). Turn out on a plate. Drop by teaspoons into the topping and shape into small horns or crescents. Place on greased baking sheet so they do not touch. Allow to rise until doubled in bulk and bake at 350° F. for 15–20 minutes. Makes 36 horns.

TOPPING Mix together 1 cup sugar, 1 teaspoon cinnamon, and ½ cup finely chopped blanched almonds.

ENGLISH MUFFINS

INGREDIENTS FOR 1 DOZEN MUFFINS
- 1 package or cake yeast
- ¼ cup lukewarm water
- 1 cup milk
- 2 tablespoons sugar
- 1½ teaspoons salt
- 3 tablespoons shortening
- 1 egg, beaten
- 4 cups all-purpose flour

Soften the yeast in the lukewarm water. Scald the milk and add to it the sugar, salt, and shortening. Cool to lukewarm. Add the egg and 2 cups of the flour and beat thoroughly. Add enough additional flour to make a moderately soft dough. Turn out on a floured board and knead until smooth and satiny. Place in a lightly greased bowl, grease surface lightly, cover, and allow to rise in a warm place until doubled in bulk (about 1½ hours). Punch down and allow to rest for 10 minutes. Roll out ¼ inch thick on a board sprinkled with white corn meal. Cut with a 3-inch cooky cutter. Sprinkle tops with corn meal, cover, and allow to rise on board until doubled (about 45 minutes). When light, bake slowly on an ungreased griddle. Have the griddle hot at first, then reduce heat so the muffins will brown slowly. Bake 7–8 minutes on each side.

CRUMPETS Make an English Muffin dough but use only 3 cups flour to make a batter. Allow the batter to rise in a warm place 3 times, 30 minutes each time, beating for 3 minutes between each rising. This beating makes the large holes characteristic of the crumpet. Bake at once by pouring batter into muffin rings set on a hot greased griddle. Fill the rings about one third full and allow them to bake, without turning, for about 20 minutes. Cool and toast and serve with butter and jam or marmalade.

MORAVIAN BREAD

- ½ recipe for Basic Sweet Dough
- 1 tablespoon melted butter
- Orange marmalade

When dough is light, punch it down and allow it to rest for 10 minutes. Pat it out on a floured board to fit a greased 9-inch square cake pan. Spread the surface with the butter. Cover with a clean towel and allow to rise for 40 minutes or until doubled in bulk. Then with the floured handle of a wooden spoon make shallow impressions at 1-inch intervals over the surface and put a teaspoon of marmalade into each hole. Bake at 400° F. for 30 minutes.

POPPY SEED BRAID

Make a sweet dough, but before adding the flour, mix in 1 cup ground poppy seeds, ½ cup chopped cooked prunes, and 2 teaspoons grated lemon rind. When the dough is light, punch down and allow it to rest for 10 minutes. Divide the dough into 5 parts and roll each part into a strip about 18 inches long. Braid 3 of these strips and place the braid on a greased baking sheet, sealing the ends. Twist the remaining 2 strips and place on top of the braid, again sealing the ends. Cover and allow to rise in a warm place until doubled in bulk (about 1 hour). Bake at 350° F. for 45 minutes. Cool and frost with Confectioners' Sugar Icing and sprinkle with nuts.

BRAIDED FRUIT BREAD

1 cake or package yeast
¼ cup lukewarm water
2 cups milk
½ cup sugar
⅓ cup butter or shortening
½ teaspoon salt
1 egg, beaten
8 cups all-purpose flour
½ cup chopped raisins
½ cup shredded citron
½ cup chopped blanched almonds

Dissolve the yeast in the lukewarm water and allow it to stand for 10 minutes. Scald the milk, add to it the sugar, butter, and salt, and allow to cool to lukewarm. Pour the milk into a mixing bowl, stir in the egg and 2 cups of the flour. Add the softened yeast and beat well. Place in a warm spot to rise for 1 hour. Add the rest of the flour and the fruit and nuts. Turn out on a floured board and knead, adding more flour, if necessary, to make a medium-firm dough. Place the dough in a lightly greased bowl, grease the surface of the dough, cover, and allow it to rise in a warm place until doubled in bulk (about 2 hours). Punch down and divide the dough into 3 unequal parts. Divide each of these 3 parts into 3 parts and braid each into 3 strands. Place the braids on top of each other, the smallest on top, the largest on the bottom. Place on a greased baking sheet, cover, and allow to rise again in a warm place until doubled in bulk (about 1 hour). Bake at 400° F. for 10 minutes. Reduce oven temperature to 350° F. and bake for about 45 minutes longer. When cool, frost with Confectioners' Sugar Icing or brush with slightly beaten egg while still warm. This makes 1 very large loaf or 2 small ones.

SPANISH SWEET BREAD

4 cups all-purpose flour, sifted
½ teaspoon salt
½ cup butter
½ cup sugar
½ tablespoon anise seeds
½ cup raisins
¼ cup chopped almonds
2 tablespoons chopped pine nuts
2 tablespoons chopped pistachio nuts
¼ cup chopped candied fruit
1 cake or package yeast
1 cup milk

Add the salt to the sifted flour and sift again. Melt the butter, add the sugar, and add to the flour mixture. Add the anise seeds, raisins, almonds, pine nuts, pistachio nuts, and fruit. Soften the yeast in the milk, which has been scalded and allowed to cool to lukewarm. Stir until the yeast is dissolved and add to the flour mixture. The dough should be soft. Allow it to rise in a warm place until doubled in bulk, punch down, and make into loaves. Allow the loaves to rise again until doubled in bulk. Bake for about 45 minutes at 350° F.

NORWEGIAN JULE KAGE

2 cakes or packages yeast
½ cup lukewarm water
2 cups milk
1 cup sugar
2 teaspoons salt
1 cup shortening
1 cup chopped raisins
½ cup shredded citron
½ cup chopped candied cherries
½ cup chopped blanched almonds
1 tablespoon ground cardamom
8 cups all-purpose flour

Dissolve the yeast in the lukewarm water. Scald the milk, add the sugar, salt, and shortening, and allow to cool to lukewarm. Add the yeast and beat in 4 cups of the flour. Place in a warm spot to rise until it is doubled in bulk. Punch down and add the fruit and nuts and the rest of the flour. Turn out on a lightly floured board and knead until smooth and satiny, adding more flour, if necessary, to make a medium-firm dough. Round up the dough, place in a greased bowl, grease the surface of the dough, cover, and place in a warm spot to double again in bulk. Punch down, knead again, form into loaves, and place in greased loaf pans. Allow to rise until doubled in bulk and bake at 400° F. for 10 minutes. Reduce oven temperature to 350° F. and bake for 50 minutes longer. When cool, frost with Confectioners' Sugar Icing and decorate with bits of fruit and nuts. Makes 3 loaves.

CHRISTMAS FRUIT BREAD

½ cup shredded citron
½ cup chopped raisins
½ cup chopped blanched almonds
½ cup chopped candied cherries
1 tablespoon grated lemon rind
1 teaspoon cinnamon
½ teaspoon ground cloves
½ teaspoon nutmeg
¼ cup brandy
1 cake or package yeast
2 tablespoons lukewarm water
1 cup milk
⅓ cup shortening
¼ cup sugar
1 teaspoon salt
1 egg, beaten
4 cups all-purpose flour

Soak the fruit, nuts, and spices in the brandy overnight. Soften the yeast in the lukewarm water. Scald the milk, add to it the shortening, sugar, and salt, and cool to lukewarm. Add the softened yeast, the egg, and 2 cups of the flour. Beat thoroughly, then add the rest of the flour. Allow to rise in a warm place until doubled in bulk, turn out on a floured board and knead, adding more flour, if necessary, to make a medium-firm dough. Allow to rise again until doubled in bulk. Punch down, knead into the dough the fruit mixture, and form into loaves. Place the loaves in greased loaf pans and allow to rise again until doubled in bulk. Brush the tops of the loaves with melted butter. Bake at 400° F. for 10 minutes, reduce oven temperature to 350° F., and bake for another 50 minutes. Cool and frost with a thin Confectioners' Sugar Icing flavored with almond extract. Makes 1 large or 2 small loaves.

APPLE BREAD

- 2 cups lukewarm, thick, unsweetened applesauce
- 1 cake or package yeast
- 2 tablespoons lukewarm water
- 2 tablespoons melted butter
- 1 teaspoon salt
- ½ cup sugar
- 4 cups all-purpose flour

Add to the applesauce the yeast which has been softened in the lukewarm water, and mix thoroughly. Stir in the butter, salt, sugar, and enough flour to make a light dough. Allow to rise in a warm place until doubled in bulk. Punch down and knead on a floured board for 3 minutes. Shape into long loaves, place almost touching on greased baking sheets, make 3 deep gashes across the top of each, cover, and allow to rise in a warm place until doubled in bulk. Bake at 400° F. for 10 minutes, reduce oven temperature to 350° F., and bake for another 50 minutes. About 10 minutes before baking is complete, brush the tops with slightly beaten egg white, sprinkle with poppy seeds, and finish baking. Makes 2 loaves.

SWEDISH TEA RING

- ½ recipe Basic Sweet Dough
- 3 tablespoons melted butter
- ½ cup brown sugar
- ½ cup raisins, if desired
- 2 teaspoons cinnamon
- ¼ cup chopped nuts

When Basic Sweet Dough is light, punch it down and allow it to rest for 10 minutes. Roll it into a rectangle about ½ inch thick and 8 inches wide. Brush with melted butter, sprinkle with brown sugar and cinnamon and raisins, if used, and roll up like a jelly roll, sealing the edge. Place on a greased baking sheet witih the sealed edge down, moisten the ends slightly and join securely to form a ring. With kitchen scissors, make deep slantwise cuts in the ring about two thirds through and at intervals of 1 inch. Turn each slice partly on its side to give a petallike appearance. If you wish to make a double ring, lift every other cut slice to the center of the ring.

Brush lightly with melted butter, cover with a towel, and allow to rise in a warm place until doubled in bulk (about 45 minutes). Bake at 350° F. for 30 minutes. Remove from the oven and while still slightly warm frost with 1 cup confectioners' sugar which has been mixed to a paste of spreading consistency with 3 tablespoons light cream. Sprinkle with chopped nuts and decorate with bits of candied fruit.

BUBBLE LOAF

½ recipe for Basic Sweet Dough
Caramel Glaze

When Basic Sweet Dough is light and doubled in bulk, punch it down and allow it to rest for 10 minutes. Break off pieces of dough about the size of walnuts and shape into balls. Place a layer of balls on the bottom of a greased loaf pan, slightly apart. Arrange a second layer on top of the first, placing the balls between the spaces in the first layer. Arrange a third layer in the same manner. Pour Caramel Glaze over all and allow to rise in a warm place until doubled in bulk (about 1 hour). Bake at 350° F. for 35 minutes and allow to cool in the pan for 5 minutes before turning out.

CARAMEL GLAZE Combine and mix thoroughly ¼ cup dark corn syrup, 1 tablespoon melted butter, 1 teaspoon lemon juice, and the grated rind of 1 lemon, if desired.

JAM SWIRL COFFEECAKE

½ recipe Basic Beaten Batter
½ cup jam or marmalade
¼ cup sugar
¼ teaspoon cinnamon

When the Basic Beaten Batter is light and doubled in bulk, stir it down. Spread the batter evenly in a greased, deep layer cake pan 9 inches in diameter. With a floured spoon make 5 grooves in a swirl design from the edge to the center. Fill the grooves with jam. Mix together the sugar and cinnamon and sprinkle over the top. Allow to rise in a warm place until doubled in bulk (about 45 minutes) and bake at 375° F. for 30 minutes.

APPLE COFFEECAKE

¼ recipe Basic Beaten Batter
4 apples

    2 tablespoons melted butter
    ¼ cup sugar
    1 teaspoon cinnamon

When the Basic Beaten Batter is light and doubled in bulk, stir it down. Spread the batter evenly in a buttered, deep layer cake pan 9 inches in diameter. Peel and slice the apples and arrange them on top in 2 circles—the slices slightly overlapping each other. Brush with the melted butter. Mix together the sugar and cinnamon and sprinkle over the apples. Allow to rise in a warm place until doubled in bulk (about 45 minutes) and bake at 375° F. for 30 minutes.

DUTCH APPLE CAKE

    ½ recipe for Basic Sweet Dough
    1 tablespoon melted butter
    2 tart apples
    2 tablespoons sugar
    ½ teaspoon nutmeg

When the Basic Sweet Dough is light, punch it down and allow it to rest for 10 minutes. Pat it out to fit a greased, 8-inch square cake pan. Brush the top with melted butter. Cover with a clean towel and allow to rise until doubled in bulk. Pare, core the apples, cut into sections ⅓ inch thick, and arrange in even rows on top of the dough, pressing the edges slightly into the dough. Sprinkle with the sugar and nutmeg mixed. Dot with butter and allow to rise another 15 minutes. Bake at 375° F. for 40 minutes. Cover top at first with buttered paper, to aid in cooking the apples. Remove paper the last 10 minutes to allow the cake to brown.

CRUMBLE COFFEECAKE

    ½ recipe Basic Beaten Batter
       or ½ recipe Basic Sweet Dough
    3 tablespoons milk
    Crumble Topping

When the Basic Beaten Batter is light and doubled in bulk, stir it down. Spread the batter evenly in a greased, 8-inch square cake pan. Brush the top with milk and sprinkle with Crumble Topping. Allow to rise until doubled (about 45 minutes). Bake at 375° F. for 30 minutes.

CRUMBLE TOPPING Mix together until crumbly ½ cup all-purpose flour, ¼ cup dry bread crumbs, 2 tablespoons sugar, 1 teaspoon cinnamon, and 2 tablespoons butter.

HONEY TWIST

⅓ recipe for Basic Sweet Dough
Honey Topping

When the Basic Sweet Dough is light, punch it down and allow it to rest for 10 minutes. Shape into a long roll about 1 inch in diameter. Coil the roll loosely into a greased, 9-inch layer pan or an 8-inch square pan, beginning at the center and working out. Brush with Honey Topping and allow to rise until doubled in bulk (about 1 hour). Bake at 350° F. for 30 minutes.

HONEY TOPPING   Combine and mix until smooth ¼ cup butter, ⅔ cup confectioners' sugar, 1 egg white, and 2 tablespoons honey.

PLAIN CINNAMON CAKE

Prepare ½ recipe Basic Sweet Dough. When light, turn it onto a floured board and pat or roll lightly to ½-inch thickness. Place in a greased, 8-inch square cake pan, brush top with melted butter, cover with a clean towel, and allow to rise until doubled in bulk. Sprinkle generously with 2 teaspoons cinnamon mixed with ½ cup sugar. Dot with bits of butter and bake at 375° F. about 15 minutes.

WHOLE WHEAT COFFEECAKE WITH DATES

½ recipe Basic Whole Wheat Sweet Dough
½ cup water
½ cup sugar
1 tablespoon flour
1 cup pitted dates, cut into small pieces
Grated rind of 1 lemon
1 teaspoon lemon juice
1 cup confectioners' sugar
1 teaspoon vanilla
2 tablespoons hot water
⅓ cup chopped nuts

Make the Whole Wheat Sweet Dough and roll it out on floured board ¼ inch thick. Combine the water, sugar, flour, and dates and cook, stirring, for about 10 minutes, or until thick. Cool, add lemon rind and lemon juice, and spread over the dough. Roll up like a jelly roll and place on a greased baking sheet with the sealed edge down. Join the ends securely to form a ring. With kitchen scissors make deep cuts in the ring about two thirds of the way through and at intervals of 1 inch. Cover with a clean cloth and allow to rise for about 40 minutes, or until doubled in bulk. Bake at 375° F. for 40 minutes. While hot, spread with icing made by combining the confectioners' sugar, vanilla, and hot water. Sprinkle chopped nuts on top. Serves 6.

HUNGARIAN COFFEECAKE

Make ½ the recipe for Basic Sweet Dough. When the dough is light, punch it down and allow it to rest for 10 minutes. Break the dough into pieces the size of walnuts and form into balls. Dip the balls in ½ cup melted butter and then roll in a mixture made of ¾ cup brown sugar, 1 teaspoon cinnamon, and ½ cup finely chopped nuts. Place a layer of the balls very lightly in a greased, 9-inch tube pan and sprinkle with raisins. Add another layer of balls and sprinkle more raisins in the crevices. Continue in this manner until all the balls are in the pan. Cover with a towel and allow to rise for about 1 hour, or until doubled in bulk. Bake at 375° F. for 35 minutes.

OREHNJACA

1 cake or package yeast
½ cup lukewarm water
⅛ cup sugar
3 egg yolks
¾ cup sugar
1 cup heavy cream
3 tablespoons butter
4 cups all-purpose flour
¼ teaspoon salt
Grated rind of ½ orange
Grated rind of 1 lemon

Soften the yeast in the lukewarm water and add the ⅛ cup sugar. Put aside in a warm place. Cream together the egg yolks and sugar. Scald the cream, stir in the butter, let cool to lukewarm, and add to the creamed egg-sugar mixture. Stir in the yeast mixture, flour, salt, orange and lemon rind, and more flour if necessary to form a soft dough. Turn out on a lightly floured board and knead for 10 minutes. Place it in a warm bowl, brush the surface lightly with melted shortening, and allow it to rise until doubled in bulk. Punch down. Divide the dough into 2 parts and roll each part out on a lightly floured board ¼ inch thick. Brush the surface lightly with melted butter. Spread with filling and roll up into 2 loaves about the size of a rolling pin. Place the rolls on a greased baking sheet and bake at 375° F. for about 1 hour.

FILLING Scald 1 pound chopped walnuts in 1 cup hot milk. Add the grated rind of 1 lemon and 1 orange, 1 tablespoon whisky, and 1 cup honey.

PUTICA

4 cups all-purpose flour
1½ cups sugar
¼ teaspoon salt
4 tablespoons soft butter
1 cake or package yeast
½ cup lukewarm milk
2 eggs, lightly beaten
½ pound chopped walnuts
¼ pound chopped raisins
¼ pound bitter chocolate, shaved
½ cup honey

In a mixing bowl combine the flour, sugar, and salt, and rub into it the soft butter. Soften the yeast in the milk and add it along with the eggs. Mix well and let rise until doubled in bulk. Roll out the dough ½ inch thick and spread with the walnuts, raisins, chocolate, and honey which have all been mixed together. Roll as a jelly roll, place on a greased baking sheet, and bake at 350° F. for 25 minutes.

ENGLISH FRUIT BUN

2 cakes or packages yeast
1 cup lukewarm water
2 tablespoons sugar
4 cups all-purpose flour
½ cup melted butter
¾ cup raisins
¾ cup currants
½ cup chopped almonds
2 tablespoons chopped candied orange peel
2 tablespoons chopped citron
¼ teaspoon ground cloves
½ teaspoon cinnamon
¼ teaspoon ginger

Soften the yeast in the water, to which has been added the sugar.

Add 2 cups of the flour and beat to a smooth batter. Cover and place in a warm spot to rise. When light and bubbly, divide the sponge in half. To one half, add half of the melted butter, the fruits, and the nuts. Sift the remaining flour together with the spices and add enough to make a stiff dough, kneading it until smooth. Put it into a greased bowl, cover, and allow it to rise. To the other half of the sponge, add the remaining butter and enough of the flour-and-spice mixture to make a stiff dough. Knead until smooth. Place it in a greased bowl, cover, and allow it to rise. When the doughs have doubled in bulk, spread out the plain, unfruited dough into a round ¼ inch in thickness. Make a ball of the fruited dough and place in the middle. Gather up the edges of the flat round, pressing them tightly together. Place the loaf, gathered edge down, on a greased baking sheet and flatten slightly. Cut through the outer dough, with scissors, all around at intervals of 2 inches. Cover and allow to rise in a warm place until doubled in bulk. Bake at 400° F. for 40 minutes. When cool, glaze with frosting and decorate with fruit and nuts.

BUTTERSCOTCH PECAN ROLL

Make ½ recipe Basic Sweet Dough. When it is light, punch it down and allow it to rest for 10 minutes. Roll it out into a rectangle about ⅓ inch thick and spread the surface liberally with softened butter and sprinkle with ½ cup brown sugar which has been mixed with 2 teaspoons cinnamon. Roll up lengthwise like a jelly roll and place seam side down in a greased loaf pan 10×5×3½ inches. Cover with a clean towel, place in a warm spot, and allow to rise until doubled in bulk. Bake at 350° F. for 30 minutes. Remove from the oven and coat the surface of the loaf with a mixture of ½ cup brown sugar and ½ cup melted butter and sprinkle over 1 cup chopped pecans. Return to the oven and bake 15 minutes longer.

GOLDEN DUKATS

Make ½ recipe Basic Sweet Dough. When it is light, punch it down and allow it to rest for 10 minutes. Roll out to ¼-inch thickness and with the cooky cutter cut the entire dough into rounds. Butter generously a round baking dish and line it with a layer of the cookies, then sprinkle with ground nuts, raisins, sugar, and cinnamon, mixed together, and sprinkle with a little melted butter. Repeat until the baking pan is half full and sprinkle the top with melted butter. Allow to rise in a warm place until the pan is full, and bake at 350° F. for 45 minutes.

In between the layers of the cookies a thick layer of jam, marmalade, or jelly may be spread, if desired.

When baked, remove from dish to serving platter, slice pie-fashion, and serve hot with a hot lemon or wine sauce.

FROSTED FRUIT LOAF

1 recipe Sweet Dough makes 3 loaves
For 1 loaf:
1 cup chopped candied fruits
½ cup confectioners' sugar
2 teaspoons milk
½ teaspoon vanilla

When sweet dough has doubled in bulk, punch it down and turn it out on a lightly floured board. Divide the dough into 3 equal pieces. Roll out 1 piece into an oblong about 1 inch thick. Sprinkle the surface with the chopped candied fruits and roll them lightly into the dough with the rolling pin. Fold both ends of the dough crosswise to the center of the dough and seal the edges and ends firmly. Place the dough in a well-greased bread pan (7½ × 3½ × 2¾ inches), cover with a towel and let rise in a warm place until doubled in bulk. Bake in a moderate oven (375° F.) about 45 minutes. Cool and ice it with a frosting made by combining the confectioners' sugar, milk and vanilla.

OLD-FASHIONED DESSERT BREAD

1 recipe Sweet Dough makes 4 cakes
For 1 cake:
¼ cup raisins
3 tablespoons butter
3 tablespoons water
⅔ cup sugar
⅓ cup brown sugar

When sweet dough has doubled in bulk, punch it down and turn it out on a lightly floured board. Divide the dough into 4 equal pieces. Roll out one piece into a circle about 8 inches in diameter and ¼ inch thick. Place it in a greased 9-inch layer cake pan, cover with a towel and let it rise in a warm place, free from draft, until doubled in bulk. Press the raisins into the dough about 1 inch apart and bake the cake in a moderate oven (375° F.) for 10 minutes. Meanwhile mix the butter, water and sugars in a saucepan and let it boil over a low heat for 5 minutes. Pour this hot syrup over the top of the cake while it is still in the oven and continue baking for about 30 minutes longer.

APRICOT PRUNE CAKE

Make ½ recipe Basic Sweet Dough and, when it is light, punch it down and allow it to stand for 10 minutes. Pat out the dough to fit a 9-inch, square cake pan. Place it in the greased pan and arrange on top in even rows alternate halves of stewed prunes and apricots. Mix together ¼ cup brown sugar, 2 tablespoons melted butter, and 1 teaspoon cinnamon and sprinkle over the fruit. Place in a warm spot to double in bulk and bake at 350° F. for 45 minutes.

BASIC RICH KUCHEN DOUGH

1 cake or package yeast
2 tablespoons lukewarm water
1 cup milk
1 cup shortening
¼ cup sugar
1 teaspoon salt
2 eggs, beaten
1 egg yolk, beaten
3 cups all-purpose flour

Dissolve the yeast in the lukewarm water. Scald the milk and stir in the shortening, sugar, and salt and cool to lukewarm. Add the softened yeast and the eggs, and enough flour to make a stiff batter. Beat well with a wooden spoon until the dough almost blisters, then knead in more flour with the hands until you have a soft dough that is not sticky. Turn out on a floured board and knead thoroughly, until the dough is smooth and satiny. Cover and allow to rise in a warm place until doubled in bulk. Punch down, allow to rise again until doubled, and make into a kuchen (see directions below). Allow to rise until doubled and bake at 350° F. for 45 minutes.

PLAIN KUCHEN

When kuchen dough is light, punch down and allow it to rest for 10 minutes. Roll out or flatten with the palms of the hands into a sheet 1 inch thick. Brush the surface of the dough with a little melted butter, roll tightly, and place in a greased loaf pan. Allow to rise again and bake at 350° F. for 45 minutes.

SOUR CREAM KUCHEN DOUGH

1 cake or package yeast
1 cup lukewarm milk
3 cups all-purpose flour
3 tablespoons sugar
1 egg, beaten
1 teaspoon salt
½ cup sour cream
½ cup soft butter

Dissolve the yeast in ½ cup of the lukewarm milk. Sift the flour into a large mixing bowl and make a nest in the center. Pour into the nest the dissolved yeast, the rest of the warm milk, sugar, egg, salt, and sour cream. Mix all together into a dough and knead until smooth and satiny, adding more flour, if necessary, to make a nonsticky dough. Cover and place in a warm spot until it has doubled in bulk. Punch down, place on lightly floured board, and knead in the butter. Knead so thoroughly that all the butter will be absorbed. Dust with flour and cover. Allow to rise again until doubled in bulk. Punch down and make into a kuchen (see directions below). Allow to rise again until doubled in bulk and bake at 350° F. for 45 minutes.

FRUIT- AND NUT-FILLED KUCHEN

When kuchen dough is light, punch down and allow it to rest for 10 minutes. Roll out 1 inch thick, spread with softened butter, and sprinkle over the surface ½ cup ground walnuts or blanched almonds, 1 cup raisins, ½ cup sugar, and 1 tablespoon cinnamon. Roll up tightly and place in large, greased tube pan. Allow to rise again and bake at 350° F. for 50 minutes.

CHOCOLATE-FILLED KUCHEN

Make a Sour Cream Kuchen Dough and when it is light, punch down and allow it to rest for 10 minutes. Roll out 1 inch thick and grate over the surface 3 or 4 ounces sweet chocolate. Roll tightly and place in buttered tube pan. Allow to rise until doubled in bulk and bake at 350° F. for 50 minutes.

MARMALADE KUCHEN

When kuchen dough is light, punch down and allow it to rest for 10 minutes. Press the dough into a well-greased, shallow pan and spread the surface generously with softened butter. Allow to rise until doubled and then with the floured handle of a wooden spoon make holes all over the surface of the dough at 2-inch intervals. Fill the holes with orange marmalade and bake at 375° F. for 40 minutes.

LAYER KUCHEN

When kuchen dough is light, punch down and allow it to rest for 10 minutes. Butter a tube pan heavily. Roll out the dough ¼ inch thick and cut dough into rounds which fit the bottom of the pan. Place the layers in the pan, one on top of the other. Brush each layer with butter and sprinkle with chopped nuts, sugar, raisins, cinnamon, and grated lemon peel. Cover and allow to rise in a warm place until doubled in bulk. Brush the top with melted butter and bake at 350° F. for 45 minutes. Cool and slice layer-cake fashion.

OPEN FRUIT KUCHENS

When kuchen dough is light, punch down and allow it to rest for 10 minutes. Flatten the dough out in a buttered, shallow, round or rectangular pan. Place regular rows of fruit on top. Sprinkle well with cinnamon and sugar and dot with butter. Allow to rise in a warm place until doubled in bulk and bake at 350° F. for 45 minutes.

Almost any fruit may be used: apples, peeled, sliced and cut into sections; peeled and halved peaches; prune plums, halved and pitted; seeded grapes; or sweet cherries.

STOLLEN

½ recipe Basic Sweet Dough
¾ cup raisins
¼ cup citron, finely shredded
¼ cup chopped candied cherries
¾ cup chopped nuts
2 tablespoons melted butter
Confectioners' Sugar Icing

When Basic Sweet Dough is light, add and knead in the raisins, citron, cherries, and nuts. Shape the dough into 2 balls and allow them to rest for 10 minutes. Flatten each ball into an oval about ¾ inch thick and brush with melted butter. Fold over like large Parker House Rolls. Pinch the ends firmly together and place them on a greased baking sheet. Brush the tops with melted butter and allow to rise until doubled in bulk (about 1 hour). Bake at 350° F. for 35 minutes. When cool, brush with Confectioners' Sugar Icing and decorate with large pieces of fruit and nuts. Makes 2 Stollen.

YEAST EGG BREADS, BRIOCHES, and BABAS

HUNGARIAN EGG DOUGH

1 cake or package yeast
2 tablespoons lukewarm water
½ cup egg yolks, beaten
½ cup melted butter
½ cup milk
2 tablespoons sugar
½ teaspoon salt
4 cups all-purpose flour

Dissolve the yeast in the lukewarm water. Mix together the egg yolks, melted butter, and milk. Add the dissolved yeast, the sugar and salt, and enough flour to make a stiff dough. Tie the dough in a cloth and place it in a bowl of water which is at room temperature. Allow it to stand until the dough rises to the surface of the water. Place the raised dough on a lightly floured board and knead thoroughly, using more flour if necessary. Place in a warm spot, cover, and allow to rise until doubled in bulk. This dough is now ready to form into loaves for bread, to be rolled into coffeecakes, or made into rolls.

COFFEECAKE Divide Hungarian Egg Dough into two parts. Pat one part into the bottom of a large, round, greased baking pan. Cover it with ½ cup chopped blanched almonds, ¼ cup sugar, ¼ cup raisins, and 1 teaspoon cinnamon. Cover this with the other part of the dough. Allow to rise until doubled in bulk and bake at 350° F. for 45 minutes. Makes 1 very large cake.

SOUR CHERRY CAKE Pat one fourth of Hungarian Egg Dough 1 inch thick into a greased loaf pan. Cover with sour pitted cherries and sugar. Cover with another inch of dough and allow to rise until doubled in bulk. Bake at 350° F. for 45 minutes. Makes 2 cakes.

ALMOND BREAD Pat Hungarian Egg Dough 1 inch thick in greased loaf pans. Brush with beaten egg white and sprinkle heavily with chopped blanched almonds and sugar. Allow to rise until doubled in bulk and bake at 350° F. for 30 minutes. Makes 4 flat loaves.

COFFEE TWISTS When kneading Hungarian Egg Dough, add ½ cup chopped raisins. When dough is light, punch down and divide into 6 parts. Form each part into a long strand and braid 3 together. Form into circles, moisten the edges, press firmly together, and place the circles on round, greased pans. Brush with beaten egg yolk. Sprinkle with sliced blanched almonds and sugar. Allow to rise until doubled in bulk and bake at 350° F. for 30 minutes. Makes 2 twists.

CINNAMON BUNS Roll Hungarian Egg Dough ½ inch thick and cut into rounds or squares. Place on greased baking sheet, brush with beaten egg yolk, and sprinkle with sugar and cinnamon. Allow to rise until doubled in bulk and bake at 375° F. for 20 minutes. Makes 2 dozen.

HORNETS' NESTS Roll Hungarian Egg Dough $\frac{1}{16}$ inch thick, brush with melted butter, and cut into strips 4×8 inches. Spread each strip with a thick coating of any good jam or filling, such as poppy seed, almond, or cheese. Roll each strip and place with the cut sides just touching in a greased cake pan. Sprinkle with sugar and allow to rise until doubled in bulk. Bake at 350° F. for 25 minutes. Makes 2 dozen.

SPAETZEL

    1 cake or package yeast
    2 tablespoons lukewarm water
    1 cup milk
    2 tablespoons butter
    1 tablespoon sugar
    ½ teaspoon salt
    5 egg yolks, beaten
    5 cups all-purpose flour
    Ground, unblanched almonds
    Bread crumbs, raisins, and cinnamon

Soften the yeast in the lukewarm water. Scald the milk and add to it the butter, sugar, and salt. Cool to lukewarm and then add the softened yeast and 2 cups of the flour. Beat well and allow to rise in a warm place until light and foamy. Stir in the egg yolks and the rest of the flour and knead well on a floured board. Allow to rise until doubled in bulk. Punch down and roll the dough into a thin sheet. Cut the dough into cooky-shaped rounds. Sprinkle a greased baking pan lightly with almonds and bread crumbs. Dip the rounds of dough in melted butter and place them in layers in the prepared pan until the pan is half full. Sprinkle each layer with ground almonds, raisins, cinnamon, and sugar and sprinkle the top with melted butter. Allow to rise until doubled in bulk and bake at 350° F. for 45 minutes. Makes 2 loaves.

Jam may be used between the layers, if desired.

PANETTONE DI NATALE, *Italian Christmas Bread*

1 cake or package yeast
¼ cup milk, scalded and cooled to lukewarm
¾ cup shortening
½ cup sugar
2 egg yolks, beaten
3 whole eggs, beaten
1 teaspoon vanilla
½ teaspoon salt
4 cups all-purpose flour
½ cup raisins
¼ cup shredded candied peel
¼ cup shredded citron
¼ cup chopped blanched almonds

Dissolve the yeast in the milk, add ½ cup of the flour, and allow to stand in a warm place until bubbly. Cream together the shortening and sugar. Add the beaten eggs and then the yeast-milk mixture. Add the vanilla, salt, and enough flour to make a dough that is soft but not sticky. Turn out on floured board and knead in the fruit and nuts. Place in a warm spot to rise until doubled in bulk. Punch down and knead again for 3 minutes. Shape into a round loaf, place in a greased baking pan, and allow to rise again until doubled in bulk. This will take longer than usual, because of the fruit. Bake at 400° F. for 10 minutes. Reduce oven temperature to 350° F. and bake for 50 minutes longer.

This may be baked in a kugelhoff pan, the bottom of which is covered with whole almonds and sprinkled with sugar.

PAN DE HUEVOS, *Mexican Egg Bread*

2 cakes or packages yeast
2 tablespoons lukewarm water
12 egg yolks
½ cup sugar
2 tablespoons melted shortening
3 tablespoons anise seed
12 egg whites, stiffly beaten
3½ cups all-purpose flour

Soften the yeast in the water and allow it to stand for 10 minutes.

Beat the egg yolks until thick and pale in color. Add the sugar gradually, continuing to beat. Then stir in the shortening and the softened yeast. Stir in the anise seed and egg whites and blend thoroughly and then add enough flour to make a dough that is light but not sticky. Allow to rise in a warm place until doubled in bulk, punch down, and knead for 3 minutes. Roll out ½ inch thick and cut into large squares. Place the squares on greased baking pans and allow to rise again until doubled in bulk. Bake at 350° F. for 45 minutes. Makes 2 loaves.

PAN DULCE, *Sweet Egg Buns*

2 cakes or packages yeast
1 tablespoon sugar
1½ cups lukewarm water
½ teaspoon salt
1½ cups sugar
2 tablespoons melted butter
4 eggs, beaten
5 cups all-purpose flour

Dissolve the yeast and 1 tablespoon sugar in the water. Allow to stand for 15 minutes and then stir in 2 cups of the flour and the salt. Allow to rise until doubled in bulk. Stir down and add the remaining sugar, melted butter, eggs, and enough flour to make a dough that is soft but not sticky. Turn out on floured board and knead until dough is smooth and satiny. Allow to rise until doubled in bulk, punch down, and knead again, using a little more flour if necessary. Form into small, round buns and place them, almost touching, on a greased baking sheet. Coat the tops with an icing made by mixing to a paste 1½ cups flour, 1 cup sugar, 1 beaten egg, ½ cup butter, ¼ cup heavy cream, and 1 teaspoon cinnamon. Allow to rise in a warm place until doubled in bulk and then bake at 350° F. for 30 minutes. Makes 4 dozen.

UKRAINIAN EASTER BREAD

2 cakes or packages yeast
2 cups milk, scalded and cooled to lukewarm
5 egg yolks, beaten
1 cup sugar
½ cup melted butter
1 cup currants
1 tablespoon vanilla
8 cups all-purpose flour

Dissolve the yeast in the milk, add 3 cups of the flour, and allow to stand in a warm place overnight. In the morning add the eggs, sugar, butter, currants, vanilla, and enough flour to make a light dough. Allow to rise in a warm place until doubled in bulk. Turn out onto a floured board and knead well, using more flour, if necessary, to make a medium dough. Put into greased loaf pans and allow to rise in a warm place until doubled in bulk. Bake at 400° F. for 10 minutes. Reduce oven temperature to 350° F. and bake for 50 minutes more. Makes 2 large loaves.

Other fruit and nuts may be added, such as chopped raisins, chopped almonds, or chopped candied peel, if desired.

KUGELHOFF

1 cake or package yeast
1 cup milk, scalded and cooled to lukewarm
1 cup butter
¾ cup sugar
5 eggs
4 cups all-purpose flour
1 teaspoon salt
Grated rind of 1 lemon
1 cup raisins
½ cup chopped blanched almonds

Soften the yeast in the lukewarm milk. Cream the butter and sugar until light and fluffy and add the eggs, one by one, creaming well after each addition. Add the yeast alternately with the flour, mixing well after each addition. Stir in the salt, lemon rind, raisins, and half the almonds. Butter a fancy kugelhoff form or tube pan, sprinkle with the remaining almonds, and pour in the batter until the form is half full. Allow to rise in a warm place until the pan is full. Bake at 400° F. for 10 minutes. Reduce oven temperature to 350° F. and bake for another 40 minutes.

KUGELHOFF WITH CHOCOLATE Make a Kugelhoff dough, omitting the raisins and nuts and adding enough flour to make a dough that is soft but not sticky. Divide the dough into two parts. Melt 2 ounces sweet chocolate in 3 tablespoons milk. Add 1 teaspoon vanilla and 2 tablespoons sugar. Mix this into one part of the dough. Roll out each part on a lightly floured sheet and place the chocolate mixture over the white dough. Roll up like a jelly roll and place in a well-buttered kugelhoff pan or tube pan. Allow to rise until doubled in bulk and bake at 400° F. for 10 minutes. Lower heat to 350° F. and bake for 45 minutes longer.

FILLED KUGELHOFF Make a Kugelhoff dough, omitting the raisins and nuts. Butter a fancy kugelhoff pan generously and pour in half the batter. Sprinkle with 3 ounces ground almonds, 2 tablespoons sugar, 3 ounces chopped raisins, 1 teaspoon cinnamon, and the grated rind of 1 lemon. Pour over remaining dough and allow to rise in a warm place until the pan is full. Bake at 350° F. for 45 minutes. Cool on a cake rack and serve dusted with powdered sugar.

FILLED EGG BREAD

1 cake or package yeast
¼ cup lukewarm water
¾ cup milk
½ cup butter
½ cup sugar
1 teaspoon salt
4 eggs, beaten
1 teaspoon vanilla
5 cups all-purpose flour
1 egg white, slightly beaten

Dissolve the yeast in the lukewarm water. Scald the milk, add the butter, sugar, and salt, and cool to lukewarm. Add the yeast, the beaten eggs, and the vanilla. Gradually mix in enough flour to make a light dough that is not sticky. Turn out on floured board and knead until smooth and satiny. Cover and allow to rise in a warm place until doubled in bulk. Combine all the filling ingredients. Divide the dough in half. Into one half knead the filling and shape it into a narrow loaf. Roll out the other half into a rectangle, place the filled loaf in the center, and fold the plain dough around it. Seal the edges and place in a greased loaf pan with the sealed edge down. Allow to rise in a warm place until doubled in bulk, brush with the egg white, and bake at 325° F. for 65 minutes. Makes 1 loaf.

FILLING
1 cup ground poppy seeds
1 cup chopped dried fruits (dates, prunes, etc.)
¾ cup chopped walnuts
½ cup chopped candied peel
¼ cup melted semisweet chocolate
½ teaspoon chocolate

BATH BUNS

1 cake or package yeast
½ cup milk, scalded and cooled to lukewarm
1 tablespoon sugar
½ cup soft butter
4 eggs, beaten
4 cups all-purpose flour
½ teaspoon salt
⅓ cup sugar
1 cup chopped blanched almonds
½ cup shredded citron
½ cup currants
½ cup chopped raisins
¼ cup candied cherries

Dissolve the yeast in the milk. Add the sugar and mix well. Add the butter, eggs, flour, and salt. Beat thoroughly and allow to rise in a warm place until very light or more than doubled in bulk. The dough should be sticky and not firm enough to roll. Stir down with a wooden spoon and work in the rest of the ingredients. Drop large spoonfuls of dough on a greased baking sheet. Allow to rise in a warm place until doubled in bulk and bake at 375° F. for 20 minutes. Remove from the oven and glaze with 1 egg yolk beaten with 1 tablespoon lukewarm water. Sprinkle thickly with sugar and return to the oven for 1 minute, to glaze.

RICH COFFEE BREAD

1 cake or package yeast
¼ cup lukewarm water
1 cup butter
4 cups all-purpose flour
1 teaspoon salt
4 tablespoons sugar
8 egg yolks
½ cup milk, scalded and cooled to lukewarm
Melted butter
1 cup chopped almonds
½ cup chopped raisins
½ cup brown sugar
1 egg white, slightly beaten

Dissolve the yeast in the water. Cut the butter into the flour, add the salt, sugar, and egg yolks, and mix thoroughly. Then add enough of the lukewarm milk to make a fairly stiff dough. Turn out on floured board and knead thoroughly, then roll out into a long rectangle. Brush the surface of the dough with melted butter and sprinkle with ¾ cup of the chopped almonds, the chopped raisins, and the brown sugar. Roll the dough into a long, thick sausage form and cut in half, lengthwise, and twist the two pieces together, forming a circle and sealing the ends. Brush with beaten egg white, sprinkle with the rest of the chopped almonds, place in a well-buttered baking pan, and allow to rise in a warm place until doubled in bulk. Bake at 350° F. for 35 minutes, or until lightly browned.

LEPENY Roll out Rich Coffee Bread very thin and cut it into large squares. Fill each square with any fruit or nut filling. Fold over the corners and seal to hold the filling intact while the Lepeny are baking. Bake at 350° F. for 25 minutes.

BRIOCHES

This famous bread of France is rich, yet peculiarly plain and simple. The dough may be shaped into the conventional pear-shaped buns or made into crescents, twists, or just plain round buns. The dough may also be used for cinnamon rolls, coffeecakes, and even doughnuts.

INGREDIENTS FOR 2 DOZEN BRIOCHES

    1 cake or package yeast
    ¼ cup lukewarm water
    1 teaspoon sugar
    4 cups sifted all-purpose flour
    ½ teaspoon salt
    2 tablespoons sugar
    1 cup butter
    6 large eggs
    Lukewarm milk

Soften the yeast in the lukewarm water with the 1 teaspoon sugar. Add just enough of the sifted flour (about 1 cup) to make a very soft dough which can be formed into a ball. Make two slits in the top, at right angles to one another, and place this ball in a bowl of lukewarm water. Place in a warm spot to rise. Within an hour the ball will rise to the surface of the water and is then ready to use.

Put the remaining flour into a large bowl and make a well in the center. Put into the hole the salt, the 2 tablespoons sugar, about 2 tablespoons milk, half the butter, and 4 eggs. Start by working the butter, eggs, and seasoning into a smooth paste, then mix in the flour, adding a little more milk, if necessary, to make a smooth dough. Knead the dough thoroughly until it is smooth and has acquired a certain amount of resilience. Make a hole in the middle of it and add 1 egg. Mix it into the paste and knead again for 2 minutes. Add the last egg in the same way.

Now work the rest of the butter until it is about the same consistency as the Brioche paste and spread it on the paste, together with the risen yeast dough, and mix, kneading small portions at a time until completely mixed. Place the dough in a greased bowl, cover, and allow it to rise until very light and more than doubled in bulk. Turn it out on a floured board and beat it with the palm of the hand. Place again in the bowl, cover, and allow it to rest in the refrigerator overnight.

Next day roll the dough into a long sausage, cut off pieces, and form into balls. Make a crisscross incision in the top of the ball and gently insert a smaller ball of the dough to make the head of the Brioche. Place in well-buttered bowl-shaped or fluted brioche molds or in small tartlet tins and allow to rise in a warm place until doubled in bulk. Brush the tops with beaten egg yolks and bake at 425° F. until brown. The baking time depends on the size of the molds, but 15–20 minutes is enough for the average individual Brioche.

NOTE: This paste can be kept for several days in the refrigerator and baked when wanted.

SAVARIN

1 cake or package yeast
½ cup lukewarm milk
2 cups all-purpose flour
4 eggs, slightly beaten
⅔ cup butter
½ teaspoon salt
1 tablespoon sugar

Soften the yeast in the lukewarm milk. Sift the flour into a bowl and add the yeast mixture. Add the eggs and work all together until the dough is elastic. Work the butter until it is softened and distribute it in small quantities over the paste, mixing it in lightly. The dough should be softer than Brioche dough. Cover and place in a warm spot to double in bulk. Work the dough again, adding the salt and sugar. Fill a well-buttered ring mold two thirds full and again allow it to rise in a warm place until it almost fills the mold. Bake at 400° F. for about 30 minutes, or until a cake tester comes out clean.

Savarin is nice served with a macédoine of cooked fruit in the center of the ring, or served plain with Apricot Sauce. It may be baked in small, individual ring molds, well buttered and sprinkled with toasted almond slivers, soaked with light syrup while still warm, and sprinkled with rum or kirsch.

BABA AU RHUM Baba paste is essentially the same as that for Savarin. Sometimes 1 tablespoon sultana raisins and 1 tablespoon currants are worked into the dough, along with the salt and sugar. Fill well-buttered ring mold or individual baking cups two thirds full with the paste, place in a warm spot, and allow to rise until it fills the mold or cups. Bake at 400° F. until lightly browned. Individual Babas will take about 15 minutes. The large mold will take 25–30 minutes. When a cake tester comes out clean it is done.

Invert the Baba on a serving plate and, while still warm, pour over a syrup made by boiling together ½ cup sugar and ¾ cup apricot juice for 10 minutes. Remove from the fire and stir in 1 teaspoon lemon juice and 2 ounces Jamaica rum. Just before serving, pour over a little more rum.

The center of the mold may be filled with ice cream, if desired, and fruit, such as apricot halves or pitted black cherries, piled high over the top.

YEAST DOUGHNUTS

Most doughnuts and crullers today are made by the quicker baking powder method (see "Quick Breads" chapter), but for a special treat, try rolling out some sweet dough ⅓ inch in thickness. Any basic sweet dough may be used, so the next time you are making sweet rolls, potato rolls, kuchens, or one of the richer egg breads, put aside enough of the dough for fried cakes.

Cut the dough with a 3-inch doughnut cutter and allow the rounds to rise on the board uncovered, in a warm place, for about 30 minutes. A light crust will form on the dough. Drop the rounds into deep hot fat (375° F.) a few at a time. As soon as a doughnut rises to the surface and begins to show a little color, turn it over. Turn again as soon as the underside is brown. Lift from the fat when lightly browned, using a long two-tined fork thrust through the hole. Drain on absorbent paper in a warm place. The frying time should not take over 3 minutes. If you do not have a deep-fat thermometer test the fat by dropping in a cube of bread. If the cube of bread browns in 50 seconds your fat is the right temperature for deep-frying doughnuts. It is not difficult to adjust the temperature by this favorite test method.

SPICED DOUGHNUTS Add a little cinnamon or nutmeg to the dough.

SUGAR DOUGHNUTS Put some fine granulated sugar into a brown paper bag, add a few doughnuts at a time, and shake gently to give an even, sugar-coated surface.

CRULLERS Crullers are doughnuts, without the hole, which have been twisted into the figure 8. Roll out sweet dough ½ inch thick and cut into strips a good ½ inch wide and about 10 inches long. Double the strip and pinch the two ends together firmly. Twist once to make a figure 8 or twice for a double twist. Allow to rise, and fry as for doughnuts. Drain and coat with sugar.

BISMARCKS Roll sweet dough ½ inch thick and cut into 3-inch rounds with a plain cooky cutter. Allow to rise, leaving them uncovered so that a light crust will form, and fry as for doughnuts. Drain and cool. In the side of each doughnut cut a slit through to the center, and insert a teaspoon of good jelly or jam. Close tightly and roll in fine granulated sugar spread on wax paper.

REFRIGERATOR DOUGHNUTS

Here is the way to have doughnuts hot and fresh each day for a week.

2 cups milk, scalded
1½ cups sugar
½ cup butter or shortening
1 teaspoon salt
1 egg, well-beaten
1 cake or package yeast
½ cup lukewarm water
6 cups all-purpose flour

Add the sugar, butter, and salt to the scalded milk and allow to cool. Add the beaten egg and the yeast, which has been softened in the lukewarm water. Work in the flour until a light dough is obtained which does not stick to the hands. Cover and allow to rise in a warm place until doubled in bulk. Punch down and roll out as much dough as is desired for a batch of doughnuts. Roll the rest in wax paper and then in a damp towel and store in the refrigerator. *Keep towel damp and dough will last for a week.* Cut the rolled dough into doughnuts, crullers, or Bismarcks. Allow to rise on board, uncovered, until doubled in bulk. Fry in deep fat. Makes 6 dozen.

KRAPFEN

1 cake or package yeast
¼ cup lukewarm water
1 tablespoon sugar
¼ cup butter
⅜ cup sugar
½ teaspoon salt
1 cup milk, scalded and cooled to lukewarm
Grated rind of 1 lemon
1 egg, well beaten
4–5 cups all-purpose flour

Soften the yeast in the lukewarm water, to which has been added the 1 tablespoon sugar. Cream together the butter and sugar, add the salt, the yeast mixture, milk, lemon rind, egg, and enough of the flour to make a dough that is soft but not sticky. Allow to rise in a warm place until doubled in bulk, knead on a lightly floured board, and roll out ¹⁄₁₆ inch thick. Cut into rounds 3 inches in diameter. Spread the edges with a little beaten egg to keep the filling from running out and spread every other round with 1 teaspoon jam, marmalade, or jelly. Place a plain round on top of each filled round and pinch the edges together. Spread with melted butter and allow to rise in a warm place for 1 hour. Fry as for doughnuts, frying the unbuttered side first. Drain on absorbent paper and dust with confectioners' sugar. Makes 4 dozen.

FASTNACHTS KUCHEN, *Fast Night Cakes* These fried cakes, which are eaten on Shrove Tuesday, the day before Lent begins, are made from Krapfen dough. Omit the grated lemon rind and add to the flour ½ teaspoon grated nutmeg. When the dough is light and doubled in bulk, knead it on a lightly floured board and roll out ¼ inch thick. Cut into squares, allow to rise ½ hour, and fry as for doughnuts in deep hot fat. Makes 4 dozen.

OLYKOEK

Make any sweet dough according to directions. Cut off small pieces and enclose in the center of each piece a few brandied raisins, a brandied cherry, or ½ teaspoon mixed citron and raisins, forming them into small balls. Let them stand in a warm place until doubled in bulk and then fry in hot, deep fat for about 2 minutes. Drain them on absorbent paper and roll them in powdered sugar. Serve warm.

Olykoeks may be sprinkled generously with rum and served with whipped cream.

CHUNK BREAD

Break off small irregular chunks of any sweet dough which has been made according to directions and allowed to rise in a warm place. Drop the chunks directly into hot, deep fat and fry as for doughnuts.

YEAST WAFFLES

½ cake or package yeast
3 tablespoons lukewarm water
1 egg, beaten
1 tablespoon melted butter
1 cup milk
2 cups all-purpose flour
½ teaspoon salt

Soften the yeast in the water and allow to stand in a warm place for ½ hour. Add the rest of the ingredients in the order given. These may be baked at once or allowed to stand in a warm place until bubbly.

FOR PANCAKES Thin the batter with ¼ cup additional milk.

FRENCH YEAST PANCAKES

1 cake or package yeast
2 tablespoons lukewarm water
2 cups all-purpose flour
2 tablespoons brandy
3 eggs
2 egg yolks
3 tablespoons butter, melted and cooled
Lukewarm milk

Soften the yeast in the water. In a warm mixing bowl combine the flour and brandy and the softened yeast. Beat together the eggs and egg yolks, add to them the butter, and stir into the flour mixture. Add enough milk to make a batter about the thickness of heavy cream. Cover the bowl with a clean towel and let it stand in a warm place for about 1 hour.

Brush a small hot frying pan (about 6 inches in diameter) with butter, and quickly pour in about 1 tablespoon of the batter, twisting the pan so that the batter covers the bottom with a thin even layer. These pancakes brown quickly so they must be turned with a broad spatula almost immediately. Let them brown on the other side. Continue cooking the batter until it has all been used, buttering the frying pan each time.

CORN MEAL GRIDDLECAKES

2 cups boiling water
1 cup corn meal
2 cups sifted all-purpose flour
1 tablespoon brown sugar
2 cups milk, scalded and cooled
1 cake or envelope yeast
2 tablespoons lukewarm water
2 eggs, beaten
1 teaspoon salt
2 tablespoons melted butter

Pour the boiling water gradually over the corn meal and beat the mush until smooth and cooled to lukewarm. Stir in the flour, sugar, and milk. Soften the yeast in the lukewarm water and let it stand for 10 minutes, then stir it into the flour-corn meal batter. Let the mixture stand all night in a warm place. In the morning stir in the beaten eggs, the salt, and the melted butter. Add enough corn meal (about 1 cup) to make a fairly thick batter and mix thoroughly. Pour the batter in small puddles on a greased griddle and bake slowly until the pancakes are brown on the underside and bubbly on top. Turn and let them brown on the other side. Serve with gobs of butter and maple syrup. Makes about 2 dozen pancakes. If you want to repeat these cakes the next day, save about 1 cup of the batter for a starter. Add to it the cup of corn meal, mixed with the boiling water and cooled to lukewarm. Stir in the flour, sugar, and milk. No additional yeast is needed. Next morning add the remaining ingredients and bake in the usual way.

BLINI

1½ cups milk
1 cake or package yeast
2 cups buckwheat flour
4 eggs, separated
½ teaspoon salt
1 tablespoon sugar
1½ cups lukewarm milk
2 teaspoons butter, melted

Scald 1½ cups of milk, cool to lukewarm, and add to it the yeast. Stir until the yeast is dissolved and add enough of the flour to make a thick sponge. Cover the bowl and allow it to rise in a warm place for about 2½ hours. Beat the egg yolks with the salt and sugar, combine with the rest of the milk, and add the butter. Stir this into the raised sponge. Mix in the remaining flour and fold in the egg whites, which have been stiffly beaten. Cover again and allow the mixture to stand for at least 30 minutes. Heat a griddle and bake small pancakes about 3 inches in diameter. The pancakes should not be thicker than ¼ inch. If they are, a little more milk should be stirred into the batter. Brown the cakes lightly on both sides and serve with butter or sour cream, cottage cheese, caviar, or smoked salmon. Makes 30 Blini.

OLD-FASHIONED BUCKWHEAT CAKES

⅓ cup flour or corn meal
2 cups scalded milk
⅔ teaspoon salt
1¼ cups buckwheat flour
1 cake or package yeast
⅓ cup lukewarm water
2 tablespoons molasses
¼ teaspoon soda

Soak the flour or corn meal in the milk and let the mixture cool to lukewarm. Stir in the salt and buckwheat flour and the yeast, which has been softened in the lukewarm water. Pour into a large bowl or pitcher and let it rise in a warm place overnight. In the morning stir in the molasses and soda. Blend well, bake as for pancakes, and serve hot with butter, maple sugar, and sausages.

RUSKS

1 cake or package yeast
¼ cup lukewarm water
1 cup milk, scalded and cooled to lukewarm
4 cups all-purpose flour
1 egg, beaten
½ cup sugar
¼ cup melted butter
½ teaspoon nutmeg
1 teaspoon salt

Soften the yeast in the water and add the milk and half the flour. Beat thoroughly and allow to rise in a warm place until light and bubbly. Then add the remaining ingredients and enough additional flour to make a medium dough. Allow to rise until doubled in bulk, punch down, and turn out on lightly floured board. Knead for a few minutes. Form into smooth, round buns and place them, not touching, on a greased baking sheet. Again allow to rise in a warm place until doubled in bulk and bake at 400° F. for 10 minutes.

Reduce oven temperature to 350° F. and bake for 15 minutes longer.

ZWIEBACK Make and bake Rusks as in the preceding recipe. When the buns are cool, slice 1 inch thick, return to the oven (300° F.), and rebake until the slices are brown on both sides.

2. Quick Breads

No household need forgo the luxury of piping-hot breads. In this chapter the quick-rising action of baking powder takes the place of the time-consuming leavening action of yeast.

Quick breads come to the rescue of busy-day meals and add glamor to otherwise dull, everyday menus.

There is no other food, for the small amount of effort expended, that affords any greater eating pleasure. Tender, flaky biscuits, with their crisp brown coats, have irresistible appeal for every taste. Light, golden muffins stimulate even the dullest palate. Have tender pancakes or waffles, hot from the griddle, for breakfast; wisps of popovers with a salad lunch; tempting coffeecakes or breads filled with fruit and nuts for any meal.

BAKING POWDER BISCUITS, DUMPLINGS, AND COBBLERS

The recipes for baking powder biscuits are many. Master just one, and then you can, by the addition of fruit or nuts, with fancy cutters and unusual-shaped tins, increase the variety to impressive proportions.

Baking powder biscuits may be rolled out, shaped into balls with the hands, dropped from a spoon to a baking sheet, flavored with fruit juices, filled with sugar, fruit, and nuts, or dipped in parsley, cheese, or spice. The basic dough may be used for shortcakes and meat pie toppings. With the addition of a little sugar and an egg, this same dough can be used for sweet breads and puddings.

BASIC BAKING POWDER BISCUITS

INGREDIENTS FOR 1 DOZEN (2½-INCH) BISCUITS

	PLAIN	RICH
All-purpose flour, sifted	2 cups	2 cups
Salt	½ tsp.	½ tsp.
Baking powder, double-action	2 tsp.	2 tsp.
Shortening, part butter	4 tbs.	6 tbs.
Milk	¾ cup	⅔ cup

METHOD

1. Preheat oven to 450° F.
2. Sift dry ingredients into mixing bowl.
3. Add the shortening and cut it lightly into the flour mixture, using a pastry blender, 2 knives, or the finger tips, until the mixture looks like coarse corn meal.
4. Mix in the milk, gradually, until a soft dough is formed. Too much milk makes the dough sticky, which is all right for drop biscuits but difficult for rolled biscuits. Too little milk makes the dough stiff, and the resulting biscuits will be dry and tough.
5. Place the dough in a mound on a lightly floured board. Knead the dough gently for about 30 seconds, turning it over 2 or 3 times to even up the texture. Handle lightly, as too much kneading at this point will toughen the biscuits.
6. Roll out dough with floured rolling pin, or pat out with floured hand (this is the easiest method for small quantity), to the desired thickness.
   For thin, crusty biscuits, roll out ½ inch thick.
   For thick, soft biscuits, roll out 1 inch thick.
7. Cut with floured biscuit cutter and place on ungreased baking

sheet. Place close together for soft sides; place apart for crusty sides.
8. Bake 12–15 minutes, or until lightly browned.

NOTE: Slightly lower temperature makes crustier biscuits.

DROP BISCUITS Here are baking powder biscuits in their easiest form. No kneading, no rolling, no cutting is necessary. Simply increase the liquid in the Basic Baking Powder Biscuit recipe to about 1 cup, to make a dough that is sticky and light enough to drop from a spoon into muffin cups or onto an ungreased baking sheet. The soft mounds will spread a little as they bake, so do not place them too close together if you want biscuits that are crusty all around. They will be crusty and rough outside and fluffy inside —perfect for fruit shortcake.

VARIETY BISCUITS AND ROLLS FROM BASIC RECIPES OR PACKAGED MIX

The following variety biscuits, except those starred, may be made from a packaged biscuit mix. Measure out 2 cups of the mix and follow the directions on the package, adding the additional ingredients as indicated.

APPLE BISCUITS Add ½ teaspoon cinnamon and ½ cup shredded apple to the flour-shortening mixture, and continue according to directions. Sprinkle tops of biscuits with cinnamon and place a thin slice of apple on top. Bake as usual.

BACON BISCUITS Add ¼ cup very crisp fried bacon bits to the flour-shortening mixture, and continue according to directions.

BACON ROLLS Roll out biscuit dough ¼ inch thick and spread with bacon drippings. Sprinkle over the surface ½ cup diced bacon which has been fried until crisp and golden brown. Roll up and cut into ½-inch slices. Place on ungreased baking sheet and bake at 450° F. for 12 minutes.

BRAN BISCUITS* Substitute ½ cup bran for ½ cup flour in Basic Baking Powder Biscuit recipe.

BUTTERMILK OR SOUR MILK BISCUITS* Omit the baking powder in Basic Baking Powder Biscuit recipe and sift ½ teaspoon soda with the dry ingredients. Use sour milk or buttermilk in place of the plain milk.

BUTTERSCOTCH BISCUITS Roll out baking powder biscuit dough ¼ inch thick, spread with butter and brown sugar, or with sugar, cinnamon, and raisins. Roll lengthwise like a jelly roll and cut into ½-inch-thick slices. Place each slice in a buttered muffin tin, in the bottom of which has been put 1 teaspoon brown sugar. Bake for 15 minutes at 425° F.

CARAWAY SEED BISCUITS Cut baking powder biscuit dough into small, thin rounds. Spread half the rounds with softened butter, sprinkle lightly with caraway seeds, cover with the remaining rounds, and bake according to directions.

CHEESE BISCUITS Add ½ cup grated cheese to flour and shortening before adding liquid. Continue according to directions and bake as usual.

CORN MEAL BISCUITS* Substitute ⅔ cup corn meal for ⅔ cup flour in Basic Baking Powder Biscuit recipe.

FRUIT BISCUITS Add ½ cup finely chopped dates, apricots, figs, or raisins to the flour-shortening mixture, and continue according to directions.

FRUIT DROPS Make a drop biscuit dough, adding 2 tablespoons sugar to the dry ingredients. Stir into the dough 1 cup finely chopped apples, 1 tablespoon grated orange rind, and ½ cup finely chopped raisins. Drop from a teaspoon onto an ungreased baking sheet and bake at 425° F. for 12 minutes.

FRUIT TURNOVERS Roll baking powder biscuit dough less than ¼ inch thick and cut into 4-inch squares. Place chopped fruit, fresh, canned, or frozen, on half of each square. Dot with butter, sprinkle with sugar, fold over to make triangles, and seal. Bake at 425° F. for 15–18 minutes. Serve with fruit sauce, if desired.

GINGER BISCUITS Add 1 beaten egg and ½ cup preserved ginger to the flour-shortening mixture. Decrease milk to ½ cup and continue according to directions.

HONEY BUNS Cream together ½ cup honey and ¼ cup butter and spread thinly in the bottom of a baking pan. Roll baking powder biscuit dough ¼ inch thick and spread with melted butter, brown sugar, cinnamon, and raisins or nuts. Roll and cut into 1-inch pieces. Place in the prepared pan and bake at 425° F. for 15 minutes. Remove from pan immediately.

JAM BISCUITS Roll and cut baking powder biscuits according to directions. Place them on an ungreased baking sheet and make a deep depression in the center top of each biscuit. Fill the depressions with jam or marmalade and bake as usual.

LEMON BISCUITS Make baking powder biscuits and cut into small rounds. Press half a lump of sugar which has been dipped into lemon juice into the top of each biscuit. Sprinkle with grated lemon rind and bake as usual.

MAPLE BISCUITS Roll baking powder biscuit dough ¼ inch thick and cut into rounds. Place the rounds in a greased baking pan, brush the tops with melted butter, and sprinkle over the top ½ cup shaved maple sugar. Bake as usual.

ORANGE BISCUITS Make the same as Lemon Biscuits, substituting orange juice and orange rind for the lemon.

PEANUT BUTTER BISCUITS* Omit salt and shortening and add ½ cup peanut butter to Basic Baking Powder Biscuit recipe.

PECAN MUFFINS Make a drop biscuit dough, adding 2 tablespoons sugar to the dry ingredients. Butter muffin tins generously and put into the bottom of each 1 teaspoon brown sugar and a few broken pecan halves. Drop biscuit dough into the prepared tins and sprinkle the tops with 1 tablespoon sugar which has been mixed with ½ teaspoon cinnamon. Bake at 425° F. for 15 minutes.

PINEAPPLE ROLLS Roll baking powder biscuit dough ¼ inch thick and spread with melted butter. Sprinkle over the surface ½ cup drained, crushed pineapple, ⅓ cup sugar, and 1 teaspoon cinnamon. Roll lengthwise and slice into 1-inch pieces. Bake in buttered muffin tins at 425° F. for 15 minutes.

SAVORY TEASERS Shape baking powder biscuit dough into small balls with the hands and dip the tops in finely chopped parsley or chives. Place plain side down on ungreased baking sheet and bake for 8 minutes.

SOUR CREAM BISCUITS Use sour cream in place of the milk, adding ½ teaspoon soda to the cream before blending it with the dry ingredients. This makes a very rich biscuit.

SURPRISE BISCUITS Roll thin layers of baking powder biscuit dough around a date which has been pitted and stuffed with half a pecan, around tiny sausages, orange sections, or apple quarters. Glaze with slightly beaten egg white before baking. Nice for hors d'oeuvre or for tea.

SWEET POTATO BISCUITS* Substitute 1 cup mashed, cooked sweet potato for 1 cup flour in Basic Baking Powder Biscuit recipe and decrease milk to about 6 tablespoons. For a sweeter biscuit, add 2 tablespoons brown sugar.

THIMBLE BISCUITS Roll baking powder biscuit dough ¼ inch thick and cut into 1-inch rounds. Bake at 350° F. for 6 minutes.

TURNOVERS Roll baking powder biscuit dough ⅛ inch thick and cut into pieces about 4×5 inches. Spread half of each piece with marmalade, jam, peanut butter, chutney, mincemeat, or a combination of butter, cinnamon, and nuts. Fold the dough over the filling and press the edges together with the tines of a fork. Cut

STEPS IN KNEADING
YEAST DOUGH, pp. 6–8

When the dough forms an irregular ball that comes away from the sides of the bowl, turn out on a lightly floured board.

With lightly floured hands, press the dough firmly into a smooth, slightly flat ball. Then, using both hands, fold the dough over on itself toward you.

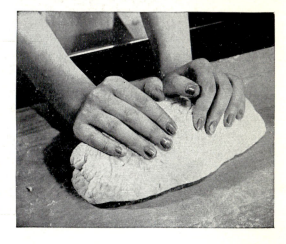

With the heels of your hands push the dough away from you. Give the dough a quarter turn and repeat until the surface is smooth and satiny.

RAISING AND PUNCHING DOWN YEAST DOUGH, p. 6-8

1. When the dough has been kneaded, shape it into a smooth ball and place it in a warm, lightly greased bowl. Always cover the bowl lightly with a towel, then set it in a warm, draft-free spot.

2. *First rising.* Two fingers pressed deeply into the dough and then withdrawn leave a slight depression if the dough has doubled in bulk.

3. Punch down after the first rising by thrusting fist into the dough. As the dough collapses, pull in the edges and fold them over into the center.

4. ABOVE: Cut the dough with a sharp knife for shaping into loaves. 5. BELOW: After the second rising a gentle finger-tip test which leaves a slight indentation tells you that the rolls or loaves are ready for the oven.

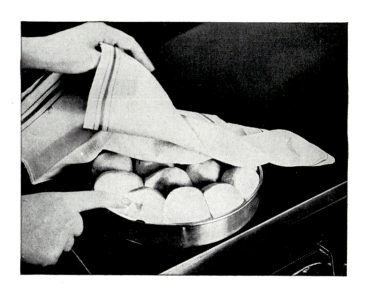

STEPS IN MOLDING YEAST BREAD, p. 8

1. Flatten the ball of dough with the palms of the hands.

5. Now fold the dough lengwise into thirds.

2. Fold it lengthwise and flatten it again.

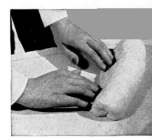

6. Seal the edges.

3. Stretch the dough gently to elongate it.

7. Form the dough into smooth roll.

4. Overlap the ends at the center and press firmly together.

8. Place the molded loaf a greased loaf pan, sea edge down.

Parker House Rolls, p. 25

Pan Rolls, p. 25

Cloverleaf Rolls, p. 26

Crescents, p. 26

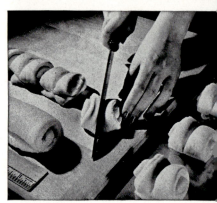

Butterflies, p. 26

Cushions, p. 27

Fan Tans, p. 26

Cloverleaf, Fan Tan, and
Crusty Rolls, pp. 26, 14

Triple Deckers, p. 27

Crossettes, p. 27

Two-in-One Twists, p. 28

Bowknots, p. 27

ABOVE, preparation of Cinnamon Pinwheels, p. 31
BELOW, preparation of Cinnamon Twists, p. 30

Preparation of Kolacky, p. 33

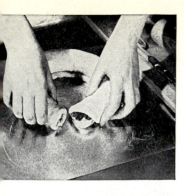

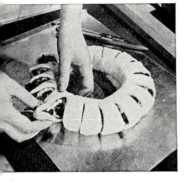

Preparation of Swedish Tea Ring, p. 45

―aration of and finished Bubble Loaf, p. 46

Apple Coffeecake, p. 46

Crumble Coffeecake, p. 47

Honey Twist, p. 48

a few small slits in the top and bake as usual.

WHOLE WHEAT BISCUITS* Use whole wheat flour in place of white in the Basic Baking Powder Biscuit recipe.

BAKING POWDER DUMPLINGS

APPLE DUMPLINGS Roll out baking powder biscuit dough ¼ inch thick and cut into large squares. Place a peeled and cored apple in the center of each square. Fill the cavity in the apple with brown sugar, a pinch of cinnamon, and dot with butter. Wrap the dough over the apple, moistening the edges with a little water and pressing them together firmly. Place them close together, sealed edge down, in a buttered baking pan. Pour over them a syrup made by boiling together 1 cup sugar and 1 cup water for 3 minutes. Bake at 400° F. for 40 minutes, or until the apples are tender, basting them from time to time with the syrup in the pan. Serve hot with cream. Other fruit dumplings may be made in the same way. Sour cherries, blueberries, or peaches make fine fruit variations for dumplings.

DUMPLINGS IN NECTAR Add 1 teaspoon cinnamon, ½ teaspoon grated lemon rind, and ½ cup seedless raisins to half the recipe for Drop Biscuits. Drop by spoonfuls into a 1-quart casserole containing 1½ cups apricot nectar or a thin, sweetened purée of any other fruit. Bake uncovered at 400° F. for 30 minutes.

FRUIT COBBLER Put 4 cups apples or peaches, thinly sliced, or blueberries into a 1½-quart casserole. Sprinkle the fruit with sugar and cinnamon and dot with butter. Make ½ the recipe for Drop Biscuits and drop by the spoonful on top of the fruit. Bake at 400° F. for 30 minutes.

RHUBARB DUMPLINGS Cut 1 pound rhubarb into 1-inch pieces and stew in 1 cup water and ½ cup sugar until tender. Add 1 cup strawberries and pour the fruit into a 1½-quart casserole. Make ½ the Drop Biscuit recipe and drop by the spoonful on top of the fruit. Bake at 400° F. for 10 minutes, cover the casserole, and bake for another 15 minutes.

PEACH COBBLER

8 peaches, peeled and sliced
Basic Baking Powder Biscuit dough
½ cup sugar
3 tablespoons peach brandy
2 tablespoons butter

Line a 3-inch-deep square cake pan with biscuit dough rolled ¼ inch thick. Fill the dish with the peeled peaches and cover the top with more biscuit dough. Do not press the edges of the biscuit dough against the edge of the pan. Prick the surface of the dough well with the tines of a fork and bake at 400° F. for 45 minutes. Remove the cobbler from the oven and lift up carefully the top biscuit crust. Sprinkle the sugar and brandy over the fruit. Add the butter and mix the fruit well with a fork. Replace the top crust and serve hot with heavy cream.

APPLE COBBLER

10 tart apples
1 tablespoon lemon juice
½ teaspoon cinnamon
¼ teaspoon salt
1 cup sugar
½ recipe for Basic Baking Powder Biscuit

Peel the apples, remove the cores, and slice them very thinly into a deep pie dish. Sprinkle the fruit with the lemon juice, cinnamon, and salt, and cover with biscuit dough crust, which has been rolled out ¼ inch thick. Do not press the topping against the edge of the dish. Prick the surface with a fork and bake at 450° F. for 10 minutes. Reduce the oven temperature to 350° F. and bake for another 35 minutes. Remove the cobbler from the oven, carefully lift up the top crust, sprinkle with the sugar, and mix it gently through the fruit. Replace the top crust and serve either hot or cold. If hot, serve with a brandy hard sauce. If cold, serve with sweet cream, plain or whipped.

FRESH CHERRY COBBLER

3 cups sour pitted cherries
1 cup sugar, or to taste
1 cup water
1 tablespoon cornstarch
2 tablespoons cold water
1 tablespoon butter
1 teaspoon cinnamon
½ recipe for Drop Biscuits

Heat the cherries with the sugar and the 1 cup water until almost boiling. Combine the cornstarch and the 2 tablespoons cold water, stir into the fruit mixture, and cook, stirring, for 3 minutes. Pour the fruit into a deep baking dish 8 inches in diameter, dot with the butter, and sprinkle with the cinnamon. Drop spoonfuls of the biscuit dough over the fruit. Bake at 400° F. for 30 minutes and serve hot with heavy cream.

APRICOT OR PEACH COBBLER Follow directions above, using ⅔ cup sugar to 3 cups peeled and sliced apricots or peaches.

BLACKBERRY COBBLER Use ¾ cup sugar to 3 cups blackberries.

FRUIT ROLY POLY

Prepare a baking powder biscuit dough and roll it out ¼ inch thick into a rectangle. Spread the surface with melted butter and then with any one of the following fruit, sugar, and spice mixtures. Roll as for a jelly roll and place seam side down on a greased baking sheet. Brush the surface with butter and bake at 400° F. for 25–30 minutes. Serve with heavy cream or any desired sauce.

FRUIT COMBINATIONS

1 cup diced apples, ½ cup raisins, 1 teaspoon cinnamon, ½ cup sugar, and ¼ cup brown sugar.

6 sliced peaches, ½ cup sugar, 1½ tablespoons lemon juice, and 1 teaspoon grated lemon rind.

1 pint blackberries, ½ cup sugar, and ½ teaspoon cinnamon.

1 pint blueberries, ½ cup sugar, juice and rind of 1 lemon.

1 pint gooseberries and ½ cup brown sugar.

1½ cups cooked and sweetened or preserved fruits.

SUET ROLY POLY

¼ pound beef suet
2 cups flour
½ teaspoon salt
2 teaspoons double-action baking powder
Jam or marmalade

Chop the beef suet very finely or put it through the finest blade of a meat chopper. Sift together into a bowl the flour, salt, and baking powder. Add the suet and mix it lightly through the dry ingredients. Moisten the mixture with a little cold water and blend into a dough, using a pastry blender or two knives. Do not use the hands, as this tends to melt the suet and toughen the dough. Turn the dough out onto a lightly floured board and roll it out into a rectangle ¼ inch thick. Spread the surface with a thin layer of jam—marmalade, plum, or gooseberry is good. Moisten the edges and roll the sheet of dough lightly as you would a jelly roll, pressing the edges down to seal thoroughly. Place it on a greased baking sheet and bake at 350° F. for 1 hour, or until nicely browned. Serve with a little hot sauce made by diluting with hot water some of the same kind of jam used in the filling.

APPLE PANDOWDY

6 tart apples
1 cup sugar
½ teaspoon cinnamon
¼ teaspoon salt
2 tablespoons butter
½ recipe Basic Baking Powder Biscuit

Pare, core, and slice the apples into a buttered casserole. Sprinkle with the sugar, cinnamon, and salt and dot with the butter. Roll biscuit dough ½ inch thick and cover the apples. Bake at 375° F. for about 35 minutes, or until the apples are tender and the crust is a golden brown. Invert on a serving dish so the apples are on top and serve with heavy cream.

ROLLED FRUIT DUMPLINGS

1½ cups sugar
2 cups water
Rich Basic Baking Powder Biscuit dough
Fruit
1 tablespoon soft butter
1 teaspoon cinnamon

Dissolve the sugar in the water and pour the syrup into an oblong baking pan 8×12×2 inches. Cook the syrup over a low heat for 5 minutes. Meanwhile make a Rich Basic Baking Powder Biscuit dough. Roll it out about ⅓ inch thick into an oblong. Spread the surface with butter, sprinkle over the fruit, cinnamon, and sugar as indicated below, and roll up into a long roll, jelly-roll fashion. Place the roll in the syrup or cut it into slices about 1½ inches thick and place the slices cut side down in the hot syrup. Bake at 450° F. for about 25 minutes, basting it occasionally with the fruity syrup in the pan. Serve warm with heavy cream.

APPLE ROLL Use 3 cups peeled, cored, and chopped apples. Sprinkle with ¼ cup sugar.

RHUBARB AND STRAWBERRY ROLL Use 2 cups rhubarb, cut

into 1-inch pieces, and 1 cup fresh strawberries, halved. Sprinkle with ¼ cup sugar.

BLUEBERRY ROLL Use 3 cups blueberries and sprinkle with 2 tablespoons sugar.

SOUR CHERRY ROLL Use 3 cups sour pitted cherries and sprinkle with ½ cup sugar.

SWEET CHERRY ROLL Use 3 cups sweet black pitted cherries. Sprinkle with 2 tablespoons sugar.

CANNED FRUIT ROLL Drain the juice from a No. 2 can of preserved fruit. Use the syrup as part of the water to make the pan syrup. Sprinkle the fruit and cinnamon over the rolled-out dough. No extra sugar is needed.

PEACH ROLL Use 3 cups fresh peaches, sliced, and sprinkle with 2 tablespoons sugar.

QUICK HOT CROSS BUNS

Make Plain Basic Baking Powder Biscuits, adding 2 teaspoons sugar to the dry ingredients. For the liquid, beat together ½ cup milk and 1 egg. Mix into the dough ½ cup currants. Cut off small pieces of the dough and roll lightly between the palms to form balls. Place on baking sheet and bake as usual. While hot, ice with confectioners' sugar icing in the form of a cross.

The dry ingredients and the shortening may be mixed the night before, leaving only the addition of the egg and milk for a quick morning mixing, before popping them into the oven. Or if you add an extra teaspoon of double-action baking powder, the rolls can be completely prepared for the oven the night before and tucked into the refrigerator, leaving only the actual baking for the next morning.

BEATEN BISCUITS

2 tablespoons lard
2 cups sifted all-purpose flour
1 teaspoon salt
5 tablespoons water

Cut the lard into the sifted dry ingredients, add the water gradually, and knead into a dough, adding a few drops more water if necessary. Turn out on a lightly floured board and knead thoroughly. Then beat with a rolling pin for about 20 minutes. When the dough has been beaten enough, you will be able to stretch it out like a ribbon. You can avoid this beating and achieve the same results by running the dough through a food chopper 4 or 5 times. Roll out the dough ¼ inch thick, cut into rounds, prick the tops with a fork, and bake on a greased baking sheet at 350° F. for 45 minutes, or until the biscuits are a delicate brown. Makes 2 dozen 1-inch rounds.

CREAM BISCUITS

2 cups sifted all-purpose flour
½ teaspoon salt
2 teaspoons double-action baking powder
6 tablespoons butter
2 cups heavy cream

Sift the dry ingredients, cut in the butter, and add the cream, working well for several minutes. Roll out ⅛ inch thick and cut into rounds. Place on ungreased baking sheet and bake at 400° F. for 12 minutes, or until they are a delicate brown.

OVEN SCONES

2 cups sifted all-purpose flour
2 teaspoons double-action baking powder
1 teaspoon salt
¼ cup sugar
6 tablespoons shortening
¼ cup currants, if desired
1 egg
1 egg, separated
½ cup milk
Sugar

Sift together the flour, baking powder, salt, and sugar. Cut in the shortening and add the currants. Beat the whole egg and the egg yolk, reserving the white for the top. Add the milk to the beaten eggs and then add this mixture to the flour mixture. Stir only enough to moisten the flour. Pat dough into a 9-inch round pan. Brush the top with egg white and sprinkle with sugar. Bake at 400° F. for 20 minutes. Cut into wedge-shaped pieces to serve.

GRIDDLE SCONES

2 cups sifted all-purpose flour
½ teaspoon soda
½ teaspoon cream of tartar
½ teaspoon salt
¾ cup buttermilk
2 tablespoons melted butter

Sift the dry ingredients together into a mixing bowl and stir in the buttermilk and butter to form a dough. Divide the dough into two parts, making a round, flat cake of each part. Divide each cake into four pie-shaped pieces. Roll each piece in flour and bake on a hot, ungreased griddle over a slow fire until well risen. Then increase the heat and brown on the underside for about 10 minutes. Turn and brown the other side for about 5 minutes.

DROP GRIDDLE SCONES Stir into the dough ¼ cup buttermilk which has been combined with 1 beaten egg and 2 tablespoons sugar. Drop the sticky batter directly onto the griddle and bake until bubbly on top, then turn and brown on the other side.

YORKSHIRE PUDDING

1 cup sifted all-purpose flour
¼ teaspoon salt
2 eggs, beaten
1 cup milk
4 tablespoons beef drippings

Sift the flour and salt together into a mixing bowl. Add the eggs and mix well. Gradually add the milk and beat with a rotary beater for 2 minutes, until it is smooth and free from lumps. Heat thoroughly a ring mold or oblong cake pan and grease it well with the beef drippings. Pour in the batter about ¼ inch deep and bake at 450° F. for 15 minutes. Reduce the heat to 350° F. and bake for 20 minutes longer. Cut into squares and place them on a hot platter around a roast of beef.

MUFFINS

Perfect muffins should be golden brown, light, tender, and fine in texture. Many variations can be made from a single basic recipe or from a packaged mix.

BASIC MUFFIN RECIPE

INGREDIENTS FOR 1 DOZEN MUFFINS

2 cups sifted all-purpose flour
2 tablespoons sugar
½ teaspoon salt
2 teaspoons double-action baking powder
1 egg, well beaten
1 cup milk
4 tablespoons butter, melted and cooled

METHOD
1. Preheat oven to 400° F.
2. Sift dry ingredients in mixing bowl.
3. Combine beaten egg and milk and pour all at once into the dry ingredients. Stir briskly until all the flour is moistened. *Do not beat until smooth.* The batter should look lumpy. Overstirring results in muffins with long holes or tunnels inside.
4. Lightly stir in the melted butter.
5. Fill greased muffin tins two thirds full.
6. Bake for 25 minutes and serve piping hot.

For sweeter muffins, increase sugar to 4 tablespoons.
For very sweet muffins, increase sugar to ½ cup.

VARIETY MUFFINS FROM BASIC MUFFIN RECIPE

APPLE MUFFINS Make Very Sweet Muffins, sifting with the dry ingredients 1 teaspoon cinnamon and folding into the batter 1 cup peeled and finely chopped apples.

ARICOT MUFFINS Make Sweet Muffins, adding ½ cup dried apricots, washed, dried, and cut in fine pieces, to the flour mixture.

BLUEBERRY MUFFINS Make Very Sweet Muffins and fold into the batter gently 1 cup washed and well-drained blueberries.

BRAN NUT MUFFINS Make Sweet Muffins, using only 1 cup flour, and add to the sifted dry ingredients 1 cup bran and ½ cup chopped nuts.

BROWN SUGAR MUFFINS Make Sweet Muffins, substituting ¾ cup brown sugar for the white sugar.

CHOCOLATE MUFFINS Make Sweet Muffins. Melt 1 square (1 ounce) chocolate with the butter and stir into the batter. Bake at 375° F. for 25 minutes.

COCOA MUFFINS Make Sweet Muffins, substituting 2 tablespoons cocoa for the same amount of flour.

CORN KERNEL MUFFINS Make Basic Muffins and fold into the batter 2 cups kernel corn, canned, fresh, or defrosted.

CRANBERRY MUFFINS Combine 1 cup raw, chopped cranberries with ½ cup sugar and fold gently into a Basic Muffin batter.

CREAM MUFFINS If cream is used instead of milk in making muffins, a very rich muffin will be the result. Use only 2 tablespoons melted butter instead of 4.

CURRANT MUFFINS Make Sweet Muffins, adding ½ cup currants, washed and dried, to the flour mixture.

DATE MUFFINS Make Basic Muffins, adding ½ cup dates, finely chopped, to the flour mixture.

JAM MUFFINS Make Basic Muffins and drop 1 teaspoon jelly or jam on top of each muffin before baking.

NUT MUFFINS Make Sweet Muffins, adding ½ cup chopped nut meats to the flour mixture.

PEANUT BUTTER MUFFINS Make Basic Muffins. Combine ¼ cup peanut butter with the milk and add to the dry ingredients along with the beaten egg. Stir in only 2 tablespoons melted butter.

PECAN MUFFINS Make Sweet Muffins, adding ½ cup chopped pecans to the dry ingredients. Place 1 tablespoon batter into small greased muffin tins, put half a pecan on top, and sprinkle with 1 tablespoon sugar which has been mixed with ¼ teaspoon cinnamon. Bake at 400° F. for 18 minutes. Makes 24 small muffins.

SOUR CREAM MUFFINS Make Basic or Sweet Muffins. Use sour cream in place of milk, adding at the same time ½ teaspoon soda dissolved in 1 tablespoon water.

SOUR MILK MUFFINS Make Basic or Sweet Muffins. Use sour milk or buttermilk for the liquid and add ½ teaspoon soda to the dry ingredients.

SPICED MUFFINS Make Sweet Muffins, sifting with the dry ingredients ½ teaspoon cinnamon, ¼ teaspoon ginger, ¼ teaspoon cloves, and ¼ teaspoon allspice.

SPICED PRUNE MUFFINS Make Sweet Muffins. Add to the sifted dry ingredients 1 teaspoon nutmeg and 1 cup chopped, cooked prunes. Fill muffin pans two thirds full and decorate the top of each muffin with half a prune and a few chopped walnuts before baking.

SURPRISE MUFFINS Make Basic Muffins. Put 1 tablespoon of batter into each greased muffin cup. Drop into the center of each 1 teaspoon currant, apple, or other jelly, or one stewed and sweetened apricot or prune, or 1 stoned date, or a piece of candied pineapple or a few chopped raisins. Add another tablespoon batter and bake as usual.

WHOLE WHEAT FRUIT MUFFINS Make Sweet Muffins, using whole wheat flour in place of plain wheat flour. Add to the dry ingredients ½ cup chopped dates and raisins.

CORN MUFFINS—SOUTHERN

2 cups corn meal
1½ teaspoons salt
2 cups boiling water
1 cup cold milk
2 eggs, well beaten

  2 tablespoons butter, melted
  4 teaspoons double-action baking powder

Mix corn meal and salt. Stir in boiling water gradually and stir until smooth. Stir in the milk, eggs, butter, and lastly the baking powder. Pour into greased muffin cups and bake for 25–30 minutes in a very hot oven (475° F.). Makes 16 muffins.

CORN MUFFINS—NORTHERN

  1 cup sifted all-purpose flour
  1 cup yellow corn meal
  ¼ cup sugar
  1 teaspoon double-action baking powder
  ½ teaspoon soda
  ½ teaspoon salt
  1 egg, beaten
  1 cup buttermilk
  3 tablespoons shortening, melted

Sift together dry ingredients. Stir in beaten egg, buttermilk, and melted shortening. Bake for 25 minutes in hot oven (400° F.). Makes 1 dozen muffins.

  If you wish to use sweet milk in place of the buttermilk, substitute 2 additional teaspoons baking powder for the soda.

CORN MEAL FRUIT GEMS

  ½ cup corn meal
  1 cup sifted all-purpose flour
  3 teaspoons double-action baking powder
  1 teaspoon salt
  6 tablespoons sugar
  2 eggs, beaten
  1 cup milk
  2 tablespoons melted butter
  1 cup raisins or currants
  1 tablespoon flour

Sift together into a mixing bowl the corn meal, the 1 cup sifted flour, baking powder, salt, and sugar. Combine the eggs and milk and stir gradually into the dry ingredients. Stir in the butter. Dredge the raisins with the 1 tablespoon flour and add to the mixture. Stir well. Fill muffin pans two thirds full and bake at 400° F. for 25 minutes. Makes 1 dozen gems.

DUTCH BABIES

3 eggs
½ teaspoon salt
½ cup sifted all-purpose flour
½ cup milk
Powdered sugar
Lemon juice

Beat eggs until very light. Add salt, flour, and milk, beating the mixture constantly until well blended and smooth. Strain the batter through a sieve to prevent any lumping and fill buttered muffin or popover tins two thirds full. Bake at 450° F. for 20–25 minutes, or until brown and crisp, gradually reducing oven temperature to 350° F. Serve hot, with powdered sugar and lemon juice.

BANANA MUFFINS

2 tablespoons butter
½ cup brown sugar
1 egg, beaten
2 bananas, mashed
2 cups sifted all-purpose flour
2 teaspoons double-action baking powder
¼ teaspoon salt
½ cup milk

Cream butter and sugar together, then stir in the egg and mashed bananas. Stir in the sifted dry ingredients alternately with the milk, mixing only as much as necessary to combine the ingredients after each addition. Fill greased muffin tins two thirds full and bake at 400° F. for 20 minutes.

HONEY BRAN MUFFINS

1 cup sifted all-purpose flour
1 teaspoon double-action baking powder
½ teaspoon soda
½ teaspoon salt
1 cup bran
⅓ cup chopped nuts
1 egg
3 tablespoons strained honey
¾ cup sour milk or buttermilk
3 tablespoons melted and cooled butter

Mix and sift the flour, baking powder, soda, and salt into a mixing bowl. Add the bran and nuts and mix thoroughly. Add the egg, honey, and milk and stir just enough to combine the ingredients.

Stir in the melted butter. Fill greased muffin tins two thirds full and bake at 425° F. for 15–18 minutes.

MOLASSES PUFFS

1 cup sifted all-purpose flour
½ teaspoon soda
½ teaspoon salt
1 egg, beaten
¼ cup melted butter
½ cup molasses
½ cup buttermilk
1 teaspoon grated lemon rind
1 teaspoon vanilla

Sift together the flour, soda, and salt. Combine egg, shortening, molasses, buttermilk, lemon rind, and vanilla. Add this to the flour mixture, stirring only enough to moisten the flour. Fill greased muffin pans two thirds full and bake at 350° F. for about 30 minutes. Makes 12 2-inch puffs.

POPOVERS

1 cup sifted all-purpose flour
½ teaspoon salt
1 cup rich milk
2 eggs, beaten
2 tablespoons melted butter

Sift together the flour and salt into a mixing bowl. Mix together the eggs and milk, then combine the dry and liquid ingredients, beating only enough to make a smooth batter. The batter should be the thickness of rich cream. Too thick a batter will keep the popovers from rising fully. Stir in the melted butter.

The best pans to use are the heavy, old-fashioned iron pans, but ovenproof glass or heavy aluminum pans are also good. Grease the pans and heat them in a 450° F. oven, then fill them half full of batter. Bake at 450° F. for 15 minutes. Reduce oven temperature to 350° F. and bake for another 30 minutes.

BAKING POWDER BREADS AND COFFEECAKES

PECAN NUT BREAD

3 cups sifted flour
4 teaspoons double-action baking powder
1 teaspoon salt
¾ cup sugar

1 cup chopped pecans
1 egg, beaten
1½ cups milk
2 tablespoons melted butter

Sift together the flour, baking powder, salt, and sugar into a mixing bowl. Add the nuts and toss lightly. Combine the egg and milk and add the flour mixture, stirring only enough to moisten the flour. Stir in the melted butter. Bake in a greased loaf pan (8½ × 3½ × 2½ inches) at 350° F. for 1 hour. Remove from pan and cool on cake rack.

DATE AND NUT BREAD

2 cups cut-up dates
1 cup broken walnuts
1 cup boiling water
¼ cup butter
¾ cup brown sugar
1 egg, beaten
2 cups sifted cake flour
½ teaspoon salt
1 teaspoon soda
5 tablespoons cold water

Pour the boiling water over the dates and nuts and allow them to stand. Cream the butter, add the sugar gradually, and cream together until light. Add the egg and beat thoroughly. Sift the flour and salt together twice. Add the soda to the dates and nuts. Add the flour and the fruit mixture alternately, beating after each addition, until the ingredients are thoroughly blended. Stir in the cold water and turn the mixture into 2 small greased loaf pans. Bake at 350° F. for 45 minutes, or until a toothpick inserted in the center comes out clean. Remove from the pans and cool on a rack.

WHOLE WHEAT NUT BREAD

1¾ cups whole wheat flour
2½ teaspoons double-action baking powder
1 teaspoon salt
¼ cup sugar
1 egg, beaten
1 cup milk
½ cup ground walnuts

Mix the dry ingredients and stir in the egg, which has been combined with the milk. Add the nuts and stir until all the ingredients are well blended. Turn into a greased loaf pan. Allow to stand in a warm place for 10 minutes and then bake at 350° F. for 45 minutes.

ORANGE DATE NUT LOAF

    2 cups sifted all-purpose flour
    ½ teaspoon salt
    2 teaspoons double-action baking powder
    ½ cup butter
    1 cup sugar
    2 eggs, beaten
    1 teaspoon grated orange rind
    2 tablespoons lemon juice
    ¾ cup milk
    ½ cup chopped walnuts
    ½ cup chopped dates

Sift the flour, salt, and baking powder together 3 times. Cream the butter, add the sugar, and continue to cream until the mixture is light and fluffy. Add the eggs and beat until smooth. Add the orange rind and then add the dry ingredients alternately with the lemon juice and milk, beating smooth after each addition. Stir in the nuts and dates. Turn into a buttered loaf pan and bake at 350° F. for 1 hour.

APRICOT BREAKFAST BREAD

    1 cup dried apricots
    ½ cup sugar
    2 cups sifted all-purpose flour
    2 teaspoons double-action baking powder
    ½ teaspoon salt
    ¼ cup butter
    1 cup milk
    2 eggs, beaten
    2 tablespoons brown sugar

Wash the apricots, cover with cold water, and simmer in a covered saucepan until they are soft. Uncover and allow to cook until the water is nearly absorbed. Beat until smooth, add the ½ cup sugar, and stir over the fire until the sugar is dissolved in the purée. Allow to cool. Sift the flour, baking powder, and salt into a mixing bowl. Cut in the butter and stir in the milk, which has been combined with the eggs. Pour ½ the batter into a buttered cake pan and cover with the apricot purée. Pour over the purée the remaining batter, sprinkle the surface with a little melted butter and sift over the top the 2 tablespoons brown sugar. Bake at 375° F. for about 30 minutes.

APRICOT BRAN BREAD

½ cup sugar
2 tablespoons butter
1 egg, beaten
1 cup sour milk
1 cup all-bran
½ cup chopped nuts
1 cup cooked, chopped apricots
2 cups sifted all-purpose flour
2 teaspoons double-action baking powder
½ teaspoon soda
½ teaspoon salt

Cream together the sugar and shortening. Stir in the egg and milk, combined. Add bran, nuts, and apricots. Beat mixture well. Add dry ingredients, which have been sifted together, and mix well. Put in a greased loaf pan and bake for 1 hour at 350° F.

CHERRY BRAN BREAD

2½ cups sifted all-purpose flour
3 teaspoons double-action baking powder
¾ cup sugar
½ teaspoon salt
1 egg, beaten
1¼ cups milk
2 tablespoons melted butter
1 cup bran
½ cup chopped maraschino cherries
¼ cup chopped nuts

Sift together into a mixing bowl the flour, baking powder, sugar, and salt. Combine the egg and milk and stir into the flour mixture. Add the butter, bran, cherries, and nuts and mix until all the ingredients are well blended.

1 tablespoon butter
¼ cup brown sugar
½ cup maraschino cherries
¼ cup chopped nuts

Melt the butter in the bottom of a loaf pan and sprinkle the sugar, cherries, and nuts evenly over the bottom of the pan. Pour the batter into the prepared pan and bake at 350° F. for 1 hour. Remove at once from the pan and cool on a rack before slicing.

HARVEST BREAD

2 cups sifted all-purpose flour
3 teaspoons double-action baking powder
¼ teaspoon salt
¾ cup sugar
¼ cup chopped candied citron
¼ cup currants
¼ cup chopped candied cherries
2 tablespoons chopped candied lemon peel
½ cup chopped nuts
2 eggs, beaten
1 cup milk
3 tablespoons melted butter

Sift together flour, baking powder, salt, and sugar. Add the fruits and nuts. Combine the eggs, milk, and melted butter. Add the liquid to the flour mixture, stirring just enough to moisten the flour. Pour into a greased, lined loaf pan (8½ ×4½ inches). Bake at 375° F. for 1 hour. Makes a 1-pound loaf.

APPLESAUCE CAKE

2 cups sifted all-purpose flour
3 teaspoons double-action baking powder
½ teaspoon salt
½ teaspoon ground cloves
½ cup chopped nuts
1 egg, beaten
¼ cup brown sugar
1 cup applesauce
¼ cup melted butter

Sift together the flour, baking powder, salt, and cloves. Add the nuts. Combine the egg, brown sugar, applesauce, and butter and stir into the flour mixture, stirring only enough to moisten the flour. Pour into a greased, lined loaf pan (8½ ×4½ inches). Bake at 350° F. for 50 minutes. Makes a 1-pound loaf.

CHOCOLATE BREAD

3 cups sifted cake flour
3 teaspoons double-action baking powder
1 teaspoon salt
1 cup brown sugar
1 egg, beaten
1¼ cups milk

4 tablespoons melted butter
2 squares unsweetened chocolate, melted

Sift together into a mixing bowl the flour, baking powder, and salt. Add the brown sugar and mix well. Combine the egg and milk and add gradually to the dry ingredients, mixing thoroughly. Add the butter and chocolate and mix again until all the ingredients are blended. Bake in a greased loaf pan (8×4×3 inches) at 350° F. for 1 hour and 15 minutes, or until done.

PAIN D'ÉPICE

1 cup plus 2 tablespoons sugar
¾ cup strained honey
2½ teaspoons soda
¼ teaspoon salt
1¼ cups boiling water
3 tablespoons rum
1 teaspoon powdered anise
2 teaspoons cinnamon
4 cups sifted all-purpose flour

Place in a bowl the sugar, honey, soda, and salt. Pour over these ingredients the water and stir until the sugar is dissolved. Stir into the mixture the rum, anise, and cinnamon and then add gradually the flour to form a smooth batter, beating thoroughly and constantly. If lumps should form, strain the whole through a sieve. Pour into a buttered tin which holds at least 6 cups liquid, and bake at 450° F. for 10 minutes. Reduce the heat to 350° F. and continue to bake for 1 hour. Remove from the pan onto a cake rack to cool. Wrap in wax paper and store in a breadbox. Allow it to stand for 1 day before slicing it paper-thin. Serve with fresh sweet butter and honey.

QUICK COFFEECAKE

2 cups sifted all-purpose flour
2 teaspoons double-action baking powder
½ teaspoon salt
½ cup sugar
6 tablespoons butter
1 egg, beaten
½ cup milk

Sift the flour, baking powder, salt, and sugar into a mixing bowl. Cut in the shortening. Combine the egg and milk and stir into the dry ingredients until the mixture is blended. Spread the dough evenly in a buttered 9-inch layer pan and bake at 400° F. for 25–30 minutes.

CRUMB TOPPING FOR QUICK COFFEECAKE Make Quick Coffeecake and spread the dough evenly in a buttered 9-inch layer pan. Brush the top with 1½ tablespoons melted butter. Mix together 4 tablespoons sugar, 1 tablespoon flour, and 1 teaspoon cinnamon and sift this mixture evenly over the top of the dough. Bake at 400° F. for 30 minutes. Cut into pie-shaped wedges while still in the pan and remove each piece to a serving dish.

FRUIT BREAD

2 cups sifted all-purpose flour
1 teaspoon salt
4 teaspoons double-action baking powder
¾ cup sugar
2 cups graham flour
1 cup candied peel, thinly sliced
1 cup chopped nuts
2 eggs, beaten
1⅔ cups milk
4 tablespoons melted butter

Sift together into a mixing bowl the white flour, salt, baking powder, and sugar. Combine the graham flour, peel, and nuts and stir into the sifted dry ingredients. Combine the eggs, milk, and melted butter and stir into the flour mixture until well blended. Spread the dough into two greased loaf pans (7×3×2½ inches) and bake at 350° F. for 1 hour. Remove from pans to cooling rack. This makes delicious sandwiches, cut very thin and spread with butter or cheese.

BRAN BREAD

1½ cups sifted all-purpose flour
3 teaspoons double-action baking powder
½ teaspoon salt
½ cup sugar
1 cup raisins
1 cup milk
3 tablespoons molasses
1½ cups whole bran
1 egg, beaten
4 tablespoons melted butter

Sift together the flour, baking powder, salt, and sugar into a mixing bowl. Add the raisins and stir. Combine the milk, molasses, bran, egg, and butter. Add to the flour mixture and stir enough to blend. Spread the dough in a greased loaf pan (8½×3½×2½ inches) and bake at 350° F. for 1 hour.

BANANA BRAN BREAD

¼ cup heavy sour cream
½ cup brown sugar
1½ cups mashed banana
1 cup bran
1½ cups sifted all-purpose flour
2 teaspoons baking powder
½ teaspoon salt
½ teaspoon soda

Blend the first four ingredients. Add dry ingredients, which have been sifted together. Put in greased loaf pan and allow to stand for 20 minutes. Bake at 350° F. for 1 hour. Makes 1 large loaf.

GINGERBREAD

1 egg, beaten
1 cup maple syrup
1 cup sour cream
2⅓ cups sifted all-purpose flour
1 teaspoon soda
2 teaspoons powdered ginger
½ teaspoon salt
4 tablespoons melted butter

Combine the egg, maple syrup, and sour cream. Sift together twice the flour, soda, ginger, and salt. Stir the liquid ingredients into the sifted dry ingredients, beating well until smooth. Add the melted butter and beat thoroughly. Pour into a buttered oblong pan and bake at 350° F. for 30 minutes. Cool on cake rack and frost with Maple Fondant Frosting.

ORANGE-FILLED COFFEECAKE

2 cups sifted all-purpose flour
¼ teaspoon salt
½ cup sugar
4 teaspoons double-action baking powder
1½ teaspoons grated orange rind
4 tablespoons shortening
1 egg, beaten
½ cup orange juice
½ cup milk

Sift dry ingredients into mixing bowl. Add orange rind and cut in shortening. Stir in the egg, which has been combined with the orange juice and milk. Spread half the mixture in greased and floured pan (8 inches square). Sprinkle with half the Orange Filling.

Add the other half of the batter and sprinkle remaining filling on top. Bake at 375° F. for 30 minutes.

ORANGE FILLING
1 cup sifted all-purpose flour
¾ cup brown sugar
2 tablespoons butter, melted
2 tablespoons orange juice
1½ teaspoons orange rind
½ teaspoon cinnamon

Mix together with a fork.

APRICOT UPSIDE-DOWN COFFEECAKE

1 recipe Quick Coffeecake
¼ cup butter
¼ cup brown sugar
16 cooked dried apricot halves

Melt the butter in an 8-inch-square pan. Sprinkle with the brown sugar and arrange the apricot halves evenly over the butter-sugar mixture. Cover with coffeecake batter and bake at 400° F. for 25 minutes.

APPLE COFFEECAKE

1 recipe Quick Coffeecake
3 medium apples, peeled and sliced
2 tablespoons melted butter
¼ cup sugar
½ teaspoon cinnamon

Spread the coffeecake batter in a buttered 9-inch layer pan and arrange the apple slices on top in circles, until the entire top of the dough is covered. Brush with the butter and sprinkle with the sugar and cinnamon. Bake at 400° F. for 25 minutes.

COFFEE RING

3 cups sifted all-purpose flour
⅓ cup sugar
3 teaspoons double-action baking powder
1 teaspoon salt
¼ cup butter
1 egg, beaten
¾ cup milk
¾ cup raisins
½ cup chopped nuts
1 tablespoon sugar

Sift the flour, sugar, baking powder, and salt into a mixing bowl. Cut in the shortening. Add the beaten egg and enough of the milk to make a dough that is soft but does not stick to the fingers. Roll out the dough ¼ inch thick into a rectangular shape. Brush the surface with a little melted butter and sprinkle with the raisins, nuts, and the 1 tablespoon sugar. Roll like a jelly roll lengthwise. Bring the ends together to make a circle and press firmly together. Place the ring on a large greased baking sheet and cut gashes around the edge with kitchen scissors, 2 inches apart. Bake at 350° F. for 30 minutes. Spread the top with Confectioners' Sugar Icing while the ring is still warm.

JAM-FILLED BREAKFAST CAKE

2 cups sifted all-purpose flour
2 teaspoons double-action baking powder
½ teaspoon salt
⅓ cup butter
1 egg, beaten
¼ cup corn syrup
½ cup milk
Jam

Sift the flour, baking powder, and salt into a mixing bowl. Cut in the butter. Mix together the egg, corn syrup, and milk and stir into the dry ingredients, mixing only enough to blend all the ingredients. Turn out on a lightly floured board and knead for 20 seconds. Roll out the dough into a rectangle ¼ inch thick. Brush the surface with melted butter and spread one third of the center with the jam, keeping it an inch away from each end. With the help of a spatula fold the two unspread edges of the dough to the center, enclosing the jam. Spread the top of the dough with jam, leaving a 1-inch margin so the filling will not run out, then fold in half. Place the dough on a greased baking sheet and cut down through the center of the top three layers of dough to within an inch of each end. Spread the dough open to expose the layers of jam and bake at 400° F. for 25 minutes. While still warm, spread the top with Confectioners' Sugar Icing.

Other excellent fillings are chutney, mincemeat, marmalade, peanut butter, or honey.

The basic dough may be varied by using orange juice and the grated rind of 1 orange in place of the milk. Chopped nuts, raisins, or chopped dried fruit may also be added to the dough if desired.

CHERRY ALMOND RING

2½ cups sifted cake flour
2½ teaspoons double-action baking powder
1 teaspoon salt
5 tablespoons butter
1 egg, beaten
⅔ cup milk
2 tablespoons sugar
1 teaspoon cinnamon
½ cup blanched almonds, shredded
½ cup candied cherries, cut in slices

Sift the flour, baking powder, and salt into a mixing bowl. Cut in the shortening. Combine the egg and milk and add gradually to the flour mixture until a dough is formed that is soft but not sticky. Roll out into a rectangle ⅓ inch thick on a lightly floured board. Spread with softened butter, sprinkle with the sugar, cinnamon, almonds, and cherries. Roll lengthwise, bring the ends together to make a circle, and press firmly together. Place the ring on a greased baking sheet and with the scissors cut ¾-inch slices almost through the roll. Turn each slice partly on its side, pointing away from the center. Place a whole cherry in the center of each slice and bake at 450° F. for 25 minutes, or until done. Ice while warm with Confectioners' Sugar Icing.

CORN BREADS

From the American Indians colonial housewives learned to use corn in many ways. From the primitive hand mortar the community mill developed, where the ripened golden grain was crushed between two stones. The stones were turned by water power, and so the meal produced became known as "water-ground" meal and is still available today in some states. The packaged steel-cut meal has far better keeping qualities than the "water-ground," but the breads they make are not like the old-fashioned corn breads.

Rhode Island johnnycake, which is baked on a griddle and is included, therefore, in the Pancakes section of this chapter, is so rich with legend and tradition that one must be daring to offer a recipe. Like the cherished corn pone and spoon bread recipes of the South, every old-colony family has its own guarded formula.

Any of these appetizing corn breads, however, traditional or not, can justly be called a truly American dish.

OLD-FASHIONED CORN BREAD

    1 cup yellow corn meal
    1 cup boiling water
    1 cup sifted all-purpose flour
    ¼ cup sugar
    3 teaspoons double-action baking powder
    ¾ teaspoon salt
    ½ cup milk
    1 egg, beaten
    3 tablespoons melted butter

Pour the boiling water on the corn meal, stirring constantly, and set aside to cool. Sift together the flour, sugar, baking powder, and salt and add these dry ingredients to the cooled mush alternately with the milk and egg. Mix thoroughly and then stir in the melted butter. Pour into a shallow pan, which has been greased and lightly floured, and bake at 450° F. for 20–25 minutes. Remove the cake from the pan and cool on a cake rack or serve hot, cut into squares, with plenty of butter.

SOUR MILK CORN BREAD

    3 cups corn meal
    2 teaspoons double-action baking powder
    1 teaspoon salt
    1 tablespoon sugar
    ½ teaspoon soda
    2 cups sour milk or buttermilk
    2 eggs, beaten
    1 cup thick sour cream

Sift together the corn meal, baking powder, salt, and sugar. Stir the soda into the buttermilk and combine with the eggs and the cream. Mix all the ingredients together and bake at 450° F. for 20 minutes.

PAN-BAKED JOHNNYCAKE

    1 cup yellow corn meal
    ½ cup sifted flour
    2 teaspoons double-action baking powder
    1 teaspoon salt
    1 tablespoon sugar
    ¾ cup milk
    2 eggs, beaten
    2 tablespoons melted butter

Mix together the corn meal, flour, baking powder, salt, and sugar. Stir in the milk, which has been combined with the beaten eggs, until all the ingredients are thoroughly combined and then stir in the butter. Pour into a greased baking pan and bake at 450° F. for 20 minutes. Serve hot. If sour milk is used add ½ teaspoon soda to the sifted dry ingredients.

SOUTHERN CORN BREAD

2 cups white corn meal
½ teaspoon soda
1 teaspoon double-action baking powder
1 cup sour milk
2 eggs, beaten
½ teaspoon salt

Mix the corn meal, soda, and baking powder together. Stir in the milk, which has been combined with the beaten eggs and salt. Pour into a greased baking pan and bake at 450° F. for 20 minutes. Serve hot.

KENTUCKY CORNCAKE

1 cup yellow corn meal
1 cup flour
3 teaspoons double-action baking powder
½ teaspoon salt
¼ cup sugar
1 cup milk
1 egg, beaten
¼ cup melted butter

Mix and sift together into a mixing bowl the corn meal, flour, baking powder, salt, and sugar. Stir in the milk, which has been mixed with the beaten egg, and lastly stir in the butter. Bake in a well-greased, 8-inch square pan at 450° F. for 20–25 minutes.

SPIDER CORNCAKE

1 egg, beaten
2 cups milk
1⅓ cups corn meal
⅓ cup sifted all-purpose flour
2 tablespoons sugar
1 teaspoon salt
2 teaspoons double-action baking powder
1 tablespoon butter

Combine the egg and 1 cup of the milk. Stir this into the sifted dry ingredients and mix thoroughly. Melt the butter in an iron skillet which has been thoroughly heated. Pour the batter into the hot pan and pour over the other cup milk. Do not stir. Bake at 350° F. for 50 minutes.

BATTER BREAD

2 eggs, well beaten
3 cups buttermilk
1 teaspoon salt
¾ teaspoon soda
1½ cups corn meal

Mix all the ingredients well and pour into a well-greased, sizzling-hot pan. Bake at 400° F. for 25–30 minutes.

SOUTHERN BATTER BREAD

2 cups sweet milk
1 cup water
1 cup corn meal
1 teaspoon salt
2 eggs, separated
2 teaspoons double-action baking powder
1 tablespoon melted butter

Heat the milk and water to nearly boiling, add the corn meal and salt, stirring briskly until the mixture thickens. Place over boiling water and cook for 25 minutes. Beat the egg yolks until thick and stir into the mush. Beat vigorously for 3 minutes, then add the baking powder. Stir in melted butter. Beat the egg whites until stiff and fold in lightly. Pour the mixture into a buttered baking dish and bake at 350° F. for 35–40 minutes.

YOGURT CORN MEAL SQUARES

1 cup sifted all-purpose flour
2 teaspoons double-action baking powder
¼ teaspoon soda
1 teaspoon salt
1 tablespoon sugar
1 cup corn meal
1 egg, beaten
1½ jars yogurt
4 tablespoons melted butter

Sift together the flour, baking powder, soda, salt, and sugar. Add 1 cup corn meal. Stir in the beaten egg and the yogurt to make a stiff batter. Stir in the butter and beat until all the ingredients are thoroughly blended. Turn into a greased baking pan and bake at 425° F. for 25 minutes. Cut into squares and serve hot with butter and jam.

NOTE: Yogurt is a cultured milk food of a custard consistency. In the United States real yogurt is made from fresh, pure, whole, homogenized cow's milk and selected strains of lactic cultures.

For other recipes using yogurt see: Yogurt Oatmeal Griddlecakes, Yogurt Waffles, Magdalena Pie.

YOGURT JOHNNYCAKE

1 cup yellow corn meal
1 cup sifted all-purpose flour
½ cup sugar
1 teaspoon salt
2 eggs, well beaten
1 cup yogurt
½ teaspoon soda

Sift together the corn meal, flour, sugar, and salt. Add the beaten eggs and mix well. Stir the soda into the yogurt and add, mixing until all the ingredients are combined. Turn into a greased baking pan and bake at 425° F. for 25 minutes.

KERNEL CORN BREAD

¾ cup yellow corn meal
2 teaspoons double-action baking powder
1 tablespoon sugar
½ cup sifted all-purpose flour
1 teaspoon salt
2 eggs, beaten
1½ cups milk
1 cup fresh corn kernels
3 tablespoons melted butter

In a mixing bowl combine the corn meal, baking powder, sugar, flour, and salt. Combine the eggs, milk, corn kernels, and butter. Add this mixture to the dry ingredients and stir quickly until mixed. Pour into a buttered casserole and bake at 375° F. for about 40 minutes, or until the bread is set. Serve hot.

CORN LACE PUFFS

½ cup corn meal
½ teaspoon salt
½ cup boiling water
2 egg whites, stiffly beaten

Combine the corn meal and salt. Pour the boiling water over this mixture, blend thoroughly, and cool. Fold in the egg whites and drop by teaspoonfuls on a greased baking sheet. Bake at 350° F. for about 30 minutes, or until the puffs are delicately browned. Serve hot with plenty of butter.

RHODE ISLAND BANNOCKS

1 quart milk
2 cups corn meal
1 tablespoon butter
½ teaspoon salt
4 eggs, separated

Scald the milk and pour it over the corn meal, which has been mixed with the butter. Add the salt and stir until the batter is quite smooth and free from lumps. Beat the egg yolks and combine with the corn meal mixture, and lastly fold in the egg whites, which have been beaten until stiff. The whites are folded in while the batter is still hot. Speed is essential to success. Pour into a buttered baking pan and bake at 450° F. for 30 minutes.

CORN PONES

3 cups white corn meal
2 teaspoons salt
1½ teaspoons double-action baking powder
¼ cup milk
1½ cups water
½ cup melted butter

Combine the corn meal, salt, and baking powder and moisten with the milk and enough of the water to make a drop batter. Allow to stand for 10 minutes, add the melted butter, and shape with the hands into round flat cakes or "pones." Place on a greased sheet and bake at 425° F. for 20 minutes. Serve very hot. Makes 1½ dozen.

HOMINY SPOON BREAD

2 cups cooked hominy grits
½ cup heavy cream
½ cup milk
½ teaspoon salt
3 tablespoons melted butter
2 eggs, separated

Heat the cooked grits with the cream and milk, stirring until it is soft and free from lumps. Add the salt, butter, and beaten egg yolks and lastly fold in the stiffly beaten whites. Pour into a buttered baking dish and bake at 350° F. for 30–40 minutes.

TO COOK HOMINY   Stir ½ cup hominy grits slowly into 2½ cups boiling water. Add 1 teaspoon salt and cook directly over the flame for 10 minutes, stirring occasionally. Then place over boiling water and cook for 2 hours.

VIRGINIA SPOON BREAD

1 cup corn meal
2 cups milk, scalded
3 tablespoons butter
3 eggs, separated
1 teaspoon salt
1 teaspoon sugar
2 teaspoons double-action baking powder

Stir the corn meal into the hot milk, add the butter, and beat until the mixture is smooth. Cool slightly and then beat in the well-beaten egg yolks. Combine the salt, sugar, and baking powder and stir in and lastly fold in the stiffly beaten egg whites. Pour into a well-buttered baking dish and bake at 375° F. for 30–40 minutes. Serve hot from the dish with a spoon.

CORN DODGER

1 cup yellow corn meal
½ cup sifted all-purpose flour
1 teaspoon salt
1½ teaspoons double-action baking powder
2 teaspoons sugar
1 cup milk
1 egg, beaten
2½ tablespoons hot bacon drippings

Sift the dry ingredients into a mixing bowl. Combine the milk and egg and stir into the dry ingredients. Beat well and then stir in the hot drippings. Pour into a hot casserole or skillet and bake at 425° F. for 30 minutes, or until golden brown. Serve hot in pie-shaped pieces.

SPOON BREAD

1 cup hot water
1 cup corn meal
2 tablespoons butter

1 tablespoon sugar
1 teaspoon salt
1 cup sour milk
½ teaspoon soda
2 eggs, well beaten

Stir the hot water into the corn meal, then add melted butter, sugar, and salt. When well blended, add the milk in which the soda has been dissolved, and lastly stir in the eggs. Pour into a hot buttered baking dish, bake at 375° F. for 30–40 minutes, and serve hot from the pan with a spoon. If sweet milk is used, omit the soda and add 2 teaspoons baking powder with the salt and sugar.

CORN STICKS

1¼ cups corn meal
¼ cup sifted all-purpose flour
2 tablespoons sugar
3 teaspoons double-action baking powder
1 teaspoon salt
1⅛ cups milk
1 egg, beaten
4 tablespoons melted butter

Place corn stick pans in the oven to heat. Sift all the dry ingredients into a mixing bowl. Combine the milk and egg and stir into the dry ingredients. Stir in the melted butter. Brush the hot corn stick pans with butter and fill them almost full with the mixture. Bake at 450° F. for 10–12 minutes. Makes 12 sticks.

DOUGHNUTS

Recent excavations in the Southwestern states revealed petrified cakes with holes. Although the aborigines may have been the first to make a doughnut of sorts, the fried cake as we know it is a direct descendant of the olykoek, which was brought to the New World by the early Dutch settlers.

PLAIN DOUGHNUTS

INGREDIENTS FOR 3 DOZEN DOUGHNUTS

3 tablespoons butter
1 cup sugar
2 eggs, beaten
3¾ cups sifted all-purpose flour
4 teaspoons double-action baking powder
½ teaspoon salt

¾ cup milk
1 teaspoon vanilla

METHOD

Cream the butter, add the sugar gradually, and cream until the mixture is light. Stir in the beaten eggs. Sift together the flour, baking powder, and salt and add these dry ingredients alternately with the milk. Stir in the vanilla.

Roll out the dough ⅓ inch thick on a lightly floured board. Use as little flour as possible in rolling out the dough, as doughnuts will toughen if handled or kneaded too much. The dough will be easier to handle if it is chilled in the icebox for 1 hour before rolling. Roll and cut a little of the dough at a time, keeping the balance in the refrigerator.

Lift the doughnuts with floured hands and drop them a few at a time into hot fat. At least 3 inches of hot fat is necessary for good results. Turn the doughnuts frequently after they rise to the surface and remove them as soon as they are nicely browned. Drain them on absorbent paper.

The temperature of the fat should be from 360° F. to 370° F. If you do not have a thermometer for deep-fat frying, drop a cube of bread into the fat. If it browns in 60 seconds the fat is at the right temperature. The correct temperature is very important in frying doughnuts. If the fat is too hot the doughnuts will not be baked through. If too cold, the fat will seep in and the doughnuts will be fat-soaked.

SUGAR DOUGHNUTS by dropping a few into a paper bag containing a little sugar. Close the bag and shake.

VARIETY DOUGHNUTS

CHOCOLATE DOUGHNUTS Increase the sugar to 1¼ cups and add 1½ squares unsweetened chocolate, melted, to the egg-sugar mixture. Chopped nuts may also be added if desired.

DROP DOUGHNUTS Drop dough from a spoon into the hot fat. For drop doughnuts the dough may be slightly softer than for rolled doughnuts.

FRUIT DOUGHNUTS Add to the dry ingredients ½ cup fruit such as raisins or chopped peel.

NUT DOUGHNUTS Add ½ cup chopped nuts (pecans or black walnuts are good) to the batter.

ORANGE DOUGHNUTS Add 1 teaspoon mace to the dry ingredients and stir in 1 tablespoon grated orange rind.

SOUR MILK DOUGHNUTS Reduce the baking powder to 2 teaspoons and add ½ teaspoon baking soda. Use sour milk or buttermilk in place of the sweet milk. Flavor with ¾ teaspoon nutmeg if desired.

SPICE DOUGHNUTS Add ½ teaspoon nutmeg and ¼ teaspoon mace to the dry ingredients.

PLAIN CRULLERS

Make Plain Doughnut dough, increasing the shortening to ¼ cup. Roll out ½ inch thick and cut into strips 8×1 inch. Twist 2 strips together, fastening the ends securely, and fry as usual.

RICH CRULLERS

4¼ cups sifted all-purpose flour
1¼ teaspoons baking soda
2½ teaspoons cream of tartar
½ teaspoon salt
1 teaspoon nutmeg
3 eggs
1 cup sugar
1 cup heavy cream

Mix and sift the dry ingredients. Beat the eggs until thick and pale in color, gradually beat in the sugar, and then stir in the cream. Gradually stir in the flour mixture, blending until almost smooth. Turn out on floured board and roll out ¼ inch thick. Cut with floured doughnut cutter and fry in deep fat as usual until golden brown.

MOLASSES DOUGHNUTS

5 cups sifted all-purpose flour
1 teaspoon baking soda
1 teaspoon salt
1 teaspoon ginger
1 egg, beaten
1 cup molasses
1 cup sour milk or buttermilk
1 tablespoon melted butter

Sift together the dry ingredients. Combine the egg, molasses, milk, and melted butter and stir into the flour mixture, until well mixed. Add a little more flour, if necessary, to make a soft dough. Turn out on floured board and roll out ¼ inch thick. Cut with a large, floured cutter, then cut again with a smaller cutter to make rings from ½ to 1 inch wide. Twist these rings into the figure 8 and fry in hot fat as usual. Drain on absorbent paper and dust generously with sugar. Makes about 3 dozen.

BRANDY DOUGHNUTS

½ cup butter
1½ cups sugar
4 eggs, beaten
1 tablespoon brandy
6 cups sifted all-purpose flour
½ teaspoon soda
1 teaspoon cream of tartar
1 cup milk

Cream the shortening and sugar. Add the eggs and brandy and mix well. Stir in the sifted dry ingredients alternately with the milk and mix to a soft dough. Chill for 1 hour and roll out thin. Cut into rounds with a floured biscuit or cooky cutter and make several gashes across the top of each. Fry in hot fat as usual. Makes 4 dozen.

BISMARCKS

Make Plain Doughnut dough and roll out ¼ inch thick. Allow the rolled dough to stand for 5 minutes and then cut into rounds with a lightly floured cooky cutter. Again allow to stand for 5 minutes. Place 1 teaspoon jam or marmalade in the center of half the rounds. Place a second round over the top of each, sandwich fashion, and seal the entire edge firmly by pressing between the fingers. Fry as usual.

POTATO DOUGHNUTS

4 tablespoons butter
¾ cup sugar
3 eggs, beaten
1 cup mashed potatoes
2¾ cups sifted all-purpose flour
4 teaspoons double-action baking powder
1 teaspoon salt
½ cup milk

Cream the butter and sugar. Mix in the beaten eggs and the mashed potatoes. Sift the dry ingredients and add alternately with the milk. If the dough is too soft to handle, depending on the moisture content of the potatoes, add a little more flour. Roll, cut, and fry as usual.

RICE CAKES

½ cup sifted all-purpose flour
3 teaspoons double-action baking powder
½ teaspoon salt
½ teaspoon nutmeg
½ cup sugar
2 cups cooked rice
3 eggs, beaten
1 teaspoon vanilla

Sift together the dry ingredients. Combine the remaining ingredients and stir them into the flour mixture, stirring until well blended. Test the consistency of the dough by dropping a spoonful into hot deep fat (375° F.) and fry to a golden brown. If the cake does not hold its shape, add a little more flour and test again. Drain on absorbent paper and sprinkle with confectioners' sugar. Makes 3 dozen.

HUSH PUPPIES

1 cup corn meal
1 teaspoon double-action baking powder
½ teaspoon salt
1 onion, minced
1 egg, beaten
¼ cup milk

Mix together the dry ingredients and the onion. Add the egg and beat vigorously. Stir in the milk and form into small patties, either round or finger-shaped. Drop into deep, smoking fat in which fish has been fried and cook until they are deep brown. Serve at once.

SWISS FRIED CAKES

1 cup light cream
2 eggs, beaten
1 teaspoon salt
2 cups sifted all-purpose flour
½ cup butter

Combine the cream, eggs, and salt and mix well. Add the flour to make a soft dough and turn out onto a floured board. Dot the dough with butter and with the hands work it into the dough. The butter should be firm but not hard. Chill the dough in the refrigerator for 1 hour and then roll out ⅛ inch thick. Cut in any desired shape, making a ½-inch gash through the center of each. Fry as usual, drain on absorbent paper, and roll in sugar while still hot. Makes 3 dozen.

DEER HORNS

½ cup butter
½ cup sugar
4 eggs, beaten
2 cups sifted all-purpose flour

Cream the butter and sugar. Add the eggs and flour and mix to a soft dough. Chill for 1 hour and roll out thin, using a little more flour, if necessary. Cut into triangles and roll as for horns or crescents. Fry in hot fat as usual. Serve hot, sprinkled with sugar. Makes 3 dozen.

FRITTERS

Fancy fruits stirred into a batter, fried in sweet butter, and served with honey was the Saracen version of what became known in France as *le beignet* and to us as the fritter.

There are many types of fritters and many ways of making fritter batters, but, like doughnuts, they are fried in deep fat, which has been heated to 370° F.

BEER BATTER FOR VEGETABLE FRITTERS

2 cups sifted all-purpose flour
1 teaspoon sugar
1 teaspoon double-action baking powder
Pinch salt
Beer

Sift together the flour, sugar, baking powder, and salt. Stir in enough beer to make a batter that is the consistency of heavy cream. Prepare vegetables such as asparagus tips, cauliflower flowerets, peeled and sliced eggplant, carrot halves, peeled small onions or onion rings, green pepper strips, or what you wish. Wash the pieces and cook them in salted water until just tender. Drain them thoroughly and sprinkle them with salt, pepper, and a few drops lemon juice. Dip them into the batter and fry in hot deep fat until nicely browned. Drain on absorbent paper.

BASIC FRITTER BATTER

2 eggs, separated
⅔ cup milk
1 tablespoon lemon juice
1 tablespoon melted butter
1 cup sifted all-purpose flour
½ teaspoon salt

Beat the egg yolks until they are thick and pale in color. Add the milk, lemon juice, and butter and blend thoroughly. Sift in the flour and salt, stirring the mixture only enough to blend it well. Do not beat. Then fold in the egg whites, which have been beaten until they are stiff but not dry. Two thirds cup flat beer may be used in place of the milk and lemon juice, if desired. Allow the beer mixture to rest for ½ hour before folding in egg whites.

CORN FRITTERS

1¾ cups sifted all-purpose flour
2 teaspoons double-action baking powder
½ teaspoon salt
¾ cup milk
1 cup corn kernels, drained, canned or fresh
1 egg, beaten
1 tablespoon melted butter

Sift together the dry ingredients into a mixing bowl. Stir in the milk, corn, egg, and butter, mixing well to blend all the ingredients. Drop by spoonfuls into deep fat (360° F.) for about 5 minutes, or until golden brown. Drain on absorbent paper.

BRANDY BATTER FOR FRUITS

1½ cups sifted all-purpose flour
2 tablespoons sugar
½ cup warm water
2 tablespoons butter, melted
¼ cup brandy
Pinch salt
2 eggs, separated

Mix the flour and sugar with the warm water and the melted butter, then continue to add enough water to obtain a smooth batter (about another ¼ cup). Cool and stir in the brandy, salt, and beaten egg yolks. The batter should now be the consistency of thick cream. Finally fold in the stiffly beaten egg whites.

WINE BATTER

1⅓ cups sifted all-purpose flour
½ teaspoon salt
2 tablespoons sugar
White wine
1 tablespoon melted butter
4 eggs whites, stiffly beaten

Sift the flour, salt, and sugar into a bowl and stir in enough white wine to make a batter the consistency of heavy cream. Stir in the butter and allow to rest for 1 hour and finally fold in the egg whites.

WITH BEER Substitute beer for the wine and omit the sugar. Beer batters may be stored for several days in the refrigerator.

FRUIT FRITTERS

FOR LARGE CANNED FRUITS, such as peaches, pears, and apricots: Drain canned fruits and dry the surface a little. Dip each piece in a fritter batter, making sure that it is completely covered. Drop into the hot fat and cook from 3-5 minutes, or until golden brown. Place the fried fritters in a shallow pan, sprinkle with sugar, and put under the broiler flame until the sugar is glazed, being very careful not to let the sugar burn.

FRESH FRUITS Peel, pit, and cut large fresh fruit in half or into slices. Sprinkle with sugar and a little lemon juice and allow to stand for about 1 hour. Then dry on absorbent paper, dip in a fritter batter, and fry as above.

FOR SMALL FRUITS AND BERRIES Wash and pick over berries, sprinkle with sugar, and allow to stand for about 1 hour. Drain berries or other small fruits thoroughly and add 2 cups of them to a fritter batter. Drop by spoonfuls into the hot fat and cook until they are golden brown all over, or for about 5 minutes. Serve hot with powdered sugar or with Sabayon Sauce.

BLUEBERRY FRITTERS

1 cup sifted all-purpose flour
1 teaspoon double-action baking powder
½ teaspoon salt
2 tablespoons sugar
2 eggs, separated
2-3 tablespoons water
¾ cup blueberries

Sift together the dry ingredients. Combine the egg yolks with the water and stir into the dry ingredients, mixing only until smooth. Fold in the stiffly beaten egg whites and lastly mix in the blueberries. Drop by spoonfuls into hot deep fat (360° F.) and cook until lightly browned. Drain on absorbent paper and serve with confectioners' sugar or a dessert sauce, such as foamy sauce or fruit sauce.

VARIATIONS Other fruits, such as diced peaches, apples,

or bananas, or other berries, may be used. If using cranberries, they must first be cooked in ½ cup water and ½ cup sugar until the skins burst, then drained and cooled.

ORANGE FRITTERS

Peel oranges and separate them into segments. Prepare a sugar syrup by boiling together 2 cups water, 1 cup sugar, and 4 tablespoons brandy. Add the orange segments and simmer gently for 10 minutes. Drain the syrup from the orange sections and allow them to cool. Dip each section in Brandy Batter and fry, a few at a time, in hot deep fat until they are delicately browned, turning them over with a wooden spoon. Drain them on absorbent paper and serve hot with the syrup, which has been boiled down to a sauce consistency.

APPLE FRITTERS À LA PRINCESSE

Pare and core some fine apples. Cut them into thick slices, sprinkle with sugar, cinnamon, and rum. Cover and allow them to stand for about 1 hour. Drain them well, adding any juice to a fritter batter. Dip them into the batter, fry as usual, and place them in a shallow pan. Sprinkle with sugar and glaze in a hot oven. Serve sprinkled with chopped pistachio nuts.

BANANA FRITTERS

Peel bananas, split them in half lengthwise, and then cut each piece in half. Put them in a shallow dish, sprinkle with powdered sugar and lemon juice, sherry, rum, or brandy to taste. Cover the dish and allow to stand for 30 minutes, turning the bananas several times. Drain them well, adding any juice to a fritter batter. Dip each piece in the batter and fry a few at a time in hot deep fat. Serve hot with sugar and any sauce desired—rum-and-butter sauce is good, or sherry sauce, depending on flavor used.

PINEAPPLE FRITTERS

Peel and cut a pineapple into slices ½ inch thick. Then cut each slice in half, sprinkle them with sugar and kirsch, and allow them to stand for 30 minutes. Drain them well, adding any juice to a fritter batter. Dip the pieces of pineapple in fritter batter and fry in deep hot fat until delicately browned. Drain, sprinkle with sugar, and glaze under the flame of the broiler.

PÂTE À FRIRE À LA CARÊME

1½ cups sifted all-purpose flour
½ teaspoon salt
⅔ cup thin cream
½ teaspoon finely grated citron
½ teaspoon finely grated angelica
½ teaspoon finely grated lemon peel
2 tablespoons melted butter
2 eggs, beaten
2 egg whites, stiffly beaten
¾ cup brandied fruits and nuts, coarsely chopped

Sift the flour and salt into a mixing bowl. To the cream add the citron, angelica, and lemon peel and heat to scalding point, strain, and allow to cool to lukewarm. Stir the flavored cream into the dry ingredients along with the butter and beaten whole eggs. Allow the mixture to rest for about 1 hour and then fold in the egg whites and brandied fruits and nuts. Fry as usual.

PETS DE NONNE

This is a cream puff paste that is cooked in deep fat.

1 cup water
½ cup butter
½ teaspoon salt
1 teaspoon sugar
1 cup sifted all-purpose or pastry flour
4 eggs
2 egg whites, stiffly beaten

Bring to a boil the water, butter, salt, and sugar. When the butter has melted and the water is rapidly boiling, remove from the heat and add all at once the flour. Hold over the flame and stir briskly until the mixture comes away from the sides of the pan and forms a smooth ball. Add 4 eggs, one at a time, beating each one in thoroughly until the mixture is smooth and glossy before adding the next.

Add a little flavoring—vanilla, lemon, brandy, or rum—and fold in the egg whites. Fill a tablespoon with the paste and with a knife slip half of it off into deep hot fat (370° F.). Then slip off the other half, making 2 beignets from each spoonful. When they are golden brown they are done. This should take about 5 minutes. Serve immediately, sprinkled with powdered sugar, or with a custard or a fruit sauce. Makes 2 dozen.

ZUCKERSTRÄUBEN

⅔ cup sifted all-purpose flour
½ teaspoon salt
4 tablespoons sugar
White wine
6 egg whites

Mix together the flour, salt, and sugar and stir in enough white wine to make a medium batter. Fold into the batter the stiffly beaten egg whites and press it through a pastry tube into deep hot fat. Remove from the fat as soon as delicately browned. Sprinkle with sugar and serve with Sabayon Sauce.

PANCAKES

Griddlecakes, flapjacks, hotcakes, pancakes—call them what you will—and their first cousin, the waffle, although included in the cookery of all nations, are among the most popular foods in America.

Boys out scouting, campers and hunters, as well as the modern homemaker, all turn to these easy-to-prepare, delightful artistocrats of hot breads for any meal.

The delicate French crêpe, blazing in a liqueur-flavored sauce, the cheese-stuffed blintzes from Russia, the Adirondack flapjack, smelling of crisply fried bacon and swimming in butter and shaved maple sugar, Rhode Island johnnycakes—all these and many, many more have in common the fact that they are baked atop the stove on a heavy, hot griddle.

BASIC PANCAKE BATTER

INGREDIENTS FOR 16 PANCAKES

2 cups sifted all-purpose flour
2 teaspoons double-action baking powder
1 teaspoon salt
2 teaspoons sugar
2 eggs, beaten
1½ cups milk
4 tablespoons melted butter

METHOD

Sift the dry ingredients into a mixing bowl. Combine the eggs and milk and stir into the dry ingredients lightly. Stir in the melted butter. Do not overmix. For thinner pancakes, add a little more milk.

TO BAKE PANCAKES

Use a heavy griddle and heat it slowly over a low, steady heat while making the batter. Test the temperature of the griddle by sprinkling on it a few drops of water. The bubbles should dance around before evaporating. Grease the griddle lightly and pour the batter from a pitcher into pools a little apart. As soon as the cake becomes puffed up and full of bubbles, turn it with a pancake flipper and brown it on the other side. Serve hot with sugar, syrup, honey, jam, or marmalade.

BUTTERMILK OR SOUR MILK PANCAKES

1½ cups sifted all-purpose flour
1 teaspoon double-action baking powder
1 teaspoon soda
½ teaspoon salt
1 tablespoon sugar
3 eggs, separated
1⅔ cups buttermilk (or sour milk)
4 tablespoons melted butter

Sift together into a mixing bowl the sifted flour, baking powder, soda, salt, and sugar. Combine the well-beaten egg yolks with the buttermilk and stir lightly into the dry ingredients. Stir in the melted butter and lastly fold in the egg whites, which have been stiffly beaten. Makes about 16 cakes.

APPLESAUCE PANCAKES Make Sour Milk Pancakes and substitute ⅔ cup unsweetened applesauce for ⅔ cup milk. Add 1 teaspoon cinnamon, if desired.

BANANA PANCAKES Add ½ cup mashed bananas and 2 tablespoons sugar to Buttermilk Pancakes.

BLUEBERRY PANCAKES Add 2 cups washed blueberries to Basic Pancake Batter and bake as usual.

WHOLE WHEAT PANCAKES Use ½ whole wheat flour and ½ all-purpose flour in making pancakes.

OATCAKES

1 cup milk
2 cups rolled oats
2 eggs, beaten
1 teaspoon sugar
½ teaspoon salt
1 teaspoon nutmeg
1 teaspoon grated lemon rind

Scald the milk and pour it gradually over the oats, stirring until combined. Allow the mixture to cool and then add the eggs, sugar, salt, nutmeg, and lemon rind. Stir until all the ingredients are well mixed and then bake in cakes on a greased griddle until they are brown on both sides. Makes about 1 dozen.

BUCKWHEAT CAKES

½ cup sifted all-purpose flour
½ teaspoon double-action baking powder
½ teaspoon salt
2 teaspoons sugar
1 teaspoon soda
1½ cups buckwheat flour
3¼ cups sour milk or buttermilk
2 tablespoons melted butter

Sift together into a mixing bowl the flour, baking powder, salt, sugar, and soda. Add the buckwheat flour and mix well. Stir in the milk and melted shortening and beat only until the batter is blended. Bake in cakes on a hot greased griddle.

YOGURT OATMEAL GRIDDLECAKES

½ cup cooked oatmeal
1 cup yogurt
1 egg, beaten
¾ cup sifted all-purpose flour
1 teaspoon soda
¼ teaspoon salt

In a mixing bowl combine the oatmeal, yogurt, and egg. Sift together the flour, soda, and salt and stir into the yogurt mixture. Beat well and bake in cakes on a hot griddle.

POTATO PANCAKES

1 cup mashed potatoes
2 cups sifted all-purpose flour
1 teaspoon salt
3 teaspoons double-action baking powder
2 eggs, beaten
1 cup milk
4 tablespoons light corn syrup
1 teaspoon nutmeg

Combine the potatoes, sifted flour, salt, and baking powder. Mix together the eggs and milk and stir lightly into the potato-flour mixture. Add the corn syrup and nutmeg and beat well. Bake on a greased griddle until the cakes are brown on both sides. Makes about 1 dozen.

LACY PANTYCAKES

½ cup sifted all-purpose flour
¾ cup sugar
1 teaspoon baking soda
1½ teaspoons double-action baking powder
1 teaspoon salt
1 cup coarsely crushed graham crackers
4 eggs, beaten
1 cup sour cream
About 3 tablespoons water

Sift together the flour, sugar, baking soda, baking powder, and salt. Add the graham crackers and fold in the eggs, which have been beaten until they are thick and pale in color. Then stir in the sour cream and the water. The batter should be just thin enough so that the cakes will run a little at the edges, when dropped on a hot griddle. The griddle should be completely covered with a thin layer of grease. Try using half butter and half bacon fat. The cakes should be dark brown in color, with a crisp, lacy surface texture and uneven edges. If they are almost impossible to turn, your batter is the right consistency. Serve hot with butter and syrup, or with powdered sugar and jam.

MARK SMITH'S FLAPJACKS

Old Mark Smith was a famous guide in the Adirondacks. Here is his recipe for pancakes:

Sift together 2 cups flour, 1 teaspoon salt, and 2 teaspoons baking powder. Add enough corn meal to make them healthy (about ½ cup). Mix the dry ingredients to a batter with water and then stir in 4 tablespoons bacon drippings from the bacon that has been fried to a golden crispness.

Cook the pancakes full size in a 10-inch frying pan that has been greased with bacon drippings. When the pancake is full of bubbles and brown on the underside, flip it over and allow it to brown on the other side. If you are expert at flipping flapjacks, you won't depend on a pancake turner—a flip of the wrist and there you are. Place the pancake on a hot plate and cover it with butter and shaved maple sugar. Pile 6 baked flapjacks on top of each other, with butter and sugar between. Cut pie fashion, serve with crisply fried bacon, and say thanks to Mark Smith.

RHODE ISLAND JOHNNYCAKES

Mix 2 cups water-ground white corn meal with 1 teaspoon sugar, 1 teaspoon salt, and then add enough warm milk to make a batter (1¼–1½ cups). It is impossible to give the exact amount of milk. It all depends on how thick you want the cakes to be. For breakfast cakes, the batter is usually made quite thin. For other meals a medium batter is desired.

Bake the batter slowly in cakes on a griddle, with just enough fat to keep them from sticking. If they are browned too quickly the meal will not be cooked.

HOECAKES

Moisten salted corn meal with scalded water or milk and allow the mixture to stand for 1 hour. Put 2 or 3 teaspoons of this on a hot greased griddle and smooth it out to make cakes about ½ inch thick. Allow the cakes to cook and when one side is brown turn over and brown the other side. Serve hot.

RAW POTATO PANCAKES

1 egg
2 cups milk
1¼ cups sifted all-purpose flour
1 teaspoon sugar
1 teaspoon salt
Dash pepper
1½ pounds potatoes
Butter or bacon drippings

Beat the egg with a little of the milk in a mixing bowl. Stir in the sifted dry ingredients alternately with the remaining milk, beating until the mixture is smooth. Wash and peel the potatoes and grate them directly into the batter and then beat thoroughly. Fry as for pancakes on a hot, buttered griddle and serve hot with crisply fried bacon or with stewed berries.

GERMAN SKILLET CAKES

6 eggs, separated
½ cup sifted all-purpose flour
1 teaspoon double-action baking powder
Pinch salt
½ cup milk

Beat the egg yolks until thick and pale in color. Sift together the flour, baking powder, and salt and add to the egg yolks alternately with the milk. When all the ingredients are combined, fold in the egg whites, which have been stiffly beaten. Melt a little butter in a skillet and pour in a tablespoon of the batter. Tip the pan so that the batter will cover the bottom of the skillet in a thin layer. When brown on one side, turn and brown the other. Serve very hot with sugar and wedges of lemon.

ROLLED CREAM PANCAKES

1 cup sifted all-purpose flour
½ tablespoon sugar
Pinch salt
3 eggs, beaten
¾ cup rich milk
2 tablespoons melted butter
1 tablespoon rum

Sift together into a mixing bowl the flour, sugar, and salt. Stir in the eggs and milk and beat until the mixture is smooth. Stir in the butter and rum and strain through a fine sieve. Cover and allow the mixture to stand for 1 hour.

Melt 1 tablespoon sweet butter in a 10-inch frying pan. Pour in about 2 tablespoons of the batter and tip the pan so that the bottom is covered with a thin layer. Cook over a gentle heat until the bottom is delicately browned. Turn the cake and allow it to brown lightly on the other side. Slide the pancakes onto a hot platter and, while still piping hot, fill them with thick sour cream or with rum-flavored Crème Pâtissière. Roll the cakes to enclose the filling and sprinkle them with chopped blanched almonds. Surround with crushed fresh strawberries and serve hot.

HUNGARIAN BERRY PANCAKES

2 cups thin sour cream
1 egg, beaten
¼ teaspoon salt
½ teaspoon ground ginger
2 cups sifted all-purpose flour
Strawberries
Sugar
¾ cup blanched, shredded, and toasted almonds

Combine the sour cream, egg, salt, and ginger and stir in the flour. Beat until the mixture is blended. It should be the consistency of thick cream. Adjust the consistency by adding a little more cream or flour. Heat a small frying pan, brush with butter, and pour in

1 generous tablespoon of the batter. Tip the pan so that the batter will flow evenly over the bottom and cook for 1 minute. Turn and brown the other side lightly. Continue to bake the cakes until all the batter has been used. Slide the baked pancakes onto a slightly floured board. Place in the middle of each 2 tablespoons strawberries, which have been cut up and sugared to taste. Roll the pancakes and place them in an ovenproof, shallow pan. Sprinkle over the tops the almonds and place under the broiler until the tops of the pancakes blister, but be careful they do not burn.

BLINTZES

Combine in a bowl to make a thin batter 1 cup all-purpose flour, 1 cup water, 2 eggs, beaten, and ½ teaspoon salt.

Heat a small frying pan (about 6 inches in diameter) and brush it very lightly with butter. Pour into it about 2 tablespoons of the batter and invert the pan over the bowl, so that the bottom will be covered by a thin layer, and allow any excess batter to drain out. Hold the pan over the flame for about 30 seconds, or until the pancake is dry. Bake on one side only. Shake the cake out onto a damp towel and repeat, first heating the pan again thoroughly, as it is the heat of the pan that almost cooks the pancake. When all the batter has been used, roll the pancakes in the damp towel until you are ready to fill and fry them.

FILLING Mash ½ pound cottage cheese with sugar and cinnamon to taste. Beat in 1 egg and add ¼ cup sultana raisins and ¼ cup shredded almonds. Vanilla, sherry, or lemon juice, or a little grated lemon rind may be added for variation, or the cheese may be thinned with sour cream. Place a teaspoon of filling in the center of each pancake and roll. Fry the pancakes until golden brown in hot melted butter, turning them so they will heat and brown on all sides. Serve with sour cream and a little jelly or jam.

SWEDISH PANCAKES

¾ cup all-purpose flour
1 teaspoon sugar
½ teaspoon salt
4 eggs, beaten
2 cups milk

Sift together into a bowl the flour, sugar, and salt. Add the eggs and milk gradually, stirring until well blended, and allow to stand for 2 hours. Fry in thin pancakes on a hot greased griddle. Roll and place on hot serving platter. Sprinkle with confectioners' sugar and serve with lingonberries.

PLÄTTAR

2 eggs
3 cups milk
3 teaspoons sugar
1⅓ cups flour
1 teaspoon salt

Beat the eggs with the milk until light and add gradually the sugar, flour, and salt and stir the batter well. Brush a heated pancake iron with a little melted butter and fry the batter in small thin pancakes until lightly browned on both sides. Serve hot with jam. Serves 6.

CRÊPES

⅔ cup sifted all-purpose flour
1 tablespoon sugar
Pinch salt
2 eggs
2 egg yolks
1¾ cups milk
2 tablespoons melted butter
1 tablespoon brandy

Sift together into a mixing bowl the flour, sugar, and salt. Beat the eggs and the yolks, combine them with the milk, and stir into the dry ingredients until smooth. Add the melted butter and brandy and allow the mixture to stand for 1 hour before using.

Grease a hot small frying pan with a little butter and pour in about 2 tablespoons of the batter, rolling the pan in a circular motion to cover the bottom evenly with a thin layer. Cook it until it is set and brown on one side (about 1 minute), turn and brown the other side. Roll or fold into quarters, place on a hot serving dish, and sprinkle with confectioners' sugar.

CRÊPES MÉNAGÈRE

1 cup sifted flour
2 tablespoons sugar
¼ teaspoon salt
4 eggs, beaten
1¾ cups milk
Flavoring

Sift together into a bowl the flour, sugar, and salt. Stir in the eggs, milk, and flavoring (vanilla, rum, brandy, orange, or lemon) and mix until the batter is smooth. Allow the batter to stand for 1 hour before using. If the batter thickens too much on standing, it should be thinned with a little milk to the consistency of light cream. Heat a small frying pan until very hot, because quick cooking is necessary for good crêpes. Grease the hot pan with enough butter to prevent the crêpes from sticking, but not enough to make them greasy. Pour in enough batter to cover the skillet with a thin layer. Tip the pan, quickly, in a circular motion so the batter will flow evenly over the bottom. When the crêpe is set and lightly browned on the underside, turn it with the help of a large spatula, and cook it until the other side is golden. Place the crêpes on a hot serving dish and sprinkle with fine sugar, or serve them with maple syrup, honey, or jam.

CRÊPES WITH KIRSCH

Make small crêpes, about 5–6 inches in diameter. Spread them with a little butter that has been creamed with sugar and flavored with a little kirsch. Roll the crêpes, place them in a shallow baking pan, sprinkle with fine granulated sugar, and glaze them very quickly under the broiler flame.

CRÊPES SUZETTE

This is only one of a great many recipes for crêpes Suzette. The crêpes themselves may be made ahead of time in the kitchen and only the sauce made at the last minute, either at the table in a chafing dish or in the kitchen. If they are finished in the kitchen, bring them flaming to the table.

Make crêpes not larger than 5 or 6 inches in diameter, and place them on a hot dish to keep warm while preparing the sauce.

THE SAUCE
4 lumps sugar
5 tablespoons sweet butter
Rind and juice of 1 orange
1 teaspoon lemon juice
¼ cup curaçao or cointreau
¼ cup benedictine or Grand Marnier
½ cup brandy, hot

Rub the lumps of sugar on the skin of the orange until they are covered with the zest from the skin. Place the lumps on a plate with 3 tablespoons of the butter and with a fork crush all together, mixing until creamy. Place the rest of the butter in a flat pan or chafing dish and add the orange juice, lemon juice, and the liqueurs. When this comes to the boil, stir in the creamed sugar-and-butter mixture. Place the crêpes in the sauce, spooning it over them so they are well covered, and fold them in quarters. Pour over the hot brandy and flame it. Serve with the sauce.

EASY CRÊPES SUZETTE

Make crêpes not larger than 5 or 6 inches in diameter, and place them on a hot dish to keep warm while making the sauce.

THE SAUCE Cream together ½ cup sweet butter and ½ cup fine granulated sugar. Add the finely grated rind of 2 oranges and the juice of 1 orange, 1 teaspoon lemon juice, and ¼ cup any desired liqueur. Spread the crêpes with this mixture, then fold or roll them and arrange them on a hot flameproof serving dish. Sprinkle them with sugar and ¼ cup brandy. Ignite and serve flaming.

CRÊPES WITH PINEAPPLE

Make a crêpe batter. Drain canned pineapple rings, slice each piece into 3 parts to make 3 very thin rings, and dry the rings on a towel. Heat and butter a very small frying pan, the bottom of which is only slightly larger than the pineapple rings. Pour in a little batter to cover the bottom and when it is set and brown on the underside, place a ring of pineapple on it. Pour another very thin layer of batter over it, turn and brown the crêpe on the other side. Place the crêpes on a hot serving platter and sprinkle with confectioners' sugar.

WAFFLES

Waffles are made from a batter slightly thicker than a pancake batter, and they are cooked in a specially constructed iron.

BASIC WAFFLE BATTER

INGREDIENTS FOR 8 WAFFLES

2 cups sifted all-purpose flour
2 teaspoons double-action baking powder
½ teaspoon salt
2 eggs, separated

1¼ cups milk
6 tablespoons melted shortening

Sift the dry ingredients into a mixing bowl and mix to a light batter with the egg yolks, which have been well beaten, and the milk. Stir in the melted shortening and then fold in the egg whites, which have been stiffly beaten.

TO BAKE WAFFLES

Most modern waffle irons are equipped with an automatic heat control and come with a complete set of instructions which should be carefully followed. In general a waffle iron should be greased with an unsalted fat before it is used for the first time. After that, if enough shortening is added to the batter, further greasing is unnecessary.

Waffle irons should be thoroughly heated before pouring in the batter. If your iron does not have a thermometer, test the heat by sprinkling the iron with a few drops of water. The water should jump around crazily before evaporating.

Pour the batter into the center of the iron until it spreads out, covering the surface. Close the iron and bake until the steaming stops. Remove with a fork and serve with butter, maple syrup, honey, or jam, according to taste.

Any leftover batter may be kept in the refrigerator in a covered container for two or three days, but it should be beaten again before using.

Waffles may be served not only with butter and syrup but with crushed and sweetened fresh fruit, with cream cheese and jelly, with such creamed mixtures as creamed chicken, oysters, shrimp, with ice cream and chocolate or butterscotch sauce.

APPLE WAFFLES Stir into the Basic Waffle Batter, before folding in the beaten egg whites, 2 cups peeled and diced apples.

BANANA WAFFLES Stir into the Basic Waffle Batter, before folding in the beaten egg whites, 1½ cups thinly sliced bananas.

COCOA WAFFLES Substitute 3 tablespoons cocoa for 3 tablespoons of the flour when making Basic Waffle Batter.

FRUIT WAFFLES Stir into the Basic Waffle Batter, before folding in the beaten egg whites, 1 cup crushed, drained berries or diced fresh or canned fruit.

NUT WAFFLES Stir into the Basic Waffle Batter, before folding in the beaten egg whites, 1 cup finely chopped nuts.

BUTTERMILK WAFFLES

1¾ cups sifted all-purpose flour
2 teaspoons double-action baking powder
1 teaspoon soda
½ teaspoon salt
3 eggs, separated
1½ cups buttermilk or sour milk
½ cup melted butter

Sift the dry ingredients into a mixing bowl and mix to a light batter with the egg yolks, which have been well beaten, and the milk. Stir in the melted shortening, then fold in the egg whites, which have been stiffly beaten. Bake in preheated waffle iron. Makes 8 waffles.

YOGURT WAFFLES Use 2 cups yogurt in place of the buttermilk in the above recipe.

SOUR CREAM WAFFLES Use 2 cups sour cream in place of the buttermilk and stir in only 2 tablespoons melted butter.

CORN BREAD WAFFLES

1½ cups corn meal
¾ cup sifted all-purpose flour
2 teaspoons double-action baking powder
½ teaspoon soda
1 teaspoon salt
2 tablespoons sugar
2 eggs, separated
1½ cups buttermilk
4 tablespoons melted butter

Sift together the dry ingredients 3 times. Beat the egg yolks and to them add the dry ingredients alternately with the milk. Stir in the melted butter and lastly fold in the stiffly beaten egg whites. This batter may be prepared several hours before needed and kept in the refrigerator. Bake in preheated waffle iron. Makes 8 waffles.

RICH DESSERT WAFFLES

1 cup sifted cake flour
2 teaspoons double-action baking powder
½ teaspoon salt
2 eggs, separated
1 cup heavy cream

Sift the dry ingredients into a mixing bowl and mix to a smooth batter with the beaten egg yolks and the cream. Then fold in the stiffly beaten egg whites and bake in a preheated waffle iron. Makes 4 waffles.

CHOCOLATE WAFFLES   Stir into the batter 2 squares melted bitter chocolate and 6 tablespoons sugar.

SPICED CHOCOLATE WAFFLES   Add to the Chocolate Waffle batter ¼ teaspoon ground cinnamon, ¼ teaspoon ground nutmeg, and 1 teaspoon vanilla.

SPONGECAKE WAFFLES

4 eggs, separated
1 cup sifted sugar
¼ cup water
1 teaspoon grated orange rind
1 cup sifted cake flour
½ teaspoon salt
1 tablespoon rum

Beat the egg yolks until light, add the sugar, and continue beating until thick. Add the water and orange rind and then stir in the cake flour, which has been sifted with the salt, to make a smooth batter. Fold in the stiffly beaten egg whites and the rum. Bake in a hot buttered waffle iron until delicately browned. Makes 6 waffles.

GINGERBREAD WAFFLES

⅓ cup butter
1 cup molasses
2 eggs, separated
2 cups sifted all-purpose flour
½ teaspoon baking soda
2 teaspoons double-action baking powder
2 teaspoons ground cinnamon
1 teaspoon ground ginger
½ teaspoon salt
½ cup sour milk or buttermilk

Cream together the butter and molasses until smooth and well blended. Add the egg yolks, one at a time, beating well after each addition. Sift the dry ingredients and add them alternately with the sour milk and beat the mixture until smooth. Fold in the stiffly beaten egg whites and bake in a hot buttered waffle iron. Serve hot with whipped cream, with applesauce, or with butter and powdered sugar.

GAUFRES PARISIENNES

¾ cup sweet butter
1 cup sugar
4 eggs, separated
1½ cups sifted all-purpose flour
⅓ cup milk
1 teaspoon vanilla

Cream the sweet butter, add the sugar gradually, and cream together until smooth and fluffy. Add the egg yolks, one at a time, beating well after each addition, then stir in the flour alternately with the milk and vanilla, beating until smooth. Lastly fold in the stiffly beaten egg whites and bake in a hot buttered waffle iron. These are delicious served with ice cream.

3. Cakes

Cakes, more than any other baked product, are symbolic of happiness in almost every land. Throughout our own lives each important event is high-lighted by a cake—the dainty, flower-wreathed christening cake; birthday cakes ablaze with candles; the magnificent, towering wedding cake; Christmas cakes; Easter cakes —all lending enchantment to these special occasions.

There is an enormous variety of cakes, some breadlike with a simple dusting of confectioners' sugar, some moist with creamy fillings and luscious icings, some large and elaborate and others small and dainty.

Today's busy homemaker needs no magic wand, no special clairvoyance, to be able to make all these and many more. No longer is it necessary to use "enough flour to make a nice stiffness . . . butter the size of an egg . . . a wineglass of sugar . . ." Thanks to the careful development and the infinite experimentation of consumer test kitchens throughout America, certain basic rules and formulae have been made available which insure success and perfect results.

BASIC RULES FOR CAKE BAKING

1. *Read recipe carefully.* Be sure you understand it before proceeding.
2. *Use the finest ingredients.* No cake can be better than the raw materials from which it is made. Use butter whenever possible, the freshest eggs, and specially prepared cake flour when it is specified in a recipe.
3. *Measure accurately.* A spoonful or a cupful means level measurements. Many a cake has been ruined by an excess of flour. Flour in cake baking should always be sifted once before measuring.
4. *Mix carefully.* If a recipe says stir, beat, or fold in, do exactly that. Trust your recipes and follow directions as given.
5. *Choose pans that fit.* Much damage can be done to a cake by using too large or too small a pan.
6. *Watch baking time and temperature.* The oven should be preheated to indicated temperature. Light the oven and set at the proper temperature before starting to mix your cake. If the oven is too slow the cake will first rise, then fall with a resulting heavy texture. If the oven is too hot the outside will bake first and form a crust, then, when the heat reaches the interior, the surface is likely to burst to allow for expansion. *Don't overbake.* Overbaking makes a cake dry. Test by inserting a wire cake tester or toothpick into the center. If this comes out clean, the cake is done. If batter adheres to it, bake a little longer, and test again. Another reliable test is to touch the top of the cake lightly with the finger. If the surface springs back the cake is finished baking. If the impression remains, bake another 5 minutes and test again.
7. *Place pans away from sides or back of oven.* Place oven rack just below the center of the oven so that the top of the cake will be about in the middle. When baking 2 layers, stagger them in opposite corners. When baking 3 layers, place the third on another rack 2 inches above or below the first, but not directly over another pan.
8. *Invest in an oven thermometer* if oven does not have a regulator.

BUTTER CAKES

BUTTER CAKES WITH BEATEN WHOLE EGGS

1. Remove butter or shortening, eggs, and milk from refrigerator about an hour before making cake.
2. Prepare pan by greasing with vegetable shortening, then shake a little flour around in it until it coats the grease with a light film. Shake out excess. Or line with wax paper, cut to fit the bottom of round pans, the bottom and 2 sides of square or oblong pans. Grease pan first, place in paper, and grease again.
3. Assemble utensils and ingredients, light oven and set at required temperature.
4. Cream the butter until soft and fluffy. A wooden spoon is best for this.
5. Add the sugar a spoonful at a time, rubbing it into the butter with the back of the spoon. For a fine-textured cake, the butter and sugar should be creamed until very light and fluffy.
6. Eggs may be broken directly into the butter-sugar mixture and vigorously beaten. It is better, though, to beat them in a separate bowl with a rotary beater until they are light before adding them. If eggs are small add an extra egg for every 3 eggs called for in the recipe. Beat the eggs into the creamed mixture.
7. Stir in some of the sifted dry ingredients, then a little liquid. Continue stirring in the dry ingredients and liquid alternately. Stir just enough after each addition to keep the batter smooth and stir gently in only one direction.
8. Pour into prepared pan or pans, spreading the batter evenly.
9. Place in preheated oven and bake for a minimum length of time. Test for doneness and bake longer if necessary.
10. Remove as soon as baking is complete and allow to stand for a few minutes to permit the cake to shrink from the sides of the pan. Loosen sides of cake with knife or spatula and turn out onto wire cake rack. Remove paper if it were used. If a warm butter cake is placed on a solid surface the bottom becomes wet and soggy.
11. Frost cake as soon as it is thoroughly cool. (See sections on frosting and decorating of cakes at end of this chapter.)

ONE-EGG WHITE CAKE

SET OVEN AT 350° F.

¼ cup butter
1 cup sugar
1 egg, beaten
2 cups sifted cake flour
2 teaspoons double-action baking powder
¼ teaspoon salt
¾ cup milk
1 teaspoon vanilla

Follow directions for Butter Cakes with Beaten Whole Eggs. Bake in two round, 8-inch layer pans for 25 minutes, or in an 8-inch square cake pan for 35 minutes.

ONE-EGG CHOCOLATE CAKE

SET OVEN AT 350° F.

¼ cup butter
1 cup sugar
1 egg, beaten
2 tablespoons cocoa
¼ cup hot water
1½ cups sifted cake flour
1 teaspoon soda
1 teaspoon double-action baking powder
1 cup sour milk
1 teaspoon vanilla

Follow directions for Butter Cakes with Beaten Whole Eggs. Dissolve the cocoa in the hot water and add after the egg. Bake in three round, 8-inch layer pans for 30 minutes. Spread Cooked Cocoa Icing (see Frostings and Fillings) between the layers and over the top and sides.

CREAM CAKE

SET OVEN AT 350° F.

2 eggs
1 cup sugar
1⅔ cups sifted all-purpose flour
2 teaspoons double-action baking powder
½ teaspoon salt
1 cup heavy cream
1 teaspoon vanilla

Beat the eggs until thick and lemon-colored. Beat in the sugar gradually. Stir in the sifted dry ingredients alternately with the cream and vanilla. Bake in two round, 8-inch layer pans for 25 minutes, or in an 8-inch square cake pan for 35 minutes.

WHIPPED CREAM CAKE

SET OVEN AT 350° F.

1½ cups heavy cream
3 eggs, well beaten
1 teaspoon vanilla
2 cups sifted all-purpose flour
1½ cups sugar
2 teaspoons double-action baking powder
½ teaspoon salt

Whip the cream until it stands in peaks but is not too stiff. Fold in the eggs and vanilla and then the dry ingredients, which have been sifted together three times. Bake in two round, 8-inch layer pans for 35 minutes.

SWEET MILK DEVIL'S FOOD

SET OVEN AT 350° F.

½ cup butter
1¼ cups sugar
2 large eggs, beaten
2 squares (ounces) chocolate, melted
1¾ cups sifted all-purpose flour
½ teaspoon salt
1 teaspoon soda
1 cup milk

Follow directions for Butter Cakes with Beaten Whole Eggs, adding the melted chocolate after the eggs. Bake in two round, 8-inch layer pans for 30 minutes, or in an 8-inch square cake pan for 45 minutes.

SOUR MILK DEVIL'S FOOD

SET OVEN AT 350° F.

½ cup butter
1½ cups sugar
2 large eggs
4 tablespoons cocoa
3 tablespoons hot coffee
1⅞ cups sifted all-purpose flour

1 teaspoon salt
1 teaspoon soda
1 cup sour milk

Follow directions for Butter Cakes with Beaten Whole Eggs. Make a smooth paste of the cocoa and hot coffee and stir in after the eggs. Bake in two round, 8-inch layer pans for 35 minutes, or in an 8-inch square cake pan for 50 minutes.

COFFEE DEVIL'S FOOD

SET OVEN AT 350° F.

½ cup butter
1¼ cups sugar
2 large eggs
1½ cups sifted all-purpose flour
½ teaspoon salt
1 teaspoon soda
1 teaspoon double-action baking powder
½ cup cocoa
1 cup hot coffee

Follow directions for Butter Cakes with Beaten Whole Eggs. Dissolve the cocoa in the hot coffee and add alternately with the sifted dry ingredients. Bake in two round, 8-inch layer pans for 30 minutes, or in an 8-inch square cake pan for 45 minutes.

CHOCOLATE LAYER CAKE

SET OVEN AT 350° F.

½ cup butter
2 cups light brown sugar
3 eggs, beaten
4 squares (ounces) bittersweet chocolate
1 cup sour milk or buttermilk
2 cups sifted cake flour
1 teaspoon soda
¼ teaspoon salt
2 teaspoons vanilla

Follow directions for Butter Cakes with Beaten Whole Eggs. Pour into two well-greased 9-inch layer cake pans and bake for 30 minutes. Turn out immediately onto cake rack, and when cool put together with Chocolate Butter Cream and frost with Mountain Cream Frosting (see Frostings and Fillings).

CHOCOLATE NUT-FILLED DEVIL'S FOOD

SET OVEN AT 350° F.

⅔ cup butter
1¾ cups sugar
2 large eggs
2 egg yolks
½ cup cocoa
½ cup warm water
2¼ cups sifted all-purpose flour
1 teaspoon soda
½ teaspoon salt
¾ cup sour milk

Follow directions for Butter Cakes with Whole Beaten Eggs. Make a smooth paste of the cocoa and warm water and blend in after the eggs.

CHOCOLATE NUT FILLING AND TOPPING Spread half the batter in an 8×12-inch pan. Mix together 3 squares (ounces) semi-sweet chocolate, melted, 6 tablespoons coffee, and 2 cups moist, shredded coconut. Spread half this mixture over the batter and put remaining batter on top. Bake for 45 minutes. Remove from the oven and spread immediately with the rest of the icing.

SPICE CAKE WITH BROWN SUGAR MERINGUE

SET OVEN AT 350° F.

⅞ cup butter
2 cups brown sugar
2 large eggs
2 egg yolks
2½ cups sifted all-purpose flour
1 teaspoon soda
1 teaspoon double-action baking powder
½ teaspoon salt
1 teaspoon cinnamon
½ teaspoon ground cloves
1 cup sour milk

Follow directions for Butter Cakes with Whole Beaten Eggs. Spread batter in an 8×12-inch cake pan and bake for 45 minutes. Remove the cake from oven. Set oven temperature at 450° F.

BROWN SUGAR MERINGUE Beat 2 egg whites with ¼ teaspoon cream of tartar until stiff enough to stand in peaks but not dry. Gradually beat in 1 cup brown sugar about 1 tablespoon at a time. Spread this meringue on the hot cake, sprinkle with ½ cup chopped nuts. Place the cake on a wet board and bake until lightly browned—about 6 minutes.

GINGERBREAD CAKE

SET OVEN AT 350° F.

  5 tablespoons butter
  ½ cup sugar
  1 egg
  ½ cup molasses
  1¾ cups sifted all-purpose flour
  2 tablespoons ginger
  1 teaspoon cinnamon
  1 teaspoon baking soda
  ½ cup buttermilk
  Juice and grated rind of 1 lemon

Follow directions for Butter Cakes with Beaten Whole Eggs. Add the molasses after the egg and then stir in the flour, sifted with the spices and soda, alternately with the buttermilk. Stir in the lemon juice and rind and pour into greased pan 10×8×1½ inches. Bake for 30 minutes, or until a cake tester inserted in the middle comes out clean. Serve hot with whipped cream sprinkled with ginger.

FLUFFY CAKE WITH MARSHMALLOW TOPPING

SET OVEN AT 350° F.

  ½ cup butter
  1½ cups sugar
  2 large eggs
  2¼ cups sifted all-purpose flour
  2½ teaspoons double-action baking powder
  ¼ teaspoon salt
  1 cup milk
  1 teaspoon vanilla

Follow directions for Butter Cakes with Whole Beaten Eggs.

MARSHMALLOW TOPPING Spread the batter in an 8×12-inch cake pan. Place marshmallows, cut in half, over the batter. Sprinkle on top ½ cup chopped nuts and ½ cup brown sugar. Bake cake and icing together for 40 minutes.

APPLESAUCE SPICE CAKE

SET OVEN AT 350° F.

  ½ cup butter
  2 cups sugar

1 large egg
1½ cups thick unsweetened applesauce
2½ cups sifted all-purpose flour
½ teaspoon salt
½ teaspoon cinnamon
½ teaspoon ground cloves
½ teaspoon nutmeg
2 teaspoons soda
½ cup boiling water

Follow directions for Butter Cakes with Beaten Whole Eggs. Blend in the applesauce after the egg. Dissolve the soda in the boiling water and add alternately with the dry ingredients. Bake in an oblong tin 8×12 inches for 55 minutes.

BANANA CAKE

SET OVEN AT 350° F.

½ cup butter
1½ cups sugar
2 large eggs
2 cups sifted all-purpose flour
2 teaspoons double-action baking powder
¾ teaspoon soda
½ teaspoon salt
¼ cup sour milk or buttermilk
1 teaspoon vanilla
1 cup mashed bananas

Follow directions for Butter Cakes with Beaten Whole Eggs. Fold in the mashed bananas at the last. Pour into two round, 9-inch layer cake pans and bake for 30 minutes, or into a 9-inch tube pan and bake for 50 minutes. Fill and top with sliced bananas and sweetened whipped cream.

MAPLE CREAM CAKE

SET OVEN AT 350° F.

½ cup butter
1½ cups brown sugar
3 eggs
2¼ cups sifted all-purpose flour
2½ teaspoons double-action baking powder
½ teaspoon salt
¾ cup milk
1 teaspoon maple flavoring
½ cup chopped walnuts

Follow directions for Butter Cakes with Beaten Whole Eggs. Stir in the chopped walnuts at the last and bake in two 9-inch layer cake pans for 20 minutes. When cool spread Sour Cream Frosting (see Frostings and Fillings) between the layers and over the top. Decorate with walnut halves.

BUTTER CAKES WITH STIFFLY BEATEN EGG WHITES FOLDED INTO BATTER

1. Remove butter or shortening, eggs, and milk from refrigerator about an hour before making the cake.
2. Prepare pans.
3. Assemble utensils and ingredients.
4. Light oven and set at required temperature.
5. Cream the soft butter, add the sugar gradually, and cream until the mixture is very fluffy.
6. Break eggs and separate the whites from the yolks. Drain the whites into a medium-sized bowl and the yolks into a smaller bowl.
7. Beat egg whites with rotary beater until they are stiff enough to stand in peaks when the beater is pulled out of them, but not dry. They should look fine-grained and glossy.
8. Beat the egg yolks until light-colored and blend them into the creamed sugar and butter. (You can use the same beater without washing it, but *never* beat egg whites with a beater that has beaten yolks without first washing it thoroughly.) If melted chocolate is included in the recipe add it now.
9. Stir in the flour, baking powder, and salt, which have been sifted together, alternately with the liquid. If recipe calls for fruit or nuts, blend them in with the last of the flour mixture.
10. Add flavoring and beat the batter just enough to be sure it is smooth.
11. Add the beaten egg whites and fold them in carefully. Use the edge of a wooden spoon or a rubber spatula and cut down through the batter to the bottom of the bowl. Turn it and bring it up along the side of the bowl, folding some of the batter over the mass of egg whites. Repeat this process of gently cutting and folding until all the egg white has been distributed evenly throughout the batter.
12. Pour the batter into prepared pans and bake according to directions.
13. Remove cake from pans, cool on wire cake racks, and then frost.

TWO-EGG CAKE

SET OVEN AT 350° F.

½ cup butter
1 cup sugar
2 eggs
1¾ cups sifted all-purpose flour
½ teaspoon salt
2 teaspoons double-action baking powder
⅔ cup milk
1 teaspoon vanilla

Follow directions for Butter Cakes with Stiffly Beaten Egg Whites Folded into Batter. Bake in two round, 8-inch layer pans for 25 minutes, or in an 8-inch square cake pan for 35 minutes.

FOUR-EGG CAKE

SET OVEN AT 350° F.

1 cup butter
2 cups sugar
4 eggs
2⅔ cups sifted all-purpose flour
2½ teaspoons double-action baking powder
½ teaspoon salt
1 cup milk
2 teaspoons vanilla

Follow directions for Butter Cakes with Stiffly Beaten Egg Whites Folded into Batter. Bake in three round, 9-inch layer pans for 30 minutes, or in an 8×12-inch oblong cake pan for 40 minutes.

CHOCOLATE NUT CAKE

SET OVEN AT 350° F.

⅓ cup butter
1 cup sugar
2 eggs, separated
2½ squares (ounces) unsweetened chocolate, melted
1½ cups sifted all-purpose flour
2 teaspoons double-action baking powder
½ teaspoon salt
1 cup milk
1 cup chopped nuts
½ cup sugar

Follow directions for Butter Cakes with Stiffly Beaten Egg Whites Folded into Batter, adding the melted chocolate after the yolks, and the nuts with the last addition of the sifted dry ingredients. Before adding the stiffly beaten whites, gradually beat into them the ½ cup sugar listed last in ingredients, then carefully fold this meringue into the batter. Bake in two round, 8-inch layer pans for 30 minutes.

FUDGE NUT CAKE

SET OVEN AT 350° F.

¼ cup butter
1½ cups sugar
2 eggs, separated
4 squares (ounces) unsweetened chocolate, melted
1¾ cups sifted all-purpose flour
2 teaspoons double-action baking powder
½ teaspoon salt
1½ cups milk
2 teaspoons vanilla
1 cup chopped nuts
½ cup sugar

Follow directions for Butter Cakes with Stiffly Beaten Egg Whites Folded into Batter, adding the melted chocolate after the egg yolks. Before adding the stiffly beaten whites, gradually beat into them the ½ cup sugar listed last, then carefully fold this meringue into the batter. Bake in two round, 9-inch layer pans for 35 minutes, or in an 8×12-inch oblong cake pan for 55 minutes.

CHOCOLATE SOUR MILK CAKE

SET OVEN AT 350° F.

½ cup butter
1⅔ cups sugar
3 eggs
3 squares (ounces) unsweetened chocolate
½ cup coffee
2 cups sifted all-purpose flour
2 teaspoons double-action baking powder
¼ teaspoon soda
½ teaspoon salt
1 cup sour milk

Follow directions for Butter Cakes with Stiffly Beaten Egg Whites Folded into Batter. Mix together the chocolate and coffee and cook, stirring constantly, until the chocolate is melted and the mixture is smooth. Cool and blend into the butter-sugar-egg yolk mixture. Bake in two round, 9-inch layer pans for 30 minutes.

NUT CAKE

SET OVEN AT 350° F.

½ cup butter
1 cup sugar
2 eggs, separated
1½ cups sifted all purpose flour
2 teaspoons double-action baking powder
½ cup milk
2 teaspoons vanilla
1 cup broken nuts

Follow directions for Butter Cakes with Stiffly Beaten Egg Whites Folded into Batter. Stir in the nuts, which have been lightly floured with 1 tablespoon flour before adding to the batter. Turn into a 10×5×3-inch loaf pan which has been lined with paper and then greased, and bake for 40 minutes, or until an inserted cake tester comes out clean. When cold, ice with Mocha Frosting.

MARBLE SWIRL CAKE

SET OVEN AT 350° F.

½ cup butter
1 cup sugar
2 cups sifted cake flour
3 teaspoons double-action baking powder
½ teaspoon salt
¾ cup milk
1 teaspoon vanilla
3 egg whites
4 tablespoons sugar

Follow directions for Butter Cakes with Stiffly Beaten Egg Whites Folded into Batter. Beat the egg whites until stiff and gradually beat into them the 4 tablespoons sugar before folding into the batter. To one fourth of the batter add the following ingredients, which have been melted together while stirring over a low flame, and then cooled:

1 square (ounce) unsweetened chocolate
1 tablespoon sugar
2 tablespoons strong coffee
¼ teaspoon soda

Grease a 10×5×3-inch loaf pan, line the bottom with wax paper, and grease again. Put the batters into the pan by tablespoonfuls, alternating white and chocolate mixtures. With a knife, cut through the batter in a wide zigzag course. Bake for 1 hour, turn out onto cake rack and, when cool, ice with Mountain Cream Frosting.

SOUR MILK BUTTER CAKE

SET OVEN AT 350° F.

    ½ cup butter
    1½ cups sugar
    2 eggs
    2¼ cups sifted all-purpose flour
    1 teaspoon double-action baking powder
    ½ teaspoon soda
    ½ teaspoon salt
    1 cup sour milk or buttermilk
    1 teaspoon vanilla

Follow directions for Butter Cakes with Stiffly Beaten Egg Whites Folded into Batter. Bake in 8-inch layer pans for 30 minutes.

GUMDROP CAKE

SET OVEN AT 325° F.

    ⅞ pound butter
    1 cup sugar
    6 eggs, separated
    4¾ cups sifted all-purpose flour
    2 teaspoons vanilla
    1 pound gumdrops, halved
    ½ cup chopped citron
    ½ cup chopped almonds
    1 cup candied cherries

Cream the butter and sugar until light and fluffy. Add the egg yolks, slightly beaten, and beat thoroughly. Stir in the vanilla and 4 cups of the flour. Dredge ¾ cup of the flour over the gumdrops, citron, almonds and cherries, mix, and stir into the batter. Beat the egg whites until stiff and fold in. Pour into two loaf pans which have been lined with heavy brown paper, greased. Bake for 1½ hours.

ORANGE LAYER CAKE

SET OVEN AT 350° F.

    1 cup butter
    2 cups fine granulated sugar
    5 eggs, separated
    3 cups sifted all-purpose flour
    3 teaspoons double-action baking powder
    ¼ teaspoon salt
    1 cup milk
    1 tablespoon orange juice
    Grated rind of 1 orange

Follow directions for Butter Cakes with Stiffly Beaten Egg Whites Folded into Batter. Fold in grated orange rind before folding in the egg whites. Pour into three well-buttered layer pans and bake for about 25 minutes, or until a cake tester inserted in the middle comes out clean. Turn out immediately onto cake rack and, when cool, put the layers together and frost with Orange Cream Frosting.

HICKORY NUT LOAF

SET OVEN AT 350° F.

    1 cup butter
    2 cups sugar
    4 eggs, separated
    1 cup chopped hickory nuts
    1 cup chopped raisins
    2½ cups sifted all-purpose flour
    ½ teaspoon soda
    Pinch salt
    ¾ cup milk
    1 teaspoon lemon juice

Follow directions for Butter Cakes with Stiffly Beaten Egg Whites Folded into Batter. Add the hickory nuts and raisins to the egg-sugar mixture. Bake in an 8-inch tube pan for about 1 hour. When cool, ice with Confectioners' Sugar Icing and decorate with halved hickory nuts.

PECAN BOURBON CAKE

SET OVEN AT 325° F.

    1 pound shelled pecans
    ½ pound seeded raisins
    1½ cups sifted all-purpose flour
    1 teaspoon double-action baking powder
    ½ cup butter
    1 cup plus 2 tablespoons sugar
    3 eggs, separated
    2 teaspoons freshly grated nutmeg
    ½ cup bourbon whisky
    Pinch salt

Break the pecans into pieces or chop them coarsely. Cut the raisins in half. Sift the flour twice and mix ½ cup of it with the nuts and raisins. Sift the remaining flour again with the baking powder. Cream the butter until soft, add the sugar gradually, and cream together until fluffy. Add the egg yolks, one at a time, beating well after each addition. Soak the nutmeg in the whisky for 10 minutes and then add it to the butter mixture alternately with the flour, mixing thoroughly after each addition. Fold into the batter the nuts and raisins and lastly fold in the egg whites, which have been beaten until stiff with the pinch of salt. Grease a tube pan—one that is large enough to hold a 3-pound cake. Line it with brown paper and grease it again. Fill the pan with the batter and let it stand for 10 minutes, to allow the mixture to settle. Decorate the top of the cake with candied cherries and large pecan halves and bake for 1¼ hours. If the top browns too quickly, cover the surface with a piece of heavy paper. Let the cake stand in the pan for 30 minutes before removing it.

WHITE LAYER CAKES USING ONLY EGG WHITES

Choose your pans and the amount of other ingredients in accordance with the amount of egg whites in your refrigerator.

SET OVEN AT 350° F.

LAYER PANS	two 8-inch	two 8-inch	two 9-inch	three 8-inch, or two 9-inch
Butter	½ cup	½ cup	½ cup	1 cup
Sugar	1⅓ cups	1½ cups	1½ cups	2 cups
Sifted all-purpose flour	2 cups	2¼ cups	2 cups	2¾ cups
Double-action baking powder	3 tsp.	3 tsp.	4 tsp.	4 tsp.
Salt	½ tsp.	½ tsp.	½ tsp.	½ tsp.
Milk	1 cup	1 cup	1 cup	1 cup
Flavoring	1 tsp.	1 tsp.	1 tsp.	1 tsp.
Egg whites	3 (⅜ cup)	4 (½ cup)	5 (⅝ cup)	6 (¾ cup)

Cream butter and sugar, add sifted dry ingredients alternately with the milk and flavoring. Fold in the egg whites and bake for 25–30 minutes.

POUND CAKE

SET OVEN AT 300° F.

  2 cups butter
  2 cups sugar
  10 egg yolks
  4½ cups sifted flour
  ½ teaspoon salt
  1 teaspoon vanilla
  10 egg whites

Follow directions for Butter Cakes with Stiffly Beaten Egg Whites

Folded into Batter. Divide the batter into two parts and put into two loaf cake tins, which have been greased, lined with wax paper, and greased again. Bake for 1 hour and 10 minutes.

ANGEL FOOD, SPONGE, AND CHIFFON CAKES

ANGEL FOOD

Angel food takes more skill to make perfectly than butter cakes. The batter must be very carefully blended with a folding motion which incorporates the flour into the stiffly beaten egg whites without releasing the air, for it is this air that makes the cake light. The whole secret is in the proper beating of the egg whites, which only experience can teach you. They must be stiff enough to hold their shape without being dry. If they are overbeaten the cake will be coarse-textured and dry. If they are underbeaten, or if the air is allowed to escape, the cake will be tough and leathery. Egg whites will beat more easily and to a greater volume if they are at room temperature, so remove them from the refrigerator about 1 hour before starting the cake.

INGREDIENTS

	8-inch tube pan	9-inch tube pan	10-inch tube pan
Egg whites	1 cup	1⅓ cups	1½ cups
Sifted cake flour	⅞ cup	1 cup	1⅛ cups
Fine granulated sugar	1¼ cups	1½ cups	1¾ cups
Salt	¼ tsp.	¼ tsp.	⅓ tsp.
Cream of tartar	1 tsp.	1⅓ tsp.	1½ tsp.
Vanilla	1 tsp.	1½ tsp.	2 tsp.

METHOD
1. Assemble ingredients and utensils, including the correct size of tube pan, which should not be greased.
2. Set oven at 325° F.
3. Sift together the flour and ¼ cup of the sugar four times and set aside. If you use squares of wax paper for this you will avoid extra washing of dishes.
4. Sift the remainder of the sugar five times and set aside.
5. Put egg whites in a big bowl and add to them the salt. Then, using a rotary beater, beat them until they are foamy. Add the cream of tartar and continue beating until they are just stiff enough to form a peak when the beater is withdrawn. Be careful

not to overbeat them until they are dry. They should look glossy and smooth.
6. Sprinkle over them 2 tablespoons of the sugar and, still using the rotary beater, beat just enough to blend. Repeat this process until all the sugar has been added.
7. Lightly beat in the vanilla and put rotary beater aside.
8. Now with a wire whip, rubber scraper, or wooden spoon start to fold in the flour. Sift about ¼ cup of the flour over the mixture and fold it in. Tip the bowl a bit and gently cut down through the mixture to the bottom of the bowl. Bring the whip or spoon across the bottom and bring it up on the other side. Hold the utensil so that it is parallel to the sides or bottom as you move. Repeat this motion, turning the bowl a little each time. Sift another ¼ cup of the flour over the mixture and repeat the folding until all the flour has been incorporated.
9. Pour the mixture into the cake pan, letting it sheet in from the mixing bowl. Run the blade of a knife through the mixture to remove any large air bubbles that might be in it and place it in the oven.
10. Bake slowly for from 40 to 60 minutes, or until a delicate brown on top. Do not overbake, as this will make the cake dry.
11. When baked, remove from the oven and invert the pan over cake rack, or over three upturned teacups. Allow to cool for 1 hour before removing it from the pan. Run a spatula around the sides and plunge it down several times around the tube to help in removing it.
12. Dust the top generously with confectioners' sugar. Never cut an angel food cake. It should be torn apart with the fingers or broken with two forks.

BROWN AND WHITE Make Angel Food, using ¼ cup less flour and sugar. Divide batter in half. Into one part fold 2 tablespoons flour and 2 tablespoons sugar sifted together. Into the other part fold 3 tablespoons cocoa and 2 tablespoons sugar sifted together. Drop by tablespoonfuls into pan, alternating cocoa and white.

CHOCOLATE Substitute ¼ cup cocoa for ¼ cup flour. Follow directions given above, sifting the cocoa along with the flour and the ¼ cup sugar. When cool, frost with Mocha Frosting, if desired.

FRUIT OR NUT Prepare ½ cup of finely chopped nuts or well-drained fruits such as pineapple, apricots, maraschino cherries. Pour into tube pan one fourth of the batter and sprinkle with fruit or nuts. Add another fourth and continue in this manner until all the batter and fruit or nuts have been used. The addition of ¼ teaspoon of almond extract gives it a nice flavor.

GOLD AND WHITE Divide finished batter in half and fold into one part 4 well-beaten egg yolks, 2 tablespoons flour, and 1 teaspoon lemon juice. Drop by tablespoonfuls into pan, alternating yellow and white.

LEMON Substitute 2 teaspoons lemon juice for the vanilla. Follow directions given above and fold in at the very last the grated rind of 1 lemon.

ORANGE Substitute 1 tablespoon orange juice for the vanilla. Follow directions given above and fold in at the very last 1 tablespoon grated orange rind.

PEPPERMINT Substitute peppermint extract for the vanilla. Follow directions given above.

CUSTARD ANGEL CAKE

SET OVEN AT 300° F.

1¼ cups sugar
½ cup water
8 eggs, separated
1 cup sifted cake flour
¼ teaspoon salt
1 teaspoon cream of tartar
1 teaspoon orange juice

Dissolve the sugar in the water and boil it until it spins a long thread (230° F.). Beat the egg yolks until they are very thick and pale in color. Pour over them very gradually the syrup, and continue beating until it has all been added and the mixture is quite thick. Sift the flour and salt together four times and fold it into the egg yolk mixture. Beat the egg whites until they are frothy, add the cream of tartar, and continue to beat until they are stiff but not dry. Fold the egg whites and orange juice into the yolk-flour mixture and pour it into an ungreased tube pan. Bake for 1½ hours, or until it is lightly brown on top and the sides of the cake have begun to shrink a little from the pan. Invert the baked cake on a rack and allow it to cool before removing it from the pan.

BASIC SPONGECAKE

Spongecakes are quite simple to make, compared to

Angel Food. The same gentle folding of the egg whites into the batter is necessary for perfection.

SET OVEN AT 325° F.

    6 eggs, separated
    1 cup sugar
    1 tablespoon lemon juice
    Grated rind of 1 lemon
    ¼ teaspoon salt
    1 cup sifted cake flour

METHOD

1. Assemble ingredients and utensils.
2. Beat the egg whites with a rotary beater until stiff but not dry, and set aside.
3. Using the same beater, beat egg yolks until they are thick and lemon-colored. NOTE: In whipping egg whites, the beater must be clean and free from fat. Egg yolk contains fat, so if you beat the egg yolks first, the beater must be carefully washed before the whites can be beaten. Avoid this by beating the whites first.
4. Gradually beat in the sugar.
5. Stir in the liquid and flavoring.
6. Fold in the sifted dry ingredients.
7. Gently fold in the stiffly beaten egg whites.
8. Turn into ungreased tube pan and bake for 40–60 minutes. Remove from oven, invert pan on cake rack or teacups, and allow the cake to cool for 1 hour.
9. Run a spatula around the outer edge and around the center tube. Shake the pan sharply, holding hand underneath to catch cake as it falls. Break into serving pieces with two forks.

GOLD CAKE

SET OVEN AT 325° F.

    ¾ cup egg yolks (about 10)
    1 whole egg
    1¾ cups sugar
    1 cup boiling water
    1 tablespoon grated orange rind
    1 tablespoon orange juice
    2 cups sifted cake flour
    1½ teaspoons double-action baking powder
    ¼ teaspoon salt

Follow directions for Basic Spongecake, beating the whole egg with the yolks. In this case no stiffly beaten egg whites are used. Bake in a 10-inch, center-tube pan for 40 minutes.

EASY SPONGECAKE

SET OVEN AT 325° F.

> 6 eggs, separated
> 1½ cups sugar
> 6 tablespoons cold water
> 2 teaspoons vanilla
> 1½ cups sifted cake flour
> 1 teaspoon double-action baking powder
> ¼ teaspoon salt

Follow directions for Basic Spongecake and bake in a 10-inch, tube-center pan for 40–60 minutes.

JIFFY SPONGECAKE

SET OVEN AT 325° F.

> 4 eggs, separated
> 1½ cups sugar
> 2 teaspoons cold water
> ½ cup hot water
> 1 teaspoon vanilla
> 1⅔ cups sifted cake flour
> ¼ teaspoon salt
> ¼ teaspoon double-action baking powder

Use an electric beater if you have one. Beat egg whites and set aside. Beat egg yolks at top speed while you sift together the flour, salt, and baking powder. Add sugar gradually while still beating at top speed. Reduce speed to medium and add the cold water, hot water, and vanilla. Remove bowl from beater, fold in dry ingredients and lastly the stiffly beaten egg whites. Pour into ungreased tube pan and bake for 40 minutes. Invert pan over cake rack until cool. This is nice frosted with a large quantity of Mountain Cream Frosting to which has been added a jar of strawberry jam and a drop of red coloring.

NOTE: To use this cake as a base for desserts or for small iced teacakes, pour it into a large shallow pan or into two round 9-inch pans to a thickness of about 1 inch and bake for 20 minutes.

JELLY ROLL

SET OVEN AT 350° F.

    5 large eggs, separated
    4 tablespoons granulated sugar
    3 tablespoons sifted all-purpose flour
    1 teaspoon vanilla
    4 tablespoons jelly

Grease a large baking sheet (18×12 inches), line with wax paper, and grease again. Add the sugar to the egg yolks and beat until they are thick and lemon-colored. Fold in carefully the flour and vanilla and lastly the egg whites, which have been stiffly beaten. Spread the mixture evenly on top of the baking sheet and bake for 12 minutes. Loosen the paper from the tin, sprinkle the top with a little granulated sugar, and turn out on wax paper. Carefully remove the paper from the bottom of the cake, sprinkle thoroughly with granulated sugar, and spread lightly with a well-flavored jelly. Roll lengthwise for a long, thin roll, or sidewise for a shorter, thicker roll.

    STRAWBERRY ROLL Place a damp towel over the Jelly Roll cake and allow it to cool for 15 minutes. Sprinkle with granulated sugar, spread with crushed and sweetened, fresh or frozen and defrosted strawberries or other fruits in season. Roll up sidewise and, when thoroughly cool, cover with a thick layer of whipped cream and decorate with whole berries.

CHOCOLATE ROLL

SET OVEN AT 350° F.

    5 large eggs, separated
    ⅔ cup sugar
    6 squares (ounces) semisweet chocolate
    3 tablespoons strong coffee
    1¼ cups heavy cream, whipped
    Cocoa

Grease a large baking sheet (18×12 inches), line with wax paper, and grease again. Melt the chocolate in the coffee by stirring it over a low flame and allow to cool a little. Add the sugar to the egg yolks and beat with a rotary beater until they are thick and lemon-colored. Stir in the melted chocolate and coffee and then fold in the egg whites, which have been beaten until stiff. Spread the mixture evenly over the prepared sheet and bake for 15 minutes, or until a knife inserted in the middle comes out clean. Do not overbake. Remove from the oven and cover with a damp towel for half an hour, or until cool. Loosen the cake from the baking sheet and dust generously with cocoa. Turn out onto wax paper (cocoa side down) and remove paper carefully from the bottom of the cake. Spread with the whipped cream, which has been sweetened and flavored to taste, and roll up like a jelly roll, rolling it sidewise rather than lengthwise to give a thin, long roll that resembles a log. To facilitate the rolling, grasp firmly each corner of the wax paper on which you turned out the cake and flip over about 2 inches of the edge on top of the spread cake. Continue to roll by further lifting of the wax paper. The last roll should deposit the log on a long board or platter. Dust the top with a little more cocoa. Serves 8.

RUM CAKE
SET OVEN AT 350° F.

    3 eggs
    1 cup sugar
    3 tablespoons cold water
    2 teaspoons vanilla
    1 cup sifted all-purpose flour
    2 teaspoons double-action baking powder

Beat eggs until light. Gradually beat in the sugar and continue beating until the mixture is thick and pale in color. Use electric beater for this, if you have one. Stir in the water and vanilla. Fold in the flour, which has been sifted three times with the baking powder. Pour into a greased 9-inch spring-form pan, and bake for 30 minutes, or until a cake tester inserted in the middle comes out clean. Keep the cake in the pan and, when cool, pour over it Rum Cream Topping. Place in the refrigerator to set and serve decorated with chopped nuts and candied cherries.

RUSSIAN TEACAKE
SET OVEN AT 350° F.

    6 egg whites
    3 egg yolks
    ¾ cup sugar
    ⅔ cup sifted cake flour
    ½ teaspoon cream of tartar
    ½ teaspoon salt

Beat the egg whites until stiff but not dry. Beat the egg yolks with the sugar until thick and pale in color and fold into the egg whites. Sift the dry ingredients together five times and fold into the egg mixture. Bake in an 8-inch center-tube pan for 1 hour. Ice top and sides with Russian Teacake Icing.

ORANGE CHIFFON CAKE

No book on baking in general would be complete without the addition of BETTY CROCKER'S CHIFFON CAKE. It is basically a spongecake, but it is made in a different way and incorporates cooking oil in the ingredients to give it a rich-tasting, unusually moist quality. It makes an excellent base for various desserts and petits fours; it is delicious frosted or plain; it is perfect to serve with ice cream or berries, or topped with a rich sauce. I have Miss Crocker's permission to reprint it here.

SET OVEN AT 325° F.
10-INCH TUBE CAKE
2¼ cups sifted Softasilk cake flour (spoon lightly into cup)
1½ cups sugar
3 tsp. double-action baking powder
1 tsp. salt
½ cup cooking oil, such as Mazola or Wesson
5 egg yolks, unbeaten
Grated rind of 2 oranges (about 2 tbs.)
Juice of 2 oranges plus water to make ¾ cup
1 cup egg whites (7 or 8)
½ tsp. cream of tartar

SET OVEN AT 350° F.
8- OR 9-INCH SQUARE CAKE
1⅛ cups flour (1 cup plus 2 tbs.)
¾ cup sugar
1½ tsp. double-action baking powder
½ tsp. salt
¼ cup cooking oil
2 egg yolks, unbeaten
1 tbs. grated orange rind
Juice of 1 orange plus water to make ⅜ cup (¼ cup plus 2 tbs.)
½ cup egg whites (4)
¼ tsp. cream of tartar

Measure and sift together into a mixing bowl the flour, sugar, baking powder, and salt. Make a well in the dry ingredients and add cooking oil, egg yolks, orange rind, and orange juice. Beat with spoon until smooth. In another bowl whip egg whites until they form *very stiff* peaks; they should be much stiffer than for angel food or meringue. *Do not underbeat.* Pour egg yolk mixture gradually over whipped egg whites, *gently* folding with rubber scraper *just* until blended. *Do not stir!* Pour into *ungreased* pan immediately. Bake Large Cake 65 minutes; Small Cake 30 minutes. The small recipe may also be baked in a 9-inch tube pan at 325° F. for 50 minutes. Immediately turn pan upside down, placing tube part over neck of funnel or bottle, or resting edges of square pan on two other pans. Let hang, free of table, until cold. Loosen from sides and tube with spatula. Turn pan over and hit edge sharply on table to loosen. Serve uniced, with whipped cream and berries, with a dessert sauce, or top with Orange Fluff Topping. Large Cake makes 16–20 servings; Small Cake, 8–10 servings.

YELLOW CHIFFON CAKE For the Large Cake, use ¾ cup water in place of the orange juice plus water. Use grated rind of 1 lemon (about 2 teaspoons) in place of grated orange rind. Add 2 teaspoons vanilla. Bake in a 10-inch tube pan at 325° F. for 55 minutes, then increase temperature to 350° F. for 10–15 minutes more. For the Small Cake, use half of amounts given.

BIT O' WALNUT CHIFFON CAKE For the Large Cake, use ¾ cup water in place of the orange juice plus water. Omit the orange rind and add 2 teaspoons vanilla. After mixing, carefully and gently fold 1 cup very *finely* chopped walnuts into batter. (Black walnuts may also be used; omit vanilla.) Bake in a 10-inch tube pan at 325° F. for 55 minutes, then increase temperature to 350° F. for 10–15 minutes more. For the Small Cake, use half of amounts given.

BETTY CROCKER PEPPERMINT CHIP CAKE

SET OVEN AT 325° F.
10-INCH TUBE CAKE
2 cups *sifted* Gold Medal "Kitchen-tested" Enriched Flour (spoon lightly into cup, don't pack)
1½ cups sugar
3 tsp. double-action baking powder
1 tsp. salt
½ cup cooking (salad) oil, such as Wesson
7 egg yolks (medium-sized), unbeaten
¾ cup cold water
1 tsp. peppermint extract*
1 cup egg whites (7 or 8)
½ tsp. cream of tartar
½ tsp. red food coloring

SET OVEN AT 350° F.
8- OR 9-INCH SQUARE CAKE
1 cup *sifted* flour
¾ cup sugar
1½ tsp. double-action baking powder
½ tsp. salt
¼ cup cooking oil
3 egg yolks (medium-sized), unbeaten
⅜ cup (¼ cup plus 2 tablespoons) cold water
½ tsp. peppermint extract*
½ cup egg whites (about 4)
¼ tsp. cream of tartar
½ tsp. red food coloring

Measure and sift together into a mixing bowl the flour, sugar, baking powder, and salt. Make a well in the dry ingredients and add cooking oil, egg yolks, water, and peppermint extract. Beat with spoon until smooth. In another bowl whip egg whites and cream of tartar until whites form *very stiff* peaks. *Do not underbeat.* Pour egg yolk mixture gradually over whipped egg whites, *gently* folding with rubber scraper *just* until blended. *Do not stir!* Sprinkle red food coloring over top of batter. Fold in with only three or four strokes to streak through batter, but not enough to blend com-

*Be sure to use peppermint extract, as oil of peppermint is much stronger.

pletely. Pour into *ungreased* pan immediately. Bake Large Cake at 325° F. for 55 minutes, then at 350° F. for 10–15 minutes; Small Cake at 350° F. for 30–35 minutes—or until top springs back when *lightly* touched. Immediately turn pan upside down, placing tube part over neck of funnel or bottle, or resting edges of square pan on two other pans. Allow to hang, free of table, until cold. Loosen from sides and tube with spatula. Turn pan over and hit edge sharply on table to loosen.

SPICE CHIFFON CAKE For the Large Cake, add 1 teaspoon cinnamon, ½ teaspoon each nutmeg, allspice, and ground cloves with the dry ingredients. Mix in 2 tablespoons caraway seed, if desired. Omit the peppermint extract and the red food coloring. For the Small Cake, use half of amounts given.

VANILLA AND ALMOND CHIFFON CAKE For the Large Cake, omit the peppermint extract and use 1 teaspoon vanilla and 1 teaspoon almond extract. Omit the red food coloring. For the Small Cake, use half of amounts given.

COCONUT CAKE

SET OVEN AT 325° F.

8 eggs
1 cup sugar
2 cups sifted cake flour
¼ cup butter, melted and cooled

Combine the eggs and sugar and beat over hot water until the mixture is warmed through. Remove from the heat and continue to beat until it is thick and pale in color. Fold in the flour and butter and bake in three greased layer pans for about 30 minutes. Remove cakes from pans and, when they are cool, spread Custard Filling between the layers. Frost the cake lavishly with Marshmallow Icing made by beating ½ cup egg whites and ¾ cup sugar over a slow fire until lukewarm and of a good spreading consistency. Flavor with 1 teaspoon vanilla. Sprinkle the icing heavily with grated fresh coconut.

SOUTHERN PECAN CAKE

6 eggs, separated
1½ cups sugar
3 tablespoons all-purpose flour
1 teaspoon baking powder
3 cups finely chopped pecans

Beat the egg yolks until they are light, add the sugar, and continue to beat until the mixture is very thick and pale in color. Mix together the flour, baking powder, and pecans and fold into the egg whites, which have been beaten until stiff. Combine this mixture with the egg yolk and sugar mixture. Bake in two layers at 350° F. for 20 minutes. Remove from pans and cool on rack. When cool, put the layers together with whipped cream flavored and sweetened to taste.

GÉNOISE

This is a very fine-textured cake which is used as the basis of some of the finest of gâteaux, petits fours, and de luxe desserts such as the baked Alaska. It is difficult to make, however, and should not be attempted by the inexperienced cook. Great care must be taken in the mixing of the ingredients, otherwise the aeration whipped into eggs and sugar will be lost, and the cake will be heavy. White butter cakes, spongecakes, or a chiffon cake make admirable substitutes.

1 cup sugar
6 eggs
1 teaspoon vanilla
1 cup sifted cake flour
¼ cup butter, melted and cooled

Combine the sugar, eggs, and vanilla in the top of a double boiler. Beat with a wire whip over very hot water for about 15 minutes, or until the mixture is warmed through and is light and creamy. Remove pan from the heat and beat with a rotary beater until it is thick, pale in color, and takes some time to level out when the beater is withdrawn. Add the flour and fold in carefully but thoroughly with a rubber scraper or a wooden spatula. Gradually and carefully fold in the butter. The butter must not be more than lukewarm, and any residue which has fallen to the bottom of the saucepan in which it was melted must not be put in. Pour the batter into a large shallow pan or two round 9-inch pans to the thickness of about 1 inch. The pans should be greased, lined with wax paper, and greased again. Bake at 350° F. for 30 minutes, or until a cake tester inserted in the center comes out clean. Remove from the pan immediately and cool on a rack.

DESSERTS—GÉNOISE OR GÉNOISE-TYPE CAKE

ORANGE DELIGHT Bake a sponge or chiffon cake in a square or oblong pan and, when it is cool, pour over it ½ cup orange juice mixed with the grated rind of 1 orange. Cover the top with peeled orange sections.

BOSTON CREAM CAKE Bake a sponge or chiffon cake in a square or oblong pan. When ready to serve, split it into two layers. Put it back together again with Custard Filling between the layers and serve with thin Chocolate Sauce.

NUT FINGERS Cut sponge or chiffon cake into small rectangles and ice them on all sides with a butter icing. Roll in chopped nuts.

ICE CREAM ROLLS Cut thin layers of sponge or chiffon cake into strips about 6 inches long and 2½ inches wide. Wrap these strips around a scoop of ice cream and pour over the top some thick Butterscotch Sauce.

PEACH AND CHERRY DESSERT Split a sponge or chiffon cake and fill with orange ice. Place it in a large serving bowl and cover with 1 dozen peaches which have been peeled and sliced. Pour over all this 1 quart brandied cherries.

COCONUT JAM ROUNDS Cut sponge, chiffon, or white butter cake into rounds, using a baking powder can or a tomato purée can which has had both the top and bottom removed. Coat the sides of the little cakes with jam and roll in freshly shredded coconut. Place them on a cooky sheet with a teaspoon of jam on top of each and bake at 350° F. for 10–15 minutes. Serve them hot with a hot Jam Sauce (see Sauces).

APRICOT CIRCLES Cut a Génoise or spongecake into rounds about ½ inch thick and 2½ inches in diameter. Pour over each piece a few drops sherry or liqueur. Place on top half an apricot, which has been cooked in syrup, and on top of each apricot place a maraschino cherry. Serve with Apricot Sauce.

HOT PEACH ROUNDS Cut a Génoise or spongecake into rounds 3 inches in diameter and ½ inch thick. Fry them in melted butter until they are lightly browned on both sides. Place them in a warm place on absorbent paper to drain. Heat halved preserved peaches in their own syrup, to which has been added a little white wine. Allow them to simmer for 2–3 minutes and then place half a peach on each slice of fried cake, hollow side uppermost. Place in each hollow 1 teaspoon black currant jelly. Place the rounds on a serving dish and strain the syrup around them. Serve hot with heavy cream.

RUM CAKE DESSERT Bake a butter cake or spongecake in a ring mold. When it is baked, remove it from the mold and cool on a rack. When cool, place it on a serving dish and pour over the following syrup:

Combine 2 cups sugar with 2 cups boiling water and ¼ teaspoon cream of tartar and boil until it forms a thick drop on the tip of a spoon. Add the juice of ½ lemon and the grated rind of 1 lemon and allow to cook for another 2 minutes. Remove the syrup from the heat and add 4 ounces Jamaica rum.

Drain two thirds of the juice from a can of halved apricots and cook them slowly for 10 minutes in the remaining juice, to which has been added a 1-inch piece of vanilla bean and a pinch salt. Pour the apricots into the hole in the middle of the cake and top with whipped cream which has been sweetened to taste.

PEACH SURPRISE Cut Génoise or spongecake into rounds about the diameter of half a peach and ½ inch thick. Rub 1 cup apricot jam through a fine sieve and place it in a saucepan with ¼ cup white wine and stir it over the fire until it is hot. Spread a little of the hot jam over the rounds of cake, place a half peach, either fresh or poached, on each, and cover the peach and the cake with meringue. Bake them in a hot oven for 10 minutes, or until the meringue is lightly browned. Serve hot with the rest of the apricot jam served separately.

FRIED CAKE Cut stale Génoise or spongecake into slices ⅓ inch thick and cut into small shapes with round, oval, or square cooky cutters. Combine ¼ cup milk, ¼ cup heavy cream, 1 tablespoon sugar, and a few drops vanilla. Dip the pieces of cake in this, allow them to drain for a few minutes on absorbent paper, and then dip them in frying batter, made by combining 1 egg yolk, a pinch salt, ½ cup warm water, and ½ cup flour and folding in the stiffly beaten whites of 2 eggs and 2 tablespoons melted butter. Fry the batter-coated rounds in hot deep fat as you would doughnuts, drain, and serve hot sprinkled with sugar.

APRICOT TIMBALES Cut Génoise or spongecake which is 3 inches thick into rounds, using a baking powder tin with both ends removed, and hollow out the center, leaving the walls about ½ inch thick. Beat the whites of 2 eggs until stiff and fold them into 2 cups apricot purée. Fill the cases with the purée and bake at 350° F. for 10 minutes. Place half of a preserved apricot on top of each timbale, decorate with cherries and slivers of angelica, and serve hot with cream or Apricot Sauce.

BASKETS Bake a Génoise or spongecake about 1½ inches deep and, when it is cool, cut it into ovals with a pastry cutter. Remove some of the center cake to make a deep hollow in each. Rub a little raspberry jam through a fine sieve and spread it around the sides of the rounds and then roll them in shredded coconut. Place a teaspoon of the jam in the hollow. Pile on top whipped cream, sweetened and flavored to taste. Decorate with glacéed cherries cut in small pieces and bits of angelica. Soak a stick of angelica about 4 inches in length in hot water until it will bend without breaking. Cut it into thin strips and place one strip across each round to form the handle of the baskets.

Another tasty combination is to use apricot jam in place of the raspberry jam and roll the rounds in chopped pistachio nuts.

ORANGE ICE BOMBE Bake sponge or Génoise cake in two melon molds and, when they are cool, scoop out the center from each mold, leaving a thick shell. When ready to serve, fill the molds with orange ice and put the two halves together to form a whole melon. Coat all over with orange ice.

ICECAPADE Bake a sponge or Génoise cake in a 9-inch round pan which is 2½ inches deep. When it is cool, scoop out the center and fill with ice cream or Rum or Vanilla Pastry Cream. Rub some apricot jam through a fine sieve and spread a thin layer of it around the outside of the cake and sprinkle thickly with chopped pistachio nuts or shredded coconut. Garnish the top with rosettes of whipped cream.

FRUIT LOAF Bake a sponge or Génoise cake in a high timbale mold and, when it is cool, cut a slice off the top and scoop out the inside. Fill with fresh fruits in season which have been sweetened to taste and flavored with a little maraschino brandy. Put on top the slice that was removed and coat all over with whipped cream. Poached or preserved fruit may be used in place of the fresh, if desired.

PEACH PYRAMID Bake a sponge or Génoise cake in a 9-inch cake pan about 2 inches deep and, when it is cool, pour over it ¼ cup sherry or madeira. Rub some apricot jam through a sieve and coat the sides and top of the cake with it. Sprinkle thickly with chopped pistachio nuts and place it on a serving dish. Whip 1 cup heavy cream, reserve a little for decoration, and pile the rest in the center of the cake in pyramid form. Drain some preserved peaches and mount them in rows all over the cream. Put the reserved cream into a pastry bag fitted with a star nozzle and pipe a small rosette of cream in between each peach half.

OEUFS EN SURPRISE Cut 1-inch-thick sponge or chiffon cake into rounds 3 or 4 inches in diameter and place half a preserved apricot on each, rounded side up. Surround each apricot with whipped cream, sweetened and flavored to taste to represent egg white. The apricot will resemble the yolk.

CREAM-FILLED STRAWBERRY CAKE Bake a sponge or Génoise cake in a large timbale mold and, when it is cool, scoop out the inside, leaving the sides and bottom ½ inch thick. Rub a little apricot jam through a sieve and spread over the outside of the cake. Cover thickly with chopped nuts and place on serving dish. Fill the inside with alternate layers of Crème Bavaroise and Strawberry Cream, allowing each layer to set before putting in the next. When ready to serve, whip 1 cup cream, flavor and sweeten it to taste, and pile it on top of the cake in pyramid shape. Cover the pyramid with halved strawberries.

CROÛTES DE PRUNES Stew ½ pound dried prunes in 1 cup water with ¼ cup claret or port, the rind of 1 lemon, and 2 tablespoons sugar, until soft. Stone the prunes, put aside the 6 nicest, and rub the rest through a fine sieve. Cut out six rounds 2½ inches in diameter from a 1-inch-thick sponge or Génoise cake, spread a layer of the prune purée on each croûte and place a whole prune on top. Whip ½ cup heavy cream, sweeten it slightly, and tint it pink. Put it into a pastry tube with a fluted nozzle and fill the stone cavity of each prune with a large rosette of the cream. Pipe a decorative border of the cream around the edge of each croûte.

CORBEILLE DE FRUITS Bake a Génoise or spongecake in a loaf pan and, when it is cool, scoop out the center to form a basket, leaving the sides and bottom about ½ inch thick. Make some Royal Icing and put it in a pastry tube fitted with a small round or fluted nozzle. Make crisscross lines on the sides of the cake to represent latticework, and in each space formed by the lines place a Crystallized Violet. Fasten the violets in place with a little of the icing. Prepare fruits in season, either fresh sugared or poached in vanilla syrup. Fill the center of the cake with the fruits and cover with whipped cream. Decorate with leaves made from angelica and with Crystallized Violets. Soak a strip of angelica in hot water until it is soft enough to bend and form it into the handle of the basket.

FRUITCAKES

CHRISTMAS FRUITCAKE

1 pound candied pineapple, cut into thin wedges
½ pound candied citron, cut into thin strips
¼ pound citron, cut into thin strips

⅛ pound candied lemon peel, cut into thin strips
⅛ pound candied orange peel, cut into thin strips
1 pound sultana raisins
½ pound seeded raisins
¼ pound currants
½ cup rum or brandy
¼ pound blanched almonds
¼ pound shelled walnuts or pecans
2 cups sifted all-purpose flour
½ teaspoon mace
1 teaspoon cinnamon
½ teaspoon baking soda
¼ teaspoon salt
¼ pound butter
1 cup sugar
1 cup brown sugar
5 eggs
1 tablespoon orange juice
1 teaspoon almond flavoring

Prepare all the fruits the day before and soak them overnight in the brandy. Cut up the nuts coarsely. Next day, grease a deep 10-inch cake pan, line it with heavy brown paper, and grease it again. Combine the fruit and nuts in a large bowl and mix them with ½ cup of the flour. Sift the remaining flour three times with the mace, cinnamon, baking soda, and salt. Cream the butter, add gradually the sugars, and cream together until well blended. Add the eggs, one at a time, beating well after each addition, and then stir in the orange juice, almond flavoring, and the flour mixture. Pour the batter over the mixed fruit and nuts and mix with both hands until combined. Lift the batter with the hands into the prepared pan, pressing it down firmly with the palms of your hands. Bake at 275° F. for 3 hours, covering the top with greased paper if it begins to brown too much. Remove cake from oven and allow to stand for 30 minutes before removing it to cake rack to thoroughly cool. Makes a 5½-pound cake.

To store for any length of time, wrap it in wax paper and store in a tightly covered container. Moisten it every 4 weeks with ½ cup brandy. Many people make their Christmas cake far ahead of time, allowing it to ripen and age for a full year before eating it.

DARK FRUITCAKE

1 pound candied cherries
2 pounds sultana raisins

5 pounds seedless raisins
2 pounds currants
1 pound blanched almonds
½ pound citron, sliced
½ pound candied orange and lemon, mixed and sliced
2 pounds butter
4 cups brown sugar
12 eggs
½ cup molasses
10 cups sifted all-purpose flour
3 teaspoons cinnamon
1 teaspoon allspice
1 teaspoon ground cloves
1 teaspoon ground nutmeg
1 teaspoon soda
2 teaspoons double-action baking powder
½ cup sherry
¼ cup vanilla
½ cup orange juice

Prepare fruit and nuts. If citron, peel, or raisins are hard, soften them by washing them and steaming for 30 minutes. Mix all together with 2 cups of the flour. Follow standard directions for Butter Cake with Beaten Whole Eggs. Stir in the molasses directly after the eggs. Add the sifted dry ingredients alternately with the liquid and stir in the floured fruit and nuts at the last. Bake in 2-pound loaf pans, 8×4×3 inches, which have been lined with heavy brown paper and then greased. Bake at 250° F. for 2 hours. Smaller cakes will require less baking time. Fill pans almost full. This recipe will make 8 loaves. Half the quantity is sufficient for most occasions.

Top with a 1-inch-thick layer of Almond Paste and ice with Confectioners' Sugar Icing.

To keep fruitcakes for a long time, store them unfrosted in a tightly covered tin box. Every month pour over ½ cup brandy.

LIGHT FRUITCAKE

1 pound sultana raisins
1 pound blanched almonds
½ pound citron, finely sliced
½ pound candied cherries
½ pound candied pineapple, finely sliced
½ pound candied orange peel, finely sliced
½ pound candied lemon peel, finely sliced

1 cup butter
2 cups sugar
1 cup white wine
4 cups sifted all-purpose flour
2 teaspoons double-action baking powder
½ teaspoon salt
8 egg whites, stiffly beaten

Prepare the fruit and nuts. If citron, peel, or raisins are hard, soften them by washing and steaming for 30 minutes. Mix all together with 1 cup of the flour. Cream the butter and sugar together until light and fluffy. Sift the dry ingredients together and add them alternately with the wine. Stir in the fruit and nuts and then fold in the egg whites. Bake in loaf pans, 8×4×3 inches, which have been lined with heavy brown paper and then greased. Bake at 250° F. for 2 hours. Makes 3 loaves.

GOLDEN FRUITCAKE

1 pound sultana raisins
1 pound figs, chopped
1 pound almonds, blanched
½ pound citron, finely sliced
1 pound candied cherries
½ pound candied pineapple, finely sliced
½ pound candied orange peel, finely sliced
½ pound candied lemon peel, finely sliced
1 pound butter
3 cups light brown sugar
8 eggs, beaten
1 cup apple jelly
6 cups sifted all-purpose flour
3 teaspoons double-action baking powder
1 teaspoon salt
2 teaspoons cinnamon
1 cup milk
2 teaspoons vanilla

Prepare fruit and nuts. If citron, peel, or raisins are hard, soften them by washing and steaming for 30 minutes. Mix all together with 2 cups of the flour. Follow standard directions for Butter Cakes with Beaten Whole eggs. Stir in the jelly (any light jelly will do) and add the sifted dry ingredients alternately with the liquid. Lastly fold in the floured fruit and nuts. Bake in loaf pans, 8×4×3 inches, which have been lined with heavy brown paper and then greased. Bake at 250° F. for 2 hours. Makes 4 loaves.

SIMNEL CAKE

¾ cup butter
2 cups sugar
4 large or 5 small eggs
2 cups sifted all-purpose flour
½ teaspoon salt
1 cup currants
1 cup finely shredded candied peel

Cream together the butter and sugar until fluffy and smooth. Add the eggs, one at a time, beating thoroughly after each addition. Dredge a little flour over the fruit. Sift the rest of the flour with the salt and add gradually. Fold in the fruit. Line a deep round cake pan with wax paper and pour in half the cake batter. Roll out Almond Paste to the size of the cake pan and place it on top of the batter. Pour in the remaining cake batter and bake at 300° F. for 1 hour. Remove cake from pan and place on wire rack to cool. When cool, decorate the top with candied peel, citron, candied cherries, and Almond Butter Frosting forced through a pastry tube to form roses, leaves, and fluted edges.

BISCHOFSBROT

5 eggs, separated
¼ teaspoon salt
1¼ cups sugar
¾ cup sliced almonds
½ cup seeded raisins
¼ cup sliced citron
2 squares (ounces) unsweetened chocolate cut into small dice
1¾ cups sifted all-purpose flour

Beat the egg yolks until light and foamy, add the salt, and add gradually the sugar, continuing to beat until the mixture is thick and pale in color. Add the almonds, raisins, citron, and chocolate and then fold in the stiffly beaten egg whites. Sift the flour over the batter and fold it in lightly. Bake in a long, narrow buttered bread mold at 350° F. for 50 minutes. Remove the cake from the tin and allow it to cool on a rack before slicing it.

WEDDING CAKE

Attractive and professional-looking wedding cakes may be made at home as successfully as any ordinary fruit cake. With the aid of a pastry tube or cake decorator it may be simply and effectively, if not elaborately, decorated and topped with the conventional bride and groom, which may be bought at any good pastry store.

¾ cup molasses
6 tablespoons water
30 ounces seedless raisins
9 ounces citron, thinly sliced
6 ounces candied cherries, halved
6 ounces candied pineapple, sliced
6 ounces blanched almonds, shredded
6 ounces pecans, coarsely chopped
1½ cups plus 3 tablespoons sifted all-purpose flour
½ teaspoon soda
1½ teaspoons cinnamon
1 teaspoon nutmeg
½ teaspoon allspice
¼ teaspoon ground cloves
¾ cup butter
¾ cup sugar
¼ ounce unsweetened chocolate, melted
4 eggs
6 tablespoons brandy

Heat the molasses and water to the boiling point. Add the fruit and nuts and cook, stirring, until the syrup has been absorbed by the fruit, or for about 5 minutes. Spread out the mixture on a large platter and allow it to cool thoroughly, stirring it occasionally.

Sift together three times 1½ cups of the flour, with the soda and spices. Cream together the butter, sugar, and chocolate and then beat in the eggs one at a time. Stir in the sifted dry ingredients alternately with the brandy. Sprinkle the remaining 3 tablespoons flour over the fruit and stir the fruit mixture into the batter. Grease a pan about 9 inches in diameter and 3 inches deep. Line the bottom and sides with 3 thicknesses of brown paper, greasing the top layer thoroughly. Pour the batter into the pan. Cover it with two layers of greased paper and then tie securely over the top two thicknesses of cheesecloth. Place the cake on a rack in a large kettle which contains about 2 inches of boiling water, cover, and steam for 2½ hours. Remove the cheesecloth and paper covers and bake at 275° F. for 3 hours. Turn out on cooling rack, remove bottom papers, and cool thoroughly. If possible, allow the cake to age for 2 or 3 days before icing it. This makes a 6½-pound cake and cuts into about 50 slices.

THREE-TIERED WEDDING CAKE

1 pound candied pineapple rings
½ pound figs
½ pound dates
¼ pound candied orange peel
¼ pound candied lemon peel
¼ pound citron
½ pound blanched almonds, halved
½ pound halved pecans
1 pound candied cherries
1 pound butter
2 cups (1 pound) brown sugar
6 eggs, separated
4 cups sifted all-purpose flour
1 teaspoon soda
1 teaspoon ground cloves
1 teaspoon nutmeg
2 teaspoons cinnamon
½ cup molasses
½ cup brandy
2 pounds seedless raisins
1 pound sultana raisins

Slice the pineapple rings into two slices, then in half crosswise. Remove the stems from the figs and cut the fruit in half lengthwise. Remove the stones from the dates and cut them with kitchen scissors into pieces not too small. Dredge the dates and pineapple pieces, separately, with 1 cup of the flour in all, tossing them well until all the pieces are well coated. Mix together the orange and lemon peel, the citron, almonds, pecans, and cherries. Cream the butter until light, add the brown sugar gradually, and continue to cream until well blended. Beat the egg yolks and stir into the butter-sugar mixture until well combined. Add the rest of the flour, which has been sifted three times with the soda and spices, alternately with the molasses and the brandy. Fold in the stiffly beaten egg whites, then the dates and, gradually, the seedless raisins and the sultanas. Grease three round or square cake tins. The first should be about 9 inches in diameter, the second 6 inches in diameter, and the third should be about 3 inches in diameter. Line them with three layers of brown paper and grease the top layer again. Put a layer of the batter in each pan. Place a layer of the pineapple down the center and fill in the spaces on either side with the mixed peel, cherries, and nuts, using about half the mixture. Cover with another layer of the batter, then place a layer of figs down the center and again fill in the side spaces with the rest of the mixed fruit and nuts and top with the remaining batter. The pans should be about two thirds full. Cover the tops of the pans with two layers of greased heavy paper and place them in larger pans containing about 1 inch hot water. Bake at 250° F., removing the water pans about 1 hour before the cakes are done. The large tier will take about 4 hours to bake, the medium tier about 3 hours, and the small tier about 2 hours. Remove cakes from cake pans, cool thoroughly, wrap in wax paper, and store in a tightly covered tin box.

When ready to frost, place the tiers one on top of the other and cover the entire surface of the cake with a thin smooth coating of a decorative frosting. Allow this coating to dry thoroughly before decorating it with more frosting put through a pastry tube or cake decorator. Top with an attractive ornament.

BRIDE'S CAKE

1¾ cups butter
2 cups sugar
8 eggs, separated
1 teaspoon almond flavoring
2 tablespoons heavy cream
2½ cups sifted all-purpose flour
1½ teaspoons double-action baking powder
¼ teaspoon salt
1 cup chopped seeded raisins
1 cup blanched almonds
1 cup citron, finely shredded

Cream the butter, gradually add the sugar, and cream together until light and fluffy. Beat the egg yolks until thick and pale in color and stir into the butter-sugar mixture, along with the almond flavoring and the cream. Beat thoroughly. Dredge a little flour over the fruit and nuts and sift the rest together with the baking powder and salt three times. Stir in the flour, add the nuts and fruit, and lastly fold in the egg whites, which have been beaten until stiff. Grease a 10-inch tube pan. Line with wax paper and grease again. Pour the batter into the prepared pan and bake at 300° F. for about 2 hours. Cool on wire cake rack and, when cool, frost the top and sides with Almond Butter Frosting, reserving enough to squeeze through pastry tube and to decorate the cake with fluted edges, flowers, and leaves.

FRUIT BUN

Sift together 2 cups all-purpose flour and ½ teaspoon baking powder. Rub into it ¾ cup butter and mix with 1 lightly beaten egg and enough cold water to make a stiff paste. Roll out two thirds of the paste on a lightly floured board large enough to line an 8-inch round cake tin which is 3 inches deep. Roll out the remaining third into a round large enough to cover the filling.
Make the filling by sifting together 2 cups flour, ½ teaspoon cream of tartar, ½ teaspoon baking soda, 1 cup sugar, 1 teaspoon ground ginger, 1 teaspoon ground cinnamon, and ¼ teaspoon black pepper. Stir into this mixture 1 pound seedless raisins, 1 pound currants, ⅓ cup citron, ⅓ cup candied orange peel, and 1 cup chopped blanched almonds. Sprinkle over it 2 ounces brandy and then add gradually about ¾ cup milk until the mixture is barely moist. Turn into the lined tin and cover with the round of pastry. Prick it all over with the tines of a fork, brush with a little beaten egg and bake at 300° F. for 2 hours.

DUNDEE CAKE

1 cup butter
⅔ cup sugar
4 eggs
½ cup blanched chopped almonds
2½ cups sifted all-purpose flour
1 teaspoon double-action baking powder
½ teaspoon salt
1 cup seedless raisins
1 cup currants
2 tablespoons orange juice
⅓ cup candied orange peel, finely cut
⅓ cup candied lemon peel, finely cut
½ cup whole blanched almonds
½ cup candied cherries

Cream the butter, add the sugar gradually, and blend well. Add the eggs, one at a time, beating well after each addition. Stir in the chopped almonds. Sift together the flour, baking powder, and salt and mix with the raisins and currants. Combine the orange juice with the orange and lemon peel and add this mixture alternately with the sifted dry ingredients, raisins, and currants. Grease two small bread pans, line them with heavy paper, and grease again. Divide the batter between the two pans and cover the top with the whole almonds and candied cherries. Bake at 250° F. for

1½ hours, covering the tops with greased paper as soon as the cake starts to brown. When baked, remove cakes from the pans and cool on cake rack.

APPLE CAKE

2 cups sifted cake flour
1½ teaspoons double-action baking powder
½ teaspoon salt
½ cup butter
½ pound apples, peeled, cored, and chopped
½ cup sugar
1 egg, well beaten
Milk to make a stiff batter

Sift together the flour, baking powder, and salt into a mixing bowl. Rub into it the butter until the flour mixture is the consistency of coarse meal. Mix the sugar and apples and stir into the first mixture. Add the egg and enough milk to make a fairly stiff batter. Pour into a large square cake pan and bake at 350° F. for 45 minutes. Serve hot from the oven with sugar and heavy cream.

PEACH UPSIDE-DOWN CAKE

9 peach halves, fresh or preserved
¼ cup soft butter
½ cup brown sugar
Maraschino cherries
½ cup butter
1 cup sugar
2 eggs, beaten
1 teaspoon vanilla
2 cups sifted cake flour
3 teaspoons double-action baking powder
1 teaspoon salt
⅔ cup milk
Whipped cream

Drain preserved peaches, or peel and stone fresh peaches. Spread the ¼ cup soft butter in the bottom of a deep 9-inch square cake pan. Sprinkle the brown sugar evenly on top of the butter and arrange the peaches cup side down on the sugar. Place whole cherries in uniform pattern between the peach halves. Cream the butter, add the sugar gradually, and cream together thoroughly. Stir in the eggs and vanilla. Sift together the flour, baking powder, and salt and add alternately with the milk. Pour the batter over the fruit and bake at 350° F. for about 45 minutes. Loosen sides of the cake with a spatula and turn out of pan, allowing the pan to rest over the cake for a few seconds, to drain out the syrup. Serve warm with whipped cream, sweetened and flavored to taste.

PINEAPPLE UPSIDE-DOWN CAKE

¼ cup butter, melted
1 cup brown sugar
1 cup pecan meats
8 slices canned pineapple
4 eggs, separated
1 tablespoon melted butter
1 teaspoon vanilla
Pinch salt
1 cup granulated sugar
1 cup sifted cake flour
1 teaspoon double-action baking powder

Pour the ¼ cup melted butter into the bottom of a 9-inch cake pan, then sprinkle evenly with the brown sugar and pecan meats. Drain the juice from a No. 2½ can pineapple slices and place the slices over the brown sugar mixture. Beat the egg yolks until thick and pale in color and then beat in the 1 tablespoon melted butter and the vanilla. Beat the egg whites with the salt until they are stiff and then beat in gradually the granulated sugar, about 1 tablespoon at a time. Fold in the yolk mixture and then fold in gradually the flour, which has been sifted with the baking powder. Pour this batter into the prepared pan and bake at 325° F. for about 30 minutes. Turn it out onto a serving platter and serve it warm.

Other fruit may be substituted for the pineapple. Canned peaches or apricots need only ½ cup brown sugar in the bottom of the pan. Fresh fruit, such as peaches, cherries, apples, may need more than 1 cup, depending upon the acidity of the fruit.

PEAR UPSIDE-DOWN CAKE

3 tablespoons butter, melted
¼ cup brown sugar
⅛ teaspoon ginger
1 tablespoon lemon juice
Pecan halves
Pear halves, peeled and cored
1½ cups sifted cake flour
2½ teaspoons double-action baking powder

½ teaspoon salt
⅓ cup butter
2 tablespoons sugar
½ cup corn syrup
2 small eggs
⅓ cup milk
1 teaspoon vanilla

Grease the sides of a 9-inch cake pan. Place the butter, sugar, ginger, and lemon juice in the bottom of the pan and add the nuts and pears so that the entire bottom surface of the pan is covered. Sift together the flour, baking powder, and salt. Cream the butter with the sugar and corn syrup until well blended. Add the eggs, one at a time, and beat well after each addition. Add the sifted dry ingredients alternately with the milk. Add the vanilla and stir until smooth. Pour the batter into the prepared pan and bake at 350° F. for about 35 minutes. Allow the cake to remain in the pan for a few minutes, to let the syrup thicken, before turning it out on a serving dish.

CHEESE CAKES

COTTAGE CHEESE CAKE

1 cup zwieback crumbs
¼ cup sugar
¼ cup melted butter
½ teaspoon cinnamon
1 pound creamed cottage cheese
¼ cup sifted cake flour
4 eggs, separated
1 cup sugar
2 tablespoons lemon juice
1½ teaspoons grated lemon rind
½ teaspoon vanilla
¼ teaspoon salt
1 cup heavy cream, whipped

Combine the zwieback crumbs, the ¼ cup sugar, melted butter, and cinnamon. Pat three fourths of this mixture on the bottom of a buttered 8-inch spring form pan. Force the cottage cheese through a coarse strainer twice with the back of a spoon, mix it with the flour, and beat thoroughly until it is as light and fluffy as possible. Beat the egg yolks, add ½ cup of the sugar, and beat until thick and pale in color. Add the lemon juice, lemon rind, vanilla, and salt and then fold in the cheese mixture. Lastly fold in the whipped cream and the egg whites, which have been beaten until stiff with the other ½ cup sugar. Blend the mixture gently but well and turn into the prepared pan. Sprinkle remaining crumbs on top. Bake at 250° F. for 1 hour. Turn off oven, open the door, and without moving the cake, leave it in oven 1 hour. Then cool thoroughly, remove spring form, and serve.

CREAM CHEESE CAKE I

Prepare the following cooky dough mixture:
1 cup sifted all-purpose flour
¼ cup sugar
1 teaspoon lemon rind
Pinch vanilla bean pulp
1 egg yolk
½ cup butter

Combine the flour, sugar, lemon rind, and vanilla bean pulp. Make a well in the center and add the egg yolk and butter. Work together quickly with the hands until well blended. Wrap in wax paper and chill thoroughly in the refrigerator for at least 1 hour. Roll out ⅛ inch thick and line the buttered bottom of a 9-inch spring form pan, trimming off the dough by running a rolling pin over the sharp edge. Bake at 400° F. for 15–20 minutes, or until light golden in color. Allow it to cool, then butter the sides of the spring form pan and place it over the base. Roll out the remaining dough ⅛ inch thick and cut it to fit the sides. Pour in the Cheese Filling and bake at 550° F. for 12 minutes. Reduce temperature to 200° F. and continue to bake for 1 hour. Turn off heat, open oven door, and allow the cake to cool in the oven for 1 hour before removing it. Cool thoroughly before cutting.

CHEESE FILLING
2½ pounds cream cheese
1¼ cups sugar
3 tablespoons flour
1½ teaspoons grated orange rind
1½ teaspoons grated lemon rind
Pinch vanilla bean pulp
5 whole eggs
2 egg yolks
½ cup heavy cream

Cream the cheese, which is at room temperature, and then beat in gradually the sugar, stirring and beating until the mixture is light and fluffy. Beat in the flour, orange and lemon rind, and vanilla bean pulp. Blend thoroughly. Add the eggs and egg yolks, one at a time, stirring lightly after each addition, and lastly fold in the heavy cream.

CREAM CHEESE CAKE II

¾ box zwieback
¼ cup melted butter
7 tablespoons sugar
1 pound cream cheese
1 teaspoon vanilla
4 tablespoons sifted all-purpose flour
Pinch salt
4 eggs, separated
1 tablespoon lemon juice
1 cup heavy cream

Roll the zwieback into fine crumbs and mix them with the melted butter and 1 tablespoon of the sugar. Press the crumbs firmly onto the bottom and sides of a well-buttered 9-inch spring form pan. Cream the cheese with the vanilla. Stir in 2 tablespoons of the sugar, the flour and salt, and cream all together until the mixture is fluffy. Beat the egg yolks, add them, and beat thoroughly. Then stir in the lemon juice and cream. Beat the egg whites until almost stiff. Add gradually the remaining sugar and continue to beat until the meringue is stiff and glossy. Fold into the cheese mixture lightly but thoroughly and pour into the prepared pan. Bake the cake at 325° F. for 1½ hours, or until set in the center. Chill the cake before removing the spring form.

FRENCH CHEESE CAKE

1 pound cream cheese
½ cup sugar
3 tablespoons flour
½ teaspoon salt
3 eggs, separated
1 teaspoon vanilla
¾ cup heavy cream, whipped
1 cup mixed seedless raisins and currants
Rich pastry dough

Put the cream cheese through a sieve and then beat it with a wooden spoon until it is light and fluffy. Sift together twice the sugar, flour, and salt. Sift the mixture a third time over the cheese and blend well. Beat the egg yolks and vanilla into the whipped cream and combine with the cheese mixture. Beat briskly until creamy and smooth, then fold in the egg whites, which have been beaten until stiff. Line an oblong cake pan about 1½ inches deep with a rich pie dough. Sprinkle the bottom with the raisins and currants and

ABOVE, preparation of Old-fashioned Dessert Bread, p. 52

BELOW, preparation of Frosted Fruit Loaf, p. 52

ABOVE, Stollen, p. 55
BELOW, Apple Dumplings, p. 77

ABOVE, preparation of Butterscotch Biscuits, p. 74

BELOW, Biscuit Bunnies. Roll out Baking Powder Biscuit Dough ½ inch thick and cut it into Easter bunny shapes.

Variations of One-egg Cake, p. 132

Variations of One-egg Cake, p. 132

Angel Food, p. 145

Ribbon Cake. Place a layer of White Cake between two layers of Devil's Food cake and frost with Mountain Cream Frosting.

Cherry Jelly Roll, p. 150

ABOVE, Squares of Angel Food
RIGHT, Sweetheart Cake
BELOW, Woolly Lamb, p. 197

ABOVE, Petits Fours, p. 190. BELOW, LEFT, Cupcakes, pp. 189–90. BELOW, RIGHT, Sweetheart Petits Fours, p. 190.

pour in the filling. Bake at 450° F. for 15 minutes to set the filling, then reduce heat to 300° F. and bake for another 30 minutes, or until the cake is firm and golden brown in color. When thoroughly cool, dust with powdered sugar and serve.

CASSATA PALERMITANA

6 eggs
1½ cups sugar
3 cups sifted all-purpose flour
2 teaspoons baking powder
Grated rind of ½ lemon

Beat eggs until creamy, add sugar gradually, and beat until thick and pale in color. Fold in the flour, which has been sifted with the baking powder, and the grated lemon rind. Pour into a buttered 9-inch spring form pan and pour over it the following filling:

1½ pounds ricotta
6 eggs
2 cups sugar
Grated rind of ½ lemon
1½ teaspoon ground cinnamon
½ cup hazelnuts, thinly sliced

Force the ricotta through a sieve twice to make sure it is smooth and free from lumps. Beat the eggs, add the sugar gradually, and beat until thick and pale. Add the lemon rind and cinnamon and lastly stir in the ricotta. Place this filling over cake batter, sprinkle with the hazelnuts, and bake at 300° F. for about 1 hour, or until a silver knife inserted in the center comes out clean.

STRAWBERRY CHEESE FLAN

Make twice the cooky dough mixture as in cake recipe above, chill it, roll it out ⅛ inch thick, and line a 12-inch buttered pie plate. Bake at 400° F. for about 15 minutes, or until light gold. Allow it to cool. Fill with Cheese Filling and bake at 450° F. for 30 minutes. Allow it to cool thoroughly and place whole strawberries in circles to cover the top completely. Glaze the surface of the strawberries with Strawberry Glaze.

STRAWBERRY GLAZE In a saucepan heat together 1 cup sugar, 1 cup water and ½ cup strawberries. Allow it to cool for 10 minutes and then pass through a fine sieve. Return the mixture to the fire, bring to the boil and stir in 2 teaspoons cornstarch, which has been mixed with ¼ cup water. Boil, stirring, for 1 minute.

JIFFY EASY-MIX CAKES

A few minutes in your electric mixer and your cake is ready for the oven.

LAZY DAISY CAKE

SET OVEN AT 350° F.

Grease generously an 8-inch square cake pan and dust it lightly with flour.

1. Sift together into a bowl
    - 1⅔ cups sifted all-purpose flour
    - 1 cup sugar
    - 2 teaspoons double-action baking powder
    - ¼ teaspoon salt
2. Add
    - ⅔ cup lukewarm milk
    - ⅓ cup soft butter
    - 1 egg, slightly beaten
    - 1 teaspoon vanilla
3. Beat with an electric mixer at top speed for 2 minutes.
4. Pour into prepared pans.
5. Bake for 35 minutes.
6. Frost, when cool, with your favorite icing.

CHOCOLATE FUDGE CAKE*

SET OVEN AT 350° F.

Grease generously two 8-inch round layer cake pans and dust them lightly with flour.

1. Mix to a smooth paste
    - 2 squares (ounces) unsweetened chocolate, melted
    - ½ cup boiling water
    - 2⅛ cups sifted cake flour
2. Sift together into a bowl
    - 1⅓ cups sugar
    - 1 teaspoon soda
    - ½ teaspoon cream of tartar
    - 1 teaspoon salt
3. Add
    - ⅓ cup shortening
    - ⅔ cup milk
    - 1 teaspoon vanilla

*Courtesy General Mills.

4. Beat with an electric mixer at medium speed for 2 minutes, scraping the sides and bottom of bowl frequently.
5. Add
    ⅓ to ½ cup unbeaten egg whites
6. Beat for 1 more minute, scraping bowl frequently.
7. Add the chocolate paste.
8. Beat for 1 more minute.
9. Pour into prepared pans.
10. Bake for 25–30 minutes.
11. Frost, when cool, with Betty Crocker Brown Beauty Icing, adding ½ cup chopped nuts to the top icing.

BETTY CROCKER CHOCOLATE CHIP CAKE

SET OVEN AT 350° F.

Grease generously two 8-inch round layer cake pans and dust them lightly with flour.
1. Sift together into a bowl
    2⅛ cups sifted enriched flour
    1½ cups sugar
    4 teaspoons double-action baking powder
    1 teaspoon salt
2. Add
    ½ cup shortening
    1 cup milk
    1 teaspoon vanilla
3. Beat with an electric mixer at medium speed for 2 minutes, scraping the sides and bottom of bowl frequently.
4. Add
    ½–⅔ cup egg whites, unbeaten
5. Beat for 2 more minutes, scraping bowl frequently.
6. Fold in carefully
    ½ cup semisweet or sweet chocolate, cut in very small pieces
7. Pour into prepared pans.
8. Bake for 30–35 minutes.
9. Spread Betty Crocker Chocolate Frosting between the layers, when cool, and frost the top and sides with Mountain Cream Frosting. Grate a little chocolate over the top.

COCONUT FLUFF CAKE

SET OVEN AT 350° F.

Grease generously two 8-inch square cake pans and dust them lightly with flour.

1. Sift together into a bowl
    - 2½ cups sifted cake flour
    - 4½ teaspoons double-action baking powder
    - 1½ teaspoons salt
    - 1¾ cups sugar
2. Add
    - ¾ cup soft butter
    - 1⅛ cups lukewarm milk
3. Beat with an electric mixer at medium speed for 2 minutes, scraping the sides and bottom of bowl frequently.
4. Add
    - 1 teaspoon vanilla
    - ⅔ cup egg whites
5. Beat for 2 more minutes, scraping bowl frequently.
6. Pour into prepared pans.
7. Bake for 35 minutes.
8. Spread Mountain Cream between layers, when cool, and frost the top and sides. Sprinkle top and sides generously with shredded coconut.

STRAWBERRY CAKE

SET OVEN AT 375° F.

Grease two 8-inch round layer cake pans and dust them lightly with flour.

1. Sift together into a bowl
    - 2 cups sifted cake flour
    - 2 teaspoons double-action baking powder
    - ½ teaspoon salt
    - 1 cup plus 2 tablespoons sugar
2. Add
    - ⅓ cup soft butter
    - ¾ cup milk
    - 1 teaspoon vanilla
3. Beat with an electric mixer at medium speed for 2 minutes, scraping the sides and bottom of bowl frequently.
4. Add
    - 1 egg
5. Beat for 1 more minute, scraping bowl frequently.
6. Pour into prepared pans.
7. Bake for 25 minutes.
8. Spread Strawberry Frosting between the layers, when cool, and on the top and sides of the cake.

THREE-LAYER BIRTHDAY CAKE*

SET OVEN AT 350° F.

Grease generously three 9-inch round layer cake pans and dust them lightly with flour.

1. Sift together into a bowl
   - 3 cups sifted cake flour
   - 3¼ teaspoons baking powder
   - 2 cups sugar
   - ½ teaspoon soda
   - 1 teaspoon salt
2. Add
   - ¾ cup shortening
   - 3 squares (ounces) unsweetened chocolate, melted
   - 1¼ cups milk
   - 1 teaspoon vanilla
3. Beat with an electric mixer at medium speed for 1½ minutes, scraping the sides and bottom of bowl frequently.
4. Add
   - 3 eggs, unbeaten
5. Beat for another 2½ minutes, scraping bowl frequently.
6. Add
   - ¼ cup milk
7. Beat for another ½ minute.
8. Pour into prepared pans.
9. Bake for 25–30 minutes.
10. Spread Peppermint Mountain Cream between layers, when cool, and frost top and sides with it, decorating top with halves of candy canes or peppermint sticks.

BETTY CROCKER MARASCHINO PARTY CAKE

SET OVEN AT 350° F.

Grease generously two 8- or 9-inch round layer cake pans and dust them lightly with flour.

1. Sift together into a bowl
   - 2¼ cups sifted cake flour
   - 1⅓ cups sugar
   - 3 teaspoons double-action baking powder
   - 1 teaspoon salt
2. Add
   - ½ cup shortening
   - ¼ cup maraschino cherry juice
   - 16 maraschino cherries, cut in quarters
   - ½ cup milk

*Courtesy General Mills.

3. Beat with an electric mixer at medium speed for 2 minutes, scraping the sides and bottom of bowl frequently.
4. Add
>½–⅔ cup unbeaten egg whites
5. Beat for 2 more minutes, scraping bowl frequently.
6. Fold in
>½ cup chopped nuts
7. Pour into prepared pans.
8. Bake for 30–35 minutes.
9. Frost with Mountain Cream, when cool, and decorate with halved maraschino cherries and bits of citron or angelica.

NUT LOAF

SET OVEN AT 350° F.

Grease generously a 10½ ×5½ ×3-inch loaf pan and line the bottom with wax paper.
1. Sift together into a bowl
>1½ cups sifted cake flour
>1 cup sugar
>3 teaspoons double-action baking powder
>1 teaspoon salt
2. Add
>½ cup soft butter
>⅔ cup milk
>1 teaspoon vanilla
3. Beat with an electric mixer at medium speed for 2 minutes, scraping the sides and bottom of bowl frequently.
4. Add
>2 eggs
>1 cup chopped nut meats
5. Beat for 2 more minutes, scraping bowl frequently.
6. Pour into prepared loaf pan.
7. Bake for 40 minutes.
8. Cool for 30 minutes. Loosen sides with a spatula and turn out on cake rack to complete the cooling.
9. Frost with 7-Minute Lemon Frosting and sprinkle top and sides with finely chopped nut meats.

CRAZY CAKE

SET OVEN AT 325° F.

1. Sift directly into an ungreased 8-inch square cake pan
>1½ cups all-purpose flour

                    1 cup sugar
                    3 tablespoons cocoa
                    1 teaspoon soda
                    1 teaspoon double-action baking powder
                    ½ teaspoon salt
2. Make 3 holes in the dry ingredients.
                    In the first put 1 tablespoon vinegar
                    In the second put 1 teaspoon vanilla
                    In the third put ¼ cup melted butter
3. Pour over
                    ¼ cup lukewarm water
4. Stir thoroughly. Use a rubber scraper to stir and lift the dry ingredients from the bottom of the pan.
5. Bake for 35 minutes.

TORTES

DOBOS TORTE

This famous torte, seven light layers high, each divided from the other by chocolate cream, was created by a famous Hungarian pastry chef, Mr. Dobos. It takes no special skill to make, but what it does require is patience.

                    7 eggs, separated
                    ¾ cup sugar
                    1 cup sifted cake flour
                    ¼ teaspoon salt

Beat the egg yolks until fluffy, add the sugar gradually, and continue to beat until the mixture is thick and pale in color. Fold in the flour and then fold in the egg whites, which have been beaten with the salt until stiff, but not dry. Grease seven shallow 8-inch layer cake pans, line the bottoms with wax paper, and grease again. The bottom tins of spring molds of the same size may be used. If you have only two or three pans, these may be prepared, the layers baked, and the operation repeated. Spread the layers evenly with 4 or 5 tablespoons of the batter and bake them at 350° F. for 8 minutes, or until the thin sheets of cake are lightly browned. Remove the pans from the oven and turn out the layers onto cake racks to cool. Remove wax paper immediately.

When all the layers have been baked and cooled, spread Chocolate Cream for Dobos Torte between the layers, saving enough of it to cover the top and sides of the cake. Place the cake in the refrigerator to chill thoroughly and then cover the top with caramelized sugar: Melt ¾ cup sugar in a small pan, then add 1 tablespoon butter and stir the mixture until it is golden brown. Use a spatula and spread the caramel over the top of the cake. This must be done quickly, or the sugar will harden. When the sugar has hardened, heat a knife and make wedge-shaped incisions around the top, through the sugar coating.

This torte will taste better the day after it is made. Keep it in the refrigerator, where it will stay fresh for a week.

BLITZ TORTE

½ cup butter
1¼ cups sugar
5 eggs, separated
1 teaspoon vanilla
1 cup sifted cake flour
1 teaspoon double-action baking powder
3 tablespoons milk
½ cup chopped blanched almonds
1 tablespoon sugar
½ teaspoon cinnamon

Cream the shortening, gradually beat in ½ cup sugar, the egg yolks, and vanilla. Sift together the flour and baking powder and add these dry ingredients alternately with the milk. Spread the mixture evenly in two shallow 8-inch round cake pans. Whip the egg whites until very light, add the remaining ¾ cup sugar gradually, and continue to beat until the egg whites are stiff. Divide this meringue equally between the two pans, spreading it lightly over the surface of the unbaked cake batter. Sprinkle the top with the almonds, the 1 tablespoon sugar, and the cinnamon. Bake at 350° F. for 30 minutes. Turn out of pans and allow the layers to cool, meringue side up, on cake racks. When cool, put the layers together with Orange or Lemon Custard Filling and spread over the top and sides Sour Cream Frosting.

HAZELNUT TORTE

1 heaping cup shelled hazelnuts
4 egg whites
1⅓ cups fine granulated sugar
3 teaspoons vanilla
1 teaspoon lemon juice
1 cup heavy cream
2 tablespoons sugar

Put the hazelnuts in a shallow pan in a hot oven (450°–500° F.) for about 10 minutes, or until the skins crack open and the nuts are toasted. Shake the pan occasionally so they will brown evenly. Empty out onto a clean towel and rub the nuts briskly together to remove the skin. Pick out the nuts, discarding the skin, and put them through a nut grater. Sift the grated nuts through a sieve to eliminate any large pieces of nuts. You should have about 1½ cups of finely powdered toasted nuts.

Beat the egg whites until stiff, then beat in gradually the 1⅓ cups sugar. Continue beating for several minutes, add 2 teaspoons of the vanilla and lemon juice, and beat for 2 or 3 minutes longer, to make sure all the sugar has been thoroughly dissolved in the egg whites. Fold in carefully 1¼ cups of the nuts and spread the mixture evenly in two 9-inch paper-lined layer cake tins. Bake at 300° F. for about 30 minutes. Remove from the oven and turn out on wire racks. Remove the wax paper immediately and allow the meringues to cool. When ready to serve, whip the cream until just stiff, add the 2 tablespoons sugar and the remaining vanilla, fold in the rest of the powdered nuts, and spread between the layers. Sprinkle the top with confectioners' sugar and serve.

SCHAUM TORTE

6 egg whites
2 cups sugar
1 teaspoon vinegar
1 teaspoon vanilla

Beat the egg whites until they are stiff enough to hold up in peaks, then beat in sugar, about 2 tablespoons at a time, three times, beating thoroughly after each addition. Beat in the vinegar and vanilla and then fold in the remaining sugar. Grease an 8-inch spring form pan and place two thirds of the mixture in it. Cut out a piece of white paper 7 inches in diameter and place it on a baking sheet. Drop the remaining meringue mixture by teaspoonfuls around the outer edge of the paper circle, forming a wreath of kisses. Place both pans in a 275° F. oven and bake for 1¼ hours. Turn off the heat, open the oven door, and allow the meringues to cool in the oven. When ready to serve, make an incision with a sharp knife around the top of the large meringue, about 1 inch from the edge, and carefully remove the center, scraping out any remaining uncooked meringue. Be very careful not to break through the bottom. Remove the shell from the spring form and place it on a serving dish. Fill the shell with whipped cream and strawberries, which have been sliced and sweetened to taste. Carefully remove the meringue wreath from the paper, wetting the back of the paper, if necessary, and place it on top of the filled shell. Decorate with whole berries. Other berries, fresh, sugared, or frozen, may be used in place of the strawberries.

The fillings for a Schaum Torte are many. Here is a pleasant one.

    4 egg yolks
    ¼ cup lime juice
    ¼ teaspoon salt
    2 cups heavy cream
    Raspberries or strawberries

Combine the egg yolks, lime juice, and salt in the top part of a double boiler. Cook over boiling water, stirring constantly, until the mixture is thick. Cool and then fold in 1 cup of the cream, stiffly whipped. Spread this cream thickly over the meringue base, cover, and chill in the refrigerator for a few hours. When ready to serve, whip the remaining cup of cream, spread it over the filling, and garnish with the meringue wreath and fresh berries.

LINZER TORTE

    1 cup sweet butter
    1 cup sugar
    3 eggs, separated
    ½ pound blanched almonds, ground
    Grated rind and juice of 1 lemon
    1 tablespoon brandy
    2 cups sifted cake flour
    1 teaspoon double-action baking powder
    Jam, jelly, or marmalade

Cream together the butter and sugar. Add the egg yolks and mix well. Add the almonds, lemon juice and rind, and brandy and combine thoroughly. Sift the flour and baking powder together three times and work into the butter-sugar mixture. Beat the egg whites until stiff and work into the dough. Pat two thirds of the dough into an 8-inch spring form pan to make a lining, having the bottom thicker than the sides. Fill with jam. Roll out the remaining dough on a lightly floured board and cut into strips. Chilling the dough will make it easier to handle. Place the strips crisscross on top of the filling and bake at 350° F. for 40–50 minutes, or until lightly browned on top. Before serving, fill the holes on top with a little more jam and sprinkle with confectioners' sugar.

This torte is sometimes baked in four round or square layers, and when the layers are cool, they are put together, each spread with a different jelly or marmalade. Apricot, strawberry, raspberry, and pineapple are favorite flavors.

CHOCOLATE TORTE

8 eggs, separated
1 cup sugar
2 squares (ounces) grated unsweetened chocolate
½ cup bread crumbs

Beat the egg yolks and sugar together until thick and pale in color. Add the grated chocolate and stir until the mixture is well combined. Add the crumbs and lastly fold in the stiffly beaten egg whites. Bake in two buttered 8-inch layer cake pans at 350° F. for 40 minutes. Remove layers from pans and cool on cake rack. When cool, split each layer in half, making four layers. Fill between the layers and cover the top and sides with the following frosting:

Mix together 1 cup sugar, 1 cup milk, and 2 ounces unsweetened chocolate, grated. Allow the mixture to boil until a soft ball is formed when dropped into cold water. Add 1 teaspoon vanilla and 1 tablespoon butter, which has been creamed thoroughly with 2 egg yolks, and beat until cool enough to spread. Whip 1 pint heavy cream and fold the chocolate mixture into the cream. Add sugar to taste.

SACHER TORTE

A delicious cake named after Frau Sacher in Vienna, who catered to the tastes of the Austrian and Hungarian nobility.

¾ cup butter
¾ cup sugar
6 eggs, separated
1 teaspoon vanilla
6 squares (ounces) unsweetened chocolate, melted and cooled
2 cups sifted cake flour

Cream the butter thoroughly, slowly add the sugar, and beat until well blended. Add the egg yolks one at a time, beating after each addition. Add the vanilla. Whip egg whites until stiff and fold them into the melted and cooled chocolate. Combine with the first mixture and fold in the sifted flour. Pour batter into two well-buttered and floured 9-inch layer cake pans and bake at 350° F. for about 25 minutes. Remove from pans and cool. Fill layers with apricot jam, then cover top and sides with Chocolate or Fudge Frosting.

MOCHA TORTE

12 ounces semi-sweet chocolate
4 large or 5 medium-sized eggs
½ cup sugar plus 1 tablespoon
½ cup unsifted all-purpose flour
4 tablespoons strong coffee

Place 8 ounces of the chocolate over boiling water until it is melted and smooth. Cut circles about 2½ inches in diameter from wax paper and spread these rounds with a thin coating of the melted chocolate. Place the spread rounds on a cooky sheet and put in refrigerator to harden.

Grease a round cake pan about 9 inches in diameter and 2 inches deep. Line the bottom with wax paper and grease again. Beat together the eggs and sugar until light in color and very thick. Use an electric beater for this, if possible. If you do not have an electric beater, place the bowl containing the sugar and eggs over hot water and beat vigorously with a rotary beater. Sift the measured flour twice and fold into the batter. Then fold in the rest of the semi-sweet chocolate, which has been melted with the strong coffee. Pour the batter into the prepared pan and bake at 350° F. for 35 minutes. Turn out immediately on a wire cake rack to cool. Frost generously with Mocha Butter Cream and make a circle of large butter cream rosettes on the top with a pastry tube. Peel off the wax paper from the back of the chocolate rounds and place them, slightly overlapping, all around the sides of the cake.

CHOCOLATE SOUFFLÉ TORTE

1 cup blanched almonds
5 ounces sweet chocolate
¼ cup cold coffee
5 eggs, separated
¾ cup sugar
¼ teaspoon salt
2 teaspoons vanilla

Place the almonds on a pie tin and bake them at 400° F., stirring them occasionally, until lightly toasted. Allow them to cool and then grind them through a meat chopper or nut grater. Place the chocolate and coffee in a saucepan over very low heat and stir until the chocolate is melted and the mixture is smooth and free from lumps. Allow it to cool slightly. Beat the egg yolks until light, add the sugar gradually, and continue to beat until the mixture is thick and pale in color. Add the salt, vanilla, and ground nuts and stir in the melted chocolate. Beat the egg whites until stiff but not dry, and fold them into the batter. Pour into a loaf pan and bake at 350° F. for 35 minutes, or until it feels firm to the touch. Turn out on a serving platter and serve hot with whipped and sweetened cream.

DATE AND WALNUT TORTE

2 eggs
1 cup sugar
2 tablespoons light cream
2 tablespoons flour
1 teaspoon baking powder
1 cup walnuts, chopped
1 cup dates, finely cut
1 teaspoon vanilla

Beat the eggs until they are very light, add the sugar gradually, and the cream, and continue to beat until thoroughly mixed. Add the flour and baking powder, mix well, and then fold in the nuts and dates. Place in an 8-inch square buttered cake tin and bake at 375° F. for 25 minutes. Cool, cut into squares, and serve with sweetened whipped cream.

ROCOCO TORTE

5 eggs, separated
5 tablespoons sugar
2 tablespoons fine bread crumbs
2 tablespoons flour
2 ounces sweet chocolate, grated

Beat the egg yolks until light. Add the sugar gradually and continue to beat until the mixture is thick and pale in color. Stir in the bread crumbs, flour, and grated chocolate, and lastly fold in the stiffly beaten egg whites. Bake in two 8-inch buttered layer cake pans at 350° F. for 30 minutes. Remove cakes from pans and cool on cake rack. When cool, fill the layers and cover the top with the following frosting:

6 tablespoons butter
2 tablespoons sugar
1 cup ground walnuts
½ cup light cream
1 teaspoon vanilla

Cream together the butter and sugar. Combine the nuts and cream and stir into the butter-sugar mixture. Add the vanilla and beat until the mixture is thick and foamy.

ALMOND TORTE

8 eggs, separated
1 cup sugar
1 pound almonds, blanched, dried, and ground to a fine meal
Pinch salt
1 teaspoon baking powder
½ teaspoon almond essence
1 teaspoon vanilla

Beat egg whites until stiff and beat into them half the sugar. Beat the egg yolks with the remaining sugar until pale in color. Fold the yolks into the whites, then carefully fold in the almond meal, salt, and baking powder. Add the almond essence and vanilla. Pour into a 9-inch spring form pan and bake at 300° F. for 1¼ hours. Cool and cover with whipped cream, to which sugar has been added to taste. Garnish with blanched almonds, slivered and sautéed in butter until lightly browned. Hazelnuts may be used instead of almonds.

ZWIEBACK TORTE

5 eggs, separated
1 cup sugar
1 cup chopped nuts
1 cup zwieback crumbs
1 teaspoon baking powder

Beat the egg yolks, add the sugar gradually, and continue to beat until the mixture is thick and pale in color. Add the nuts and zwieback crumbs and fold in the stiffly beaten egg whites and the baking powder. Bake in two round 8-inch layer cake pans at 350° F. for 20 minutes. Fill the layers and cover the top and sides with sweetened whipped cream flavored with sherry or madeira. Garnish the top with pecan halves.

ORANGE WALNUT TORTE

6 eggs, separated
1 cup sugar
1 cup finely ground walnuts
Grated rind of 1 orange
2 tablespoons orange juice
1 cup lady fingers, rolled fine
Pinch salt

Beat the egg yolks until light, gradually add the sugar, and continue to beat until the mixture is thick and pale in color. Add the walnuts, orange rind and juice, lady fingers, and salt and combine. Then fold in the stiffly beaten egg whites. Butter two 9-inch layer cake pans and dust them with fine bread crumbs. Fill them three fourths full and bake at 350° F. for 30–35 minutes. When cool, spread one layer with thick pineapple or apricot jam. Place the second layer carefully on top and cover all over with whipped cream or Cocoa, Mocha, or Chocolate Frosting. Other nuts may be used, such as almonds, filberts, or hazelnuts. Lemon rind and juice may be used in place of the orange rind and juice.

VANILLA TORTE

4 eggs, separated
1½ cups sugar
5 unsalted soda crackers, rolled fine
1 teaspoon double-action baking powder
1 teaspoon vanilla
1 cup heavy cream, whipped
½ cup finely chopped nut meats

Beat the egg yolks with the sugar until thick and pale in color. Stir in the cracker crumbs, baking powder, and vanilla and then fold in the egg whites, which have been beaten until stiff. Turn the mixture into two buttered 9-inch layer cake pans and bake at 350° F. for 25 minutes. Cool the layers on a cake rack and then put them together with half the whipped cream. Sprinkle the top of the cake with the chopped nuts, dust with confectioners' sugar, and decorate with the remaining whipped cream.

WALNUT TORTE

2½ cups ground walnuts
¾ cup sugar
7 egg whites

Mix together the walnuts and sugar. Beat the egg whites until stiff and fold in the walnut-sugar mixture. Divide evenly between three greased and floured 9-inch round cake pans and bake the layers at 400° F. for 15–20 minutes, or until delicately browned. Let the layers cool in the pans before removing them.

FILLING

½ cup sugar
3 egg yolks
3 tablespoons strong black coffee
½ cup chopped walnuts
1 tablespoon sugar

Combine the sugar, egg yolks, and coffee and stir briskly over a low flame until the mixture is thick and creamy. Do not let it boil. Cool. Mix the walnuts with the 1 tablespoon sugar and stir over the fire until browned. Fold the walnuts into the coffee cream and spread between the layers. Sprinkle top layer with confectioners' sugar.

THOUSAND LEAVES TORTE

1⅔ cups sifted all-purpose flour
1 cup sweet butter
4 tablespoons ice water
Applesauce
Vanilla Cream (see Fillings for Swedish Pastry)
1 cup confectioners' sugar
1½ tablespoons milk
1 teaspoon lemon juice
1 cup heavy cream, whipped
Fruit peel and almonds

Sift the flour into a mixing bowl and cut in the butter, using a pastry blender or two knives. Add the ice water gradually and work with a wooden spoon to a smooth dough. Cover and chill for 1 hour. Divide the dough into seven equal parts. Roll out each part very thinly on wax paper and cut into a circle about 8 inches in diameter. Place the circles, along with the wax paper beneath them, on baking sheets, brush with ice water, sprinkle with sugar, prick with a fork, and bake at 450° F. for 6 minutes, or until lightly browned. Cool, remove the wax paper, and spread the layers alternately with sweetened applesauce and Vanilla Cream. Combine the confectioners' sugar, milk, and lemon juice into a smooth icing and frost the top. Decorate the top with strips of fruit peel and shredded almonds and cover the sides with rosettes of whipped cream forced through a pastry tube.

LITTLE CAKES AND PETITS FOURS

Most cake batters may be baked in cupcake size as well as in the regulation round or square tins. Packaged cake mixes are also very adaptable to this purpose. Only the baking time will differ, and this, naturally, depends on the size of cupcakes being made. Cupcakes 2½ inches in diameter are nice for everyday use. For special occasions and for afternoon tea, bake them in very tiny 1-inch-in-diameter fluted cups. When cool, ice them around the top and sides and sprinkle with chopped nuts or shredded coconut, or decorate them gaily with candied fruits.

VANILLA CUPCAKES

2¼ cups sifted cake flour
¼ teaspoon salt
3 teaspoons double-action baking powder
1 cup sugar
½ cup melted butter
¾ cup milk
2 eggs, beaten
1 teaspoon vanilla

Sift the dry ingredients into a mixing bowl. Combine the butter, milk, eggs, and vanilla and stir gradually into the dry ingredients. Fill small, buttered muffin tins or fluted baking cups two thirds full and bake at 375° F. for 10–20 minutes, depending on size of cups. Frost the top and sides with white or tinted Mountain Cream or Butterfly Frosting and sprinkle with shredded coconut.

CHOCOLATE CUPCAKES

½ cup butter
1 cup brown sugar
1 egg
1 square (ounce) unsweetened chocolate, melted
1½ cups sifted cake flour
1 teaspoon soda
¼ teaspoon salt
½ cup sour milk

Cream the butter, add the sugar gradually, and cream together until light. Add the egg and melted chocolate. Sift together the flour, soda, and salt and stir this mixture in alternately with the sour milk. Fill tiny fluted cups two thirds full and bake at 350° F. for 10–15 minutes. Frost the sides and tops with Coffee Icing, making a rosette on top of each and rolling the sides in grated sweet chocolate.

FRUIT OR NUT CAKES

⅓ cup butter
1 cup sugar
1 egg, beaten
1½ cups sifted cake flour
2 teaspoons double-action baking powder
½ cup milk
1 teaspoon vanilla
1 cup seeded raisins or chopped nuts

Cream the butter, add the sugar gradually, and cream together until light. Stir in the egg. Sift the dry ingredients and add them alternately with the milk and vanilla. Stir in the raisins or nuts. Fill small, buttered fancy cupcake pan two thirds full with the batter and bake at 350° F. for 10–20 minutes, depending on the size of the cups. When cool, frost with any desired icing and sprinkle the tops with finely chopped nuts.

COCOA CUPCAKES

½ cup butter
1 cup sugar
1 egg, beaten
1½ cups sifted cake flour
⅓ cup cocoa
2 teaspoons double-action baking powder
½ cup milk
2 teaspoons vanilla

Cream the butter, add the sugar, and cream together until light and fluffy. Stir in the beaten egg and then add the sifted dry ingredients alternately with the milk and vanilla. Fill small, buttered fancy cupcake pan two thirds full with the batter and bake at 350° F. for 10–20 minutes, depending on the size of the cups. Cool and frost the tops and sides with Fudge or Chocolate Frosting and sprinkle the sides with chopped toasted almonds or pistachio nuts.

PETITS FOURS

Any cake may be used for these tiny decorated cakes, but the most suitable is a fine-textured butter, sponge, Génoise, angel food, or chiffon cake. Bake the cake in buttered, shallow pans about ¾ inch thick and, when it is cool, cut it into small squares, crescents, hearts, diamonds, oblongs, or rounds, using a sharp knife or deep cooky cutters. Spread the top of each cake with tinted Butterfly Frosting and decorate with colored candies, candied fruit, nuts, or coconut. Petits Fours may be completely covered with Fondant Icing in a variety of colors and flavors. Keep the Fondant Icing warm and creamy over hot water. Place the pieces of cut cake on a knife or two-tined fork and dip them quickly in the warm fondant. Place them on wax paper for several hours to dry and then decorate them with pistachio nuts, halved, strips of candied peel, candied cherries and pineapple, with candied rose leaves or violets. Dip the end of the ornaments in a little of the icing to make them stick.

FILLED PETITS FOURS

Bake a butter, sponge, chiffon, angel food, or Génoise cake in a flat pan about 1 inch thick and, when it is cool, cut it into small circles, diamonds, or squares with a sharp knife or with deep cooky cutters. Split each piece, hollow out the centers, and fill with whipped cream, Almond Paste, or Crème Pâtissière. Put together in pairs and dip into warm, delicately tinted and flavored Fondant. Place on wax paper to dry for several hours and then decorate with nuts and candied fruit and crystallized flowers, as in the recipe above.

CRUMB CAKES

Crumble stale cake into a bowl. Moisten the crumbs slightly with a desired flavoring, such as maraschino cherry juice, rum, brandy, or sherry, and mix to a paste with corn syrup. Form the mixture into tiny balls, dip in warm Plain Fondant Frosting, allow them to dry slightly, and then roll them in grated chocolate, finely chopped nuts, or coconut.

MARSHMALLOW CAKES

Bake a butter, angel, sponge, chiffon, or Génoise cake in a flat pan not more than 1 inch deep and, when cool, cut it into rounds slightly larger than a marshmallow. Split marshmallows in half and place half on each cake round. Sprinkle with a little grated sweet chocolate or with a mixture of sugar and cinnamon and bake at 350° F. until the marshmallow slightly melts.

LADY FINGERS

3 eggs, separated
⅓ cup fine granulated sugar
1 teaspoon vanilla
Pinch salt
3 tablespoons hot water
½ cup sifted cake flour
1 teaspoon double-action baking powder

Beat the egg whites until stiff and beat in the sugar a little at a time. Beat the egg yolks until thick and add to the egg whites along with the vanilla, salt, and hot water. Then fold in the flour, which has been sifted twice with the baking powder. Put the batter in a pastry tube, fitted with a plain round tube. Squeeze out 2½-inch strips, not too close together, onto cooky sheets which have been covered with heavy paper. Sprinkle with powdered sugar and bake at 350° F. for 8 minutes, or until a very delicate brown. The fingers should still feel soft to the touch when removed from the oven. Cool slightly and remove from the paper, wetting the back of the paper, if necessary. Brush the flat side of half the fingers with egg white and press the underside of a second cake on each. Or they may be sandwiched together with Confectioners' Sugar Icing or with jam or jelly. Makes about 1½ dozen whole lady fingers.

MADELEINES

1 lump sugar
1 orange or lemon
¾ cup sugar
1¼ cups sifted cake flour
10 tablespoons (1¼ bars) sweet butter
3 eggs
2 egg yolks
1 tablespoon brandy
Pinch salt

Rub the lump of sugar over the skin of an orange or lemon until it is well saturated with the fruit oil or zest. Then crush or grate the sugar. Sift together the ¾ cup sugar and flour and stir in the crushed sugar. Melt the butter and skim off the white foam that forms on the top. Put a few drops of this clarified butter into eighteen small, shell-shaped tins. Tip the madeleine shells so that the butter will completely coat them. Drain the excess butter back into the rest of the butter and keep it warm.

Beat together the eggs and yolks. With a wooden spoon stir in gradually the sugar-flour mixture. Add the brandy and salt and continue to stir until the batter is smooth and free from lumps, then beat vigorously for 1 minute. Stir in the warm butter, being careful not to include any sediment which has settled to the bottom of the saucepan in which the butter was heated. Place the batter in an enamel pan on a very low flame and stir vigorously for 1–2 minutes, or until the mixture becomes thin and is heated through. Pour immediately into the buttered shells, filling them not quite full, and bake them at 350° F. for 8 minutes, or until a delicate brown. Turn immediately onto cake rack, shell side up, to cool.

INDIANS

Pull an angel food cake apart with two forks into irregular

pieces about 1 inch in size. Place the pieces on a knife or two-tined fork and lower them into Chocolate Fondant Frosting, which is kept warm over boiling water. Allow them to dry on wax paper.

LITTLE FRUITED CAKES

¼ cup citron, finely shredded
¼ cup candied cherries, cut into small pieces
¼ cup shredded blanched almonds
½ cup chopped raisins
2 tablespoons rum
1 cup butter
1 cup sugar
5 eggs, separated
2½ cups sifted all-purpose flour
¼ teaspoon salt

Combine the fruit and nuts and moisten with the rum. Cream the butter until light and add gradually the sugar, creaming together until fluffy. Add the egg yolks, one at a time, stirring well after each addition, and then gradually stir in the sifted flour. When all the flour has been incorporated, add the fruits and nuts and lastly fold in the egg whites, which have been beaten with the salt until stiff. Fill tiny fluted baking cups three fourths full with the mixture and bake at 325° F. for 25–30 minutes, or until the cakes are delicately brown.

PALETS DE DAMES

4 tablespoons currants
2 tablespoons rum
½ cup butter
½ cup sugar
3 eggs
⅞ cup sifted all-purpose flour

Soak the currants in the rum for 1 hour. Cream the butter until light, add the sugar, and cream together until fluffy. Add the eggs, one at a time, beating well after each addition. Then stir in the flour and, when well combined, stir in the currants and the rum in which they have been soaked. Place the mixture in a pastry tube, fitted with a large round tube, and pipe mounds about the size of macaroons on a buttered and floured baking sheet. Bake at 400° F. for 10–12 minutes. Remove from the sheet and cool on a cake rack.

RECIPE ADJUSTMENT CHART FOR HIGH-ALTITUDE BAKING

	3000 ft.	5000 ft.	7000 ft.
BAKING POWDER For each teaspoon used in recipe *reduce*	⅛ tsp.	⅛–¼ tsp.	¼–½ tsp.
SUGAR For each cup used in recipe *reduce*			1–2 tbs.
LIQUID For each cup used in recipe *increase*	1–2 tbs.	2–3 tbs.	3–4 tbs.

SHORTENING
In making very rich cakes at high altitudes it is sometimes necessary to reduce the shortening 1–2 tablespoons.

CAKE DECORATING

HOW TO FROST A CAKE

Not all cakes need a frosting. Some people prefer a plain pound cake, an angel cake, or a sponge cake with only a little confectioners' sugar sifted over the top. Others prefer a thin layer of butter and sugar icing spread on top and sides to flatter and to keep a cake moist for a longer time. Still others like thin layers of cake, heavily filled and lavishly decorated with swirls of creamy, fluffy frosting. Sometimes the same frosting is used for filling between the layers, but often a different filling is preferable.

Select a plate that will set off the cake to the best advantage. It should be flat and at least 3 or 4 inches larger in diameter than the cake itself. A paper doily 2 inches larger in diameter than the cake adds a dainty touch.

Place the doily in the center of the cake plate. To protect the plate and doily from being soiled while icing the cake, tear off a large square of wax paper. Fold it into a triangle and cut across the crease with a sharp knife. Fold each of the triangles in half into two smaller triangles and again cut across the crease. You now have four triangles of approximately the same size. Place one on the plate with the point slightly overlapping the center. On the opposite side place another with its point overlapping the first point. Place the other two triangles opposite each other in the same manner in the spaces not covered by the first two pieces.

Be sure the cake is thoroughly cool. Brush off any excess crumbs adhering to it, and trim off any ragged edge with kitchen scissors. If it is a layer cake, place one layer in the center of the cake plate and spread it smoothly with frosting or filling. Place the second layer on top. If more layers are to be added, continue spreading each layer with frosting or filling. If the layers slide, anchor them by inserting a wire cake tester or a fine knitting needle through the layers. This can be removed when the filling sets.

Next spread the frosting from the top edge down over the sides, making sure that all the cake is well covered. Pile the remaining frosting on top and spread it lightly to the edges, swirling it attractively with a spatula as you spread.

If you wish to sprinkle the top and sides with grated chocolate, coconut, or finely chopped nuts, this should be done while the frosting is still moist. When cake is iced, carefully pull out wax paper triangles from under it.

TO DECORATE A CAKE

There are so many intriguing effects that may be accomplished in the decoration of cakes that it is possible, in this book, to give only a glimpse, with enough hints to enable you to do a fairly professional job on the next birthday cake or even a wedding cake. Of course a great deal depends on the individual. Expert handling of a pastry bag takes practice, and only practice can supply the necessary technique. Again, cake decorating needs an artist's eye and hand. We have all seen cakes ingeniously embellished with latticework, with scrolls and delicately tinted flowers. Similar effects may be achieved in the home by buying, from your local pastry shop, sugar ornaments and placing them artistically on a smoothly iced cake, securing them with a little dab of the frosting. Or you may, if time and inclination permit, make your own Pulled Sugar flowers, Crystallized Violets, clusters of Marzipan fruits, and delicately tinted pastry-tube rosettes and fluted edgings.

SIMPLE DECORATIVE TOUCHES

CONFECTIONERS' SUGAR Place a fancy paper doily or a paper-pattern cut-out of your own design on top of the cake. Sprinkle the doily or pattern heavily with confectioners' sugar through a fine sieve, then carefully lift the paper pattern up and away. The design will be embossed on the top of the cake.

CANDIES Buy tiny colored or silver candies to use for forming borders, designs, or letters. With a toothpick draw a design lightly on the frosting and sprinkle the design with the candies.

FRUIT Candied fruit can be used to make many decorative effects. Cut candied or maraschino cherries to form the petals of flowers. Use strips of citron for the stems and leaves. Clusters of raisins with toasted almonds, and bits of candied orange or lemon peel make attractive arrangements.

CHOCOLATE Melt chocolate over boiling water with 1 teaspoon butter for every ounce of chocolate used. When the chocolate is melted, beat the mixture until smooth. This may be dripped over swirls of fluffy topping or it may be poured over the top of a smoothly iced cake, allowing it to run down the sides in irregular design. Again it may be brushed on a smooth icing which has been allowed to dry a little, in a pattern or design much as you would paint a picture. Grated chocolate either sweet or bitter, according to taste, may be sprinkled over the top and sides of a white fluffy icing while the icing is still moist.

FLOWERS Dainty fresh flowers or a spray of greenery make charming decorations. Try placing small flowers in a "jigger" glass and inserting it in the center of a frosted tube cake. Place a tiny spray of fresh violets or rosebuds in one corner of a frosted heart-shaped cake. Or make a circle on top of a frosted cake with fresh pansies or daisies and a garland of the same flowers, or their leaves, around the plate.

ANIMAL CRACKERS Place iced animal crackers around the sides of a frosted cake, or stand them up in a circus design on top. These as well as peppermint sticks, suckers, or large gumdrops are a delight to children.

COCONUT, PLAIN, TOASTED, OR TINTED Sprinkle it over the top of fluffy frostings and press it against the sides of a cake while the frosting is still soft.

TO TINT COCONUT Dilute a few drops of vegetable food coloring with a little water and sprinkle it over the coconut. Rub the coconut between the palms of the hands until it is evenly tinted.

TO TOAST COCONUT Spread the coconut in a thin layer on a baking sheet. Place it in a 350° F. oven and allow it to bake until it is a golden brown, stirring it frequently so that it will toast evenly on all sides.

VALENTINE CAKE

Frost the sides of a square cake lavishly with Mountain Cream which has been tinted a very delicate pink. Spread the top smoothly but at least 1 inch thick with the same frosting and then scoop out a large heart in the center about ½ inch deep, leaving a raised border of the frosting all around. Sprinkle the raised border heavily with plain coconut—like a doily valentine.

A WOOLLY LAMB

Once again lamb molds are available in kitchenware stores and departments, and every cake-loving family, with or without children, should have one.

Make a butter cake or pound cake batter. You won't need it all for the lamb, so use the remaining batter to make cupcakes. Grease both halves of the lamb mold generously and dust them with flour. Pour the batter into the front half of the mold—the side with the face on it—until it comes right up to the top, being careful to get the batter well into the nose and ears. Cover with the back half of the mold and bake at 375° F. for about 40 minutes. Remove the mold from the oven and gently remove the back half to test. If the cake is done, replace the back half and allow it to stand for 10 minutes before removing it from the mold. If it is not quite done, replace the back half and return it to the oven for another 5 minutes. When removing the cake from the mold, remove the back half first and then the front half. Allow the lamb to cool standing erect.

When cool, cover the lamb with Mountain Cream and sprinkle it all over lavishly with shredded coconut. Use raisins for the eyes and a small piece of cherry for the mouth. Tint some more shredded coconut a pale green and spread it around the lamb for grass. Put a tiny silver bell on a satin ribbon and tie it around the lamb's neck with a bow on one side, and, if you wish, scatter a few rosebuds or violets, fresh or crystallized, in the coconut grass.

A SPRING BONNET

Make two layers of a cake, one in a 9-inch round layer cake pan for the brim and one in a 1-pound coffee can for the crown. Grease the pans generously and line the bottoms with wax paper. Grease the paper and fill the pans half full with the batter. Bake them at the required temperature for the type of cake batter made, until a cake tester comes out clean. Remove the cakes to a rack to cool and, when they are cool, place the 9-inch layer on a cake plate. Frost it smoothly with a Vanilla or Orange Cream Frosting. Place the crown on top and ice it also. Make a band around the brim where it joins the crown with Chocolate Butter Icing or surround the crown with a circle of Spun Sugar. Place a nosegay of flowers on the side, either fresh or made from Pulled Sugar or Marzipan.

HOW TO DECORATE WITH A PASTRY BAG

To add professional decorative touches to a cake you will need an assortment of pastry tubes and several bags in varying sizes. You may buy washable ones or you may make your own. To make temporary bags, cut rectangles of sturdy paper or parchment into triangles. For small ones make the rectangle 8×10 inches; for larger ones 12×14 inches. Roll each triangle into a cone shape and fold down the top points of the cone to secure it. By using several bags, a variety of colors may be employed without having to empty and wash the bag for each different color.

Cut the tips off the paper cones with sharp scissors to make holes of varying sizes according to the size of line you are going to make. For writing, snip off the very tip of the cone to make a tiny opening. If a large enough piece is cut from the end it is possible to insert standard pastry tubes.

Spoon a little Butterfly or Royal Frosting into the cornucopia and force it well down to the tip. Close the bag to prevent the frosting from coming out by folding over the top.

To tint frostings, use vegetable food coloring very sparingly, keeping the colors delicate, and work the frosting until the shade is evenly distributed throughout.

The best way to learn how to manipulate a pastry bag is to try out the different tubes at different angles, using varying degrees of pressure, and just see what happens. Use an inverted cake pan covered with wax paper and practice making straight lines, curves, flutings, and rosettes. Cut out a cardboard design, place it on the paper, and see if you can outline it with a fine line of frosting.

Most pastry bags or cake decorators come with a complete set of instructions for making flowers. Roses are the most difficult to form, but other flowers, such as daisies, violets, or forget-me-nots, are quite easy. Make them on wax paper, let them dry overnight, peel them off the paper, and store in the refrigerator until needed. These may be made at your leisure and kept until needed.

To make violets, squeeze out four dots of lavender icing in a circle touching each other and leaving a little space in the center and a larger space at the base of the circle. Make a larger dot, like a lip, at the base and drop a speck of yellow icing in the center.

Four small dots of pale blue frosting close together with a yellow dot in the center make forget-me-nots. Thin leaves of white or yellow frosting radiating from a circle about the size of a pea, with a flat yellow or brown center, make a daisy.

When ready to decorate, cover the entire cake with a thin layer of the frosting and let it dry. Plan your design and mark the exact center of the cake with a pinprick. Divide the circumference, according to your design, into equal sections and also mark with a pinprick. Then outline your design lightly on the frosting with a toothpick, keeping it simple and allowing it to flow with the shape of the cake. If an ornament or an inscription is to be used in the center of the cake, be sure to leave room for it. Start decorating the center of the cake and work toward the edge and finally down the sides. Always pipe a heavy line around the bottom of the cake or, if tiers are used as in a wedding cake, where each tier joins the other.

Apply any ornaments being used with a little bit of the frosting. Place them on lightly without pressing them into the cake.

PULLED SUGAR

4 cups sugar
1 cup water
1 tablespoon glucose
¼ teaspoon cream of tartar

Dissolve the sugar and water in a saucepan. Add the glucose and cream of tartar, cover the saucepan, and bring the mixture to a rapid boil. Remove cover and let it boil until it reaches the hard crack stage (312° F.), or until ½ teaspoon dropped into very cold water separates into hard brittle threads. Remove the saucepan immediately from the fire and dip the pan into cold water to prevent further cooking. Pour the syrup on a lightly oiled marble slab or heavy plate and, as it cools, lift the edges toward the center with a spatula. When it is cool enough to handle, roll it into a ball and with the fingers pull from the sides, turning the sides over and over into the center. The sugar will soon take on a white sheen. Work in a warm room, close to the heat of an oven, if necessary.

To make pulled sugar candies, pull out a small piece of the sugar with the thumb and forefinger. Cut off this portion and shape it into a petal. Form the petals into a flower arrangement, making the stem and leaves from green pulled sugar.

The sugar may be tinted with a few drops of liquid vegetable food coloring, while it is in the liquid stage, but use the dyes with a gentle hand and keep the colors delicate.

SPUN SUGAR

Spun sugar makes a charming bed on which to place an artistically iced cake or cake dessert. It probably adds more grace to a dessert than any other decoration and is, of course, a delight to children.

    3 cups sugar
    1 cup water
    1 teaspoon glucose
    ¼ teaspoon cream of tartar

Dissolve the sugar in the water, add the glucose and cream of tartar, cover the saucepan, and bring the mixture to a rapid boil. Remove the cover and let it boil to the hard crack stage (312° F.), or until ½ teaspoon dropped in very cold water separates into hard brittle threads. Remove from the fire immediately and dip the pan in cold water to prevent further cooking. Set the syrup in a warm place.

Oil the handles of 2 long wooden spoons and place them 2 feet apart on a table with the handles projecting over the side. Weigh down the handles so the spoons will stay put and be sure to cover the table and the floor beneath the handles with paper. Then take several forks (an egg beater works as well), dip them into the syrup, and move them back and forth quickly over the handles. Repeat this operation until you have a mass of sugar strands resembling silk. Trim off the ends and shape the mass into a ring, a mold, or into the shape desired.

CRYSTALLIZED VIOLETS

Remove violets from their stems and with a small brush coat each flower with the slightly beaten white of an egg. Dip in very fine granulated sugar and place the flowers on a plate which has been liberally sprinkled with fine granulated sugar. Sift a little more sugar lightly over the petals and set them in a warm place near the stove to dry. Rose petals may be crystallized in this way.

ALMOND PASTE

Almond paste may be purchased already prepared, or it may be made at home by pounding blanched almonds into a paste and kneading in the oil which is forced out by the pounding. It should be very smooth and free from hard particles. Blanch the almonds by pouring boiling water over the shelled nuts. Let them stand in the hot water for about 3 minutes, or until the skins may be easily rubbed off. Dry them on a clean towel and let them stand in a warm place for about 3 hours before pounding them.

MARZIPAN

Marzipans are miniature fruits, flowers, or vegetables molded from pure Almond Paste or from a combination of paste and sugar. The paste may also be rolled out like a dough and cut out into fancy shapes and figures. Marzipans make attractive decorations for cakes and pastries.

MARZIPAN BASE I

1 cup Almond Paste
1 egg white, beaten stiff
Pinch salt
½ teaspoon orange flower water
1 teaspoon lemon juice
1½ cups confectioners' sugar

With a wooden spoon combine the Almond Paste and egg white. Add the salt, orange flower water, and lemon juice and then start beating in the sugar. When the mixture gets too stiff to work easily with the spoon, mix in the remaining sugar until you have a soft sweet dough. Store in a tightly covered container in the refrigerator for at least a day before using.

MARZIPAN BASE II

2 cups sugar
1 cup light cream
Pinch salt
2 teaspoons cornstarch
2 cups Almond Paste
⅓ cup orange juice
1 teaspoon lemon juice

In a saucepan combine the sugar, cream, salt, and cornstarch. Bring the mixture to a boil and allow it to boil until it spins a long thread (238° F.). Remove from the fire, stir in the Almond Paste, orange and lemon juice, and blend thoroughly. Let the mixture cool and then form it into flowers much in the same manner as you would work with clay, or roll it out into a thin sheet, using a small quantity at a time, and cut it with a sharp knife into petals and leaves.

MARZIPAN DAISIES

Cut out circles of Almond Paste and slash it all around down to the center, leaving about 1/8 inch at the center uncut. Color a little Marzipan Base a rich yellow and place a round piece over the circular center. Smooth the petal edges and lift them slightly to simulate the petals of a daisy. Make Black-eyed Susans in the same way, using yellow Marzipan for the leaves and dark brown for the center.

MARZIPAN VIOLETS

Cut out circles about 1 inch in diameter from Almond Paste or Marzipan Base, which has been tinted a delicate violet. Cut the circles into five petals, leaving a small center intact. Place a tiny dot of yellow for the center, and twist and curl the petals, crushing them gently together to look like a violet.

MARZIPAN WILD ROSES

Color Almond Paste or Marzipan Base a delicate pink and cut rounds, about the size of a half dollar, out of a small quantity that has been rolled out quite thin. Cut the rounds into four leaves, leaving the center intact. Place a lot of yellow in the center and curl the petal edges upward and toward the center.

MARZIPAN FRUIT

STRAWBERRIES Color Almond Paste or Marzipan Base with red vegetable coloring. Roll a small portion with the hands into a small ball. Flatten one side to form the top and shape the opposite side into a rounded point to simulate a strawberry. Roll in granulated sugar which has been colored red, and attach a small piece of green-colored Marzipan, which has been formed into a hull, on the top.

APPLES, PEARS, AND PEACHES Form small pieces of Marzipan Base or Almond Paste into the shape of these fruits. Dilute red, yellow, and green vegetable dyes with a little water and brush over the surface of the little miniatures, making them as realistic as possible. Insert a little stem with a leaf attached in the top of each.

ORANGES AND LEMONS Shape small pieces of orange-colored Almond Paste or Marzipan Base into oranges and insert a small stem with a leaf attached to each. Lemons should be molded from yellow-colored Marzipan.

PEAS IN THE POD Color Marzipan Base with a mixture of green and yellow vegetable dyes to make a pea-green color. Roll it out quite thin and cut it into canoe-shaped pieces. Press the pointed ends together in the shape of a pod and place tiny peas of the paste in each pod.

LEAVES Roll out green-colored Almond Paste or Marzipan Base very thin. Place a cardboard cut-out of the desired leaf on the paste and cut around it with a sharp knife. Leaf-shaped cooky cutters may be used. Mark out the veins with the blunt end of a toothpick and pipe a little paste, which has been thinned with water and colored either a darker or lighter hue of green, into the grooves.

4. Cookies

Even a child can make them and should! Many of today's fine cooks began their climb to culinary distinction via the cooky jar. Many children have been instilled with a love of baking because they were encouraged to mix, roll, and cut a dough into circles or stars or elephants and to stand anxiously on guard beside the oven door until their cookies emerged delicate, golden, and fragrant. Many creative minds first expressed themselves through the medium of a cooky dough instead of potter's clay.

Cookies may be plain-Jane ginger, oatmeal, or peanut butter or they may be as petite, sugar-encrusted, icing-embroidered, and intriguing as time and inclination permit.

It would not be difficult to write an entire book on cookies, but since this book is covering a larger field, the oddities and infinite varieties of cooky land have been left by the wayside. The old-time favorites, however, are here—suitable for all occasions: hearty cookies for the lunchbox or between-meal snacks; dainty, rich cookies so perfect for tea or a light dessert; enchanting, decorative cookies for parties and holidays; gay, traditional cookies from other lands. Enough and more to spare are the cookies in this chapter. So let's keep the cooky jar filled to the brim—a symbol of peace, comfort, and security in this land of plenty.

HOW TO MAKE COOKIES

1. Assemble ingredients and utensils.
2. Grease baking sheets or pans lightly with vegetable shortening. Most recipes require the use of two baking sheets. While one is in the oven the other may be filled. Remove the crumbs from the used sheet with a spatula and regrease before using it again.
3. Light the oven and set it at the right temperature if cookies are to be baked immediately, or 15 minutes before you wish to bake them.
4. Cream the shortening and butter together until light and fluffy. Part margarine may be used, but all butter gives the best flavor.
5. Blend in beaten eggs and then stir in the sifted dry ingredients alternately with any liquid and flavoring called for in the recipe, mixing enough to combine the ingredients thoroughly after each addition.
6. Drop, roll, and cut, or chill the dough according to the particular cooky being made.
7. Bake according to directions but *watch baking time carefully*. It it difficult to give the absolute cooking time as much depends on the size and thickness of the cookies. *Overbaking* makes cookies hard and dry. Crisp cookies are done when they are delicately and evenly browned. Drop cookies may be tested by touching the center lightly with the finger tip. If the impression does not remain the cookies are finished baking. If your oven bakes unevenly, turn the pan halfway through the baking period.
8. Remove cookies from the sheet with a spatula as soon as they come from the oven and place them on a wire rack to cool. Do not stack hot cookies or they will stick together.
9. Store crisp cookies in a can with a loose-fitting cover. If they become soft in humid weather they may be dried in a warm oven. Store soft, chewy cookies in an airtight container or crock.

BASIC COOKIES

BASIC DROP COOKIES

The easiest and quickest of all cookies are made by this method. The dough is soft and sticky. Scoop up a heaping teaspoon of the dough and with another spoon, or with a rubber scraper, push the dough onto a greased baking sheet. Place the mounds well apart to allow for spreading during baking.

Drop dough can be made stiffer by the addition of a little flour. It can then be rolled into small balls with floured hands, placed on the baking sheet, and flattened with a knife or the tines of a fork. The dough may also be thinned with a little liquid and spread in a pan or on a sheet, baked, and cut into squares while still warm.

BROWN SUGAR DROP COOKIES

1 cup soft butter
2 cups brown sugar
2 eggs
3½ cups sifted all-purpose flour
1 teaspoon soda
1 teaspoon salt
½ cup sour milk

Cream the butter and sugar together, add the eggs, and blend thoroughly. Sift together the dry ingredients and add them alternately with the sour milk, stirring well after each addition. Drop about 2 inches apart on a lightly greased baking sheet and bake at 400° F. for 8 minutes. Makes 6 dozen cookies.

FRUIT DROPS Mix into the dough 1 cup broken nuts, 2 cups candied cherries, cut into halves, and 2 cups chopped dates. Place half a nut on top of each cooky.

NUT DROPS Mix into the dough 1 cup coarsely chopped nuts and 1 teaspoon vanilla.

COCONUT DROPS Mix into the dough 1 cup moist shredded coconut and 1 teaspoon vanilla.

CHOCOLATE DROPS Mix into the dough 1 cup sweet or semi-sweet chocolate, cut into small bits and 1 teaspoon vanilla.

COFFEE SPICE DROPS Add to the sifted dry ingredients 1 teaspoon nutmeg and 2 teaspoons cinnamon. Substitute cold coffee for the sour milk.

HERMITS Mix into the dough 2 cups seeded raisins, 1 cup chopped nuts and 1 teaspoon vanilla.

BASIC REFRIGERATOR COOKIES

Cutterless cookies freshly baked on a moment's notice. The dough is firm. The first addition of the dry ingredients is quickly and easily worked in. When the mixture becomes too stiff to stir, work in the dry ingredients with the back of a spoon (a wooden spoon is best) or mix with your hands. Because of the firmness of the dough, nuts or fruits should be added before adding the flour. Shape the dough into long, even rolls, as large in diameter as you want your cookies to be. Wrap tightly in wax paper and chill in refrigerator for several hours or overnight or for a week. If you have refrigerator molds, pack the dough into them very firmly. Butter or ice cream cartons make excellent substitutes for commercial molds.

When ready to bake cookies, remove the wax paper and cut the dough into thin slices. Use a very sharp knife and draw it back and forth in a sawing motion, pressing lightly. Do not press too hard or allow the dough to become softened or the cookies will be out of shape.

VANILLA REFRIGERATOR COOKIES

1 cup soft butter
½ cup white sugar
½ cup brown sugar
2 eggs, beaten
2 teaspoons vanilla
2¾ cups sifted all-purpose flour
½ teaspoon soda
½ teaspoon salt

Cream the butter and sugar together until light and fluffy. Add the eggs and vanilla and blend thoroughly. Mix in the dry ingredients, which have been sifted together. Shape into long, smooth roll about 2½ inches in diameter, wrap in wax paper, and chill in refrigerator. With a sharp knife cut into slices less than ⅛ inch thick. Place the slices a little apart on a lightly greased baking sheet and bake at 400° F. for 6 minutes. Makes 6 dozen cookies. Refrigerator cookies may be decorated with bits of candy, nuts, or icing.

NUT REFRIGERATOR COOKIES Add 1 cup coarsely chopped pecans, almonds, or walnuts before adding the dry ingredients.

CHOCOLATE REFRIGERATOR COOKIES Mix 2 squares (ounces) unsweetened chocolate, melted and cooled, into the butter-sugar mixture.

FRUIT AND NUT REFRIGERATOR COOKIES Mix ½ cup cut-up

fruit (dates, raisins, candied fruits) and ½ cup chopped nuts into the butter-sugar mixture.

CINNAMON REFRIGERATOR COOKIES Add 2 teaspoons cinnamon to the dry ingredients and omit the vanilla.

ORANGE-ALMOND REFRIGERATOR COOKIES Mix 1 tablespoon grated orange rind and ½ cup chopped blanched almonds into the butter-sugar mixture.

COOKY SANDWICHES Sandwich round or square, very thin, refrigerator cookies together with vanilla, chocolate, or fruit-flavored icing.

BASIC ROLLED COOKIES

The old-time favorite. The dough should be soft but not sticky. A brief chilling of any dough that is to be rolled (1 hour or more) makes it easier to handle without the further addition of flour. Too much flour makes a cooky dry, tough, and flavorless.

When your dough is the right consistency the rolling is easy. Work with half the quantity at a time, keeping the rest in the refrigerator until ready to use. Flour the board and rolling pin lightly, using only enough flour to keep the dough from sticking. Roll the dough out from the center with a light motion to the thickness required in the recipe. Roll very thin for crisp cookies, thicker for soft cookies, but always roll gently.

Have a variety of cutters of all sizes and shapes on hand and cut out the cookies as close together as possible, as the first rolling is always the tenderest. Dip the cutter in flour each time before using to keep the dough from sticking.

For parties or special holidays draw your cooky pattern on cardboard and cut it out. Place it on top of the dough and cut around it carefully with a floured sharp knife.

BUTTER COOKIES

1 cup soft butter
½ cup sugar
1 egg, beaten
3 teaspoons vanilla
3 cups sifted all-purpose flour
½ teaspoon double-action baking powder

Cream together the butter and sugar until light and fluffy, then stir in the egg and vanilla. Sift together the flour and baking powder, and mix in gradually, adding more if necessary to make a dough that is light but not sticky. Chill and roll out $\frac{1}{16}$ inch thick. Cut into desired shapes and place on lightly greased baking sheet. Bake at 425° F. for 6 minutes or until delicately browned. Makes 8 dozen 1½-inch cookies.

LEMON COOKIES Use 2 teaspoons grated lemon rind and 1 teaspoon lemon juice in place of the vanilla.

NUT COOKIES Mix into the dough 1 cup finely chopped nuts.

CHOCOLATE COOKIES Mix 2 squares (ounces) unsweetened chocolate, melted and cooked, into the sugar-butter mixture. Bake at 350° F. for 10 minutes.

TURNOVERS Cut into 3-inch rounds and place a rounded teaspoon of any desired filling on each. Fold over like a turnover and press the edges together with the floured tines of a fork. Bake at 400° F. for 8 minutes.

FILLED COOKIES Cut with a fancy cutter into scalloped rounds, diamonds, hearts, or any desired shape, but cut two of each. Place one cut-out on a lightly greased baking sheet, spread filling over it almost to the edges, cover with matching cut-out, and press the edges together with the floured tines of a fork.

BASIC PAN COOKIES

Chewy, moist, and easy to make. The dough should be moist and sticky.

Spread the dough into a greased square or oblong pan, bake and, while still warm, cut into squares or bars. Remove them from the pan and cool on a wire rack. When cool, roll in confectioners' sugar.

BROWNIES

2 squares (ounces) unsweetened chocolate
¼ cup butter
1 cup sugar
2 eggs, beaten
1 cup sifted all-purpose flour
½ teaspoon double-action baking powder
½ teaspoon salt
1 cup chopped nuts
1 teaspoon vanilla

Melt the chocolate and butter together over boiling water. Stir in the other ingredients and mix thoroughly. Pour mixture into an 8-inch square pan, lightly greased, and bake at 350° F. for 30 minutes, or until the top has a dull crust. A slight imprint will be left when the top is touched lightly with the finger. Cool slightly, cut into bars about 1½×2 inches. Cool and roll in confectioners' sugar. Makes 20 bars.

THIN BROWNIES Chop nuts very fine and spread dough into oblong pans (9×13×2 inches). Sprinkle with ¾ cup finely sliced almonds or pistachio nuts and bake for 8 minutes. Cut immediately into squares or diamonds and remove from the pans to cool.

DATE BROWNIES Add 1 cup finely cut-up dates to the dough.

SUGAR COOKIES

CRISP SUGAR COOKIES

½ cup butter
¾ cup sugar
1 egg, beaten
1½ cups sifted all-purpose flour
½ teaspoon double-action baking powder
½ teaspoon salt
2 tablespoons heavy cream
1 teaspoon vanilla

Cream the butter, add the sugar gradually, and cream together until light and fluffy. Add the egg and mix thoroughly. Sift together the dry ingredients and add alternately with the cream and vanilla, mixing well after each addition. Chill dough for 1 hour in refrigerator and then roll out 1/16 inch thick. Cut into shapes, place on greased baking sheet, sprinkle with fine granulated sugar, and bake at 400° F. for 6 minutes. Makes 5 dozen 2-inch cookies.

These cookies are nice cut into very small rounds—about 1 inch in diameter—and then sandwiched together with chocolate, vanilla, or fruit-flavored sugar icing.

GRANDMOTHER'S SUGAR COOKIES

¾ cup butter
1 cup sugar
1 egg
1 egg yolk
1 tablespoon heavy cream
1 teaspoon vanilla
1½ tablespoons caraway seeds

1¾ cups sifted all-purpose flour
1 teaspoon double-action baking powder
½ teaspoon salt

Cream the butter, add the sugar gradually, and cream together until light and fluffy. Beat the egg and egg yolk together and stir into the butter-sugar mixture. Add the cream, vanilla, caraway seeds, and the dry ingredients, which have been sifted together. Mix into a dough, wrap in wax paper, and chill in the refrigerator for at least 1 hour. Roll out on floured board ¼ inch thick and cut into rounds 2½ inches in diameter. Place on greased baking sheet 1 inch apart, sprinkle with fine granulated sugar, and bake at 375° F. for 8 minutes. Makes 2 dozen large cookies.

VANILLA DROP COOKIES

½ cup butter
1 cup sugar
1 egg
1 egg yolk
1½ cups sifted all-purpose flour
1 teaspoon double-action baking powder
½ teaspoon salt
¼ cup milk
1 teaspoon vanilla

Cream the butter, add the sugar gradually, and cream together until light and fluffy. Beat the egg and egg yolk together and stir into the butter-sugar mixture. Sift the dry ingredients and add them alternately with the milk and vanilla. Drop by the teaspoonful on baking sheet which has been lined with greased brown paper and bake at 400° F. for 10 minutes. Makes 4 dozen 2½-inch cookies.

SOUR CREAM COOKIES

½ cup butter
1 cup sugar
1 egg, beaten
3¼ cups sifted all-purpose flour
½ teaspoon soda
½ teaspoon salt
1 teaspoon double-action baking powder
½ teaspoon nutmeg
½ cup thick sour cream

Cream the butter, add the sugar gradually, and cream together until light and fluffy. Add the egg and mix thoroughly. Sift together the dry ingredients and add them alternately with the sour cream. Chill for 1 hour in refrigerator. Roll out on floured board ¼ inch thick and cut into rounds 2½ inches in diameter. Place on greased baking sheet 1 inch apart and bake at 400° F. for 10 minutes. Makes 2½ dozen large cookies.

SOUR MILK COOKIES

½ cup butter
1 cup sugar
1 egg, beaten
2 cups sifted all-purpose flour
½ teaspoon soda
½ teaspoon salt
½ cup sour milk
1 teaspoon vanilla

Cream the butter, add the sugar gradually, and cream together until light and fluffy. Add the egg and mix thoroughly. Sift together the dry ingredients and add them alternately with the sour milk and vanilla. Drop by the teaspoonful on greased baking sheet. Sprinkle with sugar and bake at 400° F. for 10 minutes. Makes 3 dozen.

BUTTERSCOTCH COOKIES

½ cup butter
2 cups brown sugar
2 eggs, beaten
3¼ cups sifted all-purpose flour
1 teaspoon double-action baking powder
1 teaspoon vanilla

Cream the butter, add the brown sugar gradually, and cream together. Add the eggs and mix thoroughly. Add the dry ingredients, which have been sifted together, and mix into a firm dough. Shape into rolls 2½ inches in diameter, wrap in wax paper, and chill in refrigerator for 2 hours or overnight. Slice ⅛ inch thick with a sharp knife, place on greased baking sheet and bake at 400° F. for 10 minutes. Makes 4 dozen cookies. Before baking, these cookies may be brushed with slightly beaten egg white and sprinkled with finely chopped nuts.

VANILLA COOKIES

1 cup butter
¼ cup sugar

    3 cups sifted all-purpose flour
    2 teaspoons vanilla

Cream the butter and sugar until light and fluffy. Add the flour and vanilla and mix thoroughly. Shape into rolls 1½ inches in diameter, roll in sugar mixed with cocoa, and wrap in wax paper. Chill in refrigerator for 2 hours or overnight. With a sharp knife slice ⅛ inch thick and place on greased baking sheet. Bake at 350° F. for 8 minutes. Makes 5 dozen cookies.

VANILLA ROCKS

    1 cup butter
    ½ cup fine granulated sugar
    1 egg yolk, beaten
    3 cups sifted all-purpose flour
    2 teaspoons vanilla

Cream the butter and sugar until light and fluffy, add the egg yolk, flour, and vanilla, and mix thoroughly. Force the dough through pastry bag with rose nozzle, making small rosettes on greased baking sheet, and bake at 350° F. about 8 minutes or until golden yellow. When cold, garnish the center of each with a small dot of jelly or a piece of maraschino cherry. Makes 4 dozen cookies.

    DIAGONALS Chill half the dough in the refrigerator for 2 hours. Roll out the chilled dough ⅛ inch thick and cut into long strips 2½ inches wide. Place these on a greased baking sheet and force the unchilled dough through a pastry bag fitted with a small fluted nozzle, making three rows on each strip. Thin dough, if necessary, with a little cream. Bake at 350° F. for 10 minutes or until lightly browned. When cold, force currant jelly through small pastry funnel between the rows and cut the strips crosswise into 1-inch diagonals.

EGG COOKIES

    2 cups butter
    1½ cups sugar
    3 hard-cooked egg yolks
    3 raw eggs, beaten
    6 cups sifted all-purpose flour
    Grated rind and juice of ½ lemon

Cream the butter and sugar and add the cooked yolks, which have been rubbed through a fine sieve. Add the flour alternately with the raw eggs. Add the lemon rind and juice and mix into a firm dough. Roll out ⅛ inch thick, brush with egg white, and cut into small rounds or squares. Place on greased baking sheet, sprinkle with chopped nuts mixed with a little sugar and cinnamon, and bake at 350° F. for 10 minutes. Makes 10 dozen cookies.

FROSTED BUTTER COOKIES

1 cup butter
4 eggs, separated
2 cups sifted all-purpose flour
1 teaspoon double-action baking powder
1 cup sugar
1 cup ground blanched almonds
Grated rind and juice of 1 lemon

Cream the butter, add the egg yolks, and mix thoroughly. Sift the flour and baking powder and stir into the butter-egg mixture. Wrap the dough in wax paper and chill in refrigerator for 2 hours or longer. Roll out ⅛ inch thick and cut into rounds. Beat the egg whites until stiff and gradually beat in the sugar. Stir in the almonds, lemon juice, and rind. Cover each round with a layer of this meringue and bake at 350° F. for 12 minutes. Makes 3 dozen cookies.

ORANGE COOKIES

¼ cup butter
1 cup sugar
Grated rind of ½ orange
4 egg yolks, beaten
2 tablespoons orange juice
2½ cups sifted all-purpose flour
2 teaspoons double-action baking powder
Pinch salt

Cream the butter and sugar until light and fluffy. Add the orange rind, egg yolks, and orange juice, and mix thoroughly. Add the flour, which has been sifted three times with the baking powder and salt. Mix into a firm dough and roll out on a lightly floured board ⅛ inch thick. Cut into rounds or squares, place on greased baking sheet, and bake at 375° F. for 8 minutes. Makes 3 dozen cookies.

BRANDY RINGS

1⅓ cups butter
¾ cup sugar
3½ cups sifted all-purpose flour
3 tablespoons brandy

Knead the butter in cold water until soft and free from salt. Pat dry and place in a mixing bowl with the sugar, flour, and brandy. Knead into a smooth, firm dough. Roll out ⅛ inch thick on a floured board and cut into long thin strips. Twist two lengths together like a cord, cut into 4-inch lengths, and shape into rings. Place on greased baking sheet and bake at 350° F. until golden in color—about 10 minutes. Makes 6 dozen cookies.

ROSETTES, *Swedish Struvor*

1 cup flour
1 cup milk
1 tablespoon sugar
2 eggs, beaten
Pinch salt

Mix together the flour, milk, sugar, eggs, and salt into a batter and beat with a rotary egg beater or whisk until the batter is smooth. Dip a rosette iron into hot deep fat (360–370° F., or until a cube of bread browns in 1 minute). Drain the iron slightly on unglazed paper and then dip it into the batter up to but not over the edge of the iron. Lower the batter-coated iron into the hot fat and let it fry for 1–1½ minutes, or until delicately browned. Loosen the rosette from the iron with a fork and drain on unglazed paper. Serve as a dessert with whipped cream, jam, or preserves. Or dust with confectioners' sugar and serve for coffee or tea. Makes 40 rosettes. Store plain rosettes in a tight container in a dry place. They will keep crisp and fresh for several weeks.

BUTTER BALLS

½ cup butter
¼ cup sugar
1 egg, separated
1 teaspoon vanilla
Grated rind of ½ lemon
Grated rind of ½ orange
1 tablespoon lemon juice
1 cup sifted all-purpose flour
½ cup ground nuts
Candied cherries

Cream the butter and sugar together, add the egg yolk and vanilla, and beat well. Add the orange and lemon rind and the lemon juice and stir in the flour. Beat hard for a few minutes, cover the bowl, and chill in refrigerator overnight. Roll into tiny balls, dip the balls in the egg white, slightly beaten, roll in nuts, and place on buttered baking sheet about 1 inch apart. Press a piece of cherry on top of each and bake at 350° F. for 15 minutes. Makes 4 dozen cookies.

DREAM DROPS

1 cup sweet butter
¾ cup sugar
2 teaspoons vanilla
2 cups sifted all-purpose flour
1 teaspoon double-action baking powder
Blanched and halved almonds

Cream the butter, add the sugar gradually, and cream together until light and fluffy. Add the vanilla and the flour sifted with the baking powder and knead into a smooth, firm dough, adding more flour if necessary. Roll out ½ inch thick, cut into small rounds 1 inch in diameter, place on greased baking sheet with half an almond on top of each round, and bake at 350° F. until lightly browned or about 15 minutes. Makes 3 dozen cookies.

ROLLED WAFERS

¼ cup butter
½ cup fine granulated sugar
¼ cup milk
1 cup sifted all-purpose flour
1 teaspoon vanilla
Grated almonds

Cream the butter, add the sugar gradually, and cream together until light. Stir in the milk a little at a time, then the flour and vanilla. Butter the back of a baking sheet and with a spatula spread the dough thinly over it. Sprinkle with almonds and score the dough in 3-inch squares. Bake at 325° F. until delicately browned—about 6 minutes. Cut the squares with a sharp knife and, while warm, roll into cornucopia shape. Fill with sweetened and flavored whipped cream before serving. Makes 4 dozen wafers.

CHOCOLATE COOKIES

CHOCOLATE DROPS

½ cup butter
1 cup sugar
1 egg, beaten
2 squares (ounces) unsweetened chocolate, melted
1¾ cups sifted all-purpose flour

    ½ teaspoon soda
    ¼ teaspoon salt
    ¾ cup sour milk
    1 cup chopped nuts
    1 teaspoon vanilla

Cream the butter and sugar, add the egg and chocolate, and mix thoroughly. Stir in the flour, which has been sifted with the salt and soda, alternately with the sour milk, mixing well after each addition. Stir in the chopped nuts and vanilla and drop by the teaspoonful on a greased baking sheet. Bake at 400° F. for 12 minutes. Cool and frost the tops with a chocolate icing. Makes 4 dozen cookies.

CRISP CHOCOLATE COOKIES

    ½ cup butter
    ½ cup sugar
    1 egg
    2 squares (ounces) unsweetened chocolate, melted
    1¾ cups sifted all-purpose flour
    ½ teaspoon double-action baking powder
    ½ teaspoon salt
    3 tablespoons milk

Cream the butter and the sugar, add the egg and chocolate, and mix thoroughly. Sift the flour with the baking powder and salt and add alternately with the milk, mixing well after each addition. Form into rolls about 2 inches in diameter, wrap in wax paper, and chill in the refrigerator for 2 hours or overnight. With a sharp knife cut into slices $\frac{1}{16}$ inch thick, place on greased baking sheet, and bake at 400° F. for 8 minutes. Makes 5 dozen cookies. If you wish, put two together sandwich fashion with a chocolate icing in between.

CHOCOLATE CHIP COOKIES

    ½ cup butter
    6 tablespoons white sugar
    6 tablespoons brown sugar
    1 egg, beaten
    1⅛ cups sifted all-purpose flour
    ½ teaspoon salt
    ¼ teaspoon soda
    1 teaspoon vanilla
    ½ cup chopped nuts
    8 ounces semi-sweet chocolate, cut into small pieces

Cream the butter, add the sugar gradually, and cream together until smooth. Stir in the egg and the sifted dry ingredients and blend thoroughly. Stir in the vanilla, nuts, and chocolate pieces and drop by the teaspoonful on greased baking sheet. Bake at 350° F. for 8 minutes. Makes 4 dozen cookies.

CHOCOLATE ALMOND COOKIES

1 cup butter
1 cup sugar
2 eggs, beaten
4 ounces almonds, grated
8 ounces sweet chocolate, grated
4 cups sifted all-purpose flour
1 teaspoon cinnamon
¼ teaspoon ground cloves
1 teaspoon double-action baking powder
3 tablespoons milk

Cream the butter, add the sugar gradually, and cream together. Stir in the eggs and mix thoroughly. Add the almonds and chocolate. Sift together the flour, cinnamon, cloves, and baking powder and add alternately with the milk. Mix well, adding more flour if necessary to make a light dough. Roll out on floured board ⅛ inch thick, cut into rounds 2½ inches in diameter, brush with slightly beaten egg white, sprinkle with sugar, and bake at 350° F. for 10 minutes. Makes 8 dozen cookies.

CHOCOLATE WALNUT COOKIES

½ cup butter
1 cup sugar
1 egg, slightly beaten
2 squares (ounces) unsweetened chocolate, melted
2 tablespoons milk
1 teaspoon vanilla
½ cup chopped walnuts
2¼ cups sifted all-purpose flour
2 teaspoons double-action baking powder
¼ teaspoon salt
½ teaspoon cinnamon

Cream the butter, add the sugar gradually, and cream together. Add the egg, chocolate, milk, vanilla, and walnuts. Sift together the flour, baking powder, salt, and cinnamon and stir into the batter gradually, mixing well after each addition. Shape into rolls 2 inches in diameter, wrap in wax paper, and chill in the refrigerator for 2 hours or overnight. With a sharp knife cut into ⅛-inch slices, place on lightly greased baking sheet, and bake at 350° F. for 10 minutes. Makes 4 dozen cookies.

CHOCOLATE STICKS

>4 eggs
>2 cups brown sugar
>1 teaspoon cinnamon
>¼ teaspoon allspice
>¼ teaspoon ground cloves
>4 ounces sweet chocolate, grated
>3 cups sifted all-purpose flour
>1 teaspoon double-action baking powder
>1 cup chopped blanched almonds
>¼ cup finely chopped citron

Beat the eggs and sugar until light and add the spices and the chocolate. Sift the flour and baking powder over the citron and almonds, mix, and then stir into the egg-sugar mixture. Mix into a light dough, adding more flour if necessary to handle it. Roll out on lightly floured board ¼ inch in thickness, cut into narrow strips about 3 inches in length, place on greased baking sheet, and bake at 350° F. for 12 minutes. Makes 5 dozen sticks.

CHOCOLATE AND VANILLA PINWHEELS

>½ cup butter
>½ cup sugar
>1 egg yolk, beaten
>1¾ cups sifted all-purpose flour
>1½ teaspoons double-action baking powder
>Pinch salt
>3 tablespoons milk
>1 teaspoon vanilla
>1 square (ounce) unsweetened chocolate, melted

Cream the butter, add the sugar gradually, and cream together. Add the egg yolk and beat well. Sift the dry ingredients and add alternately with milk and vanilla. Divide the dough in half and stir the chocolate, which has been cooled, into half the dough. Wrap each half in wax paper and chill in the refrigerator for 1 hour. On a lightly floured board roll out the plain vanilla dough into a thin oblong sheet. Then roll out the chocolate dough to the same size and thickness and place atop the vanilla dough. Roll together tightly as for a jelly roll and with a sharp knife slice ⅛ inch thick and place cut side down on greased baking sheet. Bake at 350° F. for 10 minutes. Makes 3 dozen pinwheels.

VARIATION Shape each half portion of dough into two rolls 1 inch in diameter. Then make 1 thick roll of all four by placing a chocolate and a vanilla roll side by side with the other two rolls on top—place the vanilla atop the chocolate and the chocolate atop the vanilla. Wrap tightly in wax paper and chill for 1 hour in the refrigerator. Slice crosswise ⅛ inch thick, place on greased baking sheet, and bake at 350° F. for 10 minutes.

CHOCOLATE PRETZELS

1 cup butter
⅔ cup sugar
1 egg, beaten
2 squares (ounces) unsweetened chocolate, melted
1½ cups sifted all-purpose flour
½ teaspoon cinnamon
1 teaspoon vanilla

Cream the butter and sugar thoroughly. Add the egg and chocolate and stir in the flour, which has been sifted with the cinnamon. Add vanilla and mix into a light dough, adding a little more flour if necessary. Wrap the dough in wax paper and chill for 1 hour in the refrigerator. Break off small pieces of dough and roll between the palms of the hands into strips the thickness of a pencil. Shape these into pretzels or figure 8s, place on greased baking sheet, sprinkle with finely chopped nuts, and bake at 350° F. for 8 minutes. Makes 3 dozen cookies.

FUDGE FINGERS

½ cup butter
1 cup brown sugar
2 eggs, beaten
⅔ cup sifted all-purpose flour
1 teaspoon vanilla
Pinch salt
1 cup chopped walnuts
2 squares (ounces) unsweetened chocolate, melted

Cream the butter, add the sugar, and cream together. Stir in the eggs, flour, vanilla, and salt and mix thoroughly. Stir in the walnuts and the melted chocolate and pour into a greased 8-inch square pan. Bake at 350° F. for 30 minutes. Cool, cut into fingers about 1½ inches × 2 inches, and roll in fine granulated sugar. Makes 20 bars.

INDIANS

½ cup butter
2 squares (ounces) unsweetened chocolate, melted
1 cup sugar
2 eggs
½ cup sifted all-purpose flour
½ teaspoon baking powder
1 teaspoon vanilla
1 cup chopped walnuts

Melt the butter and chocolate over a slow fire. Beat the sugar and eggs together, add the melted chocolate-butter mixture and the rest of the ingredients, and beat for 4 minutes. Pour into buttered 8-inch square pan and bake at 350° F. for 20 minutes. Cool, cut into squares, and dust with powdered sugar. Makes 20 bars.

OATMEAL COOKIES

CRISPY OATMEAL COOKIES

1 cup butter
1 cup brown sugar
1 cup white sugar
2 eggs, beaten
1½ cups sifted all-purpose flour
1 teaspoon soda
1 teaspoon salt
3 cups quick-cooking rolled oats
1 teaspoon vanilla

Cream the butter, add the sugar gradually, and cream together. Add the eggs and mix thoroughly. Stir in the flour, soda, and salt, which have been sifted together, and then stir in the oats and vanilla. Shape into rolls about 2½ inches in diameter, wrap in wax paper, and chill in the refrigerator for 2 hours or overnight. Slice with a sharp knife ⅛ inch thick and place 1 inch apart on a lightly greased baking sheet. Bake at 400° F. for 10 minutes. Makes about 5 dozen.

TRILBIES

1 cup butter
1 cup brown sugar
½ cup milk
2 cups quick-cooking rolled oats
2 cups sifted all-purpose flour
3 teaspoons double-action baking powder
1 teaspoon salt

Cream the butter and sugar together. Stir in the milk and oats. Sift together the flour, baking powder, and salt, add to the oat mixture, and mix into a firm dough. Wrap in wax paper and chill in the refrigerator for 2 hours. Roll out on a floured board ⅛ inch thick and cut into small rounds, squares, or diamonds. Place on buttered baking sheet and bake at 350° F. for 12 minutes. When cool, sandwich two cookies together with the following Date Filling: Chop ½ pound pitted dates and cook with ½ cup sugar and 1 cup water, stirring frequently, until smooth and thick. Makes 3 dozen.

SCOTTISH FANCIES

1 egg, lightly beaten
½ cup sugar
1 teaspoon melted butter
1 cup quick-cooking rolled oats
½ cup grated coconut
½ teaspoon salt
½ teaspoon vanilla

Combine the egg and sugar, add the butter, and stir in the remaining ingredients. Drop by the teaspoonful on a greased baking sheet 1½ inches apart. Dip a fork into cold water and spread each spoonful into a circle. Bake at 350° F. for 10 minutes or until delicately browned. Makes 2 dozen cookies.

SIMPLE OAT COOKIES

3 cups quick-cooking rolled oats
⅔ cup butter
½ cup sugar

Mix the ingredients in a mixing bowl and knead with the fingers until well blended. Roll the dough into small balls and place on buttered baking sheet. Dip a fork into cold water and flatten each ball, crosswise. Bake at 325° F. for 8 minutes or until lightly browned. Makes 4 dozen cookies.

OATMEAL MOLASSES COOKIES

¼ cup soft butter
1¼ cups sugar
2 eggs, beaten
6 tablespoons molasses
1¾ cups sifted all-purpose flour
1 teaspoon soda
1 teaspoon salt

1 teaspoon cinnamon
2 cups quick-cooking rolled oats
½ cup chopped nuts
1 cup seedless raisins

Cream the butter and sugar together. Add the eggs and molasses and mix thoroughly. Sift together the flour, soda, salt, and cinnamon and add to the molasses mixture. Stir in the oats, nuts, and raisins. Drop by the teaspoonful onto greased baking sheet and bake at 400° F. for 10 minutes. Makes 5 dozen cookies.

OATMEAL DROP COOKIES

1 cup butter
1 cup sugar
2 eggs, beaten
2 cups sifted all-purpose flour
1 teaspoon double-action baking powder
½ teaspoon soda
½ teaspoon salt
1 teaspoon cinnamon
2 cups quick-cooking rolled oats
3 tablespoons milk
1 cup seedless raisins
1 cup chopped nuts

Cream the butter and sugar, add the eggs and the flour, baking powder, soda, salt, and cinnamon, which have been sifted together. Stir in the oats, milk, raisins, and nuts. Drop by the teaspoonful on a greased baking sheet, 1 inch apart, and bake at 350° F. for 12 minutes. Makes 4 dozen cookies.

DATE-FILLED OAT SQUARES

1½ cups quick-cooking rolled oats
2 cups sifted all-purpose flour
½ teaspoon soda
½ teaspoon salt
1 cup brown sugar
1 cup chopped walnuts
1½ cups butter, melted
Date Filling

Combine the oats, flour, soda, salt, sugar, and walnuts and stir in the melted butter. Put half of this mixture into a buttered 8-inch square pan, spread with Date Filling, and pat the rest of the mixture on top. Bake at 325° F. for 30 minutes. Cut while warm into squares and sprinkle with confectioners' sugar. Makes 16 2-inch squares.

DATE OATMEAL COOKIES

¾ cup butter
1 cup sugar
2 eggs, beaten
3 tablespoons light cream
1 teaspoon vanilla
2 cups sifted all-purpose flour
¾ teaspoon soda
1 teaspoon salt
2 cups quick-cooking rolled oats
1½ cups chopped pitted dates
½ cup chopped nuts

Cream the butter, add the sugar gradually, and cream together. Add the eggs, cream, and vanilla and mix thoroughly. Add the flour, soda, and salt, which have been sifted together, and then stir in the oats, dates, and nuts. Mix into a fairly stiff dough. Form the dough into balls about the size of walnuts and place on greased baking sheet 1 inch apart. Flatten to ¼ inch thick and bake at 375° F. for 12 minutes. Makes 4 dozen cookies.

GINGER AND SPICE COOKIES

CRISP GINGER COOKIES

½ cup butter
½ cup sugar
1 egg, beaten
¼ cup molasses
2¼ cups sifted all-purpose flour
1 teaspoon soda
½ teaspoon salt
1½ teaspoons ginger

Cream the butter, add the sugar gradually, and cream together until light and fluffy. Add the egg and molasses and mix thoroughly. Add the dry ingredients, which have been sifted together, and mix into a soft dough. Shape into rolls about 2 inches in diameter, wrap in wax paper, and chill in the refrigerator for 2 hours. Slice ⅛ inch thick with a sharp knife, place on greased baking sheet, and bake at 400° F. for 10 minutes. Makes 5 dozen cookies.

GINGER WAFERS

¼ cup butter
¼ cup sugar
¼ cup molasses

1 egg, beaten
1 teaspoon ginger
¼ teaspoon soda
1½ cups sifted all-purpose flour

Cream the butter, gradually beat in the sugar, molasses, and egg. Sift together the ginger, soda, and flour and stir into the mixture, adding more flour if necessary to knead into a firm dough. Roll out very thin on a lightly floured board, cut into rounds or squares, and bake at 350° F. for 6 minutes, being very careful not to let them burn. Makes 4 dozen cookies.

THICK MOLASSES COOKIES

¾ cup butter
1 cup brown sugar
1 egg
4 tablespoons molasses
2¼ cups sifted all-purpose flour
½ teaspoon salt
2 teaspoons soda
1 teaspoon cinnamon
1 teaspoon ginger
½ teaspoon ground cloves

Cream the butter, add the sugar gradually, and cream together. Add the egg and molasses and mix thoroughly. Add the dry ingredients, which have been sifted together, and mix into a firm dough. Shape into round balls about the size of walnuts, dip the tops into fine granulated sugar, and place 1 inch apart on a greased baking sheet. Bake at 375° F. for 12 minutes. Makes 3 dozen cookies.

GINGER SNAPS

¾ cup butter
2 cups sugar
2 eggs, beaten
½ cup molasses
2 teaspoons vinegar
3¾ cups sifted all-purpose flour
1½ teaspoons soda
2 teaspoons ginger
½ teaspoon cinnamon
¼ teaspoon ground cloves

Cream the butter, add the sugar gradually, and stir in the eggs, molasses, and vinegar. Add the dry ingredients, which have been sifted together, and mix into a light dough. Shape into round balls about the size of walnuts and place 1 inch apart on a greased baking sheet. Bake at 350° F. for 12 minutes. Makes 5 dozen cookies.

CHRISTMAS GINGER SNAPS

⅔ cup brown sugar
⅔ cup molasses
1 teaspoon ginger
1 teaspoon cinnamon
½ teaspoon ground cloves
2 teaspoons soda
⅔ cup butter
1 egg
5 cups sifted all-purpose flour

Combine the sugar, molasses, and spices and stir over a low flame until the mixture reaches the boiling point. Stir in the soda and pour over the butter in a mixing bowl. Stir until the butter has melted. Add the egg, sift in the flour, and blend thoroughly, adding more flour if necessary to make a light dough. Knead on floured board, wrap in wax paper, and place in the refrigerator for 2 hours. Roll out ⅛ inch thick and cut into fancy shapes, using fancy cutters or cardboard cut-outs of Christmas trees, Santa Claus shapes, hearts, stars, angels, children, or animals. Place on greased baking sheet and bake at 325° F. for 10 minutes. When cool, decorate with sugar icing piped through the fine nozzle of a pastry tube. Makes 6 dozen cookies.

ALMOND GINGER SNAPS

1 cup butter
1 cup sugar
½ cup molasses
3 teaspoons ginger
2 teaspoons cinnamon
1 teaspoon ground cloves
1 cup blanched almonds
4 cups sifted all-purpose flour
1 teaspoon baking soda

Cream the butter and sugar until light and fluffy. Add the molasses, spices, and almonds. Stir in the flour, which has been sifted with the soda, and place on floured board. Knead, adding more flour if necessary, until smooth. Shape into two rolls about 2 inches in diameter, wrap in wax paper, and chill in the refrigerator for 2 hours or overnight. Slice ⅛ inch thick with a sharp knife, place on greased baking sheet, and bake at 325° F. for 8 minutes. Makes 5 dozen cookies.

GINGERBREAD HOUSE

1½ cups heavy cream
2½ cups brown sugar
1 cup molasses
1 tablespoon ginger
1 tablespoon grated lemon rind
3 teaspoons soda
8 cups sifted all-purpose flour

Whip the cream until thick but not stiff. Beat in the sugar gradually, then stir in the molasses, ginger, and lemon rind, and continue to stir until thoroughly mixed. Add the flour, which has been sifted with the soda, turn out onto floured board, and knead, adding more flour if necessary, until smooth. Chill in the refrigerator overnight. Roll out dough ⅛ inch thick on a greased and floured baking sheet. Have ready cardboard cut-out pattern for a house. Place pattern on dough and cut around, using a sharp pointed knife. (Cut leftover dough into animal and children shapes.) Brush with water to give a smooth surface and bake at 250° F. for 15 minutes. Let cool on the sheet. Remove carefully with spatula, dip the edges in hot sugar syrup, and build your house. Decorate with sugar icing forced through a very fine nozzle of a pastry tube.

GINGER CREAMS

½ cup shortening
1 cup sugar
1 egg
1 cup molasses
4 cups sifted all-purpose flour
2 teaspoons soda
½ teaspoon salt
2 teaspoons cinnamon
2 teaspoons ginger
1 teaspoon nutmeg
1 teaspoon ground cloves
1 cup hot water

Cream the butter, add the sugar gradually, and cream together. Add the egg and molasses and mix thoroughly. Sift the dry ingredients and add them alternately with the hot water, mixing well after each addition. Drop by the teaspoonful onto a greased baking sheet and bake at 400° F. for 8 minutes. While slightly warm, cover the tops with sugar icing. Makes 8 dozen cookies.

SPICE COOKIES

5 eggs
2 cups brown sugar
1 teaspoon vanilla
3½ cups sifted all-purpose flour
1 teaspoon ground cloves
1 teaspoon ginger
2 teaspoons cinnamon
1 teaspoon soda

Beat the eggs until light and gradually stir in the sugar. Add the vanilla and stir in the dry ingredients, which have been sifted together, adding more flour if necessary to make a soft dough. Drop by the teaspoonful on greased baking sheet and bake at 375° F. for 12 minutes. Makes 6 dozen cookies.

SPICE RAISIN COOKIES

⅔ cup butter
1½ cups brown sugar
2 eggs, beaten
1 cup seedless raisins
1 teaspoon soda
3 tablespoons sour milk
3 cups sifted all-purpose flour
1 teaspoon ground cloves
2 teaspoons cinnamon
Pinch salt

Cream the butter and sugar together, add the eggs and raisins. Dissolve the soda in the sour milk and add alternately with the dry ingredients, which have been sifted together. Mix thoroughly into a soft dough and drop by the teaspoonful on a greased baking sheet. Bake at 375° F. for 12 minutes. Makes 5 dozen cookies.

CHRISTMAS SPICE COOKIES

2 cups brown sugar
½ cup honey
¼ cup butter
3 cups sifted all-purpose flour
3 teaspoons double-action baking powder
1 teaspoon cinnamon

¼ teaspoon ground cloves
¼ teaspoon nutmeg
1 egg
2 tablespoons milk
¼ cup finely ground citron
Grated rind and juice of ½ lemon

Combine the sugar and honey and stir over a slow fire until the sugar is dissolved. Stir in the butter and let the mixture cool. Mix together the dry ingredients and stir in alternately with the egg, which has been beaten with the milk. Add the citron, lemon rind and juice, and more flour, if necessary, to make a dough that is light but easy to handle. Roll out on a lightly floured board ⅛ inch thick and cut into fancy shapes. Place on greased baking sheet and bake at 350° F. for 8 minutes. Makes 6 dozen cookies.

HONEY AND SPICE COOKIES

3 cups sifted all-purpose flour
1 teaspoon allspice
½ teaspoon cinnamon
1 teaspoon soda
3 eggs, slightly beaten
3 tablespoons honey
Grated rind and juice of ½ lemon
Pecans, almonds, or walnuts

Sift the dry ingredients into a mixing bowl. Stir in the eggs, honey, the lemon rind and juice, and knead into a firm dough. Roll out ¼ inch thick on a lightly floured board and cut into 2½-inch rounds. Place the rounds on a greased baking sheet, brush with slightly beaten white of egg, place half a nut on each cooky, and bake at 350° F. for 15 minutes. Makes 3 dozen cookies.

CARDAMOM COOKIES

1 cup butter
1 cup sugar
2 eggs, beaten
4 cups sifted all-purpose flour
2 tablespoons crushed cardamom seeds
Grated rind of 1 lemon

Cream the butter and sugar together, stir in the rest of the ingredients, adding more flour if necessary to make a firm dough. Roll out ⅛ inch thick, cut into small rounds, place on greased baking sheet, and bake at 350° F. for 8 minutes. Makes 6 dozen cookies.

ANISE COOKIES

    3 eggs
    1 cup sugar
    2 cups sifted all-purpose flour
    1 tablespoon ground anise seed
    ½ teaspoon double-action baking powder

Beat the eggs until very light, add the sugar, and beat vigorously for several minutes. Sift in the flour, which has been mixed with the anise seed and baking powder, and beat again for 5 minutes. Drop by the teaspoonful on well-greased and floured pans about 1 inch apart. Let stand overnight in a warm place, uncovered, to dry. Bake at 350° F. for 8 minutes. Makes 3 dozen cookies.

FRUIT AND NUT COOKIES

FRUIT DROPS

    ½ cup butter
    1 cup brown sugar
    1 egg, beaten
    1¾ cups sifted all-purpose flour
    ½ teaspoon soda
    ½ teaspoon salt
    ⅓ cup sour cream
    1 cup chopped pitted dates
    1 cup candied cherries, halved
    1 cup chopped almonds or pecans

Cream the butter, add the sugar gradually, and cream together. Stir in the egg and add the sifted dry ingredients alternately with the sour cream, mixing well after each addition. Stir in the dates, cherries, and nuts and drop by the teaspoonful on a greased baking sheet. Place half a nut on top of each spoonful and bake at 400° F. for 12 minutes. Makes 3 dozen cookies.

RAISIN COOKIES

    ½ cup butter
    1 cup sugar
    2 eggs, beaten
    ½ cup molasses
    1 cup seedless raisins
    2½ cups sifted all-purpose flour
    2 teaspoons double-action baking powder
    Pinch salt
    1 teaspoon cinnamon

1 teaspoon nutmeg
¼ teaspoon ground cloves
2 tablespoons milk

Cream the butter and sugar together, add the eggs, molasses, and raisins, and mix thoroughly. Sift the dry ingredients and add with as much of the milk as necessary to make a medium dough. Roll out on lightly floured board, cut into rounds or squares, and bake at 350° F. for 12 minutes. Makes about 4 dozen cookies.

DATE AND NUT STICKS

2 eggs
1 cup sugar
2 cups chopped pecans
2 cups chopped pitted dates
½ cup candied cherries, cut
1 teaspoon vanilla
⅔ cup sifted all-purpose flour
1 teaspoon baking powder

Beat the eggs and sugar together until light, add the nuts, dates, cherries, and vanilla. Sift in the flour and baking powder and mix thoroughly. Spread in an 8-inch square pan and bake at 350° F. for 20 minutes. Cut into strips while still warm. Makes 32 sticks.

HERMITS

1 cup butter
2 cups brown sugar
2 eggs, beaten
2 cups sifted all-purpose flour
1 teaspoon soda
1 teaspoon salt
2 teaspoons cinnamon
1 teaspoon nutmeg
½ cup strong cold coffee
2 cups seedless raisins
½ cup chopped pitted dates
1 cup chopped nuts

Cream the butter, add the sugar gradually, and cream together. Add the eggs and mix thoroughly. Dredge 2 tablespoons flour over the raisins, dates, and nuts and sift the rest with the soda, salt, cinnamon, and nutmeg. Add these dry ingredients alternately with the coffee, mixing after each addition. Stir in the raisins, dates, and nuts and drop by the teaspoonful on a greased baking sheet. Bake at 400° F. for 8 minutes. Makes 8 dozen cookies.

ROLLED DATE COOKIES

Crisp Sugar Cooky dough
¼ cup melted butter
1 cup chopped pitted dates
½ cup chopped walnuts
¼ cup sugar
½ teaspoon cinnamon

Follow the recipe for Crisp Sugar Cookies. Roll the dough out into a large thin sheet on a lightly floured board, brush with the butter, sprinkle with the dates, nuts, sugar, and cinnamon. Roll up like a jelly roll and cut into pieces ½ inch thick. Place on greased baking sheet and bake at 350° F. for 15 minutes. Makes 2 dozen rolls.

FILLED COOKIES

⅔ cup butter
½ cup brown sugar
1 egg, well beaten
1 teaspoon vanilla
3 cups sifted all-purpose flour
2 teaspoons double-action baking powder
¼ teaspoon salt
⅓ cup milk
Date Filling

Cream the butter, add the sugar gradually, and cream together until light and fluffy. Add the egg and vanilla. Sift the dry ingredients and add alternately with the milk, a little at a time, beating after each addition until smooth. Chill for 2 hours in the refrigerator. Roll out ⅛ inch thick on a lightly floured board and cut into 2½-inch rounds. Place 1 teaspoon Date or Fig Filling on a circle, place another round on top, and press the edges together with the tines of a fork dipped in flour. Place on lightly greased baking sheet and bake at 400° F. for 12 minutes. Makes 3 dozen cookies.

FIG COOKIES

½ cup butter
1 cup brown sugar
2 eggs, beaten
1 teaspoon soda
2 tablespoons sour cream
½ teaspoon cinnamon
1 cup chopped figs
2 cups sifted all-purpose flour

Cream the butter and sugar together, add the eggs, and mix thoroughly. Dissolve the soda in the sour cream and add along with the cinnamon and figs. Sift in the flour a little at a time, mixing well after each addition and adding more flour if necessary to make a dough easy to roll out. Roll out on lightly floured board, cut into rounds or squares, and bake at 350° F. for 12–15 minutes. Makes about 4 dozen cookies.

PINEAPPLE DROPS

⅔ cup butter
1¼ cups brown sugar
2 eggs, beaten
¾ cup canned, shredded pineapple, well drained
1 teaspoon vanilla
2 cups sifted all-purpose flour
1½ teaspoons double-action baking powder
¼ teaspoon soda

Cream the butter, add the sugar gradually, and cream together until light and fluffy. Stir in the eggs, pineapple, and vanilla. Sift in the dry ingredients a little at a time, beating after each addition until smooth. Drop by the teaspoonful on greased baking sheet and bake at 400° F. for 10 minutes. Makes 4 dozen cookies.

PEANUT BUTTER COOKIES

½ cup butter
½ cup peanut butter
½ cup white sugar
½ cup brown sugar
1 egg, beaten
½ teaspoon vanilla
1¼ cups sifted all-purpose flour
½ teaspoon soda

Cream the butter and peanut butter until smooth, add the sugar gradually, and cream together until light and fluffy. Add the beaten egg and vanilla and stir in the flour, which has been sifted with the soda. Drop by the teaspoonful on a greased baking sheet and press flat with a fork dipped in flour. Bake at 350° F. for 8 minutes. Makes 3 dozen cookies.

QUICK NUT PATTIES

1 egg
1 cup sugar
1 cup chopped nuts
5 tablespoons all-purpose flour

Beat the egg and sugar until thick and pale in color. Stir in the nuts and the flour and mix thoroughly. Drop by the teaspoonful on a greased baking sheet and bake at 375° F. for 10 minutes. Makes 2 dozen cookies.

WALNUT SQUARES

1 egg
1 cup brown sugar
1 cup chopped walnuts
1 teaspoon vanilla
⅔ cup sifted all-purpose flour
½ teaspoon soda
Pinch salt

Beat the egg and sugar together until smooth. Stir in the nuts and vanilla and the flour, which has been sifted with the soda and salt. Spread in a greased 8-inch square pan and bake at 325° F. for 25 minutes. Cut into squares while still warm. Cool and roll in powdered sugar. Makes 64 1-inch squares.

WALNUT STICKS

2 eggs
1 cup brown sugar
1 cup chopped walnuts
⅔ cup sifted all-purpose flour

Beat the eggs and sugar until light, add the nuts, and mix in the flour thoroughly. Spread on greased cooky sheet and bake at 350° F. for 15 minutes. Cut into 3-inch strips while still warm. Makes 6 dozen strips.

PUMPKIN COOKIES

½ cup soft butter
1¼ cups brown sugar
2 eggs, beaten
1½ cups cooked and sieved pumpkin
2½ cups sifted all-purpose flour
3 teaspoons double-action baking powder
1 teaspoon cinnamon
½ teaspoon nutmeg
½ teaspoon salt
¼ teaspoon ginger
1 cup seeded raisins
1 cup chopped nuts

Cream the butter and sugar together until light and then stir in the eggs and pumpkin purée. Sift the dry ingredients and add, stirring until well blended. Stir in the raisins and nuts. Drop by the teaspoonful onto greased baking sheet and bake at 400° F. for 15 minutes. Makes 3 dozen cookies.

BLACK WALNUT AND COCONUT BARS

½ cup butter
½ cup brown sugar
1 cup sifted all-purpose flour

Cream the butter, add the sugar gradually, and beat until smooth. Stir in the sifted flour and spread the mixture in the bottom of an 8-inch square cake pan. Bake at 375° F. for 20 minutes.

FILLING
2 eggs
1 cup brown sugar
1 teaspoon vanilla
2 tablespoons all-purpose flour
Pinch salt
1 cup chopped black walnuts
½ cup shredded coconut

Beat the eggs with the sugar until light and fluffy and add the vanilla. Sift the flour and salt over the nuts and coconut and stir into the butter-sugar mixture. Pour this batter over the baked crust and continue baking at 375° F. for another 20 minutes. Cool a little and cut into oblong bars. Makes 24 bars.

HONEY BARS

1 cup fine granulated sugar
1 cup honey
1 cup blanched and halved almonds
2 cups sifted all-purpose flour
½ teaspoon nutmeg
¼ teaspoon ground cloves
¼ cup lemon juice
2 tablespoons citron, finely cut

Combine the sugar and honey and stir over a low flame until it reaches the boil, add the almonds, and mix thoroughly. Cool slightly and then stir in the sifted dry ingredients alternately with the lemon juice, mixing well after each addition. Add the citron and more flour if necessary to make a firm dough. Wrap in wax paper and chill in the refrigerator overnight or longer as this dough will keep, unbaked, for a week. Roll out ½ inch thick, place on greased baking sheet, and bake at 375° F. for 15 minutes. While still warm, cut into strips 1 inch × 2 inches, and frost. Makes 6 dozen bars.

HONEY NUT TARTS

1 cup sweet butter
2 egg yolks
1 cup sour cream
2 cups sifted all-purpose flour
Pinch salt

Cream the butter until very soft, add the egg yolks, and beat until smooth. Stir in the sour cream alternately with the flour and salt, adding more flour if necessary to make a firm dough. Wrap in wax paper and chill in the refrigerator for 1 hour. Roll out 1/8 inch thick on a lightly floured board and cut into rounds 3 inches in diameter. Put a teaspoon of filling on one side, fold over the other side, and crimp the edges with the tines of a fork, dipped in flour. Place on greased baking sheet and bake at 350° F. for 8 minutes. Makes 3 dozen tarts.

HONEY NUT FILLING
1 cup chopped nuts
1 cup sugar
1 cup honey
1 teaspoon cinnamon

Combine all the ingredients into a paste.

CLOVERLEAF COOKIES

1 cup sweet butter
4 tablespoons confectioners' sugar
1 cup cake flour
2 teaspoons vanilla
1 cup ground blanched almonds

Cream the butter, add the sugar, and cream together. Add the flour, vanilla, and nuts and knead into a firm dough. Shape into small balls the size of large marbles and place three together with a small piece of candied cherry in the center. Bake at 350° F. for 15 minutes. Makes 2 dozen cookies.

ROCKS

1 cup butter
1½ cups brown sugar
2 eggs, beaten

3 cups sifted all-purpose flour
1 teaspoon soda
2 teaspoons cinnamon
½ teaspoon salt
1 cup seedless raisins
1 cup chopped nuts

Cream the butter, add the sugar gradually, and cream together. Add the eggs and mix thoroughly. Add the dry ingredients, which have been sifted together, stir in the raisins and nuts, and mix into a firm dough. Drop by the teaspoonful on a greased baking sheet and bake at 350° F. for 15 minutes. Makes 4 dozen cookies.

COCONUT ICEBOX COOKIES

⅔ cup butter
¾ cup sugar
1 egg, beaten
1 teaspoon vanilla
1½ cups shredded coconut
1¾ cups sifted all-purpose flour
1½ teaspoons double-action baking powder
Pinch salt

Cream the butter, add the sugar, and cream together until light and fluffy. Stir in the egg, vanilla, and coconut and then the sifted dry ingredients. Mix thoroughly, shape into rolls 1½ inches in diameter, wrap in wax paper, and chill in the refrigerator for 1 hour. With a sharp knife slice ⅛ inch thick, place on lightly greased baking sheet, and bake at 400° F. for 6 minutes. Makes 5 dozen cookies.

ALMOND STICKS

1 cup butter
1 cup sugar
2 eggs, beaten
2 cups sifted all-purpose flour
2 cups ground blanched almonds
Grated rind of 1 lemon
1 egg yolk, beaten

Cream the butter, add ¾ cup sugar, and cream together. Add the eggs, flour, 1¾ cups of the almonds, and the lemon rind and knead to a firm dough, adding more flour if necessary. Roll out ⅛ inch thick on a lightly floured board, cut into strips, and place on greased baking sheet. Brush with the beaten egg yolk, sprinkle with ¼ cup sugar, and ¼ cup almonds, and bake at 350° F. for 8 minutes. Makes 4 dozen 3-inch strips.

ALMOND SHORTBREAD

1 cup butter
½ cup fine granulated sugar
2 cups sifted all-purpose flour
1 cup grated blanched almonds
Pinch salt

Cream the butter and sugar until light and fluffy. Dredge the flour over the nuts and work in the flour, nuts, and salt, adding more flour if necessary to make a firm dough. Shape the dough into 2-inch rolls, wrap in wax paper, and chill in the refrigerator for 2 hours. With a sharp knife slice ⅛ inch thick, place on greased baking sheet, and bake at 350° F. for 10 minutes. Makes 4 dozen cookies.

ALMOND TARTS

⅔ cup sweet butter
⅓ cup sugar
1 egg yolk
½ cup grated blanched almonds
1¾ cups sifted all-purpose flour
Pinch salt

Cream the butter and sugar together until light and fluffy. Add the egg yolk, almonds, flour, and salt and mix thoroughly, adding more flour if necessary to make a firm dough. Chill in the refrigerator for 1 hour or longer. Butter small fluted tins and coat the inside with dough, using well-floured thumbs. Bake at 325° F. for 10 minutes, allow to cool in the tins, unmold, and serve filled with whipped cream topped with a little jam. Makes 3 dozen tarts.

ALMOND WAFERS

½ cup butter
½ cup sugar
1 tablespoon all-purpose flour
2 tablespoons milk
⅔ cup ground blanched almonds

In a saucepan combine all the ingredients and stir over a low fire until the butter is melted and the ingredients are well mixed. Drop by the teaspoonful on greased and floured baking sheet 2 inches apart and bake at 350° F. for 8 minutes. While still hot, shape quickly around a broom handle or rolling pin. Makes 4 dozen cookies.

PECAN WAFERS

½ cup butter
1 cup brown sugar
2 eggs, beaten
4 tablespoons all-purpose flour
¼ teaspoon salt
1 teaspoon vanilla
½ cup chopped pecans

Cream the butter, add the sugar gradually, and cream well together. Add the eggs, flour, salt, vanilla, and nuts and mix thoroughly. Drop by the teaspoonful on greased baking sheet 1½ inches apart and bake at 325° F. for 8 minutes. Makes 2 dozen cookies.

MACAROONS AND KISSES

MERINGUE KISSES

4 egg whites
Pinch salt
1 cup fine granulated sugar
1 teaspoon vanilla, lemon, or almond flavoring

Beat the egg whites with the salt until stiff enough to form peaks, but not dry. Gradually beat in the sugar, about 1 tablespoon at a time, beating well after each addition and making sure the sugar has dissolved before adding more. Beat in the flavoring. Moisten a heavy board and cover it with a layer of heavy, unglazed paper. Drop the meringue by the teaspoonful, 1 inch apart. Sprinkle with fine granulated sugar and bake in a very slow oven (250° F.) for 1 hour or until the tops are crisp and delicately tinged with brown. Makes 48 kisses.

MARGUERITES Flavor meringue with vanilla and fold in 1 cup finely chopped nuts. Drop by the teaspoonful on small chocolate or vanilla wafers. Sprinkle with granulated sugar and bake at 300° F. for 30 minutes. Makes 48 marguerites.

MERINGUE DROPS Put meringue in a pastry bag and make small rosettes or drops not more than ¾ inch in diameter on unglazed paper placed on a heavy wet board. Sprinkle with fine granulated sugar and bake at 250° F. for 35 minutes. Put the bases of two drops together with sugar icing.

PECAN KISSES

1 egg white

Pinch salt
1 cup brown sugar, sifted
1 cup chopped pecans

Beat the egg white with the salt until stiff. Fold in the sugar and nuts. Drop by the teaspoonful in small piles ½ inch apart on greased baking sheet. Bake at 250° F. for 45 minutes. Makes 2 dozen kisses.

CHOCOLATE KISSES

3 egg whites
½ cup sugar
2 squares (ounces) unsweetened chocolate, grated
1 teaspoon vanilla

Beat the egg whites until very stiff and fold in the sugar, chocolate, and vanilla. Drop by the teaspoonful on greased baking sheet and bake at 250° F. for 1 hour. Makes 3 dozen kisses.

COCOA KISSES

2 egg whites
1¼ cups sugar
2 tablespoons cocoa
½ teaspoon cinnamon
½ cup chopped blanched almonds

Beat the egg whites until they are stiff enough to form peaks and then gradually beat in the sugar a little at a time. Fold in the other ingredients lightly and drop the mixture by the teaspoonful on heavy paper which is placed on a wet board. Bake at 250° F. for 1 hour, or until crisp and delicately browned. Makes 2 dozen kisses.

COCONUT KISSES

2 egg whites
¾ cup fine granulated sugar
1 cup shredded coconut

Beat the egg whites until they are stiff enough to form peaks and then gradually beat in the sugar a little at a time. Fold in the other ingredients lightly and drop the mixture by the teaspoonful on heavy paper which is placed on a wet board. Bake at 250° F. for 1 hour, or until crisp and delicately browned. Makes 3 dozen kisses.

NUT KISSES Fold in ¾ cup chopped nuts such as hickory nuts, blanched almonds, filberts, in place of the coconut.

FIG OR DATE KISSES Fold in 1 cup dried figs or dates which have been softened by steaming, in place of the coconut.

DATE AND NUT KISSES   Fold in 1 cup pitted and chopped dates, and 1 cup chopped blanched almonds, or walnuts, in place of the coconut.

PISTACHIO KISSES   Fold in 1 cup pistachio nuts in place of the coconut. Add a drop of green coloring.

BROWN SUGAR MACAROONS

1 cup light brown sugar
1¼ cups pecans, finely ground
1 egg white, unbeaten

Knead all the ingredients together and roll into small balls the size of a marble. Place 2 inches apart on greased baking sheet and bake at 300° F. for 15 minutes. Makes 2 dozen macaroons.

CORNFLAKE MACAROONS

3 cups cornflakes
Pinch salt
1 cup shredded coconut
½ cup corn syrup or honey
½ cup sugar
2 eggs, beaten
1 teaspoon vanilla

Combine all the ingredients and roll into balls the size of walnuts. Place well apart on a greased baking sheet and bake at 300° F. for 30 minutes. Chopped nuts may be substituted for the coconut and ½ cup melted sweet chocolate may be substituted for the ½ cup sugar. Makes 3 dozen macaroons.

CHOCOLATE MACAROONS

¼ cup ground blanched almonds
2 squares (ounces) unsweetened chocolate, grated
½ cup sugar
2 egg whites, stiffly beaten
½ teaspoon vanilla

Mix the almonds, chocolate, and sugar to a smooth paste and fold into the egg whites. Stir in the vanilla and drop by the teaspoonful on heavy paper, lightly greased. Bake at 325° F. for 30 minutes. Makes 2 dozen macaroons.

COOKIES FROM OTHER LANDS

FINNSKA KABOR

¾ cup butter
¼ cup fine granulated sugar
2 cups sifted all-purpose flour
1 teaspoon almond extract
1 egg white, slightly beaten
¼ cup confectioners' sugar
½ cup finely chopped almonds

Cream the butter and sugar until light and fluffy, and then work in the flour and almond extract. Roll out on a lightly floured board ¼ inch thick and cut into strips about ¾ inch × 2 inches. Brush the top of the strips with the egg white and sprinkle with the confectioners' sugar mixed with the almonds. Place on greased baking sheet and bake at 350° F. for 15 minutes. Makes 5 dozen strips.

RUSSIAN NUT BALLS

1 cup butter
½ cup fine granulated sugar
2¼ cups sifted all-purpose flour
Pinch salt
1 teaspoon vanilla
1 cup finely chopped nuts

Cream the butter and sugar until light and fluffy. Work in the flour and salt, the vanilla, and the nuts and mix into a firm dough. Form the dough into small balls—about 1 inch in diameter—place on greased baking sheet and bake at 400° F. for 15 minutes. Roll immediately in confectioners' sugar, cool, and roll again in the sugar. Makes 5 dozen cookies.

BORRACHITOS

1 cup butter
⅔ cup sugar
2 egg yolks
½ teaspoon salt
3 cups sifted all-purpose flour
Claret wine, enough to make a soft cooky dough

Cream shortening, add sugar, egg yolks, and salt, mixing well. Add flour alternately with wine until all of the flour is used and a soft cooky dough is obtained. Run through a pastry tube in small amounts (or drop from a teaspoon) and bake at 375° F. for 8 minutes. Sprinkle cookies with a little sugar and powdered cinnamon as soon as they are removed from the oven. Makes 6 dozen cookies.

PETITS GÂTEAUX TAILLES

>1 cup soft butter
>1 cup fine granulated sugar
>2½ cups sifted all-purpose flour
>Pinch salt
>1 teaspoon vanilla

Cream butter and sugar together until light and fluffy. Stir in the flour, salt, and vanilla and mix into a firm dough. Shape the dough into a roll 2 inches in diameter, wrap in wax paper, and chill in the refrigerator for 2 hours. Slice $\frac{1}{16}$ inch thick with a sharp knife, place on buttered baking sheet, and bake at 400° F. for 8 minutes. Makes 6 dozen cookies.

Petits Gâteaux Tailles may be delicately colored with a few drops of food coloring and the flavor changed accordingly: red food coloring—flavor with rose water; green food coloring—flavor with peppermint or wintergreen; yellow food coloring—flavor with almond.

SCOTCH SHORTBREAD

>1 cup butter
>10 tablespoons fine granulated sugar
>2½ cups all-purpose flour

Sift the flour and sugar together three times and mix it into the butter with the finger tips until the mixture is the consistency of corn meal. Turn out on floured board and knead, adding a little more flour, until the mixture begins to crack. Roll out ⅜ inch thick, and cut into small, fancy shapes. Bake at 325° F. for 20 minutes, or until very lightly browned. Do not overbake. Makes 2 dozen small cookies.

SCOTCH WAFERS

>½ cup molasses
>½ cup butter
>1 cup sifted all-purpose flour
>⅔ cup fine granulated sugar
>1 tablespoon ginger

Bring the molasses to the boiling point, remove from the heat, and add the butter. Then gradually add the sifted dry ingredients, stirring constantly. Drop by the half teaspoonful on greased baking sheet, 2 inches apart. Bake at 300° F. for 10 minutes. Remove from the pan while still warm and shape over the handle of a wooden spoon into cornucopias. Makes 2 dozen wafers.

DUTCH SQUARES

1 pound butter
2 cups light brown sugar
2 teaspoons vanilla
¼ teaspoon salt
4½ cups sifted all-purpose flour
4 cups chopped pecans or black walnuts

Cream the butter until soft and fluffy and gradually work in the sugar. Stir in the vanilla, salt, and part of the flour. When the mixture becomes too firm to stir, work in the remaining flour with the hands and then work in 2 cups of the chopped nuts. Cover a baking sheet about $\frac{3}{16}$ inch thick with this dough. This quantity will cover two sheets. Glaze the top with the slightly beaten white of an egg and cover thickly with chopped nuts, using about 1 cup for each sheet. Bake at 350° F. for 15 minutes and cut into small squares or oblongs while still warm. Makes about 6 dozen squares.

MANDELCHEN

2 cups grated blanched almonds
½ cup fine granulated sugar
½ cup butter

Mix the almonds and sugar and work in the butter, kneading into a very stiff paste. Chill in refrigerator for 1 hour, then roll out $\frac{1}{16}$ inch thick on a floured board. Place on greased baking sheet and bake at 350° F. for 6 minutes or until lightly browned. When cool, sprinkle with confectioners' sugar. Makes 4 dozen cookies.

SPRINGERLE

2 eggs
1 cup sugar
2 cups sifted all-purpose flour
2 teaspoons ground anise seed

Beat the eggs and sugar until light and pale in color. Mix in the flour, sifted with the anise seed, and knead to a stiff paste, adding more flour if necessary. Roll out ⅛ inch thick and press down on floured springerle board, if you have one, in order to emboss the design. Cut out into squares, place on greased baking sheets which have been sprinkled with anise seed, and let dry at room temperature overnight or for 10 hours. Bake at 325° F. until pale yellow or for 8 minutes. Makes 4 dozen cookies.

LEBKUCHEN

1 cup honey
¾ cup brown sugar
1 egg, beaten
1 tablespoon lemon juice
1 teaspoon grated lemon rind
2¾ cups sifted all-purpose flour
½ teaspoon salt
½ teaspoon soda
1 teaspoon cinnamon
1 teaspoon ground cloves
1 teaspoon allspice
½ cup finely cut citron, candied orange and lemon peel
½ cup chopped blanched almonds

Bring the honey to a boil, let it cool, and add the brown sugar, egg, lemon juice and rind. Sift together the flour, salt, soda, cinnamon, cloves, and allspice and stir into the honey mixture. Stir in the fruit and nuts. Mix thoroughly and spread ¼ inch thick in a large shallow pan. Bake at 375° F. for 20 minutes. While warm, frost with Orange Sugar Frosting and cut into oblongs. Remove from the pan and cool on a wire rack. Makes 6 dozen 2×3-inch cookies.

The dough may be placed in the refrigerator overnight and then rolled out ½ inch thick and cut into large rounds with a floured cooky cutter. Decorate with blanched almonds and citron and bake and frost as above.

DANISH ALMOND WREATHS

1 egg yolk
½ cup sugar
¼ cup grated blanched almonds
1 teaspoon vanilla
2½ cups sifted all-purpose flour
1 cup melted butter

Beat the egg and sugar until light and pale in color. Add the almonds and vanilla and stir in the flour gradually, mixing well after each addition. Finally stir in the melted butter, mix thoroughly, and place the dough in the refrigerator for 20 minutes to cool. Then force it through a fluted nozzle of a pastry tube on a greased baking sheet in the shape of wreaths or the letter S. Bake at 350° F. until they are tinged with gold—about 8 minutes. Do not overbake. Makes 4 dozen cookies.

SPRITZ   These cookies are made in the same way and with the same dough as the Danish Almond Wreaths, except that 6 bitter almonds are blanched and grated in place of the ¼ cup almonds.

SWEDISH MACAROONS

1⅓ cups blanched and dried almonds
1½ cups fine granulated sugar
2 egg whites

Grind the almonds twice, the second time with the sugar. Work to a smooth paste, adding the egg whites gradually. Force the mixture through a fluted pastry tube into rosette clusters, wreaths, or figure 8s and decorate with pieces of candied cherries. Bake at 325° F. until pale yellow—about 30 minutes. Makes 2 dozen macaroons.

KROM CAKES

Golden, fragile, waferlike biscuits may be easily made with the light cast-aluminum krom iron now being made in this country. A different and delicious sweet for tea or dessert. Store them in a tight container in a dry place and they will keep crisp for several weeks.

3 eggs
½ cup sugar
1 cup sifted all-purpose flour
½ cup cold water
¼ pound butter, melted and cooled
¼ teaspoon cardamom

Beat the eggs and sugar together until thick and pale in color. Stir in the flour, water, melted butter, and cardamom. Place the batter in a small pitcher and heat the krom iron on both sides over a low steady flame. Brush the inside of the iron with a little melted butter, pour about 1 tablespoon of the batter into the center of the iron, and close it. Let the wafer cook for about 1 minute, or until it stops steaming, turn the iron and let the cake cook for about ¾ minute on the other side, or until the wafer is golden brown. Open the iron, remove the krom cake with a fork, and quickly roll it over the wooden stick or a broom handle. They may also be shaped into cones or into small baskets. Serve them as tea cookies dusted generously with confectioners' sugar, or serve them as a dessert filled with ice cream, whipped cream, or Crème Pâtissière.

The batter will thicken on standing and should be thinned occasionally with a little cold water. The thinner the batter, the more fragile will be the wafers.

PFEFFERNUESSE

1 cup soft butter
1½ cups sugar
3 eggs, beaten
5 cups sifted all-purpose flour
1 teaspoon salt
4 teaspoons double-action baking powder
1 teaspoon cinnamon
1 teaspoon nutmeg
1 teaspoon ground cloves
½ teaspoon white pepper
1½ cups milk
½ cup water
Grated rind of 1 lemon
1 teaspoon anise seed
1 cup chopped almonds

Cream butter and sugar, add eggs, and mix well. Sift together the dry ingredients and add them alternately with the liquid. Add the lemon rind, anise seed, and almonds and blend thoroughly. Drop by the teaspoonful on lightly greased baking sheet and bake at 350° F. for 15 minutes. Remove from the sheet and, while still warm, dust with confectioners' sugar. Makes 5 dozen cookies.

BERLINER KRANZER

1½ cups soft butter
1 cup sugar
2 teaspoons grated orange rind
2 eggs, beaten
4 cups sifted all-purpose flour

Cream together the butter and sugar and stir in the orange rind and eggs. Add the flour and mix all together thoroughly. Chill the dough for at least 1 hour. Break off small pieces and roll out about 6 inches long and ¼ inch thick. Bring the ends together and tie into a single knot. Place on a lightly greased baking sheet and glaze with a light meringue made by beating 1 egg white until stiff and gradually beating into it 2 tablespoons sugar. Press bits of red candied cherries and green citron on the center of the knot to form berries and leaves. Bake at 400° F. for 10 minutes. Makes 6 dozen cookies.

NORWEGIAN MANDELKAKER

1 cup soft butter
½ cup sugar
1 egg, beaten
1⅔ cups sifted all-purpose flour
½ teaspoon double-action baking powder
3 teaspoons cinnamon
1 teaspoon ground cardamom
½ cup chopped toasted almonds

Cream together the butter and sugar and stir in the egg. Sift together the dry ingredients and add to the butter-sugar mixture, blending thoroughly. Mix in the almonds and chill the dough for at least 1 hour. Roll into little balls about 1 inch in diameter and place them on a greased baking sheet. Flatten them slightly and glaze the tops with 1 egg yolk slightly beaten with 1 tablespoon water. Top each cooky with half a blanched almond and bake at 375° F. for 10 minutes. Makes 4 dozen cookies.

SWEDISH SAND TARTS

⅓ cup blanched and dried almonds
4 unblanched almonds
⅞ cup soft butter
¾ cup sugar
1 egg, beaten
1¾ cups sifted all-purpose flour

Grind the almonds on the fine blade of the food chopper twice and mix into them thoroughly the butter, sugar, and egg. Then stir in the flour and chill the dough for at least 1 hour. Press the dough into tiny fluted tart forms to coat the inside. Place the molds on a baking sheet and bake at 350° F. for 12 minutes or until delicately browned. Loosen the cookies from the molds and turn them out on a wire rack to cool. Makes 3 dozen cookies.

ZUCKER HÜTCHEN

6 tablespoons soft butter
½ cup sugar
1 egg yolk
2 tablespoons heavy cream
1⅜ cups sifted all-purpose flour

½ teaspoon double-action baking powder
¼ teaspoon salt
¼ cup finely cut-up citron

Cream together the butter and sugar and stir in the egg yolk and cream. Sift together the dry ingredients and stir into the butter-sugar mixture. Mix in the citron. Chill the dough for 1 hour or more and then roll out ⅛ inch thick. Cut into 2-inch rounds. Heap 1 teaspoon Meringue in the center of each round to make it look like the crown of a little hat. Place them 1 inch apart on a greased baking sheet and bake at 350° F. for 12 minutes or until lightly browned. Makes 4 dozen cookies.

GOOSNARGH

4 cups sifted all-purpose flour
¼ cup fine granulated sugar
1 teaspoon coriander
1¾ cups butter

Sift together three times the flour, sugar, and coriander and finally sift it into a mixing bowl. Add the butter and with the hands work all the ingredients into a firm dough. Knead on lightly floured board and roll out ⅛ inch thick. Cut out with a 3-inch cutter, prick all over with the tines of a fork, and bake at 325° F. until delicately browned. When cool, dust with confectioners' sugar. Makes 3 dozen.

MARZIPAN COOKIES

2 cups blanched almonds
½ cup bitter almonds
2½ cups confectioners' sugar
2 egg whites, unbeaten

Dry the almonds overnight and grind very finely. Sift the sugar over them and mix thoroughly. Knead to a stiff paste, adding the egg whites gradually. More egg white may be added if needed. Roll with the hands, on a board sprinkled with confectioners' sugar, ½ inch thick and cut into crescents, hearts, etc. Bake until lightly browned at 325° F. for 30 minutes.

CHRISTMAS AND OTHER HOLIDAY COOKIES

Christmas cookies are as vital a part of our Yuletide preparations as are the plum puddings and the fruitcakes. In every Christian country throughout the world special festive cookies are made for Christmas. These we have borrowed in profusion and have incorporated them so intimately into our own holiday preparations that we no longer think of them as belonging to any country but our own. Spicy sugared cookies from Moravia, made in the shapes of animals, birds, and angels; large-tummied Santa Clauses from Belgium; fragile almond-flavored sand bakelser from Sweden; nut-studded strips from Finland; rich buttery shortbread from Scotland; gay little Berliner Kranzer wreaths and mandelkaker from Norway —all these and many more have become an essential part of our holiday preparations.

Butter cookies of all shapes—stars, bells, trees, toys, and animals, gaily decorated with colored icings and bits of candied fruits and nuts, accentuate the spirit of Christmas, but no cooky brings as much joy to the children throughout the world as the spicy gingerbread man, with an almond for a nose, raisins for eyes, and bits of candied-cherry buttons down his vest.

GINGERBREAD MAN

Trace the pattern for a gingerbread man or make your own design on cardboard, and cut it out. Flour the cut-out lightly and place it on the dough. Use any one of the gingerbread cooky doughs in this book. Cut carefully around the cut-out and place the cookies on a greased baking sheet. Make eyes, nose, and buttons from raisins, bits of candied fruit or nuts, and bake.

Decorate the baked gingerbread men with Quick Decorator's Frosting or Colored Sugar:

QUICK DECORATOR'S FROSTING. Mix about 1 tablespoon water with 1 cup confectioners' sugar to make a paste of a consistency that will hold its shape, yet soft enough to be easily forced through a pastry tube. Tint the paste with a drop of food coloring.

COLORED SUGAR Rub a drop of food coloring into a few tablespoons granulated sugar and place in a warm oven, with the door open, to dry.

OTHER SHAPES

Many children's books, even comic books, contain figures of animals and birds that may be traced on cardboard for cooky cut-outs.

STARS Bake in star shape. When cool, cover with Decorator's Frosting and sprinkle with blue sugar.

WREATHS Cut cookies out with a scalloped cutter. Remove the centers with a smaller scalloped cutter and bake. When cool, cover with white Decorator's Frosting, sprinkle with green sugar, and form clusters of berries and leaves from bits of candied cherries and green citron.

COOKY TREE ORNAMENTS Loop a piece of string and press the ends into the dough at the top of each cooky on the underside before baking. Decorate and hang on the Christmas tree.

MONKEY FACES Use any drop cooky dough. Place 3 raisins on each cooky to form the eyes and mouth. The cookies will take the shape of amusing faces during the baking.

VALENTINE COOKIES Make any rolled sugar cooky dough. Cut into heart shapes, brush with beaten egg white, and sprinkle with red sugar. Bake and decorate with red and white colored frosting.

GEORGE WASHINGTON'S BIRTHDAY Place halves of candied cherries rounded side up on cookies and form a stem and leaves from a little green citron. Or cut out cookies in the shape of a hatchet and decorate with cherries.

BIRTHDAY PLACE CARDS Cut sugar cookies into oblong shapes and bake. When cool, decorate and write names with colored icing.

FLOWER COOKIES Color sugar cooky dough with a little pink or yellow food coloring. Cut out with a scalloped cutter and bake. When cool, decorate with colored frosting and place a bit of cherry or fruit for the center.

TO PACK COOKIES FOR GIFTS

Cake tins, loaf pans, copper saucepans, or ring molds make attractive as well as useful containers in which to pack gift cookies. Line the container with wax paper, fill with your prettiest cookies, wrap in cellophane, and tie with a large, gay ribbon.

5. Pies, Pastries, and Puddings

There are pies for every taste and for every occasion. They may be broken down into five main classifications:
1. Two-crust pies
2. Open-faced, one-crust pies, tortes, and kuchens
3. Creamy and chiffon fillings for baked pie shells
4. Deep-dish pies
5. Individual pies, tarts, and turnovers

No pie can be any better than the pastry that complements it, and the making of tender, flaky pastry is largely a matter of experience and technique.

SHORTENING Butter, lard, or any of the commercial vegetable shortenings may be used. Each lends its own characteristic to the pastry, and the selection or combination chosen is, to a great extent, a matter of personal taste.

Some discriminating palates insist upon all butter. True, butter gives a fine flavor not obtained by any other shortening, but the moisture present in the butter develops the gluten of the flour and makes a crisp pastry, which is fine for very thin, delicate tart shells. The butter, however, should be washed. For very fine pastries the butter should be melted or clarified and then strained into a clean bowl, care being taken not to include the curds and sediment which settle to the bottom. The clarified butter should be chilled before using.

Lard is a great favorite with many, but it is extremely soft and tends to work out on the board, thereby requiring the use of additional flour, which produces a soft, inferior pastry. Pastry made from lard or suet has a flavor which is excellent for meat pies and casserole toppings but which is not so suitable for dessert pies. A fine quality leaf lard should be used.

Vegetable shortenings have a firm consistency which makes them ideal for piecrust, but lacking in flavor, owing to their blandness, if not combined with at least a little butter.

The ideal home pastry, tender and flavorful, is made from half vegetable shortening worked first into the flour until the mixture has the consistency of coarse corn meal. Then the butter is added and broken up with the finger tips into small nuggets and distributed evenly throughout the mixture.

Flakiness depends greatly on the proportion of shortening to flour used. The larger the amount of shortening, the flakier will be the crust.

WATER The liquid used in a plain pastry is generally water, although milk, buttermilk, eggs, and sour cream are used in many specialty pastries. A fine, flaky pastry may be completely ruined by the tricky business of adding the water to the fat and flour mixture. Too little water produces a crust that is crumbly rather than flaky, while too much water makes a tough, leathery crust. Since flour absorbs warm water more readily, the water used should be icy cold, and it should be distributed evenly throughout the fat-flour mixture until the particles adhere together.

Sprinkle the ice water over the fat and flour and press the particles gently together. Set aside any small lumps of dough that form until you have a firm ball of dough, which is easy to handle but neither sticky nor crumbly, and which cleans the bowl.

If the weather is warm or the room in which you work is overheated, chill the fat-flour mixture in the refrigerator before adding the ice water.

Roll out the pastry on a lightly floured board with a light, deft motion, rolling it from the center to the edge and keeping it circular. If it sticks, loosen it from the board or table with a spatula and give it a half twist. Try not to turn the dough over, as there is the danger of rolling in too much flour, which will toughen the pastry. Chilling the dough before rolling makes it easier to handle.

In general, pies should be baked for 10 minutes in a hot oven (450° F.). The temperature should then be lowered to moderate (350° F.), and the baking completed.

PLAIN PASTRY

INGREDIENTS FOR A TWO-CRUST 9-INCH PIE

2 cups sifted all-purpose flour
1 teaspoon salt
⅔ cup shortening
4 tablespoons ice water

METHOD

1. Sift flour and salt into a mixing bowl.
2. Add half the shortening and cut it into the flour and salt mixture, using two knives, cutting crosswise through the fat and flour until the mixture looks like coarse meal. You may also use a fork or pastry blender, or your finger tips, dipping them in the flour, and with the aid of the thumb breaking the shortening into small particles.
3. Add the remaining shortening and quickly work or cut it into small pieces about the size of navy beans or large peas.
4. Sprinkle the ice water lightly over the mixture and work it in gently. Add only enough water to make it possible to gather the dough together with the fingers so that it cleans the bowl. Form the dough into a ball, wrap in wax paper, and chill.
5. Cut the dough in half a little off center, using the larger part for the bottom crust, and roll it out on a lightly floured board. Roll it gently from the center to the edge, giving it a slight twist occasionally to keep it from sticking and to keep it circular, until it is large enough to fit the pan with a ½-inch overlap. It should not be more than ⅛ inch thick.
6. Fold the pastry in half and then into quarters and transfer it to the pan. Unfold it and fit it into the pan without stretching it. Allow it to cover the rim of the pan nicely and then trim off any overhanging edges with kitchen scissors.

7. Brush the surface with 1 teaspoon melted butter and place it in the refrigerator to chill.
8. Roll out the other half of the dough for the top crust, keeping it circular and a little thinner than the bottom crust. Make it large enough to extend 1 inch beyond the edge of the pan. Fold it in half and again into quarters and with a sharp knife make several slits through the pastry to allow for the escape of steam. Unfold onto wax paper, place on large plate or baking sheet, and chill in the refrigerator while preparing the filling.
9. Fill the pastry-lined pan with your desired filling. Moisten the edge of the pastry with a little cold water. Place the pastry top evenly over the filling, allowing it to fall loosely in place. Trim off any extra pieces with kitchen scissors, but leave ½ inch overhanging the edge of the pan.
10. Fold the overhanging edge neatly under the edge of the lower crust. Flute the edge by taking hold of the rim of pastry with the thumb and forefinger of both hands. Pull the rim held by the right hand toward you a little. Then move the right hand along the rim ½ inch and place the left thumb and forefinger in the indentation made by the right hand. Pull the right hand again toward you and repeat this all around the edge, making deep indentations until it is fluted.
11. Bake according to directions for each recipe.

FOR A SHINY TOP CRUST   Brush the top lightly with milk just before baking.

FOR A GLAZED CRUST   Brush the top with 1 egg yolk beaten lightly with 1 teaspoon cold water.

LATTICE-TOP PIES   Allow the bottom pastry to hang ½ inch over the edge of the pan. Roll the pastry for the top the exact size of the pan and cut it into strips ½ inch wide. Lay half the strips about 1 inch apart one way across the filling. Then place the other half of the strips diagonally across to make diamond-shaped openings. Seal the ends of the strips to the pastry on the edge of the pan. Moisten the overhanging edge with a little cold water, turn it over the ends of the strips, and flute in the regular way. The edge may be crimped with the tines of a fork, if you wish.

To interweave the strips, place half the strips one way on wax paper. Weave the other strips in and out across the other way, beginning with the center strip and working out to the sides. Chill thoroughly, transfer to the top of the filling, seal and flute.

PASTRY FOR A 6-INCH PIE   You will need only half the ingredients for a standard 6-inch pie.

SERVINGS

A 9-inch pie serves 8
An 8-inch pie serves 6
A 6-inch pie serves 4

FLAKY PASTRY

Make Plain Pastry and chill as usual. Roll it out lengthwise 1/3 inch thick and spread the surface with thin shavings of hard butter. Fold into thirds, lapping one part over the other, then roll out thin and fold again. Chill in the refrigerator for several hours or overnight before rolling out and lining pie plate.

RICH FLAKY PASTRY

Make Flaky Pastry as above and roll dough out lengthwise 1/3 inch thick. Spread the surface again with thin shavings of hard butter. Fold into thirds, lapping one part over the other, then roll out thin and fold again. Chill in the refrigerator for several hours or overnight before rolling out and lining pie plate and using for various other pastry desserts.

NOTE: Adding the flakes of butter once will make a pastry rich and flaky enough for ordinary use.

CHEESE PASTRY

Make Plain Pastry according to directions and roll it out very thin. Sprinkle it with grated American cheese, fold over, press the edges together, and roll out again. Fold as before and chill before using it to line the pie plate.

POT CHEESE PASTRY

INGREDIENTS FOR A TWO-CRUST, 9-INCH PIE

2 cups sifted all-purpose flour
1 tablespoon sugar
Pinch salt
1 cup butter
1/2 pound pot cheese
1/2 cup sour cream

Sift flour, sugar, and salt into a mixing bowl. Cut in the butter until the mixture is like coarse meal. Then cut in the cheese until it is distributed in fine pieces throughout the flour-butter mixture. Add cream to make a smooth dough, cover, and chill in the refrigerator overnight. Then roll out to line pie plate.

WALNUT PASTRY

This is a delicious pastry for fruit pies or tarts. Try it with a Honey Apple Pie.

INGREDIENTS FOR A TWO-CRUST 9-INCH PIE

1½ cups sifted all-purpose flour
Pinch salt
½ cup ground walnuts
½ cup butter
3 tablespoons ice water

Sift flour and salt into bowl. Add the walnuts and then cut in the butter. Add the ice water slowly to form a dough. Chill and roll out for a two-crust 9-inch pie.

SOUR CREAM PASTRY

INGREDIENTS FOR A TWO-CRUST 9-INCH PIE

2 cups sifted all-purpose flour
Pinch salt
1 tablespoon sugar
1 cup butter
1 egg yolk
1 cup sour cream

Sift flour, salt, and sugar into mixing bowl. Cut in the butter and add the egg yolk and enough of the sour cream to make a smooth dough. Roll out thin and fold like a napkin. Wrap in wax paper and chill in the refrigerator overnight. When ready to make the pie, roll out two crusts according to general directions.

CREAM CHEESE PASTRY

INGREDIENTS FOR A TWO-CRUST 9-INCH PIE

1 cup butter
8 ounces cream cheese
½ cup cream
Pinch salt
2½ cups sifted all-purpose flour

Cream together the butter and cheese until light and fluffy. Stir in the cream and salt and mix until all the ingredients are well combined. Stir in the flour and mix into a smooth dough. Chill in refrigerator before rolling out to line pie plate or tart tins or for various other pastries. This pastry will keep for several days in the refrigerator and is excellent used for:

APPLE CREAM PIE Roll out Cream Cheese Pastry and line plate in the regular fashion. Fill with thinly sliced apples in straight rows, spread thickly with sugar, dust with cinnamon, dot with butter, and bake at 350° F. for 35 minutes, or until the apples are tender. Remove from oven and pour over ½ cup heavy cream. Serve hot or cool.

COOKIES Roll out a small amount of Cream Cheese Pastry very thin. Boil 1 cup sugar with ⅓ cup water and a pinch cream of tartar until it spins a long thread. Add 1 cup ground pecans. Spread this filling along one half of the pastry and roll up like a jelly roll. Cut into slices ¼ inch thick, place on greased cooky sheet, and bake at 350° F. for 10 minutes, or until lightly browned.

STRAWBERRY TARTS Roll out a small amount of Cream Cheese Pastry very thinly, and cut it into circles about 2 inches in diameter. Spread half the circles with strawberry jam, cover with the other half of the circles sandwich fashion, and seal the edges together with the tines of a fork. Place the tarts on a greased baking sheet and bake at 350° F. for 10 minutes, or until lightly browned.

SWEET PASTRY

2 cups flour
1 cup sugar
½ cup shortening, part butter
2 eggs, beaten

Sift the flour and sugar into a mixing bowl. Cut in the shortening and add as much egg as necessary to make a pastry dough. Chill before rolling out. Roll out on a lightly floured board, line the pie plate with it and chill again before filling and baking.

FOR PUFFED STRIPS ON TOP Reserve one third of the dough and to it add 1 teaspoon baking powder and 2 tablespoons milk. Mix again and roll out. Cut into strips but do not cross them on top of the filling. These puffed strips are very nice for fruit or berry pies.

TWO-CRUST PIES

APPLE PIE

Use tart, juicy pie apples. Peel, quarter them, remove the cores, and slice thinly. The amount of sugar used depends on the tartness of the apples and the desired taste.

INGREDIENTS FOR A 9-INCH PIE

6 cups sliced apples
¾ to 1 cup sugar
1 teaspoon cinnamon or nutmeg
2 tablespoons butter

Fill a pastry-lined pie pan with the sliced apples. Sprinkle with sugar and cinnamon and dot with butter. Cover with pastry and bake at 450° F. for 10 minutes. Reduce heat to 350° F. and continue to bake for 30–40 minutes, or until the crust is nicely browned and the apples are soft when tested with a fork. Serve warm with a wedge of fine cheddar cheese, or with heavy cream.

APPLE PECAN RAISIN Sprinkle over the apples ½ cup seedless raisins and ½ cup chopped pecans. Dust the baked pie with confectioners' sugar and serve hot with heavy cream.

HONEY APPLE PIE

3 cups sliced apples
½ cup honey
2 tablespoons butter
1 teaspoon cinnamon
1 teaspoon vanilla
Pastry for two-crust pie

Fill a pastry-lined pie plate with the apples, pour over the honey, sprinkle with cinnamon, dot with butter, and sprinkle with vanilla. Adjust the top pastry and bake at 350° F. for 35 minutes. Walnut Pastry is delicious for this pie.

APPLE CRUMB PIE

Line a 9-inch pie plate with Sour Cream Pastry and fill with coarsely grated apples. Sprinkle over sugar to taste, a little cinnamon, and 2 tablespoons bread crumbs. Dot with butter and cover the top with pastry. Brush the surface with milk and bake at 450° F. for 10 minutes. Reduce temperature to 350° F. and bake for 25 minutes longer, or until the crust is a golden brown.

FRESH RHUBARB PIE

Select early tender strawberry rhubarb. Remove the leaves, wash the stalks, and cut into 1-inch pieces. The amount of sugar will have to be adjusted to the tartness of the rhubarb and to the individual taste.

INGREDIENTS FOR A 9-INCH PIE

2 pounds (4 cups) cut-up rhubarb
2 tablespoons flour
1½–2 cups sugar
2 tablespoons butter
Pastry for two-crust pie

Line a 9-inch pie plate with your favorite pastry and chill it thoroughly. Combine the flour and sugar and sprinkle one fourth of it over the bottom of the pastry. Fill with the rhubarb, piling it up in the center, and sprinkle with the remaining sugar and flour mixture. Dot with butter and cover with pastry. Sprinkle top crust with sugar and bake at 450° F. for 10 minutes. Reduce heat to 350° F. and bake for about 45 minutes longer, or until the crust is nicely browned and the rhubarb is soft.

FRESH CHERRY PIE

1 quart sour cherries, pitted
1 cup sugar
1 tablespoon cornstarch
Pastry for two-crust pie

Place the cherries and their juice in a saucepan. Add the sugar, which has been mixed with the cornstarch, bring to a boil, and cook, stirring, until slightly thickened. Line a 9-inch pie plate with pastry, fill with the fruit, and cover with a lattice topping. Bake at 375° F. for 45 minutes, or until the pie is delicately browned.

MINCEMEAT FOR PIE

The first mincemeat recipe of which we have record dates as far back as 1486. It was made of hare, pheasant, partridge, pigeons, and two conies, spiced and cooked. Down through the centuries this recipe became modified to what we know today as a combination of suet, meat, currants, and spices.

There are many formulae for mincemeat and much controversy as to what rightfully belongs in it. Here is one for those of you who wish to make your own, although many prefer to buy one of the many excellent cooked mincemeats in the stores today.

INGREDIENTS FOR FIVE 9-INCH PIES

½ pound lean boiled beef, chopped
½ pound beef kidney suet, chopped
3¾ pounds raw apples, peeled and chopped
½ pound currants
1 pound seeded raisins, chopped
1 tablespoon salt
3 ounces each candied orange rind, lemon rind, and citron, chopped
Grated rind of 2 lemons
5 cups brown sugar
3 tablespoons cinnamon
2 teaspoons nutmeg
1 teaspoon ginger
½ teaspoon ground cloves
5 cups cider

Combine all ingredients in a large kettle and simmer very gently for 2 hours, stirring occasionally. Cool and place in clean quart jars, seal tightly, and store in a cool place. It will keep for 6 months.

TO MAKE PIE

Line a 9-inch pie plate with pastry, fill with mincemeat, and cover the top with pastry according to standard directions. Bake at 450° F. for 10 minutes, reduce temperature to 350° F. and continue baking for about 30 minutes longer. While the pie is still hot, insert a small funnel into one of the slits in the crust and pour in ¼ cup brandy. Serve warm.

FRESH PEAR PIE

8 large pears
½ cup sugar
1 tablespoon lemon juice
Grated rind of ½ lemon
½ teaspoon vanilla
Nutmeg
Pastry for two-crust pie

Line a 9-inch pie plate with pastry. Peel, quarter, and halve the pears and then slice them as you would an apple. Fill the pastry-lined pan with the slices, sprinkle over them the sugar, lemon juice, lemon rind, vanilla, and a dusting of nutmeg. Cover with a lattice topping and bake at 450° F. for 10 minutes. Reduce the heat to 350° F. and bake for another 30 minutes, or until the piecrust is lightly browned and the pears are tender.

FRESH PLUM PIE

3 cups pitted fresh plums
1¼ cups sugar
2 tablespoons flour
Pinch salt
2 tablespoons lemon juice
Pastry for two-crust pie

Line a 9-inch pie plate with pastry and fill with the plums. Combine the sugar, flour, and salt and sprinkle over the plums. Sprinkle with the lemon juice and cover with pastry. Bake at 450° F. for 10 minutes, reduce temperature to 350° F. and bake for another 35 minutes.

FRESH PEACH PIE

8 peaches
1 cup sugar
2 tablespoons flour
Pinch salt
½ teaspoon almond extract
Pastry for two-crust pie

Peel peaches, remove the pits, and slice. Line a pie plate with pastry and fill it with the peaches. Combine the sugar, flour, and salt and sprinkle over the peaches. Drip over the almond extract, cover with pastry, and bake at 450° F. for 15 minutes. Reduce oven temperature to 350° F. and bake for another 30 minutes. Serve warm.

FRESH PINEAPPLE PIE

2 eggs
1½ cups sugar
1 tablespoon lemon juice
3 cups shredded fresh pineapple
Pastry for two-crust pie

Beat the eggs slightly and combine with the sugar, lemon juice, and pineapple. Line a pie plate with pastry and pour in the filling. Cover with pastry and bake at 450° F. for 10 minutes. Reduce oven temperature to 350° F. and bake for another 30 minutes, or until the crust is nicely browned and the pineapple is tender.

TO USE CANNED PINEAPPLE Reduce sugar to ½ cup.

PINEAPPLE AND STRAWBERRY PIE Use 1½ cups shredded fresh pineapple and 1½ cups sliced strawberries.

RAISIN PIE

⅓ cup lemon juice
1 teaspoon grated lemon rind
½ cup orange juice
2 teaspoons grated orange rind
1 cup light brown sugar
Pinch salt
2 cups seeded raisins
1¾ cups water
4½ tablespoons flour
Pastry for two-crust pie

Combine the lemon juice and rind, orange juice and rind, sugar, salt, raisins, and 1½ cups of the water and heat to boiling. Mix the flour to a paste with the remaining water and stir gradually into the hot mixture. Cook, stirring, for about 5 minutes, or until thickened. Line a pie plate with pastry, pour in the filling, and cover the top with pastry or with a lattice topping. Bake at 450° F. for 10 minutes, reduce oven temperature to 350° F. and bake for another 30 minutes.

BLUEBERRY OR BLACKBERRY PIE

3 cups berries
½–¾ cup sugar
1 tablespoon flour
⅛ teaspoon salt
Pastry for two-crust pie

Wash and sort the berries. Line a 9-inch pie plate with pastry and fill it with the berries. Combine the sugar, flour, and salt and sprinkle over the berries. Cover with pastry and bake at 450° F. for 10 minutes. Reduce temperature to 350° F. and bake for another 35–40 minutes, or until the crust is nicely browned and the berries are tender.

CRANBERRY PIE

1 pound cranberries
2 cups sugar
2 tablespoons flour
Pinch salt
Pastry for two-crust pie

Wash the cranberries and cut them in half. Line a 9-inch pie plate with pastry and fill it with the cranberries. Combine the sugar, flour and salt and sprinkle over the top of the berries. Dot with butter, and cover with pastry. Bake at 450° F. for 15 minutes. Reduce the temperature to 350° F. and bake for another 35 minutes. Serve hot or warm. One half cup seeded raisins makes a nice addition to this pie.

PRUNE PIE

1 pound prunes
½ cup sugar
1 tablespoon lemon juice
1 tablespoon butter
½ teaspoon cinnamon
Pastry for two-crust pie

Wash prunes and soak for 30 minutes in hot water to cover, add sugar and lemon juice, then cook them slowly in the same water until almost soft. Drain, reserving the juice, remove the stones, and cut the prunes in half. Line a pie plate with pastry and put in it the prunes. Cook the prune juice until it has reduced to about 2 tablespoons and pour this liquor over the prunes in the pie plate. Dot with butter, sprinkle with cinnamon, and cover the top with pastry or with a lattice topping. Bake at 450° F. for 10 minutes, reduce temperature to 350° F. and bake for another 30 minutes, or until the crust is lightly browned.

FRESH STRAWBERRY OR RASPBERRY PIE

3 cups berries
1 cup sugar
1 tablespoon cornstarch
Pinch salt
Pastry for two-crust pie

Wash the berries, sort, and hull them. Line a 9-inch pie plate with pastry and fill it with the berries. Mix together the sugar, cornstarch, and salt and sprinkle the mixture over the top of the berries. Dot with butter. Cover with pastry or with a lattice topping and bake at 450° F. for 10 minutes. Reduce temperature to 350° F. and bake for another 30 minutes, or until the crust is nicely browned. Serve slightly warm.

GRAPE PIE

4 cups Concord grapes
¾ cup sugar
1½ tablespoons lemon juice
1 tablespoon orange rind

      1 tablespoon quick-cooking tapioca
      Pastry for two-crust pie

Slip the pulp out of the grapeskins, reserving the skins. Cook the pulp over a low flame, stirring, until the seeds loosen and then press it through a sieve to remove the seeds. Combine the pulp and skins with the sugar, lemon juice, orange rind, and tapioca and mix thoroughly. Allow the mixture to stand for 5 minutes while you line a 9-inch pie plate with pastry. Pour the filling into the lined plate and place a lattice of pastry over the top. Bake at 450° F. for 10 minutes, lower the heat to 350° F. and bake for 30 minutes longer, or until the crust is nicely browned.

VINEGAR PIE

      2 cups water
      1 cup brown sugar
      1 cup vinegar
      2 tablespoons butter
      ½ cup flour
      Pastry for two-crust pie

Combine the water, sugar, and vinegar, and bring the mixture to a boil. Add the butter and stir until it melts, and then stir in the flour, which has been mixed to a smooth paste with a little cold water. Continue to stir until the mixture is thick. Line a 9-inch pie plate with pastry, pour the filling into the crust, and cover it with lattice strips of pastry. Bake at 450° F. for 10 minutes, reduce the heat to 350° F. and bake about 25 minutes longer, or until the pastry is delicately browned and the filling is firm.

TORTA DE RICOTTA

      1½ pounds ricotta
      ¼ pound toasted almonds, chopped
      4 eggs
      ⅓ cup sugar
      1 teaspoon vanilla
      Flaky Pastry

Line a 9-inch pie plate with Flaky Pastry and cut enough strips to make a lattice topping. Rub the cheese through a fine sieve and stir into it the chopped almonds. Beat the eggs with the sugar until well combined and fluffy and add to the cheese mixture along with the vanilla. Beat until the mixture is smooth and thoroughly blended. Turn into the prepared pie plate, place lattice strips of pastry over the top, pinching the edges firmly together. Bake at 350° F. for about 45 minutes, or until the filling is firm and the pastry is golden brown. Remove from the oven and cool before serving. Sprinkle the top generously with confectioners' sugar.

ONE-CRUST PIES

Use only half the ingredients that you would use for a two-crust pie and follow the directions for making pastry. Do not divide the dough in half, but roll it out on a lightly floured board into a circle 1 inch larger all around than the pan. Fit the pastry loosely into the pan, trim off the ragged edges with kitchen scissors, leaving ½ inch overhanging. Moisten the rim of the pie pan with a little cold water. Fold the overhanging pastry back and under, pressing it onto the moist rim. Flute the edge in the usual way and brush the surface with 1 teaspoon melted butter. Chill thoroughly before adding the desired filling. Fill and bake according to directions with each recipe.

CUSTARD PIE

3 whole eggs or 6 yolks
½ cup sugar
¼ teaspoon salt
¼ teaspoon nutmeg
2⅔ cups milk
Pastry for one-crust pie

Beat the eggs or yolks slightly, beat in the sugar, salt, nutmeg, and milk. Line a 9-inch pie plate with pastry and chill as usual. Pour in the custard and bake at 450° F. for 15 minutes. Reduce the temperature to 350° F. and bake for another 15 minutes until almost set. Custard pies should be still a bit soft in the center when removed from the oven. The pie will continue to cook after removal from the oven long enough to set the center. Serve cold.

COCONUT CUSTARD PIE Substitute 1 teaspoon vanilla for the nutmeg and add 1 cup shredded coconut to the custard mixture. Sprinkle a little more coconut over the top and bake as above.

RICH CUSTARD PIE, *Crème de la Crème*

3 cups heavy cream
⅓ cup sugar
6 egg yolks
Vanilla
Flaky Pastry for one-crust pie

Heat the cream over boiling water until it is hot but not scalding.

Stir in the sugar until it is thoroughly dissolved. Beat the egg yolks lightly and pour over them the hot cream, stirring constantly. Flavor with vanilla. Line a 9-inch pie plate with Flaky Pastry and sprinkle over the bottom ½ cup brown sugar. Pour in the custard and bake at 350° F. for 35 minutes, or until almost set in the center. Serve with a fruit sauce or Sabayon Sauce.

APPLE OR PEACH CUSTARD PIE

2 large apples or peaches
3 eggs, separated
⅔ cup sugar plus 6 tablespoons
2 cups milk
3 tablespoons nuts, finely chopped
Pastry for one-crust pie

Make your favorite pastry for a one-crust pie, line a 9-inch pie plate, and chill as usual. Peel, core, and slice the apples or peaches and place them on the bottom of the pastry. Beat the egg yolks and the ⅔ cup sugar until they are well combined and then gradually beat in the milk. Pour this egg-sugar-milk mixture over the sliced fruit and bake at 450° F. for 10 minutes. Reduce oven temperature to 325° F. for 30 minutes. Cool and top with a meringue made by beating the egg whites until stiff and then gradually beating into them the 6 tablespoons sugar. Fold in the nuts and bake at 350° F. for 15 minutes, or until the meringue is lightly browned.

RASPBERRY CUSTARD PIE

2 cups hot milk
4 tablespoons sugar
6 egg yolks, beaten
1 box raspberries
3 tablespoons sherry
Whipped cream
Pastry for one-crust pie

Combine the milk and sugar and pour gradually over the beaten egg yolks, stirring rapidly. Line a 9-inch pie plate with pastry and strain into it the custard mixture. Bake at 350° F. for 35 minutes, or until almost set in the middle. Cool. Wash and pick over the raspberries and pass them through a fine sieve. Sweeten the resulting purée with sugar to taste. Pour the sherry over the surface of the custard, spread a layer of the raspberry purée on top, and serve with whipped cream.

WINE CUSTARD PIE

2 cups white wine
½ cup sugar
6 egg yolks, slightly beaten
2 tablespoons heavy cream
2 teaspoons sherry
Flaky Pastry for one-crust pie

In the top of a double boiler combine the white wine and sugar. Heat but do not boil. When hot, pour it over the egg yolks, stirring constantly. Stir in the cream and sherry. Line a 9-inch pie plate with Flaky Pastry, strain into it the custard, and bake at 350° F. for 45 minutes. Serve this pie very cold, garnished with brandied cherries, if desired.

PUMPKIN PIE

2 cups mashed pumpkin, fresh, frozen, or canned
½ teaspoon salt
2 cups rich milk
2 eggs, beaten
⅔ cup brown sugar
2 tablespoons granulated sugar
2 teaspoons cinnamon
½ teaspoon nutmeg
½ teaspoon ginger
¼ teaspoon ground cloves
Pastry for one-crust pie

Make your favorite pastry for a one-crust pie, line a 9-inch pie plate, and chill as usual. Combine the ingredients in the order given and strain into the chilled pastry-lined pie pan. Bake at 450° F. for 15 minutes. Reduce temperature to 350° F. and bake for about 40 minutes longer, or until almost set in the center. Serve warm or cold and garnished with sweetened whipped cream, if desired.

PUMPKIN CREAM PIE

2 cups strained, cooked pumpkin, fresh, frozen, or canned
2 teaspoons cinnamon
⅔ cup brown sugar
½ teaspoon ginger
½ teaspoon salt
1½ cups milk
2 eggs, well beaten
½ cup heavy cream
Pastry for one-crust pie

ABOVE, Holiday Cake, with confectioners' sugar decoration, p. 195. BELOW, Flower Cake, p. 196

Strawberry Shortcake made with Rich Baking Powder Biscuits, p. 73

Fruitcakes, pp. 159–62

Brownies, p. 209

Fig-filled Cookies, p. 232

Refrigerator, Dropped, and Rolled Cookies

Chocolate and Vanilla Pinwheels, p. 219

Deep-dish Peach Pie, p. 297

Fresh Cherry Pie, p. 260

Open Peach Pie

Old-time Tarts

Chocolate Cream Pie and Tarts, p. 285

Combine the pumpkin, cinnamon, sugar, ginger, and salt. Add slowly the milk and beat with a rotary beater until thoroughly blended. If you have a blender, use it instead of the rotary beater to blend the mixture. Stir in the eggs and cream. Line a 9-inch pie plate with your favorite pastry and pour in the pumpkin mixture. Sprinkle the top with cinnamon and bake at 325° F. for 50 minutes. Serve warm with whipped cream, if desired.

NEW ENGLAND SQUASH PIE

2 cups squash purée
1 cup sugar
1 teaspoon cinnamon
1 teaspoon nutmeg
¼ teaspoon salt
½ teaspoon ginger
¼ teaspoon mace
3 eggs, beaten
1 cup heavy cream
4 tablespoons brandy
Pastry for one-crust pie

Steam squash, peel it, and rub enough through a sieve to make 2 cups purée. Allow it to cool while you line a 9-inch pie plate with pastry. Stir into the cooled purée the sugar, cinnamon, nutmeg, salt, ginger, and mace and mix thoroughly. Then stir in the eggs, cream, and brandy. Pour the mixture into the pastry-lined plate and bake at 450° F. for 10 minutes. Reduce the temperature to 350° F. and bake for about 40 minutes longer, or until almost set in the center. Serve warm or cold and garnished with whipped cream, sweetened and flavored to taste.

KENTUCKY CHESS PIE

3 egg yolks
1 egg white
1 cup sugar
2 tablespoons flour
½ cup melted butter
5 tablespoons milk
½ teaspoon vanilla
Pastry for one-crust pie

Beat the egg yolks and the white. Combine the sugar and flour and add to the eggs. Stir in the butter, milk, and vanilla. Line an 8-inch pie plate with pastry and pour the mixture into it. Bake at 400° F.

for 35 minutes, or until set. When it is cool, cover it with meringue and bake at 300° F. for 15 minutes, or until the meringue is lightly browned.

SHOOFLY PIE

1 cup boiling water
¾ teaspoon soda
¾ cup molasses
2 cups sifted flour
1 cup brown sugar
½ cup butter
Pinch salt
Pastry for one-crust pie

Pour the boiling water over the soda and stir it into the molasses. Line a 9-inch pie plate with pastry and chill as usual. In a bowl combine the flour, sugar, butter, and salt. Rub the mixture between the hands until it forms crumbs. Pour the molasses mixture into the pastry shell, sprinkle the crumbs on top, and bake at 350° F. for 35 minutes, or until the crumbs are golden.

MOLASSES PIE

½ cup pecan meats, broken
3 eggs
1 tablespoon flour
1 cup sugar
1 cup molasses
2 tablespoons melted butter
Pinch salt
Pastry for one-crust pie

Make your favorite pastry for a one-crust pie, line an 8-inch pie plate, and chill as usual. Sprinkle the nuts on the bottom. Beat the eggs, flour, and sugar together until well combined. Add the molasses, melted butter, and salt and mix thoroughly. Pour over the nuts in the crust and bake at 450° F. for 10 minutes. Reduce temperature to 300° F. and bake for another 30 minutes. Cool and top with whipped cream, if desired.

SWEET POTATO PIE

4 eggs, beaten
1½ cups mashed sweet potatoes
⅓ cup sugar
2 tablespoons honey

⅔ cup milk
½ cup crushed black walnuts
⅓ cup orange juice
1 teaspoon vanilla
Pastry for one-crust pie
1 cup cream, whipped
1 tablespoon grated orange peel
½ teaspoon nutmeg

Combine the sweet potatoes, eggs, and sugar. Add the honey, milk, nuts, orange juice, and vanilla and mix thoroughly. Line a 9-inch pie plate with pastry and pour in the sweet potato mixture. Bake at 450° F. for 10 minutes. Reduce the temperature to 350° F. and bake for another 30 minutes, or until almost firm. Cool and spread the top with the whipped cream, which has been mixed with the grated orange peel and the nutmeg.

Crushed pineapple or apricot purée may be substituted for the walnuts, if desired.

PECAN PIE

4 eggs, beaten
1 cup light brown sugar
1 tablespoon flour
1 cup dark corn syrup
Pinch salt
3 tablespoons melted butter
1 cup pecan meats, coarsely chopped
2 teaspoons vanilla
Pastry for one-crust pie

Combine the eggs, sugar, and flour. Stir in the corn syrup, salt, melted butter, pecan meats, and vanilla. Line a 9-inch pie plate with pastry and pour into it the filling. Bake at 450° F. for 10 minutes. Reduce oven temperature to 350° and bake for 30 minutes longer. Chill and serve with whipped cream, sweetened and flavored to taste.

SOUR CREAM PECAN PIE

1 teaspoon flour
½ teaspoon ground cinnamon
¼ teaspoon ground cloves
1 cup thick sour cream
2 eggs, well beaten
1 cup sugar
1 teaspoon grated lemon rind

1½ cups broken pecan meats
Pastry for one-crust pie

Combine the flour, cinnamon, and cloves and blend with a little of the sour cream to make a smooth paste. Stir in the rest of the sour cream, the eggs, sugar, and lemon rind. Line an 8-inch pie plate with pastry and distribute the pecan meats evenly over the bottom. Pour over the pecan meats the sour cream-egg mixture and bake at 450° F. for 10 minutes. Reduce the temperature to 325° F. and bake for about 40 minutes longer, or until the filling is almost set in the middle. Serve hot or cold.

FUDGE PIE

½ cup butter
1 cup sugar
1 teaspoon vanilla
2 egg yolks, unbeaten
2 squares (ounces) unsweetened chocolate, melted
⅓ cup sifted flour
2 egg whites
⅛ teaspoon salt
½ cup heavy cream, whipped
2 tablespoons chopped pecan meats
Pastry for one-crust pie

Cream the butter, add the sugar gradually, and cream together until light and fluffy. Add vanilla and blend. Add the egg yolks, one at a time, beating well after each addition. Add the melted chocolate and mix well. Add the flour and blend. Beat the egg whites with salt until stiff but not dry and fold into the batter. Line a 9-inch pie shell with pastry and pour the mixture into it. Bake at 375° F. for 45 minutes, or until pie is completely puffed across top. Cool. Top with whipped cream and sprinkle with pecan meats.

The same chocolate filling baked in a greased pie pan at 375° F. for 35 minutes, which has *not* been lined with pastry, can then be served in pie-shaped pieces, something like a moist brownie in triangle shape.

COTTAGE CHEESE PIE

1 pint cottage cheese
1 cup sugar
2 eggs, beaten
1 teaspoon butter

Pinch salt
¼ teaspoon nutmeg
Pastry for one-crust pie

Cream the cottage cheese with the sugar until well blended. Stir in the eggs, butter, salt, and nutmeg, mix thoroughly, and put through a fine sieve to remove any lumps. Turn into an 8-inch unbaked pie shell and bake at 325° F. for 40 minutes.

PINEAPPLE CHEESE PIE

½ pound cottage cheese
1 cup sugar
¼ cup soft butter
½ cup sifted all-purpose flour
¼ teaspoon salt
2 eggs
¾ cup milk, scalded and cooled
1 teaspoon vanilla
2½ cups (No. 2 can) crushed pineapple
1 tablespoon cornstarch
¼ cup water
Pastry for one-crust pie

Rub the cheese through a fine sieve, add slowly the sugar, and mix thoroughly. Add the butter and beat until the mixture is light and well combined. Stir in the flour and salt. Add the eggs, one at a time, alternately with the milk, beating well after each addition. Stir in the vanilla. Heat the crushed pineapple. Make a paste of the cornstarch and water and stir into the hot pineapple. Let the thickened pineapple cool and then turn it into an unbaked 9-inch pie shell. Pour the cheese mixture over this and bake at 450° F. for 10 minutes. Reduce the temperature to 350° F. and bake for 30 minutes longer, or until the cheese is set. Chill the pie before serving it.

SWITZERLAND SWISS CHEESE PIE

½ pound grated Switzerland Swiss cheese
1 tablespoon flour
3 eggs
1 cup light cream
Rich Flaky Pastry for one-crust pie

Dredge the cheese with the flour and spread it evenly over the bottom of a 9-inch pie plate which has been lined with Rich Flaky Pastry. Beat the eggs thoroughly, combine them with the light cream, and pour this mixture over the grated cheese. Bake at 400°

F. for 15 minutes, then reduce the heat to 300° F. and continue to bake for 30 minutes, or until almost set.

CHOCOLATE CAKE PIE

1 cup sugar
2 tablespoons all-purpose flour
Pinch salt
3 eggs, separated
2 squares (ounces) unsweetened chocolate, melted
1 cup rich milk
Pastry for one-crust pie

Make your favorite pastry, line a 9-inch pie plate, and chill as usual. Sift together the sugar, flour, and salt. Beat the egg yolks until light and fluffy and stir in the sifted dry ingredients. Stir in the melted chocolate and the milk. Beat the egg whites until stiff and fold in the chocolate-egg yolk mixture. Pour into the prepared pan and bake at 450° F. for 15 minutes. Reduce the temperature to 350° F. and bake for another 30 minutes.

PINEAPPLE CAKE PIE Omit the chocolate and add 1 teaspoon grated lemon rind, 2 tablespoons lemon juice, and ½ cup drained crushed pineapple.

STRAWBERRY CAKE PIE Omit the chocolate and add 1 tablespoon lemon juice and ½ cup strawberry purée.

LEMON CAKE PIE

½ cup butter
1 cup sugar plus 2 tablespoons
4 eggs, separated
2 tablespoons all-purpose flour
Grated rind of 1 lemon
Juice of 2 lemons
1 cup rich milk
Pastry for one-crust pie

Cream the butter and sugar. Beat the egg yolks until light and stir into the butter-sugar mixture along with the flour and the grated lemon rind. Add the lemon juice and milk and mix thoroughly. Beat the egg whites until stiff and fold them into the lemon custard. Turn into a 9-inch pie plate, which has been lined with pastry, and bake at 450° F. for 15 minutes. Reduce oven temperature to 350° F. and bake for another 30 minutes.

FRUIT-FILLED TORTES

PÂTE BRISÉE, *Flan Pastry*

1 cup flour
1 egg yolk
1 tablespoon sugar
½ cup butter
Grated rind of 1 lemon
Pinch salt

Sift the flour onto a pastry board or into a bowl. Make a well in the center of the flour and put into it the egg yolk, sugar, butter, lemon rind, and salt. Mix these center ingredients into a smooth paste and then quickly work in the flour, adding a very little ice water to moisten the dough, if necessary. Press the dough, with the fingers, into a 9-inch pie plate, or chill it for 1 hour in the refrigerator and roll it out ¼ inch thick to fit a flan ring. This paste or dough is known also as Pâte à Foncer, or Mürbe Teig, and is used for many types of kuchens, fruit pies, and desserts.

Chill the lined pie plate or flan ring for 30 minutes before covering it with fruit, sugar, and spices.

SOUR CREAM PASTRY FOR OPEN FRUIT PIES

1 cup butter
2¼ cups sifted all-purpose flour
2 teaspoons sugar
Pinch salt
2 egg yolks
1 tablespoon lemon juice
½–¾ cup thick sour cream

Work the butter with ¼ cup of the flour to a smooth paste and chill it in the refrigerator. Sift the remaining flour, sugar, and salt into a mixing bowl. Stir in the egg yolks, lemon juice, and enough sour cream to make a smooth dough. Roll out the dough to a thickness of ½ inch and flatten the butter paste in the center of it. Fold the ends of the dough over the butter, dust lightly with flour, and lightly roll out again quite thin. Fold into thirds, lapping one part over the other, and chill in the refrigerator for 1 hour. Roll out and chill again three times before using for lining a pie plate.

APPLE OR PEACH TORTE

Line a pie plate or flan ring with Pâte Brisée. Core, pare, and cut the fruit into eighths. Place the sections in circles on top of the dough. Sprinkle over ½ cup sugar and ½ teaspoon nutmeg or 1 teaspoon cinnamon. Dot generously with butter and bake at 350° F. for 15 minutes. Beat the yolk of an egg with 3 tablespoons heavy cream and drip this over the fruit. Continue baking for 20 minutes, or until the dough is lightly browned and the fruit is tender.

PRUNE KUCHEN

Wash 1 quart fresh prune plums, make four incisions lengthwise to within ½ inch of one end and remove the pits. Place these upright in an attractive pattern on top of a pie plate or flan ring lined with Pâte Brisée. Sprinkle with ¾ cup sugar, 1 tablespoon lemon juice, and 1 teaspoon cinnamon. Dot with butter and bake at 350° F. for 45 minutes, or until the dough is lightly browned and the fruit is tender.

BLUEBERRY TORTE

Line a pie plate or flan ring with Pâte Brisée. Wash and pick over 1 quart blueberries and fill the lined pan with them. Sprinkle with ½ cup sugar, 2 tablespoons lemon juice, and 1 teaspoon cinnamon. Bake at 350° F. for 15 minutes. Beat the yolk of an egg with 3 tablespoons heavy cream and drip this over the berries. Continue to bake for another 20 minutes, or until the dough is lightly browned.

GOOSEBERRY TORTE

Line a pie plate or flan ring with Pâte Brisée. Wash and pick over 1 quart ripe gooseberries and fill the lined pan with them. Sprinkle over them 1 cup sugar and bake at 350° F. for 20 minutes. Beat the yolk of an egg with 3 tablespoons heavy cream and drip this over the berries. Continue to bake for another 15 minutes, or until the dough is lightly browned and the fruit is tender.

CHERRY TORTE COUNTRY STYLE

This may be made as either a pudding or a pie. For a pudding, do not line the pie plate with pastry. For a pie, line a 9-inch pie plate with Flaky Pastry or Pâte Brisée. Fill the pastry with 2 cups sweet pitted cherries. Combine the following ingredients and pour over the cherries:
    1 egg, beaten
    3 tablespoons flour

½ cup heavy cream
1 tablespoon sugar
Pinch salt

Bake at 375° F. for 30–35 minutes, or until the top is browned.

APPLESAUCE TORTE

Line a pie plate with Pâte Brisée. Fill the lined plate three fourths full with sweetened applesauce and then arrange thin apple slices on top, overlapping them in an orderly fashion. Sprinkle with sugar and bake at 350° F. for 35 minutes, or until the crust is browned. When cool, glaze the top with Apricot Glaze.

CHERRY KUCHEN

PASTRY
1½ cups sifted all-purpose flour
Pinch salt
1 tablespoon sugar
½ teaspoon double-action baking powder
½ cup butter
2 egg yolks, beaten
2 tablespoons water

FILLING
1 quart cherries
½–¾ cup sugar
1 teaspoon cornstarch
2 eggs, beaten
½ cup heavy cream
½ teaspoon salt

Sift together into a mixing bowl the flour, salt, sugar, and baking powder. Cut in the butter until the mixture is like coarse meal. Add the beaten egg yolks and as much of the water as needed to make a pastry dough. Chill the dough for 1 hour and then spread it out ⅛ inch thick into a 9×12-inch baking pan, pressing it with the palm of the hand. Bake at 450° F. for 15 minutes.

Pit the cherries and drain them, reserving the juice. Mix them with the sugar and spread them over the tart shell. Bake at 375° F. for 10 minutes and then allow the kuchen to cool.

Moisten the cornstarch with a little cold water and stir it into the cherry juice. Add the eggs, cream, and salt and cook, stirring, over boiling water until the mixture is thick. Cool slightly and pour over the cherries.

BLUEBERRY KUCHEN

Make Sour Cream Pastry for Open Fruit Pies or the same pastry as that used for the Cherry Kuchen, chill, line a flan ring or 9-inch pie plate with it, and bake at 450° F. for 15 minutes.

    1 quart blueberries
    1 cup sugar
    2 tablespoons lemon juice
    ½ cup heavy cream
    3 egg yolks, beaten
    ⅛ teaspoon salt

Mix the blueberries and ½ cup of the sugar together and turn them into the partially baked kuchen shell. Bake at 375° F. for 10 minutes, sprinkle the berries with the lemon juice, and then allow the kuchen to cool.

Combine the cream, egg yolks, salt, and the remaining sugar and cook, stirring, over boiling water until the mixture is thick. Cool slightly and pour over the blueberries.

HUNGARIAN PLUM PITÉ

    ½ cup butter
    1 cup sugar
    2 eggs
    1 cup flour
    1 teaspoon double-action baking powder
    Pinch salt
    ½ teaspoon almond extract
    1 quart plums
    1 teaspoon cinnamon
    Whipped cream

Cream the butter until light and fluffy. Add ½ cup of the sugar and cream together thoroughly. Add 1 egg and beat well. Add the other egg and beat until the mixture is light. Sift together the flour, baking powder, and salt and stir into the egg-butter-sugar mixture until well mixed. Stir in the almond extract. Spread the mixture into a buttered deep square pan. Cut the plums in halves, remove pits, and place them in rows over the batter, skin side down, pressing them slightly into the dough. Sprinkle with the other ½ cup sugar and the cinnamon and bake at 350° F. for about 30 minutes. Cut into squares and serve with sweetened and flavored whipped cream.

MAGDALENA PIE

Make Graham Cracker Pastry Shell to fit 8-inch pie tin.

FILLING

1 cup brown sugar
4 tablespoons butter
1 cup fresh cranberries
1 large apple, cored and thinly sliced
¼ cup raisins

Combine all the ingredients in a saucepan and cook over medium flame for about 5 minutes, stirring constantly. Lower the flame, cover the saucepan, and continue cooking until the apple slices are soft, or for about 10 minutes. Pour the mixture into the prepared shell and bake at 350° F. for 10 minutes. When cool, spread the top of the pie with a topping made of 1 jar yogurt and 6 tablespoons honey mixed together. The topping may be sprinkled with a few graham cracker crumbs, if desired.

CREAM AND CUSTARD PIES

BAKED PASTRY SHELLS

Roll out pastry, line pan, flute the edge, and chill as usual. After chilling, prick the surface of the pastry with a fork to release the air between the crust and the pan and to prevent it from puffing during the baking. Bake in a very hot oven (450° F.) for 15 minutes, or until a golden brown. Cool thoroughly before adding the filling.

MERINGUE TOPPING

2 egg whites
Pinch salt
¼ teaspoon cream of tartar
6 tablespoons fine granulated sugar

Beat egg whites with the salt until frothy, add the cream of tartar, and continue beating until the whites are stiff enough to hold a peak when the beater is withdrawn. Add the sugar very gradually, beating until all the sugar has been added and the mixture is stiff and glossy. Pile the meringue lightly on cooled pie filling, allowing it to touch the edge of the crust all the way around to prevent it from shrinking. Make attractive swirls or peaks. Bake at 350° F. for 15 minutes, or until a delicate brown. Allow to cool at room temperature.

BRAZIL NUT PASTRY SHELL

Mix 2 cups ground brazil nuts with 4 tablespoons sugar and press it firmly onto the bottom and sides of a 9-inch pie plate.

MERINGUE PASTRY SHELL

3 egg whites
Pinch salt
¼ teaspoon cream of tartar
¾ cup fine granulated sugar
1 teaspoon vanilla

Beat the egg whites and salt until foamy. Add the cream of tartar and continue to beat until the egg whites will stand in a soft peak when the beater is withdrawn. Gradually beat in the sugar, about 1 tablespoon at a time, and continue to beat until the sugar is completely blended and the mixture is very stiff and glossy. Beat in the vanilla. Spread the meringue thickly over the bottom and sides, building it up a good ½ inch above the edge of the plate to form a nestlike shell. Bake the shell at 300° F. for 50 minutes, or until the meringue is dry and delicately colored. Loosen it from the pan while still warm and allow it to cool before adding the filling.

ZWIEBACK PASTRY SHELL

Crush 1 box zwieback with a rolling pin and put through a sieve. Crush again any large pieces which remain in the sieve. Combine 1½ cups crumbs with 3 tablespoons sugar and ¼ cup melted butter. Butter a pie plate generously and press the mixture on the sides and bottom. Chill in refrigerator for a short time. Zwieback pastry shells may be flavored with a little grated lemon rind and a little cinnamon, if desired.

GRAHAM CRACKER PASTRY SHELL Make the same as for Zwieback Pastry Shell.

WAFER SHELL

Crush 1 box vanilla, chocolate, or ginger wafers and put through a sieve. Crush again any large pieces which remain in the sieve. Mix the crumbs with ¼ cup each sugar and melted butter. Butter a pie plate generously and pat the cooky crumbs thickly over the bottom and sides. Chill in the refrigerator for a short time.

CORNFLAKE SHELL

Combine 2 cups crushed cornflakes with ½ cup melted butter, 4 tablespoons sugar, and 1 teaspoon cinnamon. Press on bottom and sides of a buttered pie plate.

COCONUT CREAM PIE

½ cup sugar
6 tablespoons all-purpose flour
Pinch salt
2 cups hot milk
1 cup grated fresh coconut
2 egg yolks
1 tablespoon butter
1 teaspoon vanilla
9-inch baked pastry shell

In the top of a double boiler combine the sugar, flour, and salt. Stir in gradually the hot milk and cook over a low flame until smooth and thickened. Stir in the coconut, place over boiling water, and cook for 15 minutes, stirring occasionally. Beat the egg yolks lightly with a little of the hot coconut cream and then stir into the remaining hot cream. Cook, stirring, for 2 minutes and remove from the heat. Beat in the butter and vanilla and cool. Pour into the baked pastry shell and chill. When ready to serve, spread the surface with sweetened whipped cream and sprinkle generously with shredded coconut or cover the top of the coconut cream with large swirls of Meringue Topping, sprinkle with shredded coconut, and bake at 350° F. for 15 minutes, or until the meringue is nicely browned.

TOASTED COCONUT CREAM PIE

1½ cups shredded coconut
⅓ cup sifted all-purpose flour
¼ teaspoon salt
1 cup sugar
½ cup cold milk
1½ cups hot milk
4 eggs, separated
2 teaspoons vanilla
9-inch baked pastry shell

Toast the coconut in a 350° F. oven until delicately browned, stirring it frequently, then let it cool. In the top of a double boiler combine the flour, salt, ¼ cup of the sugar and the cold milk. When the mixture is smooth, stir in the hot milk, place the saucepan over boiling water, and cook, stirring, until thickened. Beat the egg yolks until lemon-colored and mix them with a little of the thickened mixture, then stir into the saucepan. Add 1 cup of the toasted coconut and cook, stirring, for 3 minutes longer. Remove from the fire and cool. Stir in the vanilla and pour the mixture into the baked pastry shell. Beat the egg whites until stiff, gradually beat in the remaining sugar, and continue beating until the meringue is thick and glossy. Spread this over the top of the pie, sprinkle with the remaining coconut, and bake at 350° F. for 15 minutes, or until the meringue is delicately browned. Cool before serving.

VANILLA CREAM PIE

⅔ cup sugar
½ teaspoon salt
2⅔ tablespoons cornstarch
1⅓ tablespoons flour
2⅔ cups milk
3 egg yolks
1 tablespoon butter
2 teaspoons vanilla
9-inch baked pastry shell

In the top of a double boiler combine the sugar, salt, cornstarch, and flour. Stir in the milk and bring the mixture to a boil over low heat and cook for 3 minutes, stirring constantly. Remove from the fire. Beat the egg yolks lightly and stir a little of the hot milk mixture into them, then blend into the hot mixture. Place over boiling water and cook for 10 minutes, stirring occasionally. Stir in the butter and cool. When cool, stir in the vanilla and pour into the baked pastry shell. Top with whipped cream or Meringue Topping.

ALMOND BAVARIAN CREAM PIE

1 tablespoon (envelope) gelatin
½ cup cold water
1 cup Almond Paste
2 cups milk
4 egg yolks, beaten
1 teaspoon vanilla
2 cups heavy cream, whipped
9-inch baked pastry shell

Soak the gelatin in the cold water. Dissolve the Almond Paste in the milk by heating the mixture over a low flame and stirring until it is smooth. Pour this gradually over the egg yolks and cook over boiling water, stirring, until heated through and slightly thickened. Add the gelatin and stir until thoroughly mixed. Then stir over cracked ice until it is cool and beginning to set. Stir in the vanilla, fold in the whipped cream, and turn into the baked pastry shell. Chill before serving.

SPANISH CREAM PIE

4 eggs, separated
½ cup sugar
2 cups hot milk
1 tablespoon (envelope) gelatin
½ cup cold water
2 teaspoons vanilla
Whipped cream
9-inch baked pastry shell

Beat the egg yolks until light. Add the sugar and beat again. Add the hot milk and cook over a low flame until it is thick enough to coat a spoon, but do not allow it to boil. Remove from the fire and stir in the gelatin, which has been soaked in the cold water. Stir over cracked ice until cool and then fold in the egg whites, which have been beaten until stiff, and the vanilla. Turn into baked pastry shell, chill, and serve topped with whipped cream.

BANANA CREAM PIE

3 tablespoons cornstarch
10 tablespoons sugar
¼ cup cold milk
1½ cups hot milk
½ cup warm heavy cream
3 eggs, separated
3 bananas
1 teaspoon vanilla
½ cup heavy cream, whipped
9-inch baked pastry shell

In the top of a double boiler mix together the cornstarch and 4 tablespoons of the sugar. Stir in the cold milk and add gradually the hot milk. Place the saucepan over boiling water and stir constantly for about 10 minutes, or until thickened. Stir in the warm cream, which has been lightly beaten with the egg yolks, and continue stirring over the boiling water for another 5 minutes. Remove the saucepan from the heat and stir in 1 banana, which has been mashed or put through a ricer. When cool, stir in the vanilla and the whipped cream. Spread half the banana cream over the bottom of the pastry shell. Slice the other 2 bananas thinly over the cream and cover with the remaining cream so that the sliced bananas are entirely covered. Spread the surface of the pie with a meringue made from the 3 egg whites and the 6 tablespoons sugar. Bake at 300° F. for 15 minutes, or until the meringue is lightly browned.

RUM CREAM PIE

6 egg yolks
⅞ cup sugar
1 tablespoon (envelope) gelatin
½ cup cold water
1 pint heavy cream, whipped
½ cup Jamaica rum
Shaved bittersweet chocolate
9-inch baked pastry shell

Beat the egg yolks until they are light, add the sugar gradually, and continue to beat until the mixture is thick and pale. Soak the gelatin in the cold water for 5 minutes and then place it over boiling water until it becomes very hot. Strain the gelatin into the egg-sugar mixture and stir briskly to thoroughly combine. Fold in the whipped cream, stir in the rum, and pour the mixture into the baked pastry shell. Chill in the refrigerator until set and then cover the top generously with the shaved curls of chocolate.

EGGNOG CREAM PIE

3 large or 4 small eggs, separated
⅓ cup sugar
1 tablespoon (envelope) gelatin
1 cup hot rich milk
1 cup heavy cream, whipped
2 tablespoons Jamaica rum
Nutmeg
9-inch baked pastry shell

In a small bowl beat the egg yolks and sugar until the mixture is thick and pale in color. Stir in the gelatin and then the hot milk. Place the bowl over boiling water and stir until it is smooth, creamy, and very hot. Stir over crushed ice until it cools and begins to set. Whip the egg whites until stiff and fold them in along with half the whipped cream. Stir in the rum and fill the baked pastry shell. Decorate the top with the rest of the whipped cream, dust with a little nutmeg, and place in the refrigerator until ready to serve.

CHOCOLATE ANGEL PIE

Make a Meringue Pastry Shell, folding into the meringue ¾ cup finely chopped walnuts or pecans and 1 teaspoon vanilla. Make a nestlike shell, building up the sides of the shell a good ½ inch above the edge of the plate. Bake at 300° F. for 50–55 minutes and allow it to cool.

4 ounces sweet chocolate
3 tablespoons strong black coffee
1 teaspoon vanilla
1 cup heavy cream, whipped

Melt the chocolate with the coffee over a low flame, stirring until the mixture is smooth. Cool and stir in 1 teaspoon vanilla. Fold this chocolate mixture into the whipped cream and turn into the Meingue Pastry Shell. Chill for 2 hours before serving.

CHOCOLATE CREAM PIE

2 eggs
2 egg yolks
6 tablespoons sugar
6 tablespoons all-purpose flour
2 tablespoons (envelopes) gelatin
16 ounces semi-sweet chocolate
10 tablespoons strong black coffee
1½ cups hot milk
4 egg whites, stiffly beaten
1 cup heavy cream, whipped
2 tablespoons rum
9-inch baked pastry shell

Put into a saucepan the eggs, egg yolks, sugar, and flour and beat until the mixture is light and fluffy. Mix in the gelatin. Break the chocolate into small pieces, add the coffee, and stir over a low flame until the chocolate is smooth and melted. Add the hot milk gradually, stirring, to the melted chocolate and then stir this chocolate milk into the egg mixture. Stir constantly over a low flame until very hot and thickened, but do not allow it to boil. Stir over cracked ice until cool. Fold in the egg whites, half of the whipped cream, and the rum. Turn into the baked pastry shell and spread the surface with the remaining whipped cream.

BUTTERSCOTCH CREAM PIE

1½ cups brown sugar
9 tablespoons all-purpose flour
Pinch salt
3 cups hot milk
3 egg yolks, beaten
3 tablespoons butter
2 teaspoons vanilla
Whipped cream, if desired
9-inch baked pastry shell

In the top of a double boiler mix together the sugar, flour, and salt. Add gradually the hot milk and the beaten egg yolks and cook over boiling water, stirring, until the mixture is smooth and thickened. Cover and cook for 10 minutes longer. Remove from the fire and stir in the butter and vanilla. Cool and pour into baked pastry shell. Serve with whipped cream, if desired.

CHARTREUSE CUSTARD PIE

2 cups hot milk
Pinch salt
4 tablespoons sugar
6 tablespoons yellow chartreuse
8 egg yolks
4 tablespoons heavy cream
9-inch baked pastry shell

Combine the hot milk, salt, sugar, and yellow chartreuse. Beat together the egg yolks and cream and pour over them the hot milk, stirring constantly. Return the mixture to the saucepan and cook over boiling water, stirring, until thickened. Stir over cracked ice until cool and turn into the baked pastry shell.

STRAWBERRY CREAM CUSTARD PIE

4 eggs, separated
1 tablespoon sugar
1 cup hot milk
½ teaspoon vanilla
2 cups heavy cream, whipped
1 pint crushed strawberries
9-inch baked pastry shell

Beat the egg yolks until light and combine them with the sugar and hot milk. Cook the mixture over boiling water, stirring constantly, until thickened. Remove from fire, add vanilla, and stir over cracked ice until it is cool. Have the pastry shell, the custard, strawberries, and whipped cream all very cold. Beat the egg whites until stiff and fold into the whipped cream. Fold in the custard, and finally the strawberries. Pile into the baked pastry shell and serve.

APPLE CUSTARD PIE

2 cups hot milk
4 eggs, separated
Sugar to taste
2 cups apple purée
9-inch baked pastry shell

Make a thick custard by mixing the hot milk and egg yolks, adding the sugar to taste, and cooking over boiling water until thickened, stirring constantly. Chill the apple purée and the custard and, when both mixtures are cold, mix them together and fold in the egg whites, which have been stiffly beaten. Turn the mixture into the baked pastry shell and chill.

PINEAPPLE CUSTARD PIE

1 fresh pineapple
½ cup sugar
3 eggs, separated
Whipped cream
9-inch baked pastry shell

Peel the pineapple and grate the pulp. Strain off enough of the pineapple juice to make 1 cup and combine this cup of juice with the sugar. Allow the juice and sugar to boil for 10 minutes. Beat the egg yolks and pour the syrup slowly over them while still beating. Return the mixture to the pan and cook over boiling water, stirring constantly, until thickened, then cool. Place the grated pineapple pulp in the bottom of the baked pastry shell, beat the egg whites until stiff, and fold them into the custard. Pour the custard over the grated pineapple and chill. Serve topped with whipped cream.

COFFEE CUSTARD PIE

5 egg yolks, lightly beaten
¼ cup sugar
1½ cups hot milk
1 cup strong black coffee
9-inch baked pastry shell
Whipped cream, if desired

Combine the egg yolks and sugar. Pour the hot milk over the eggs and sugar, stirring rapidly. Add the coffee and strain the mixture into a saucepan. Cook over boiling water, stirring, until thickened, then remove from the fire and stir over cracked ice until cool. Pour into baked pastry shell and chill. Serve with whipped cream.

COCONUT CUSTARD PIE

1 fresh coconut
1 cup sugar
6 egg yolks
9-inch baked pastry shell

Make a thin syrup from the coconut milk and the sugar. Grate the coconut meat, add to the syrup, and allow the mixture to boil for 10 minutes. Remove from the fire to cool slightly while you beat the egg yolks. Continue beating while you pour the coconut-syrup mixture over the eggs. Return to the saucepan and cook over boiling water, stirring, for about 10 minutes longer, or until the mixture coats the spoon. Stir over cracked ice until cool and pour into baked pastry shell. Top with a meringue and bake at 350° F. for 15 minutes, or until nicely browned.

STRAWBERRY TART

2 cups sifted all-purpose flour
4 egg yolks
4 tablespoons sugar
Pinch salt
4 tablespoons butter
Pastry Cream
Strawberries
6 tablespoons red currant jelly
1 tablespoon water

Put the flour on a pastry board and make a well in the center. In the well put the egg yolks, sugar, salt, and butter. Mix the center ingredients to a smooth paste and quickly work in the flour, adding a few drops ice water, if necessary, to make a dough. Roll out the dough, not too thin, and carefully line a flan ring, which has been placed on a baking sheet, and trim off the edge neatly. Cover the pastry with wax paper and place a little rice on top of the paper to help the dough keep its shape during the baking. Bake at 350° F. for 35 minutes, or until golden brown on top. Remove the paper and rice and allow the cake shell to cool.

When it is cool, fill it level full with Rum or Vanilla Pastry Cream, and cover the top carefully with strawberries. Combine the jelly and water and stir it over a low flame until it is smooth and syrupy. Allow it to cool a little and then brush it over the strawberries.

MERINGUE PIES

LEMON MERINGUE PIE

2 cups sugar
9 tablespoons all-purpose flour
Pinch salt
2½ cups hot water
6 egg yolks, beaten
4 tablespoons butter

½ cup lemon juice, or to taste
4 teaspoons grated lemon rind
9-inch baked pastry shell

In the top of a double boiler mix together the sugar, flour, and salt. Gradually stir in the water and then the beaten egg yolks. Cook over boiling water, stirring constantly, until thickened and smooth. Cover and cook for 10 minutes. Add the butter, lemon juice, and lemon rind. Cool and pour into the baked pastry shell. Cover with Meringue Topping and bake at 350° F. for 15 minutes, or until lightly browned.

LEMON FLUFF PIE

4 eggs, separated
1 cup sugar
½ cup lemon juice, or to taste
Grated rind of 1 lemon
9-inch baked pastry shell

In the top of a double boiler combine the slightly beaten egg yolks, ½ cup of the sugar, and the lemon juice and rind and cook over boiling water, stirring, until the mixture is thickened. Cool. Beat the egg whites until stiff, gradually beat in the remaining sugar, and fold into the lemon custard. Turn into the baked pastry shell, piling it high in swirls, and bake at 350° F. for about 15 minutes, or until a golden brown.

LIME MERINGUE PIE

7 tablespoons cornstarch
2½ cups sugar
2 cups boiling water
5 eggs, separated
Grated rind of 2 lemons
¼ teaspoon salt
½ cup unstrained lime juice
2 drops green vegetable coloring
9-inch baked pastry shell

Sift together into the top of a double boiler the cornstarch and 1¾ cups of the sugar. Stir in gradually the boiling water, then stir over direct heat until the mixture thickens and bubbles. Place over boiling water and cook for 10 minutes longer. Beat the egg yolks with a little of the hot thick syrup and then stir them into the rest of the syrup. Stir in the lemon rind, salt, lime juice, and vegetable coloring and continue to cook over boiling water until the mixture is thick and smooth, stirring constantly. Cool and pour into the baked pastry shell.

Beat the egg whites until stiff, gradually add the remaining sugar, and continue to beat until the meringue is thick and glossy. Spread this meringue evenly over the filling, sprinkle lightly with a little more sugar, and bake at 350° F. for 15 minutes, or until the meringue is lightly browned.

APRICOT FLUFF PIE

4 egg whites
Pinch salt
¼ cup sugar
1½ cups apricot purée
1 tablespoon lemon juice
9-inch baked pastry shell

Beat the egg whites with the salt until stiff. Gradually beat in the sugar and continue beating until the meringue is stiff and glossy. Stir the lemon juice into the apricot purée and then fold this mixture into the meringue. Turn into the baked pastry shell and bake at 350° F. for about 20 minutes, or until a golden brown on top.

LIME FLUFF PIE

4 eggs, separated
¾ cup sugar
Pinch salt
Juice of 2 limes, or to taste
Grated rind of 2 limes
1 drop green vegetable coloring
9-inch baked pastry shell

Beat the egg yolks and 4 tablespoons of the sugar together. Add the salt, lime juice and rind and cook over boiling water until thick. Remove from the fire, stir in the vegetable coloring, and cool slightly. Beat the egg whites until stiff, gradually beat in the remaining sugar, and fold this meringue into the lime custard. Pile the mixture lightly in the baked pastry shell, chill, and serve; or bake at 350° F. for 15 minutes, cool, and serve.

CHIFFON PIES

LEMON CHIFFON PIE

1 tablespoon (envelope) gelatin
¼ cup cold water

1 cup sugar
½ cup lemon juice
Pinch salt
4 eggs, separated
1 teaspoon grated lemon rind
Whipped cream, if desired
9-inch baked pastry shell

Soak the gelatin in the cold water for 5 minutes. In the top of a double boiler combine ½ cup of the sugar, the lemon juice, salt, and the slightly beaten yolks of the eggs. Cook over boiling water, stirring, until the mixture coats the spoon. Stir in the softened gelatin and the lemon rind and cool. Beat the egg whites until stiff. Gradually beat in the remaining sugar and continue beating until the meringue is stiff and glossy. Fold this into the cooled custard, turn into the baked pastry shell, and chill. Whipped cream may be spread on top at serving time, if desired.

ORANGE CHIFFON PIE Make according to the directions for Lemon Chiffon Pie. Substitute 1 teaspoon lemon juice, 1 tablespoon grated orange rind, and ½ cup orange juice for the lemon juice and rind.

LIME CHIFFON PIE

4 eggs, separated
1 cup sugar
½ cup lime juice
1 tablespoon (envelope) gelatin
½ cup cold water
Grated rind of 1 lime
Pinch salt
Whipped cream
9-inch baked pastry shell

Beat the egg yolks lightly and stir in ½ cup of the sugar and the lime juice. Cook the mixture over boiling water until it coats the spoon. Soak the gelatin in the cold water for 5 minutes and stir into the hot custard. Add the rind and stir over cracked ice until the mixture begins to thicken. Beat the egg whites with the salt until stiff and then gradually beat in the remaining sugar and continue beating until the meringue is thick and glossy. Fold this into the lime custard and pour into the baked pastry shell. Just before serving, spread the surface with whipped cream.

APRICOT CHIFFON PIE

1 tablespoon (envelope) gelatin
¼ cup cold water
½ cup apricot juice
½ cup sugar
Pinch salt
2 tablespoons lemon juice
1 cup cooked apricots, puréed
1 cup heavy cream, whipped
9-inch baked pastry shell

Soak the gelatin in the water for 5 minutes and then heat the mixture over hot water until the gelatin is dissolved. Combine the apricot juice, sugar, salt, and lemon juice and stir in the dissolved gelatin. Add the apricot purée, which must be cool, and mix thoroughly. Fold in the whipped cream. Fill the baked pastry shell with the mixture and chill. Serve topped with additional whipped cream, if desired.

COFFEE CHIFFON PIE

1 tablespoon (envelope) gelatin
¾ cup strong black coffee
4 egg yolks
1 cup sugar
Pinch salt
1 tablespoon lemon juice
4 egg whites, stiffly beaten
Whipped cream
9-inch baked pastry shell

Soak the gelatin in ¼ cup of the cold coffee for 5 minutes. In the top of a double boiler combine the egg yolks, ½ cup of the sugar, the salt, and the remaining coffee. Cook over boiling water, stirring, until the mixture coats the spoon. Stir in the dissolved gelatin and the lemon juice and cool. Beat the egg whites until stiff, gradually beat in the remaining sugar, and fold into the coffee mixture. Fill the baked pastry shell with the mixture and chill. Serve topped with whipped cream.

BUTTERSCOTCH CHIFFON PIE

1 tablespoon (envelope) gelatin
¼ cup cold water
3 eggs, separated
1 cup hot milk

½ cup brown sugar
¼ teaspoon salt
1 teaspoon vanilla
1 cup heavy cream, whipped
9-inch baked pastry shell

Soak the gelatin in the cold water for 5 minutes. In the top of a double boiler combine the egg yolks, hot milk, sugar, and salt, and cook over boiling water until the mixture coats the spoon, stirring constantly. Add the gelatin and stir until it is thoroughly dissolved. Cool. Stir in the vanilla, fold in the stiffly beaten egg whites and the whipped cream. Turn into the baked pastry shell and chill well before serving.

RUM CHIFFON PIE

1 tablespoon (envelope) gelatin
4 tablespoons dry white wine
1½ cups top milk
¾ cup brown sugar
3 eggs, separated
Pinch salt
½ cup heavy cream, whipped
3 tablespoons Jamaica rum
Grated sweet chocolate
9-inch baked pastry shell

Soak the gelatin in the wine for 5 minutes. Combine the milk, sugar, egg yolks, and salt in the top of a double boiler and cook over boiling water, stirring, until the mixture coats the spoon. Add the softened gelatin and stir until it is thoroughly dissolved, then stir over cracked ice until the custard is thick and cool. Fold in the stiffly beaten egg whites and the whipped cream, alternately with the rum. Fill the baked pastry shell and grate a little sweet chocolate over the top. Chill thoroughly before serving.

MAPLE CHIFFON PIE

1 tablespoon (envelope) gelatin
¼ cup cold water
½ cup milk
½ cup maple syrup
¼ teaspoon salt
3 eggs, separated
1½ cups heavy cream, whipped
2 teaspoons vanilla
9-inch baked pastry shell

Soak the gelatin in the cold water for 5 minutes. In the top of a double boiler combine the milk, maple syrup, and salt. Beat the egg yolks lightly and stir into the milk and maple syrup. Cook the mixture over boiling water, stirring, until it coats a spoon. Then add the gelatin and stir until it is thoroughly dissolved. Let cool. Fold in the stiffly beaten egg whites, half the whipped cream, and the vanilla and turn into the baked pastry shell. Chill and decorate the top with the remaining whipped cream before serving.

STRAWBERRY CHIFFON PIE

1 tablespoon (envelope) gelatin
¼ cup cold water
4 eggs, separated
1 tablespoon lemon juice
¾ cup sugar
Pinch salt
1 cup strawberry pulp and juice
Whipped cream
9-inch baked pastry shell

Soften the gelatin in the cold water. In the top of a double boiler combine the slightly beaten egg yolks, lemon juice, ½ cup of the sugar, and the salt. Cook over boiling water, stirring, until the mixture coats the spoon. Stir in the softened gelatin and the strawberry pulp and juice and cool. Beat the egg whites until stiff. Gradually beat in the sugar and continue beating until the meringue is stiff and glossy. Fold this into the cooled strawberry custard and turn into the baked pastry shell. Chill. Before serving, spread the surface with a layer of whipped cream and decorate lavishly with whole hulled berries.

ALMOND CHOCOLATE CHIFFON PIE

½ cup shredded blanched almonds
1 tablespoon (envelope) gelatin
¼ cup cold water
2 squares (ounces) unsweetened chocolate
1 tablespoon strong black coffee
⅔ cup sugar
¼ teaspoon salt
½ cup hot milk
1 teaspoon vanilla
2 cups heavy cream, whipped
9-inch baked pastry shell

Toast the almonds in a 350° F. oven until a golden brown, stirring them frequently so they do not burn. Soak the gelatin in the cold water for 5 minutes. Melt the chocolate with the coffee over boiling water and, when the mixture is smooth, stir in the sugar, salt, and hot milk. Cook for 3 minutes, stirring constantly, then stir in the softened gelatin until thoroughly dissolved. Stir the mixture over cracked ice until thickened and cool, then beat with a rotary beater, adding the vanilla. Fold in the whipped cream, reserving enough to decorate the top, and 2 tablespoons of the almonds. Sprinkle the remaining almonds over the bottom of the baked pastry shell, turn the chocolate mixture into the shell, and chill well. Just before serving, decorate the top with the remaining whipped cream forced through a pastry bag with a fancy tube.

BLACK BOTTOM PIE

4 eggs, separated
1 cup sugar
1¼ tablespoons cornstarch
2 cups hot rich milk
1 tablespoon (envelope) gelatin
¼ cup cold water
2 squares (ounces) unsweetened chocolate, melted and cooled
1 teaspoon vanilla
¼ teaspoon cream of tartar
3 tablespoons Jamaica rum
1 cup heavy cream
2 tablespoons fine granulated sugar
Shaved bittersweet chocolate
9-inch baked pastry shell

In the top of a double boiler combine the egg yolks, ½ cup of the sugar, the cornstarch, and the hot milk. Cook the mixture over boiling water, stirring, until it coats the spoon. Soak the gelatin in the cold water for 5 minutes and stir it into the hot custard. Divide the custard into two parts. To one part add the melted chocolate and the vanilla and pour it into the baked pastry shell. Chill until the chocolate mixture is set. Allow the other half of the custard to cool. Beat the egg whites with the cream of tartar and gradually add the remaining sugar, beating until smooth and glossy. Fold this into the cooled custard along with the rum and cover the chocolate layer in the pastry shell with the rum mixture. When ready to serve, spread the surface with the cream, which has been whipped and sweetened with the fine granulated sugar, and sprinkle the top with shavings of chocolate. A Wafer Shell made of chocolate, vanilla, or ginger wafers is excellent with this filling.

PINEAPPLE CHIFFON PIE

1 tablespoon (envelope) gelatin
¼ cup cold water
4 eggs, separated
1 tablespoon lemon juice
¾ cup sugar
1 cup crushed fresh pineapple
Pinch salt
Whipped cream
9-inch baked pastry shell

Soften the gelatin in the cold water. In the top of a double boiler combine the slightly beaten egg yolks, lemon juice, ½ cup of the sugar, the crushed pineapple, and the salt. Cook, stirring, over boiling water until the mixture coats the spoon. Stir in the gelatin and cool. Beat the egg whites until stiff. Gradually beat in the remaining sugar and continue beating until the meringue is stiff and glossy. Fold this into the cool pineapple custard and turn into the baked pastry shell. At serving time spread the surface with whipped cream.

If canned crushed pineapple is used, reduce the amount of sugar combined with the egg yolks to ¼ cup.

NESSELRODE PIE

1 tablespoon (envelope) gelatin
1½ cups milk
3 eggs, separated
⅓ cup chopped raisins
2 tablespoons ground blanched almonds
1 cup macaroon crumbs
1 teaspoon vanilla
1 tablespoon rum or brandy
Pinch salt
⅓ cup sugar
2 tablespoons shaved unsweetened chocolate
9-inch baked pastry shell

Soften the gelatin in ¼ cup of the milk. Scald the remaining milk in a saucepan placed over boiling water. Beat the egg yolks slightly and stir into them the scalded milk. Return the egg-milk mixture to the saucepan and stir over the boiling water until the mixture coats the spoon. Remove from the heat and stir in the softened gelatin. Add the raisins, almonds, macaroon crumbs, vanilla, rum or brandy, and the salt. Stir the mixture over cracked ice until it cools and begins to set. Beat the egg whites until stiff, add the sugar gradually, and continue beating until stiff and glossy. Fold into the custard and turn into baked pastry shell. Chill and serve sprinkled with shaved chocolate.

DEEP-DISH PIES

Deep-dish pies are generally one-crust fruit pies with a pastry crust arranged over, instead of under, the fruit.

Place prepared, sliced fruit or berries in a baking dish or deep pie pan, heaping the fruit slightly in the center. Sweeten and season to taste. Most fruit is improved by a long squirt of lemon juice, a little grated lemon or orange peel, a dash of cinnamon or nutmeg, or a few drops vanilla, according to individual preference. If the fruit is dry, a little water is added and often a small cup is inverted in the center of the dish to draw up some of the juice during baking, so it will not boil over.

Any desired pastry may be used to cover the fruit. Moisten the edge of the dish with cold water; roll out pie pastry ⅛ inch thick and about 1 inch larger in diameter than the dish. Fold over in half, cut slits near the center to allow for the escape of steam, and place the folded crust over half of the filled dish. Unfold and trim off all but ½ inch of the overhanging edge. Fold this edge under and press the double edge against the moistened rim with the floured tines of a fork. Brush the top with a little melted butter and bake at 450° F. for 10 minutes, then reduce the temperature to 350° F. and bake for 30–35 minutes longer, or until the filling is tender and the crust is browned.

Apples, cherries, apricots, peaches, and berries of all types are especially suited to deep-dish pies. Juicy fruits should have a little flour, cornstarch, or quick-cooking tapioca added. Two tablespoons flour or 1 tablespoon cornstarch or quick-cooking tapioca is usually sufficient for 4 cups fruit.

DEEP-DISH FRUIT PIES

⅔–1 cup sugar
1 tablespoon lemon juice
½ teaspoon grated lemon rind
2 tablespoons flour
Pinch salt
3 cups fresh fruit or berries
1 tablespoon butter
Pastry for one-crust pie

Mix together the sugar, lemon juice and rind, flour, and salt and combine this mixture with the prepared fruit. Turn into an 8-inch baking dish and dot with the butter. Roll out pastry or baking powder biscuit dough ⅛ inch thick, cover the top of the dish, fluting the edge and pressing it against the edge of the dish, prick the surface with a fork, and bake at 450° F. for 10 minutes. Reduce oven temperature to 350° F. and bake for another 35 minutes.

DEEP-DISH APPLE PIE

10 tart cooking apples
¾ cup sugar
¾ cup brown sugar
2 teaspoons cinnamon
Grated rind and juice of 1 lemon
¼ cup water
3 tablespoons butter
Pastry for one-crust pie

Wash, peel, core, and finely slice the apples into a round, 2-quart baking dish. Sprinkle each layer as you slice with the sugars, which have been mixed with the cinnamon and lemon rind. Pour over the water and the lemon juice and dot with 2 tablespoons of the butter. Cover with pastry in the regular way. Melt the remaining butter and with it brush the surface of the pastry and bake at 450° F. for 10 minutes. Reduce the temperature to 350° F. and bake for another 50 minutes, or until the apples are tender and the crust is lightly browned. Serve hot with heavy cream.

DEEP-DISH BLUEBERRY PIE

1 cup sugar
2 tablespoons cornstarch
½ teaspoon salt
3 cups blueberries
2 tablespoons butter
1 tablespoon lemon juice
Pastry for one-crust pie

Mix together the sugar, cornstarch, salt, and blueberries. Cook the mixture over a low flame, stirring constantly, for about 10 minutes, or until slightly thickened. Stir in the butter and lemon juice and pour into a rectangular baking dish about 7×10×2 inches. Roll out the pastry ⅛ inch thick and cut it into strips ½ inch wide. Weave the strips into a latticework and place it over the fruit. Cut a strip of pastry ¾ inch wide and place it around the edge of the dish, over the ends of the lattice strips. Flute with the fingers and bake at 425° F. for about 25 minutes.

DEEP-DISH RHUBARB PIE

2 pounds strawberry rhubarb
1½ cups sugar
2 tablespoons flour
Flaky Pastry for one-crust pie

Wash the rhubarb and remove leaves. Cut the stalks into 1-inch pieces and mix with the sugar and flour. Place the mixture in a deep pie dish, with an egg cup or custard cup in the center to draw up the juice and prevent the crust from sagging. Cover the dish with Flaky or Rich Flaky Pastry, pressing the edge to the dish with the tines of a fork, and slashing the top of the dough in several places to allow for the escape of steam. Bake at 450° F. for 10 minutes. Reduce heat to 350° F. and continue to bake for 25 minutes. Sprinkle the crust with sugar and return to the oven for another 10 minutes, until the sugar is melted.

PEACH SKILLET PIE

Make a Rich Baking Powder Biscuit dough. Roll it out ⅛ inch thick and place it over a heavy skillet, allowing the dough to hang over the edge. Fill with sliced peaches, sprinkle with ½ cup sugar, ½ teaspoon salt, ½ teaspoon cinnamon, and 1 teaspoon lemon juice. Dot with 2 tablespoons butter and fold the overlapping dough toward the center, leaving the center uncovered. Bake at 450° F. for 10 minutes. Reduce oven temperature to 375° F. and bake for another 30 minutes.

APPLE PANDOWDY

6 large apples
½ cup sugar
½ teaspoon cinnamon
¼ teaspoon nutmeg
¼ teaspoon salt
½ cup molasses
¼ cup water
3 tablespoons butter
Pastry for two-crust pie

Line a deep pie dish or casserole with pastry. Mix together the apples, sugar, cinnamon, nutmeg, and salt and fill the casserole. Add the molasses and water, dot with butter, and cover with pastry. Press the edges of the crust firmly against the rim of the casserole and bake at 425° F. for 45 minutes, decrease temperature to 325° F. and bake for another 15 minutes, or until the crust is brown and the apples are tender. Remove from the oven and, with a knife, chop the pastry and fruit and mix all together. If the apples are dry or not sweet enough, add a little more water and molasses. Return to the oven and bake at 325° F. for another 30 minutes. Serve hot with heavy cream.

INDIVIDUAL PIES, TARTS, AND TURNOVERS

Small pies, tarts, and turnovers are individual desserts just large enough to serve one person.

SMALL CLOSED PIES   Pastry for a two-crust pie will make 6 closed individual pies. Mix and handle the pastry according to directions for two-crust pies. Line tart shells, individual pie pans, or muffin cups with the pastry, flute the edges, and add any fruit filling desired just as you would for a two-crust pie. Cover with the top crust and bake at given temperature, reducing the baking time by about 10 minutes.

OPEN SMALL PIES OR TARTS   Pastry for a two-crust pie will make 12 3-inch tarts. Flaky Pastry is especially nice for these little pastries, and variety pastries such as Cream Cheese are often suitable. Roll out the chilled dough to about ⅛ inch in thickness and cut it into twelve circles about 5 inches in diameter. Line plain or fluted tart shells, being careful not to stretch the dough. Trim the edges to about ½ inch beyond the edge of the pan. Moisten the rims of the pans with a little cold water, fold the overlapping edge back, and flute it with the fingers or press with a fork. Use any of the fillings given for one-crust pies, such as Custard, Pumpkin, or Lemon Cake, and bake at given temperature, reducing baking time by about 15 minutes.

TO BAKE TART SHELLS   Line tart pans in the regular way. With a fork, prick small holes generously over the sides and bottom of each tart to prevent puffing and bake at 425° F. for 10–12 minutes, or until lightly browned. Attractive tart shells may be made by fitting the rounds of dough over the backs of muffin tins, pricking the dough thoroughly, and making six pleats at regular intervals around the shell.

FRESH FRUIT OR BERRY FILLINGS   Pile fresh sliced fruit or berries into baked tart shells. Soften a little jelly over hot water, adding about 1 tablespoon of hot water to every 4 tablespoons of jelly used. Currant jelly is good for dark fruits such as blueberry or strawberry; a light-colored jelly should be used for peaches or apricots. Pour a little melted jelly over the fruit and place the tarts in the refrigerator. As the jelly sets again, it will give a shiny glaze to the fruit. Decorate with whipped cream before serving. Or fill the baked shells with sweetened and flavored whipped cream, place sliced fruit or berries on top, and glaze with jelly. Another day, spread 1 tablespoon whipped cream cheese in each shell and top with sugared fruit or berries.

FRUIT AND CREAM FILLINGS   Baked tart shells may also be partially filled with Pastry Cream. The fruit is placed on top and glazed with melted jelly. A little whipped cream piped around the edge of each tart before serving adds an attractive touch.

CREAM FILLINGS   The various creams, custards, meringue, and chiffon fillings used for large baked pastry shells are all suitable for tarts. Make the fillings according to the recipes in the chapter. The filling for a 9-inch baked pastry shell will fill 8 3-inch baked tart shells.

TURNOVERS   Roll out pastry ⅛ inch thick and cut into 4-inch rounds or squares. This is an excellent way to use leftover trimmings of pastry. Place marmalade, jam, chutney, or fruit fillings on half of each pastry, fold it over to form half a circle or a triangle, moisten the edges with a little water, and seal the edges by pressing them together with the tines of a fork. Prick small steam vents and bake at 425° F. for 15 minutes.

TARTES AUTRICHIENNES

8 large tart apples
½ cup water
1¼ cups sugar
½ cup seedless raisins
Juice of 1 lemon
Grated rind of 1 lemon
½ teaspoon cinnamon
¼ pound butter
½ cup shredded blanched almonds
Pastry for two-crust pie

Peel, quarter, and core the apples and place them in a saucepan with the water and sugar. Bring to a boil and cook until the apples are tender. Put the apples and juice through a fine sieve and add to the resulting purée the raisins, lemon juice and rind, cinnamon, and butter. Return the mixture to the fire and simmer for 15 minutes, or until thick, stirring occasionally. Roll out pastry and line small tart pans. Fill the lined pans with the apple mixture and bake at 425° F. for 10 minutes. Sprinkle the top of each tart with shredded almonds and bake for 10 minutes longer. Serve hot with heavy cream.

BLACK CHERRY TARTS

3 tablespoons cornstarch
1¼ cups sugar
Pinch salt
½ cup cold milk
1½ cups hot milk
3 egg yolks, beaten
1 teaspoon vanilla
½ cup water
2 cups black pitted cherries
½ cup heavy cream, whipped
8 flaky baked tart shells

In the top of a double boiler mix together the cornstarch, ¼ cup of the sugar, and the salt. Stir in the cold milk to make a smooth mixture and then gradually add, stirring constantly, the hot milk. Stir the mixture over a low flame until thickened and smooth, place over boiling water, and cook for 10 minutes. Stir a little of this hot thick mixture into the egg yolks and then gradually stir them into the rest of the thickened mixture. Continue to cook over boiling water for 2 minutes, stirring constantly. Remove from the fire, stir in the vanilla, and cool. In a saucepan combine the remaining sugar and the ½ cup water. Bring it to a boil and allow it to cook for 5 minutes. Then add the cherries, cover, and simmer gently for 15 minutes. Remove the cherries from the syrup with a slit spoon and spread them out on a platter to cool. Continue to cook the syrup gently until it is very thick. When the custard is cool, fold into it the whipped cream and spread a layer of custard in each tart shell. Cover the custard with cherries and pour a teaspoon of the thickened syrup over the top of each.

FRESH PEACH TARTS

Fill baked tart shells level with whipped cream sweetened and flavored to taste. Place over the cream slices of fresh peaches and brush the surface of the sliced peaches with a little apricot or peach jam which has been heated with an equal amount of water. Sprinkle over all some blanched almonds which have been shredded and baked in the oven to a golden brown.

APRICOT RUM TARTS

⅓ cup brown sugar
2 tablespoons cornstarch
1¼ cups apricot juice
2 tablespoons butter
6 ounces cream cheese
2 tablespoons Jamaica rum
12 apricot halves, fresh, cooked, or canned
1 cup heavy cream, whipped
12 baked tart shells

Combine the sugar and cornstarch. Gradually stir in the apricot juice and add the butter. Bring the mixture to a boil and cook for 15 minutes, stirring constantly, until smooth and thickened. Beat the cream cheese with the rum until it is smooth and whipped and place about 2 tablespoons in each tart shell. Place a half apricot, rounded side up, on top of the cream cheese and pour over a good tablespoon of the thickened apricot juice. Make a fluted edge of whipped cream around the edge of each tart.

STRAWBERRY TARTS

3 tablespoons all-purpose flour
3 tablespoons sugar
1 egg
1 egg yolk
2 teaspoons gelatin
¾ cup hot milk
2 egg whites, stiffly beaten
½ cup heavy cream, whipped
2 tablespoons Jamaica rum
6 individual flaky tart shells, baked
Strawberries, whole or halved
2 tablespoons currant jelly
¼ cup heavy cream

In a saucepan combine the flour, sugar, egg, and egg yolk and beat until smooth. Stir in the gelatin and add gradually the hot milk. Stir over a low flame until it almost reaches the boiling point. Then place the saucepan over a bed of cracked ice and stir until it is cool and beginning to set. Stir in the egg whites, the whipped cream, and the rum. Fill the tart shells with this Rum Pastry Cream. Cover the top with strawberries and glaze the strawberries by brushing them with the currant jelly, which has been melted over a little warm water until it is thin enough to spread. Whip the remaining cream and use it to pipe a line around the edge of each tart.

ALMOND TARTS

1½ cups chopped blanched almonds
2 eggs, beaten
6 tablespoons sugar
2 tablespoons rum
1 egg white, stiffly beaten
Flaky Pastry for one-crust pie

Line six tart shells with Flaky Pastry and chill. Place the almonds on a pie plate in a 450° F. oven for 10 minutes, or until lightly browned, stirring them frequently to prevent them from burning. Combine 1 cup of the almonds with the eggs, sugar, and rum and then fold in the egg white. Fill the shells level, sprinkle the tops with a little granulated sugar, and bake at 350° F. for 15-20 minutes, or until golden brown. Dust with confectioners' sugar and the remaining chopped browned almonds.

COCONUT TARTS

½ cup butter
1½ cups sugar
3 eggs
3 egg yolks
2 cups freshly grated coconut
1 teaspoon vanilla
Pastry for two-crust pie

Cream the butter until soft, add the sugar gradually, and cream together until light and fluffy. Beat the eggs and egg yolks together and stir into the butter-sugar mixture. Then stir in the coconut and vanilla.

Line twelve small tart tins with pastry, fill them with the coconut-egg mixture, and bake at 350° F. for 25-35 minutes, or until a golden brown.

RAISIN TARTLETS

1 pound raisins
1 dozen walnut halves

   3 tablespoons lemon juice
   ¼ cup brown sugar
   Flaky Pastry for two-crust pie

Line twenty small tartlet pans with Flaky Pastry. Put the raisins and nuts through a food chopper, using a medium blade, and moisten with the lemon juice. Stir in 2 tablespoons of the brown sugar and place 1 tablespoon of the mixture in each prepared tartlet pan. Sprinkle the surface of each tart with a little of the remaining brown sugar and bake at 400° F. for 15–20 minutes.

TRANSPARENT TARTS

   ½ cup butter
   2 cups sugar
   5 eggs
   3 tablespoons lemon juice
   Pastry for two-crust pie

Line twelve tart pans with pastry. Cream the butter until soft, add the sugar gradually, and cream together until light and fluffy. Then beat in the eggs one at a time. Stir in the lemon juice and turn into the prepared tart pans. Bake at 400° F. for 5 minutes. Reduce temperature to 350° F. and bake for about 10 minutes longer, or until firm.

SPICECAKE TARTS

   ½ cup currant jelly
   2 cups sifted cake flour
   ¾ teaspoon soda
   Pinch salt
   1 teaspoon cinnamon
   ¼ teaspoon ground cloves
   ½ cup raisins
   ¼ cup chopped nuts
   ⅔ cup butter
   ¾ cup sugar
   2 eggs, beaten
   ⅔ cup molasses
   ⅔ cup milk
   Pastry for two-crust pie

Line fifteen small-sized tart pans with pastry and place 1½ teaspoons of the jelly in the bottom of each. Sift together into a bowl the flour, soda, salt, cinnamon, and cloves, stir in the raisins and nuts. In another bowl cream the butter until soft. Gradually add the sugar and cream together until light and fluffy. Beat in the eggs and molasses and then stir in the flour-nut mixture, alternately with the milk. Turn into the prepared tartlet pans, filling them three fourths full, and bake at 425° F. for 5 minutes. Reduce temperature to 375° F. and bake for about 15 minutes longer.

CHESS TARTS

½ cup butter
1 cup sugar
2 eggs
1 teaspoon vanilla
½ cup thick sour cream
1 cup chopped walnuts
1½ cups raisins
Whipped cream
12 unbaked tart shells

Cream the butter until light. Add the sugar gradually and cream together until fluffy. Add the eggs, one at a time, and beat after each addition. Stir in the vanilla, cream, nuts, and raisins. Partially fill the pastry-lined tart pans with this mixture and bake at 425° F. for 10 minutes. Reduce the oven temperature to 325° F. and bake until the filling is firm. Serve with whipped cream.

MIXED FRUIT TURNOVERS

⅔ cup cooked prunes
⅓ cup cooked apricots
¼ cup sugar
1 tablespoon cornstarch
¼ teaspoon salt
1 tablespoon lemon juice
Pastry for two-crust pie

Combine all the ingredients and stir over a low flame for 5 minutes. Roll out pastry ⅛ inch thick and cut into 4-inch squares. Place a spoonful of filling on half of each square, moisten the edges, and fold the pastry over to form triangles. Seal the edges by pressing them together with the tines of a fork, prick the surface to allow for the escape of steam, place on baking sheet, and bake at 425° F. for 15 minutes.

PRESERVED FRUIT TURNOVERS

1 No. 2 can preserved fruit
2 tablespoons brandy

Pastry for two-crust pie

Drain the juice from a No. 2 can of preserved apricots, pears, pineapple slices, apples, or peaches. Pour the brandy over the fruit and allow it to marinate for ½ hour. Roll out pastry ⅛ inch thick and cut into 4-inch squares. Place half an apricot, apple, or peach or pineapple slice on half of the square, moisten the edges with juice, and fold over into a triangle. Press the edges together with the tines of a fork and place on a greased baking sheet. Bake at 450° F. for 15 minutes.

PUFF PASTRY TURNOVERS

Make half the recipe for Puff Pastry, wrap it in wax paper, and leave in the refrigerator overnight. Next day roll it out ⅛ inch thick and cut it into 3-inch circles. Place a teaspoon of good fruit jam or marmalade in the center of each. Moisten the edges with beaten egg and fold over each circle in half. Press the edges together with a fork dipped in flour and brush the surface with beaten egg. Chill in refrigerator for 1 hour, then bake at 450° F. for 10 minutes, reduce oven temperature to 350° F. and bake for another 5–10 minutes, watching carefully so that they do not burn. Remove from the oven, cool, and sprinkle with confectioners' sugar.

POACHED PEACH TURNOVERS

12 fresh peach halves
1 cup water
½ cup sugar
1-inch stick cinnamon
½ teaspoon vanilla
4 tablespoons brown sugar
2 tablespoons butter
Pastry for two-crust pie

Poach the peach halves in the water, to which has been added the sugar, cinnamon, and vanilla, until just tender when pierced with a fork. Roll out pastry ⅛ inch thick and cut into twelve 4-inch squares. Place a peach half on half of each pastry square and fill the hollow with 1 teaspoon brown sugar and ½ teaspoon butter. Fold over to form a triangle. Press the edges together with a floured fork, prick the surface of each turnover, and chill. Bake at 450° F. for 15 minutes.

Pear halves or small apple halves may be used in place of peaches.

CHERRY TURNOVERS Mix together 2 cups drained, pitted

sour cherries, fresh or canned, ½ cup sugar, 2 tablespoons quick-cooking tapioca, and 1 cup diced marshmallows. Roll out pastry ½ inch thick. Proceed as directed above. Bake at 450° F. for 15 minutes.

CURRANT AND HONEY TURNOVERS For the filling, cook 2 cups dried currants in water to cover until the currants are plump and the water has practically evaporated. Stir in ⅓ cup sugar, 2 tablespoons lemon juice, 2 tablespoons honey, and 2 tablespoons butter. Roll out pastry ¼ inch thick, cut in 4-inch rounds, and proceed as directed above. Bake at 450° F. for 15 minutes.

MARMALADE TURNOVERS

Roll out your favorite pastry ⅛ inch thick and cut into circles 4 inches in diameter. Heap 1 tablespoon marmalade or chutney or guava paste in the center of each circle. Add a small piece butter, sprinkle with cinnamon, and close the pastry around the filling, pressing the edges firmly together. Place them on a buttered baking sheet and bake at 400° F. for 20 minutes, or until the pastry is lightly browned.

BANBURY TURNOVERS

½ cup sugar
1 tablespoon flour
1 egg, slightly beaten
1 cup seedless raisins
¼ cup chopped nuts
1 tablespoon lemon juice
2 tablespoons grated lemon rind
Pastry for two-crust pie

Roll out pastry ⅛ inch thick and cut into 4-inch squares. Combine the sugar and flour and stir into the egg. Add the remaining ingredients and mix thoroughly. Place a spoonful of filling on half of each square, moisten the edges, and fold the pastry to form a triangle. Seal the edges by pressing together with the tines of a fork and prick the surface. Bake at 425° F. for 15 minutes. Makes 1½ dozen.

FRIED PRUNE TURNOVERS

1 recipe Baking Powder Biscuit dough
2½ cups chopped cooked prunes
½ cup chopped nuts

1 tablespoon lemon juice

Roll out biscuit dough ¼ inch thick and cut into rectangles about 4×2 inches. Mix together the prunes, nuts, and lemon juice and place 1 tablespoon of the filling on half of each rectangle. Fold over and press the edges together with a floured fork. Fry in deep fat (375° F.) for about 3 minutes, or until lightly browned. Makes 8 turnovers. Drain on absorbent paper and dust with confectioners' sugar while still warm.

VARIATIONS Any thick filling is suitable for these turnovers, such as: thick fruit purées, seasoned to taste; Mincemeat; chutney, guava butter, jam, or jelly, slightly beaten.

DATE AND NUT FILLING Cook together ½ cup chopped dates, ¼ cup chopped walnuts with ½ cup water and 1 tablespoon orange juice until thick, stirring constantly.

A FEW BAKED PUDDINGS

APPLE BROWN BETTY

6 tart apples, pared, cored, and sliced
1⅓ cups moist bread crumbs
¾ cup sugar
1 teaspoon cinnamon
2 tablespoons butter
Juice and rind of 1 lemon
⅓ cup water

Place half the apples in a buttered casserole. Combine the bread crumbs, sugar, and cinnamon, sprinkle half of this mixture over the apples, and dot with half the butter. Repeat with the remaining apples, crumbs, and butter. Sprinkle with lemon juice and rind, add the water, cover, and bake at 375° F. for 45 minutes. Serve with a Hard Sauce or a Foamy Sauce. Serves 6–8.

RHUBARB BROWN BETTY

¼ cup sugar, brown or white
Grated rind of 1 lemon
¼ teaspoon nutmeg
¼ cup butter, melted
2 cups bread crumbs
2 cups stewed rhubarb

Mix together the sugar, lemon rind, and nutmeg. Pour the melted butter over the bread crumbs and mix well. Cover the bottom of a buttered pudding dish with one third of the crumb mixture and spread over it 1 cup stewed rhubarb. Sprinkle with half the sugar mixture, then repeat the layers, covering finally with the remaining crumbs. Bake at 350° F. for 40 minutes, covering for the first 15 minutes to prevent the crumbs from browning too rapidly. Serve hot with cream. Serves 4–6.

BLACK CHERRY PUDDING

2 cups preserved black cherries
1 cup sifted cake flour
1½ teaspoons double-action baking powder
¼ teaspoon salt
½ teaspoon cinnamon
¼ cup butter
⅔ cup sugar
2 eggs, beaten
¼ cup milk
¼ cup hot water
1 teaspoon vanilla
Whipped cream

Heat the cherries and juice to the boiling point. Sift together the flour, baking powder, salt, and cinnamon. Cream the butter, add the sugar gradually, and cream together until light and fluffy. Add the eggs and beat until blended. Then stir in the flour alternately with the milk and water, beating until smooth after each addition. Stir in the vanilla. Place the hot fruit in a buttered baking dish, pour the batter on top, and bake immediately at 400° F. for 25–30 minutes, or until the cake is done. Serve warm with whipped cream.

Any canned or stewed fruit, such as blueberries, peaches, apricots, or raspberries, may be substituted for the cherries. Serves 6.

DUTCH APPLE PUDDING

2 cups sifted all-purpose flour
3 teaspoons double-action baking powder
½ teaspoon salt
2 tablespoons sugar
¾ cup butter
1 egg, beaten
¾ cup milk
⅓ cup brown sugar
1 teaspoon cinnamon
½ teaspoon nutmeg
2 cups thinly sliced apples

Sift together into a mixing bowl the flour, baking powder, salt, and sugar. Cut in ½ cup of the butter. Combine the egg and milk and stir into the flour mixture, stirring only enough to make a soft dough. Mix the remaining butter, brown sugar, cinnamon, and nutmeg and spread this mixture over the bottom of an 8-inch square pan. Cover with the apple slices and turn the dough on top. Spread the dough out evenly and bake at 350° F. for 1 hour. Serve hot with heavy cream. Serves 6.

HOT COCOA PUDDING

1 cup sifted all-purpose flour
2 teaspoons double-action baking powder
½ teaspoon salt
¾ cup sugar
6 tablespoons cocoa
½ cup milk
2 tablespoons melted butter
1 cup chopped nuts
1 cup brown sugar
1¾ cups hot water
Whipped cream, if desired

Sift together into a mixing bowl the flour, baking powder, salt, sugar, and 2 tablespoons of the cocoa. Stir in the milk and melted butter and mix until smooth. Add the nuts and spread the batter into a buttered baking pan. Sprinkle the surface with the brown sugar mixed with the remaining cocoa and pour the hot water over the entire mixture. Bake at 350° F. for 40 minutes. Cut the solid cake part into squares and serve with a little of the sauce from the pan over each piece. Top with whipped cream if desired. Serves 4.

LEMON CUSTARD PUDDING

¼ cup sifted all-purpose flour
1 cup sugar
¼ teaspoon salt
2 teaspoons grated lemon rind
¼ cup lemon juice
2 eggs, separated
1 cup milk

Sift together into a mixing bowl the flour, sugar, and salt. Stir in the lemon rind, juice, well-beaten egg yolks, and the milk. Beat the egg whites until stiff and fold into the egg-yolk batter. Pour into an 8-inch casserole, place the casserole in a pan containing about 1 inch hot water, and bake at 350° F. for 40–45 minutes. Serve warm, plain or with whipped cream. Serves 4.

CRUMB CAKE PUDDING

1 cup dry cake crumbs
½ cup milk
¼ cup butter
1 cup sugar
3 egg yolks, beaten
1 cup peach preserves
1 cup chopped nuts
Whipped cream

Soak the cake crumbs in the milk, adding a little more milk to completely moisten them, if necessary. The amount will depend on the dryness of the crumbs. Cream the butter, add the sugar gradually, and cream together until light and fluffy. Stir in the egg yolks and the soaked crumbs and mix thoroughly. Then stir in the preserves and nuts. Turn into a buttered baking dish and bake at 300° F. for about 1 hour, or until firm. Serve with whipped cream. Serves 4–6.

OLD-FASHIONED BREAD PUDDING

1½ cups diced stale bread
3 cups milk
2 eggs, beaten
½ cup sugar
¼ teaspoon salt
1 teaspoon cinnamon
½ cup raisins

Soak the bread in the milk in a buttered baking dish. Combine the eggs, sugar, salt, and cinnamon and stir into the bread mixture. Stir in the raisins and place the dish in a pan containing about 1 inch hot water. Bake at 350° F. for 45 minutes, or until almost set in the center. Serve with a Lemon or Jelly Sauce. Serves 4.

OLD-FASHIONED COTTAGE PUDDING

¼ cup butter
¾ cup sugar
1 egg, well beaten
1¾ cups sifted all-purpose flour
3 teaspoons double-action baking powder
½ teaspoon salt
¾ cup milk
1 teaspoon vanilla

Cream together the butter and sugar. Beat in the egg. Sift together the flour, baking powder, and salt and stir these ingredients into the butter mixture alternately with the milk and vanilla. Bake at 350° F. for 25–30 minutes. Serve with a Lemon Sauce. Serves 4.

6. Fine Pastries

PÂTE À CHOUX, *Cream Puff Pastry*

½ cup hot water
¼ cup butter
Pinch salt
½ teaspoon sugar
½ cup all-purpose flour
2 eggs, unbeaten

Pour the hot water over the butter in a saucepan and stir until the butter is melted. Add the salt and sugar and then place on the fire and bring the mixture to a rapid boil. Add the flour all at once, raise the saucepan over the heat, and stir vigorously with a wooden spoon until the mixture comes away from the sides of the pan and forms a ball in the center. Remove from the fire and add the eggs, one at a time, beating vigorously with the spoon after each addition until the batter is thick and glossy.

CREAM PUFFS

Make Pâte à Choux and shape on a greased baking sheet by dropping the batter from a tablespoon or a teaspoon, depending on the size of the puff desired. Bake at 400° F. for 10 minutes. Lower the temperature to 350° F. and bake until the puffs are free from beads of moisture. The time required will depend on the size of the puff, but if they are underbaked, they will collapse when removed from the oven. Large puffs will need from 30 to 45 minutes' baking. When the puffs are cool, split and fill them with whipped cream, ice cream, Chocolate Bavarian Cream, or Crème Pâtissière. Makes 6 large puffs or 18 tiny ones.

ÉCLAIRS

Shape Pâte à Choux with a pastry bag fitted with a ½-inch flat nozzle into strips 1×4 inches on a greased baking sheet. Bake as for Cream Puffs, cool, split, and fill as desired. Makes 6 éclairs.

RINGS

Shape Pâte à Choux into rings about 3 inches in diameter on a greased baking sheet. Bake as for Cream Puffs, cool, split, and fill with whipped cream. Cover with chocolate frosting and sprinkle with shredded almonds. Makes 6 rings.

CROWN

Make a circle with Pâte à Choux about 8 inches in diameter on a greased baking sheet. Brush the surface with beaten egg and sprinkle with slivered blanched almonds. Bake as for Cream Puffs. When cool, split and fill with large rosettes of Chocolate Pastry Cream alternated with rosettes of whipped cream.

CREAM PUFF TRIPLETS

Drop three tiny mounds of Pâte à Choux close enough together so they will bake as one puff. When cold, lift the upper part of each puff and fill each with a Pastry Cream or ice cream of a different color. Dust the tops with confectioners' sugar.

CROQUEMBOUCHE

This is a very beautiful and effective dessert made of small Cream Puffs mounted into a pyramid.

Make Flaky Pastry, roll it out, and cut it 9 inches in diameter or into the size of circle that you wish the base of your Croquembouche to be. Bake at 350° F. for 10 minutes, or until lightly browned, and then let it cool.

Make small Cream Puffs, about the size of large walnuts, and using three times the recipe for Pâte à Choux. Let them cool and fill them with Crème Bavarois or Crème à l'Anglaise Collée.

Make some Caramel Syrup (see Gâteau St. Honoré).

Place the Flaky Pastry base on a large serving plate. Dip the bottoms of the little Cream Puffs in the Caramel Syrup and place a row of them all around the outside edge of the base. Place a second row of the puffs on top of the first row over the spaces between each puff. Continue building the pyramid in this way until you finally top it with one Cream Puff.

The Croquembouche may be served garnished with whipped cream and the rest of the Caramel Syrup or sprinkled generously with confectioners' sugar. Serves 12.

RELIGIEUSE

Make a small baked tart shell about 3 inches in diameter for each person to be served and when they are cool fill them with Crème Pâtissière which has been flavored with a little coffee extract.

For each tart shell you will need to make three small Eclairs, not larger than your first finger, and one tiny Cream Puff. Fill the Éclairs and the Cream Puffs with whipped cream. Fit the ends of three Éclairs into the filled tart shells, pushing them well into the cream, and bring them together at the top, forming a triangle. Dip the bottom of a Cream Puff in Caramel Syrup (see Gâteau St. Honoré) and place it on top of the Éclair triangle. Decorate in between each Éclair with Mocha Butter Cream, forced through the fluted nozzle of a pastry tube, and top the puff with a rosette of the Mocha Cream.

PÂTE FEUILLETÉE, *Puff Pastry*

Many of the mouth-watering delicacies on a tray of French pastry are based on puff pastry. Strips of the paste may be wound around cone-shaped molds. These spirals are baked, cooled, and then filled with Crème Pâtissière or whipped cream. Squares or circles may be filled with fruit, marmalade, or jam, folded, sealed, and baked. Baked strips are put together with whipped cream to make the ever-popular Napoleons. Tiny shells or *bouchées* make delightful and dainty desserts when filled with any one of the many creams, fruit, berries, or preserves. These, as well as the turnovers, may be filled with savory mixtures for a tasty hors d'oeuvre.

Puff pastry makes a festive topping for deep-dish pies, with decorative pieces of the paste in the shape of leaves, rosettes, stars, etc., arranged on top.

> 1 pound sweet butter
> 4 cups all-purpose flour (1 pound)
> 1 teaspoon salt
> 1½ cups ice water

Wash the butter by putting it into a bowl of cold water and kneading it with your hands until it is the consistency of putty. Remove it from the water, squeeze it in a clean cloth to extract any water that may have been trapped in it, and chill in the refrigerator.

Sift the flour and salt into a bowl or in a mound on a board. Add the ice water gradually, mixing as little as possible in combining it. It must never be worked. Add only enough of the water to form the dough into a smooth ball that has about the same consistency as the washed butter. This is called the *détrempe*. The weight of the washed butter should be half the weight of the *détrempe*.

Place the dough on a lightly floured board and roll it out ½ inch thick into a rectangle. Turn the dough so that it is horizontally in front of you. Shape the butter into a flat cake about ½ inch thick and place it in the center of the dough. Fold the flap of dough on the left to cover the butter, then fold the flap of dough on the right over the left flap. The butter is now completely covered. Press the edges of the dough firmly together to enclose as much air as possible and leave in a cold place for about 20 minutes.

Now gently roll the paste away from you to make a long rectangle about ½ inch thick and 20 inches long. The enclosed butter should not be allowed to break through the surface of the dough. This is one of the secrets of puff pastry. If you allow the butter to break through, it means you are losing the enclosed air and it is this air that is going to make the pastry puff. When you have rolled out the rectangle, turn it so that it is horizontally in front of you and fold as you did before—left over to the right and right over to the left. This rolling, turning, and folding is called a "turn." Make another turn and again allow the dough to remain in a cold place for 20 minutes. Make two more turns and chill again. Repeat, making six turns in all, and chill for 15 minutes, or until ready to use. After rolling and cutting the dough into whatever shape you desire, chill it again before baking. The paste should be ice-cold when placed in the oven. It may be kept several days in the refrigerator in a bowl covered with a cloth wrung out of cold water, but in this case the last two turns are not made until it is going to be used. This amount of dough will make 12 large patties or 2 vol-au-vents.

PUFF PASTRY SHELLS

Roll out Puff Pastry ¼ inch thick and cut into rounds with a floured cutter, either plain or fluted. Nests of cutters designed to cut out circles of paste from ½ inch to 6 inches or more in diameter are available. These are not essential, however, as cardboard patterns may be placed on the dough and a sharp-pointed knife used to cut around them.

Cut the centers from two thirds of the rounds, leaving rings of dough. Brush the edge of an uncut round with cold water, place a ring on top, dampen the top of this, and place a second ring on top. Press lightly together each time. Place the shells on a baking sheet covered with a double thickness of heavy brown paper. Brush the tops with beaten egg and chill thoroughly.

The baking of Puff Pastry requires as much care and judgment as the making of the dough. Puff Pastry needs a hot oven, the greatest heat coming from the bottom, so that it may rise properly. When it has risen to its full height, lower the temperature to moderate.

Bake in a hot oven (450° F.) for 10 minutes. Reduce the temperature to 350° F. and bake for 15–25 minutes, depending on the size of the shell. Shells 3 inches in diameter will need 25 minutes. Reduce oven temperature to 300° F. and bake for another 10 minutes, or until the shells are a golden brown. The baking will have to be watched carefully as Puff Pastry burns easily. When the shells are well risen, a second cold baking sheet should be placed under the first one to prevent burning the bottoms. If the pieces of Puff Pastry cut out from the circles are going to be used for little shell caps, they should be baked separately.

MILLE FEUILLES, *Napoleons*

Roll Puff Pastry into a rectangle ¼ inch thick and cut into strips 2½ inches wide. Place the strips on a baking sheet which has been lined with several layers of heavy brown paper, prick with a fork, and chill thoroughly. Bake at 450° F. for 10 minutes. Reduce temperature to 350° F. and bake for another 10 minutes. Place another cold baking sheet under the pastry, reduce oven temperature to 300° F. and bake for another 10 minutes, or until a golden brown. Cool thoroughly and cut into 3-inch bars. Sandwich two bars together with Pastry Cream or whipped cream and dust the tops generously with confectioners' sugar. Makes 18 Napoleons.

GODCAKES

Roll out Puff Pastry ¼ inch thick and cut into 3-inch squares. Place on one corner of each a teaspoon of marmalade or Currant Filling. Moisten the edges of the pastry, fold over from corner to corner to make small triangles, and seal the edges securely with the floured tines of a fork. Place the turnovers on a baking sheet which has been lined with several layers of brown paper and chill thoroughly. Bake at 450° F. for 10 minutes. Reduce oven temperature to 350° F. and bake for another 10 minutes. Place a cold baking sheet under the Godcakes, reduce temperature to 300° F. and bake until golden brown. Makes 18 turnovers.

CURRANT FILLING   Mix together ¾ cup currants, ⅓ cup lemon peel, finely chopped, ½ teaspoon nutmeg, ½ teaspoon allspice, ¼ cup sugar, and ¼ cup butter. Heat slowly and cook, stirring, for about 10 minutes.

PEACH HEARTS

Roll Puff Pastry ¼ inch thick and cut into heart shapes. Chill and bake according to directions for Napoleons. Cool and place a spoonful of peach jam in the center of each. Pipe a fluted edge of whipped cream around the jam. Makes 24 hearts.

BANANA JALOUSIE

Roll Puff Pastry ⅛ inch thick and press it over the backs of small oval or round tart tins. Chill and bake according to directions for Napoleons. Remove from the tins and cool. When ready to serve, spread a thin layer of pineapple jam on the inside of the shell, cover this with overlapping layers of bananas, glaze with a little pineapple jam which has been melted with a little hot water, and pipe a fluted edge of sweetened whipped cream all around. Makes 36 tarts.

MARRON STARS

Roll Puff Pastry ¼ inch thick and cut into small star shapes. Chill and bake according to the directions for Napoleons. When cool, place a glacéed chestnut in the center and surround it with little rosettes of delicately colored frosting. Makes 24 stars.

MARMALADE SQUARES

Roll Puff Pastry ¼ inch thick and cut into 3-inch squares. Turn the points over to the middle, wet slightly, and press down tightly. Bake according to directions for Napoleons and, when cool, place a spoonful of marmalade or jam in the center of each. Makes 18 squares.

PUFF PUFFS

Roll Puff Pastry ¼ inch thick and cut into rounds about 2 inches in diameter. Chill and bake according to directions for Napoleons. When cool, place a small filled Cream Puff on top, fastening it in place with Caramel Syrup (see Gâteau St. Honoré). Decorate with a rosette of whipped cream on top and pipe a fluted line of cream around the base of each puff. Makes 24.

BERRY BASKETS

Roll Puff Pastry ¼ inch thick and cover the outsides of small tart tins with it to form baskets. Cut narrow strips of the paste to form handles and place the strips over the outsides of tart tins, the same size as used in making the baskets. Chill and bake according to directions for Napoleons. The handles will take less baking time than the baskets and must be watched carefully. When cold, fill the baskets with fresh berries, sweetened to taste. Top with whipped cream and fasten on the handles with Caramel Syrup (see Gâteau St. Honoré). Makes 18 baskets.

GREEK SANDWICHES

Roll Puff Pastry ¼ inch thick into a long strip on a board sprinkled with granulated sugar. Sprinkle the top side with granulated sugar. Now fold over 2 inches of the narrow edge of the paste near you. Fold the paste at the farther end the same width. Repeat this folding until the folds meet, then place one fold over the other. Slice ¼ inch thick and place the slices, cut side up, on a baking sheet which has been lined with a double thickness of heavy paper.

Chill and bake according to directions for Napoleons. Cool and sandwich together with whipped cream. Dust the tops with confectioners' sugar. Makes 18 sandwiches.

GÂTEAUX D'AMANDE

Puff Pastry
½ cup Almond Paste
1 cup Crème Pâtissière

Roll Puff Pastry ⅓ inch thick and cut into a circle about 9 inches in diameter. Mix together thoroughly the Almond Paste and Crème Pâtissière and spread this mixture over the circle of pastry about ½ inch thick, leaving a ½-inch border of pastry around the edge. Moisten this edge and cover with another circle of Puff Pastry. Seal the top and bottom together by pressing firmly all around with the thumb. Brush the top with an egg beaten with a little milk and prick the top with a sharp-pointed knife, making a design. Place on a baking sheet lined with brown paper and chill for 30 minutes. Bake at 450° F. for 10 minutes, or until the pastry has puffed and started to become crusty. Reduce temperature to 350° F. and bake for another 25 minutes. Reduce temperature to 300° F. and bake for another 10 minutes, or until the cake is a golden brown. While hot, sprinkle the top with confectioners' sugar.

GÂTEAU ST. HONORÉ

Roll Puff Pastry about ¼ inch thick into a circle 9 inches in diameter. Then, with a pastry tube, form an edge about ¾ inch thick all around the circle with Pâte à Choux. Brush the top of the Pâte à Choux with beaten egg mixed with a little milk and bake at 425° F. for 10 minutes. Reduce temperature to 350° F. and bake for another 20–30 minutes, or until the edge has puffed and is dry.

Meanwhile, make some small Cream Puffs, brush with the beaten egg and milk, and bake according to directions for Cream Puffs. When the small puffs are cold, fill them with Crème Pâtissière or whipped cream. Dip the small filled puffs in Caramel Syrup and arrange them around the edge of the cake. Fill the center with Crème St. Honoré and top with whipped cream.

CARAMEL SYRUP   Combine 1 cup sugar with ⅓ cup water and ¼ teaspoon cream of tartar and cook over low heat, without stirring, until the syrup turns to amber color.

APRICOT SANDWICH

Roll Puff Pastry ¼ inch thick and cut into pieces 3 inches long and 2 inches wide. Place them on a baking sheet which has been lined with a double thickness of heavy paper and chill thoroughly. Bake according to directions for Napoleons, cool, and sandwich two pieces together with apricot jam. Cover the tops with confectioners' sugar or a chocolate frosting. Makes 18 sandwiches.

HUNGARIAN PUFF PASTRY

1 pound sweet butter
1 pound pastry flour (4 cups)
2 egg yolks
Pinch salt
1 cup ice-cold milk
Juice and rind of ½ lemon

Make a paste of the butter and 1 cup of the flour. Flatten it into a cake and place in the refrigerator to harden. Make a dough of the remaining ingredients, using just as much of the milk as necessary to form a smooth dough. Divide the dough in half and roll out each part into a rectangle ½ inch thick. Flatten the butter between the two layers of dough and roll out gently until the butter is forced to 1 inch from the edge all the way around. Fasten the edges of the dough and gently roll out into a long rectangle as thin as possible without allowing the butter to break through. Turn the dough until it is horizontally in front of you and fold the ends to the center (see the method described in recipe for Puff Pastry). Leave in the refrigerator overnight. In the morning, roll out very thin, turn and fold, and return to the refrigerator for 1 hour. Repeat this process three times. Then roll out ¼ inch thick, cut with a hot knife into strips 2×3 inches, place on a baking sheet which has been lined with a double thickness of heavy paper, and chill thoroughly. Bake at 450° F. for 10 minutes. Reduce temperature to 350° F. and bake for another 10 minutes. Place a cold baking sheet under the pastry, reduce temperature to 300° F. and bake until golden brown. When cold, dust the tops with confectioners' sugar. Makes 18 pastries.

KIPFELS Roll out Hungarian Puff Pastry ⅛ inch thick. Cut into 3-inch squares and roll into horns, sealing the overlapping edge. Chill and bake as directed above. Cool and fill with chopped nuts, fruit, and whipped cream. Makes 24 horns.

LADY LOCKS Roll out Hungarian Puff Pastry ⅛ inch thick and cut into strips 1 inch wide and 10 inches long. Wind each strip around buttered metal tubes, or lady lock forms, overlapping the edges tightly. Start at the wide part of the tubes but do not roll quite to the ends. Place 1 inch apart on baking sheet which has been covered with a double layer of brown paper and bake as directed above. Slip off the tubes, cool, and when ready to serve, fill with Pastry Cream or whipped cream which has been sweetened and flavored to taste. Makes 24 lady locks.

TIROLER

½ recipe Hungarian Puff Pastry
6 eggs, separated
6 tablespoons sugar
½ pound ground nuts

Beat the egg yolks and sugar until thick and pale in color. Add the nuts and fold in the egg whites, stiffly beaten. Line a baking pan with the Puff Pastry rolled out to less than ¼ inch in thickness. Spread the egg mixture over it, cover with a second layer of pastry, brush with beaten egg, and bake at 350° F. for 35 minutes, or until a golden brown. Dust with confectioners' sugar and cut into serving squares.

CROISSANTS

French croissants combine the technique of Puff Pastry, whereby air is rolled into the dough to make them rise, with the leavening action of yeast. They are similar to Danish or Swedish Pastry.

2 cakes or packages yeast
¼ cup lukewarm water
4 cups sifted pastry flour
½ teaspoon salt
1 tablespoon sugar
1½ cups rich milk
¾ pound butter

Soften the yeast in the lukewarm water and mix it into a dough with 1 cup of the flour. Form into a round ball, cut a cross in the top, cover, and put in a warm place to rise. When the "starter" has doubled in bulk, sift the remaining flour, salt, and sugar into a bowl. Add the milk, stirring and working it into a smooth dough. Add the starter and combine. Cover with a towel and allow to stand in a warm place for 15 minutes. Wash the butter (see Puff

Pastry) and press it in a cloth to remove any excess water. Roll out the dough into a sheet about ½ inch thick and turn it so it is horizontally in front of you. Spread the butter on top of the dough. Fold one third of the dough over the center third and then fold the remaining dough on top, making three layers. The open ends of the dough should be facing you. Roll out, turn, and fold again. Chill for several hours or overnight. When ready to use, roll, turn, and fold again twice more and chill for 1 hour. Cut the dough in half and roll out each part into a circle ¼ inch thick. Cut each circle into sixteen triangles. Starting with the broad side of the triangle, roll up each piece and turn the ends toward each other to form a crescent. Place on a greased baking sheet, cover, and allow to rise in a warm place for about 1 hour, or until doubled in bulk. Brush with beaten egg yolk mixed with a little cold milk and bake at 400° F. for 5 minutes. Reduce temperature to 350° F. and bake for 15 minutes longer, or until the crescents are golden brown.

SWEDISH OR DANISH PASTRY

2 cakes or packages yeast
1 tablespoon sugar
¼ cup lukewarm water
3¾ cups sifted pastry flour
1½ cups sweet butter
1 cup cold milk
1 egg, beaten
¼ cup sugar

Soften the yeast with the 1 tablespoon sugar in the lukewarm water. Sift ⅓ cup of the flour onto the butter, work together until well combined, and then chill in the refrigerator. Add the milk, egg, and the ¼ cup sugar to the yeast mixture. Add the flour gradually and beat with a wooden spoon until the dough is smooth and glossy. The dough should be soft but not sticky. Roll it out on a well-floured board into a 14-inch square. Roll out the butter into a rectangle 6×12 inches and place it over half of the dough. Fold over the uncovered side of the dough and press the edges together. Now roll out the dough into a long rectangle, turn it so it is horizontally in front of you, and fold into three parts from left to right, as though folding a napkin. Repeat this rolling, turning, and folding operation three times, and then chill for 30 minutes, or overnight. Repeat the rolling, turning, and folding operation three times, cut into desired shapes, fill, roll (see shapes and fillings below), and place on greased baking sheets. Chill again for at least 2 hours before baking. Bake immediately on removing from refrigerator in a 400° F. oven for 5 minutes; reduce oven temperature to 350° F. and bake for another 10 minutes, or until delicately browned. The surface of each pastry may be brushed with beaten egg before baking, if desired.

While hot, frost the tops with confectioners' sugar mixed to a paste with a little milk or cream. The filled and rolled pastry will keep in the refrigerator on baking sheets for a week. They may be removed and popped into a hot oven when ready to use. Any leftover baked pastry may be reheated before serving again. Makes about 40 small pastries.

CRESCENTS Roll out dough ¼ inch thick and cut into long strips 5 inches wide. Cut the strips into triangles 3 inches wide at the base. Place a teaspoon of filling on the base and roll up, curving the ends toward the middle to form a crescent.

ENVELOPES Roll dough out ⅛ inch thick and cut into 4-inch squares. Spread with 1 tablespoon of the filling and fold the corners toward the center, pressing down the edges firmly.

COCKSCOMBS Roll out dough ⅛ inch thick and cut into long strips 5 inches wide. Spread lightly with filling and fold one third over the middle third. Then fold over the remaining third. Slice across the folds ½ inch thick and place cut side down on greased baking sheets. Cut five deep gashes in the side of each.

SCHNECKEN Roll out dough into a rectangle ¼ inch thick and spread with the filling. Roll as you would a jelly roll and, with a hot knife, cut into ½-inch slices.

FILLINGS FOR SWEDISH OR DANISH PASTRY

ALMOND PASTE Grind 1 cup blanched almonds and mix with ½ cup sugar. Add 1 egg and beat until the mixture is smooth.

PECAN PASTE Grind 1 cup pecan meats and mix with ½ cup brown sugar. Add 1 egg, a pinch cinnamon, if desired, and beat until the mixture is smooth.

WALNUT PASTE Grind 1 cup walnut meats and ½ cup raisins. Mix with ½ cup sugar and ¼ teaspoon cinnamon.

VANILLA CREAM In the top of a double boiler combine 1 egg yolk, 1 tablespoon flour, 1 tablespoon sugar, and ½ cup milk. Cook over boiling water, stirring constantly, until thick. Cool, and stir in 1 teaspoon vanilla.

AUSTRIAN PASTRY ROLL

2½ cups sifted all-purpose flour

Pinch salt
2 tablespoons sugar
1 cup sweet butter
½ cup heavy cream
1 egg yolk
½ pound chopped walnuts
½ cup chopped seeded raisins
1 tablespoon cinnamon
½ teaspoon nutmeg
¼ teaspoon ground cloves
½ cup milk

Sift together the flour, salt, and 1 tablespoon of the sugar into a bowl, rub in the butter, and mix into a dough by gradually adding the cream, which has been lightly beaten with the egg yolk. Form the dough into a ball, wrap in wax paper, and chill in the refrigerator. In a saucepan combine the walnuts, raisins, the remaining sugar, the cinnamon, nutmeg, cloves, and milk and stir over the fire until just heated through. Place this mixture in the refrigerator to cool.

Roll out the dough into a rectangle and spread with the nut and raisin paste. Roll up like a jelly roll, place on a greased baking sheet, and bake at 425° F. for about 45 minutes. Cool and serve with heavy cream. Serves 8.

LOVE LETTERS

¾ cup butter
1½ cups flour
6 egg yolks
Pinch salt

Make dough of these ingredients, cover, and put in refrigerator overnight. Fold sugar, nuts, and cinnamon into the egg whites. Cut pastry into twenty-two pieces and roll out very thin into squares. Place filling in the centers, fold into thirds, then fold the ends over into thirds, making square envelopes. Bake at 350° F. till golden brown—about 20 minutes. When done, remove at once to a platter. When cool, dust with powdered sugar mixed with a little cinnamon.

FILLING
¾ cup fine granulated sugar
1 cup ground blanched almonds
½ teaspoon cinnamon
6 egg whites, beaten stiff

FLAKY PASTRY BERRY ROLL

1 quart berries
1⅓ cups sugar
1 teaspoon nutmeg
1 teaspoon lemon juice
Flaky Pastry for two-crust pie
1 tablespoon flour
2 tablespoons butter
Juice of 1 orange

Wash and pick over the berries. Sprinkle them with 1 cup of the sugar, the nutmeg, and lemon juice. Roll out the pastry very thin into a rectangle. Sprinkle it with the flour, dot with 1 tablespoon of the butter, and distribute the fruit mixture evenly over the surface. Roll tightly as you would a jelly roll and place on a baking sheet. Bake at 350° F. for 30 minutes, basting it with a sauce made by combining the other tablespoon butter, melted, the remaining sugar, and the orange juice. Serves 8.

LITTLE FRIED PIES

Make Flaky Pastry for a two-crust pie and chill it for about 1 hour. Roll it out on a floured board very thin and cut it into 3-inch squares. Place 2 tablespoons of fruit filling in the center of each square, moisten the edges with cold water, and fold the pastry over to make a triangle. Seal the edges by pressing with the tines of a fork. Allow the little pies to stand for a few minutes and then drop them, a few at a time, into hot deep fat (365° F.). Allow the pies to fry until golden brown, remove them to a piece of absorbent paper to drain, sprinkle with confectioners' sugar, and serve hot. Makes 10 pies.

FILLINGS Fresh slices of apples, peaches, or apricots should be parboiled or steamed until tender. Drain the slices and add sugar and cinnamon to taste. Canned sliced fruit may be drained, sugared, and flavored to taste.

HUNGARIAN PITÉ

1⅛ cups butter
2½ cups sifted pastry flour
2 egg yolks, beaten
3 tablespoons heavy cream

Cut the butter into the flour, add the egg yolks and enough cream to make a soft dough. Place in the refrigerator for 1 hour and then roll out on a floured board into a long rectangle. Turn the rectangle so that it is horizontally in front of you and fold into three parts like a napkin (see Puff Pastry). Chill for ½ hour and repeat the rolling, turning, folding, and chilling twice more. Then roll out half the dough and line an 8-inch square baking pan. Spread the desired filling over the dough and cover with the other half of the dough rolled out into a solid sheet or cut into strips. Prick all over with a fork and bake at 350° F. for about 40 minutes. Cool, dust with confectioners' sugar, cut into squares, and pile high on the serving dish. Makes 16 2-inch squares

ALMOND FILLING
4 egg yolks
½ cup sugar
1 cup ground almonds
Juice of ½ lemon
Grated rind of ½ lemon
4 egg whites, beaten stiff

Beat the egg yolks until light, add the sugar gradually, and beat together until thick and pale in color. Stir in the almonds, lemon juice and rind, and fold in the egg whites.

CHEESE FILLING
1 pound dry cottage cheese
1 tablespoon sugar
Pinch salt
Grated rind of ½ lemon
2 tablespoons melted butter
2 egg yolks
4 egg whites, beaten stiff

Press the cheese through a fine sieve and combine it with the sugar, salt, lemon rind, melted butter, and egg yolks. Mix thoroughly and then fold in the egg whites.

POZUNSKI ROSCICI

3½ cups sifted pastry flour
½ pound butter
Pinch salt
1 cup thick sour cream
1 cake or package yeast
2 tablespoons lukewarm water
4 egg yolks

In one bowl combine the flour, butter, and salt, and rub together as for piecrust. In another bowl combine the sour cream, the yeast, which has been softened in the water, and the egg yolks, and mix thoroughly. Pour this mixture into the flour mixture and mix just enough to form it into a soft dough, adding a little more flour if necessary. Place in the refrigerator overnight. Roll this dough out very thin and cut into 4-inch squares. Spread with jam, jelly, or nuts, fold into triangles, and seal by pressing the edges with the floured tines of a fork. Bake at 400° F. for about 20 minutes. Roll in confectioners' sugar while still hot. Makes 24.

BAKLAVA

5 cups sifted pastry flour
¼ teaspoon double-action baking powder
1 teaspoon salt
5 eggs, beaten
5 tablespoons vegetable oil
¾ cup lukewarm water
1½ cups sifted cornstarch
2 cups finely chopped walnuts
1½ pounds butter
½ teaspoon flour
2¼ cups melted vegetable shortening
1 cup honey
1 cup water

In a mixing bowl combine the flour, baking powder, and salt. Add the eggs and the vegetable oil and knead for 15 minutes, adding the lukewarm water a little at a time, forcing the dough from the edges to the center of the bowl. Keep the hands slightly oiled while kneading.

Put a little of the cornstarch on a pastry board. Divide the dough into four equal parts. Make each part into a long roll and divide each into five equal parts. This gives you twenty pieces of dough. Form these into balls, roll them in oil, and place them in an oiled pan. Cover with a towel, place another pan over it, and allow it to rest for 2 hours.

Cover a table top at least 4 feet square with an oilcloth. Sift cornstarch lightly over this and place on it one of the balls of dough. Roll out the dough to the size of a dinner plate. Then work the dough over a wooden rod ¾ inch thick and 4 feet long, pressing the dough out lightly with your hands until it is about 2 feet in diameter. To roll the dough evenly, unroll it from the rod away from you, then roll it onto the rod again, starting from the edge in front of you. Keep the oilcloth sprinkled with cornstarch to prevent the dough from sticking. Fold the circle in half and then in half again and set it aside, covering it with a clean towel. Continue until all the twenty balls are rolled and folded, one on top of the other beneath the towel.

Open and spread out five of the folded circles, one on top of the other. Place a large square pan in the center of these and cut the dough around it. Place each flat piece in the pan with all the cuttings. Repeat with five more sheets of dough and sprinkle evenly with the chopped walnuts. Place the remaining sheets of dough in the pan in the same way until they have all been cut and added, placing the last cuttings beneath the last square sheet. With a sharp knife, cut the dough diagonally into five sections in both directions, making twenty-five diamond-shaped cakes. Allow to rest for 2 hours.

Melt the butter, add the flour, and allow it to simmer on a very low fire for about 20 minutes, or until it forms a white foam. Skim off the foam and pour the butter into a saucepan very carefully so as not to disturb the salt that has settled to the bottom of the saucepan. Add the vegetable shortening to the melted butter and keep this mixture at the simmering point while the Baklava is baking.

Allow the oven to get very hot (450° F.), then turn it down to 350° F. Pour 1½ cups of the butter-shortening mixture over the dough, place it in the oven, and bake for 7 minutes. Pour over another 1½ cups of the fat mixture, reduce the oven temperature to 325° F. and bake for another 7 minutes. Pour in the remainder of the fat mixture, reduce the oven temperature to 300° F. and bake for 20 minutes longer. Remove the Baklava from the oven, drain off all the fat possible through a fine sieve, return the Baklava to the oven and bake for another 5 minutes. Again drain off any remaining fat and bake for another 5 minutes.

When ready to serve, pour the honey, which has been boiled with the water to a thick syrup, around the edge of the pan and between the cut pastry, with a few drops on top, and serve immediately with a garnish of whipped cream.

STRUDELS

Why doesn't the American housewife make a strudel at least once a week—apple or cherry in season, nut or cream cheese or Tyrolese, according to mood?

For years I waited patiently and then not so patiently for a friend of mine, who was born and raised in Bavaria where the strudel is as popular as it is in Austria and Hungary, to show me how to make one, and finally I took the bull by the well-known horns.

Before you could say *Apfelstrudel* three times, I had a very soft, malleable paste which I pulled up and away from and slapped down again hard against the pastry board one hundred times. The spirit had moved me; the results were more than gratifying, and I discovered to my delight that a strudel is no more difficult to make than apple pie, and a great deal more fun! I discovered that four hands are not essential to pulling out the dough into a great thin sheet—you can do it alone; that the filling must be distributed fairly evenly and thinly over two thirds of the sheet; that the dough and filling must be rolled lightly and loosely—and don't spare the butter.

The strudel is best when served still warm from the oven with a dusting of confectioners' sugar and a dash of whipped cream. It is not a dessert that keeps well for another day, but all or part of an unbaked strudel can be kept, covered with wax paper, in the refrigerator for one or several days depending on the filling and baked when needed. Strudels with fruit fillings such as apple or peach should not be refrigerated for more than a day.

STRUDEL DOUGH

3 cups sifted pastry flour
2 eggs, lightly beaten
½ teaspoon salt
3 tablespoons vegetable oil
⅔ cup warm water
1 cup butter

Sift the flour onto a pastry board or enamel table and make a well in the center. In the well put the eggs, salt, and oil and work up a soft dough with the warm water. With one hand, pick up the dough and crash it down again on the table. Repeat this about one hundred times until the dough leaves the board and your hands clean. Scrape together every bit of the dough, using a spatula if necessary, dust with a little flour, and form into a smooth ball. Brush the top with oil, cover with a heated bowl, and allow to rest from 30 minutes to 1 hour.

Spread a clean cloth over a large table (about 3×5 feet) and sprinkle lightly but thoroughly with flour. Place the dough in the middle and roll it out into a large oblong, turning it several times to prevent its sticking to the table, and rolling the outer edges as thinly as possible. Now reach under the dough and start stretching gently from the center to the outer edge, working around the dough until it is as thin as paper and hangs over the edges of the table. Do not pull the dough. Some people work with the backs of their hands. I keep my hands palms up with the fingers straight out, working with a circular motion under the dough. You will soon find the method most convenient to you, and any way is all right providing you do not tear the dough, for it cannot be mended.

With kitchen scissors, cut away the thick edge that overhangs the table and allow the sheet to dry a little while you make the filling. Allow it to lose its stickiness but do not allow it to become brittle. Brush the entire surface with melted butter, sprinkle with bread crumbs, and cover from a half to two thirds of the surface with filling. Fold over the overhanging flaps on the ends and sides, butter the turned-up edges, and then with the aid of the tablecloth start to roll the dough over, pulling the cloth and dough toward you. The last roll should deposit the strudel on a well-buttered baking sheet. Roll fairly loosely to give room for expansion. Brush the surface with melted butter and bake at 350° F. until a golden brown (45–50 minutes), basting it several times during the baking with melted butter. Sprinkle generously with powdered sugar and serve warm with unsweetened whipped cream. Makes 12–15 servings. The trimmings of dough may be kneaded with a little flour, rolled out, and, when dry, cut into broad noodles.

APFELSTRUDEL

Strudel Dough
¼ pound butter, melted
½ cup fine bread crumbs
6 tart apples, peeled, cored, and finely sliced
1 cup sugar
1 teaspoon cinnamon
1 cup raisins
1 cup chopped walnuts or almonds, if desired

Make and stretch Strudel Dough according to instructions. Brush the dough with some of the melted butter, sprinkle two thirds of the surface with the bread crumbs and the apples. Sprinkle over this the sugar, cinnamon, raisins, and nuts. Roll, place on a buttered baking sheet, brush with butter, and bake at 350° F. for 45–50 minutes, basting it frequently with melted butter.

PEACH STRUDEL Use peaches in place of the apples.

SOUR CHERRY STRUDEL Use 2 pounds sour cherries, pitted, in place of the apples. Omit the raisins.

SWEET CHERRY STRUDEL Use 2 pounds sweet black cherries, pitted, in place of the apples. Decrease sugar to ½ cup and omit the cinnamon and raisins.

CREAM CHEESE STRUDEL

Strudel Dough
1 cup butter
⅔ cup sugar
8 eggs, separated
Pinch salt
Grated rind of 1 lemon
1⅔ cups sour cream
1 pound cream cheese
1 cup sultana raisins

Make and stretch Strudel Dough according to instructions. Cream ⅔ cup of the butter, add the sugar gradually, and cream together until light and fluffy. Beat the egg yolks and stir into the butter-sugar mixture, along with the salt, lemon rind, and sour cream. Cream the cream cheese until soft and press it through a fine sieve to remove any lumps, then combine with the first mixture and put it all through the sieve again. Beat the egg whites until stiff and fold in. Spread this mixture about 1 inch thick over about two thirds of the surface of the Strudel Dough, sprinkle with the raisins, and roll the strudel very loosely. Melt the remaining butter and brush the surface of the strudel generously. Place it on a buttered baking sheet and bake at 350° F. for about 45 minutes, or until nicely browned, basting several times throughout the baking.

COTTAGE CHEESE STRUDEL

Strudel Dough
1 tablespoon butter
½ cup sugar
6 eggs, separated
1 pound cottage cheese
1 cup sour cream
½ teaspoon cinnamon
¼ cup melted butter
Grated rind of 1 lemon

Make and stretch Strudel Dough according to instructions. Cream the tablespoon butter with ¼ cup of the sugar and stir in the beaten egg yolks. Press the cottage cheese through a fine sieve and stir into the butter-sugar-egg yolk mixture. Stir in the sour cream and fold in the egg whites, beaten until stiff.

Sprinkle the surface of the Strudel Dough with some of the melted butter, the remaining sugar, mixed with the cinnamon and the grated lemon rind. Over ⅓ of the surface spread the cheese mixture, and roll. Place the strudel on a buttered baking sheet, brush with more melted butter and bake in a 350° F. oven for 45 minutes, or until golden-brown, basting several times throughout the baking.

TYROLESE STRUDEL

Strudel Dough
1 cup butter
½ cup sugar
6 eggs, separated
⅔ cup chopped nuts
¼ cup sliced dates
¼ cup sliced figs
1 cup chopped raisins
Grated rind of 1 lemon
½ teaspoon cinnamon

Make and stretch Strudel Dough according to instructions. Cream ⅔ cup of the butter until light, add the sugar gradually, and cream together until light and fluffy. Stir in the beaten egg yolks and then add the nuts, dates, figs, raisins, lemon rind, and cinnamon. Fold in the egg whites, which have been beaten until stiff. Melt the remaining butter and sprinkle some of it over the surface of the Strudel Dough. Spread the filling over about half of the surface and roll. Place the strudel on a buttered baking sheet, brush with more of the melted butter, and bake at 350° F. for 45 minutes, or until nicely browned, basting several times with the remaining melted butter throughout the baking period.

ALMOND STRUDEL

Strudel Dough
6 eggs, separated
6 tablespoons sugar
1 cup ground blanched almonds
1 cup fine bread crumbs
Juice and grated rind of 1 lemon
1 cup raisins
½ cup melted butter

Make and stretch Strudel Dough according to instructions. Beat the egg yolks with the sugar until thick and pale in color, add half the almonds, half the bread crumbs, the juice and rind of the lemon, and fold in the egg whites, stiffly beaten. Brush the surface of the Strudel Dough with part of the melted butter and sprinkle with the remaining almonds, bread crumbs, and the raisins. Spread the egg mixture over one third of the dough, not too close to the edge. Roll, brush with butter, and bake at 350° F. for 45 minutes, basting several times with the remaining butter. Serve hot or cold with Sabayon Sauce.

CHOCOLATE STRUDEL

Strudel Dough
6 eggs, separated
6 tablespoons sugar
4 ounces bittersweet chocolate, grated
1 cup walnuts, finely ground
1 teaspoon vanilla
½ cup melted butter
½ cup fine white bread crumbs

Make and stretch the Strudel Dough according to instructions. Beat the egg yolks with the sugar until thick and light in color. Add the chocolate, nuts, and vanilla and fold in the egg whites, stiffly beaten. Brush the surface of the Strudel Dough with part of the melted butter and sprinkle with the bread crumbs. Spread the chocolate-egg mixture over one third of the dough, not too close to the edge. Roll, brush with butter, and bake at 350° F. for 45 minutes, basting several times with the remaining melted butter.

LEMON STRUDEL

Strudel Dough
6 eggs, separated
1 cup sugar
Juice of 3 lemons
3 teaspoons cornstarch
⅓ cup water
Grated rind of 1 lemon
½ teaspoon double-action baking powder
½ cup melted butter

Make and stretch Strudel Dough according to instructions. Beat the egg yolks with the sugar and lemon juice until pale in color. Dissolve the cornstarch in the water and mix with the egg-yolk mixture. Cook over boiling water, stirring until thickened. Add the lemon rind and cool. Beat the egg whites with the baking powder until stiff and fold into the cooled mixture. Sprinkle the Strudel Dough with some of the melted butter, spread the filling over one third of the dough, and roll. Place the strudel on a greased baking sheet and bake at 350° F. for 45 minutes, basting several times with the remaining butter.

POPPY SEED STRUDEL

Strudel Dough
1 cup ground poppy seeds
1½ cups sugar
1 teaspoon cinnamon
1 cup raisins
½ cup heavy cream
1 large apple
Grated rind of 1 lemon
½ cup melted butter

Make and stretch the Strudel Dough according to instructions. Mix the ground poppy seeds with 1 cup of the sugar. Add the cinnamon and the raisins. Brush the entire surface of the dough with melted butter and sprinkle with the remaining sugar. Spread the poppy seed mixture over one third of the dough and then sprinkle with the cream. Grate the apple and the lemon rind over the surface, roll, brush with some of the butter, and bake at 350° F. for 45 minutes, basting several times with the remaining butter.

SOUR CREAM STRUDEL

Strudel Dough
1 tablespoon butter
½ cup sugar
5 eggs, separated
1 cup sour cream
Grated rind of 1 lemon
½ cup melted butter
½ cup bread crumbs
½ cup chopped nuts
1 cup raisins

Make and stretch Strudel Dough according to instructions. Cream the 1 tablespoon butter and the sugar until light and fluffy. Add the beaten egg yolks, then the sour cream and lemon rind, and fold in the egg whites, stiffly beaten. Brush the surface of the dough with some of the melted butter, sprinkle evenly with the crumbs, nuts, and raisins. Spread the filling on one third of the dough, not too close to the edge. Roll, brush with butter, and bake at 350° F. for 45 minutes, basting several times with the remaining butter.

LAYER STRUDEL

Prepare twice the amount of Strudel Dough in the basic recipe at the beginning of this chapter, cut it in half, and stretch one half at a time. Allow it to dry until it is no longer sticky but not until it is brittle and cut it into sheets the size of a large baking pan. Butter the baking pan and place three or four layers of dough one on top of the other, buttering each layer generously. Butter the top layer, sprinkle with sugar and cinnamon, chopped nuts, and a few raisins. Continue until half of the leaves have been used. Now spread with any desired strudel filling and continue piling leaves on the top in the same way as on the bottom. Butter the top generously and bake at 350° F. for 45 minutes or until golden brown. Cut into serving squares, dust with powdered sugar, and serve with unsweetened whipped cream.

7. Frostings, Fillings, Sauces

DECORATIVE FROSTINGS

ROYAL ICING

3 egg whites
2 cups sifted confectioners' sugar
½ teaspoon cream of tartar
1 drop ultramarine blue vegetable food coloring

Place the egg whites in a round-bottomed bowl and add about one third of the sugar. Beat with a wooden spoon until the mixture is smooth and creamy. Then add the cream of tartar and, if no other coloring is to be used, the ultramarine. This is to make the icing a pure, cold white and will counteract any slight yellowing that might occur. Add more sugar and beat. Continue beating, adding the remaining sugar until the mixture is the right consistency. For spreading, it should be the consistency of heavy cream. For ornamenting, it should be so thick that a peak, made when the spoon is withdrawn, will remain. The more you beat, the fluffier and lighter will be the icing, so use an electric beater if you have one. When finished, cover with a damp cloth until ready to use.

If you wish to color it delicately with a drop of vegetable food coloring, omit the ultramarine.

CONFECTIONERS' SUGAR ICING

Combine ¾ cup confectioners' sugar and 2 tablespoons hot milk. Beat until smooth and flavor with vanilla.

ORANGE SUGAR FROSTING

Mix into a smooth paste 6 tablespoons orange juice, 2¼ teaspoons grated orange rind, and 3¾ cups confectioners' sugar.

UNCOOKED BUTTER FROSTINGS

[handwritten: 16 oz. Icing Sugar]

These frostings are simple and quick to make. They spread easily and stay moist. Sifted confectioners' sugar is beaten into creamed butter. Then some liquid is added to bring it to the proper spreading consistency. Milk or cream are the usual liquids used, but different flavors may be made by using instead fruit juices, brandy or rum, or liqueurs.

VANILLA BUTTER FROSTING

4 tablespoons butter
4 cups sifted confectioners' sugar
¼ cup heavy cream, scalded
1 teaspoon vanilla

Cream the butter until light and gradually beat in the sugar, alternating with the hot cream, until the mixture is the right spreading consistency. Flavor with vanilla.

BUTTERFLY FROSTING

4 tablespoons butter
5 cups sifted confectioners' sugar
2 egg whites
2 tablespoons heavy cream
1½ teaspoons vanilla
¼ teaspoon salt

Cream the butter. Add part of the sugar gradually, blending after each addition. Add the remaining sugar alternately with the egg whites, then the cream, until it is the right spreading consistency. Beat thoroughly after each addition. Add the vanilla and salt.

FOR COLORED DECORATIVE FROSTING Divide frosting into as many parts as you wish colors. Keep one part white. To another part stir in 1 square (ounce) unsweetened chocolate, melted, and 1 tablespoon light cream. Tint the remaining frostings with a tiny bit of yellow, green, or pink food coloring to give delicate shades.

While using this frosting, keep the containers covered to avoid the formation of a crust. If necessary, thin occasionally with a few drops cream.

ALMOND BUTTER FROSTING

4 tablespoons butter
2 cups confectioners' sugar
1/8 teaspoon salt
1 teaspoon almond flavoring
3 tablespoons light cream

Cream butter thoroughly. Add sugar gradually, together with the salt and flavoring. Stir until fluffy, adding cream gradually to make it the right consistency.

BROWNED BUTTER FROSTING

1/4 cup butter
2 cups sifted confectioners' sugar
2 tablespoons heavy cream
2 teaspoons vanilla
1 tablespoon hot water

Melt the butter in a saucepan until it is lightly browned. Remove from the fire and stir in the sugar, cream, vanilla, and hot water. Beat until the mixture is smooth and a good spreading consistency.

CHOCOLATE BUTTER FROSTING

3 squares (ounces) unsweetened chocolate
3 tablespoons butter
2 cups sifted confectioners' sugar
Pinch salt
5 tablespoons hot light cream
1 teaspoon vanilla

Melt the chocolate and butter over hot water and beat until it is smooth and free from lumps. Stir the sugar and salt into the hot cream, add the melted chocolate-butter mixture and beat well. Stir in the vanilla and a little hot milk, if the frosting is too stiff to spread nicely.

COCOA BUTTER FROSTING

4 tablespoons butter
6 tablespoons cocoa
5 tablespoons scalding-hot milk
2 cups sifted confectioners' sugar
1 teaspoon vanilla

Melt together over hot water the butter and cocoa and beat until the mixture is smooth. Pour the hot milk over the sugar and stir until the sugar is dissolved. Stir in the vanilla and then the hot cocoa mixture. Beat until the frosting is thick enough to spread.

MOCHA FROSTING

4 cups sifted confectioners' sugar
4 teaspoons cocoa
Pinch salt
¼ cup butter
4-5 tablespoons strong black coffee
1 teaspoon vanilla

Sift together the sugar, cocoa, and salt. Cream the butter until it is fluffy. Add the sugar mixture alternately with the coffee, beating after each addition until the frosting is smooth. Add the vanilla and continue to beat until the frosting is very fluffy.

BROWN BEAUTY ICING

Combine in a bowl 1 cup sifted confectioners' sugar, 3 egg yolks, 3 tablespoons milk, 2 squares (ounces) unsweetened chocolate, melted, 3 tablespoons soft butter, and 1 teaspoon vanilla. Beat with a rotary beater until the mixture is the right consistency to spread.

FONDANT FROSTINGS

A candy thermometer should be used in cooking the syrup for fondant frostings in order to have exactly the right stage for beating into a creamy icing. These frostings harden quickly, and a certain amount of technique is needed in spreading them over a cake. They may be kept soft and workable over boiling water.

PLAIN FONDANT FROSTING

2 cups sugar
1 cup water
½ teaspoon cream of tartar, or
2 tablespoons light corn syrup

In a saucepan combine the ingredients and stir over a low flame until the sugar is dissolved. Cover and bring to a rapid boil. Uncover and continue to boil, without stirring, until a small amount of syrup forms a soft ball when dropped into cold water, or to 238° F. on a candy thermometer. Remove from the fire and allow it to cool to lukewarm. Then beat with a wooden spoon until the syrup becomes white and creamy. Spread quickly over the cake. If it becomes too dry for smooth spreading, add a little hot water and beat until smooth. The fondant may be delicately tinted with vegetable food coloring and flavored as desired.

DIPPING WITH FONDANT Make Plain Fondant Frosting and keep it soft over boiling water, stirring in a few drops boiling water if the mixture becomes too stiff. Add any flavoring or vegetable coloring desired, but stir as little as possible to avoid crystallization. Lower small cakes or cookies into the liquid fondant on a dipping fork. Raise the cake and draw the dipping fork lightly across the edge of the pan to remove any excess fondant, then invert the dipped cake onto a platter or wax paper. Work quickly so that the fondant will not become too thick. If it should thicken, however, add a few more drops boiling water to bring it back to the right consistency. Decorate the little cakes with a bit of candied fruit or rind, nuts, or tiny sugar flowers.

CHOCOLATE FONDANT FROSTING

3 cups sugar
¼ teaspoon cream of tartar
⅓ cup butter
1 cup milk
4 squares (ounces) unsweetened chocolate
1 teaspoon vanilla

In a saucepan combine the sugar, cream of tartar, butter, milk, and chocolate. Bring slowly to a boil, stirring only until the sugar is thoroughly dissolved, and cook until it forms a very soft ball when a small amount is dropped into cold water (232° F.). Stir the mixture occasionally to prevent burning. Remove from fire and allow it to cool to lukewarm. Add the vanilla and beat until it becomes creamy and barely holds its shape. Spread quickly on the cake. If it becomes too dry for smooth spreading, add a little hot water and beat.

MAPLE FONDANT FROSTING

1⅓ cups sugar
⅔ cup grated maple sugar
½ cup butter
⅔ cup light cream

Combine all the ingredients in a saucepan. Bring to a boil and cook until it forms a soft ball when tried in cold water or to 234° F. on a candy thermometer. Allow it to cool and then beat until it is the right consistency to spread.

CREAMY COOKED FROSTINGS

VANILLA CREAM FROSTING

½ cup butter
2½ tablespoons cake flour
Pinch salt
½ cup milk
3 cups sifted confectioners' sugar
1 teaspoon vanilla

In a saucepan melt the butter. Remove from the fire and stir in the flour and salt. Stir in gradually the milk, bring the mixture to a boil, stirring constantly, and boil for 1 minute. Remove from heat. Stir in the confectioners' sugar, set saucepan over cracked ice, and beat until the mixture is the right consistency to spread. Stir in the vanilla. Frost cake and decorate with walnut halves.

ORANGE CREAM FROSTING

¼ cup butter
4 tablespoons cake flour
Pinch salt
½ cup orange juice
3 cups sifted confectioners' sugar
1 tablespoon grated orange peel

In a saucepan melt the butter, remove from the heat, and stir in the flour and salt. Stir in gradually the orange juice, bring to a boil, stirring constantly, and allow it to boil for 1 minute. Don't be alarmed if the mixture curdles. Remove again from the heat and stir in the sugar. Place the saucepan over cracked ice and beat until the mixture is the right consistency to spread. Stir in the grated orange peel.

VARIATIONS
1. Add ½ cup chopped nut meats.
2. Brown the butter before adding the flour.
3. Reduce butter to ¼ cup and stir in 2 ounces unsweetened chocolate, melted, after the sugar has been added.

CHOCOLATE BUTTER CREAM

4 squares (ounces) unsweetened chocolate
2 tablespoons hot water
4 egg yolks
¼ teaspoon salt
½ cup sugar
1 cup sweet butter

Melt the chocolate and water over a flow flame, stirring constantly until the chocolate is melted and the mixture is smooth. In the top of a double boiler beat the egg yolks and salt until they are light. Gradually beat in the sugar and then the melted chocolate. Cook over boiling water, stirring constantly, until the mixture is smooth and thick. Remove from the heat and beat in the butter, bit by bit. Chill the frosting until it is a good spreading consistency.

MOCHA BUTTER CREAM

1 cup sugar
⅓ cup water
⅛ teaspoon cream of tartar
4 egg yolks
1½ cups sweet butter
5 ounces semi-sweet chocolate
4 tablespoons strong coffee
2 tablespoons Jamaica rum

In a saucepan combine the sugar, water, and cream of tartar. Stir over a low flame until the sugar is dissolved and then boil rapidly until the syrup spins a long thread. Beat the egg yolks until thick and then gradually beat in the syrup and continue beating until the mixture is stiff. Then beat in the sweet butter bit by bit. Pour the coffee over the chocolate and stir the mixture over a low flame until the chocolate is melted and the mixture is smooth. Stir this into the butter cream along with the rum. Chill in the refrigerator until it is the right consistency to spread. This takes a lot of beating, so use your electric beater if you have one.

In warm weather or in a hot kitchen, this frosting has a tendency to become soft. The cake should be kept in a cool place or in the refrigerator until serving time.

BETTY CROCKER CHOCOLATE FROSTING

Mix together in a saucepan 1¼ cups sifted confectioners' sugar, ⅛ teaspoon salt, 5 tablespoons cocoa, 2½ tablespoons all-purpose flour. Stir in 1½ tablespoons butter and ½ cup milk. Place over low heat and allow it to boil slowly for 7 minutes, or until very thick, stirring constantly. Cool. Stir in ½ teaspoon vanilla.

COOKED COCOA ICING

- 2 tablespoons cornstarch
- 2 cups granulated sugar
- 4 tablespoons cocoa
- 2 cups boiling water
- 4 tablespoons butter

In a saucepan combine the cornstarch, sugar, and cocoa. Stir in the water and cook over a low flame, stirring constantly, until thick. Remove from heat, stir in the butter until it is melted, and cool.

CHOCOLATE CREAM FOR DOBOS TORTE

- 5 squares (ounces) unsweetened chocolate
- 2 tablespoons coffee
- 4 egg yolks
- ¼ teaspoon salt
- ½ cup sugar
- 1 cup sweet butter

Melt the chocolate with the coffee in a saucepan placed over boiling water, stirring constantly until the chocolate is melted and the mixture is smooth and free from lumps. Beat the egg yolks with the salt until light, add the sugar gradually, and continue to beat until the mixture is thick and pale in color. Beat the egg mixture into the chocolate, and cook over the hot water for 5–6 minutes, stirring constantly, or until the mixture is thick and smooth. Allow it to cool slightly while you cream the butter. Add the creamed butter bit by bit to the chocolate cream, beating briskly after each addition. Chill the filling, stirring occasionally, until it has reached a spreading consistency.

MOCHA FILLING AND FROSTING

    1 tablespoon flour
    3 tablespoons sugar
    1 egg
    ½ cup strong coffee
    1 teaspoon vanilla
    ⅓ cup butter
    ½ cup confectioners' sugar
    ½ cup finely chopped blanched almonds

In a saucepan combine the flour, sugar, egg, and coffee. Cook over boiling water, stirring constantly, until thick. Remove from heat and stir in the vanilla and the confectioners' sugar and butter, which have been creamed together into a smooth paste. The almonds may be stirred into the icing or sprinkled on top after cake is iced.

RUSSIAN TEACAKE ICING

    3 egg yolks
    ⅜ cup sugar
    1 tablespoon flour
    ¾ cup hot milk
    1 tablespoon (envelope) gelatin
    ¼ cup cold water
    1 teaspoon vanilla
    1 cup heavy cream, whipped

Beat egg yolks until thick and lemon-colored. Beat in gradually the sugar, which has been sifted with the flour. Stir in the hot milk, place over boiling water, and cook, stirring, for 3 minutes. Add the gelatin, which has been soaked in the cold water for 5 minutes, and stir until it is completely dissolved. Stir in the vanilla and cool. When cool, fold in the cream. Ice cake and sprinkle top and sides with chopped nuts.

RUM CREAM TOPPING

    1 tablespoon (envelope) gelatin
    ¼ cup cold water
    2 cups hot milk
    ¾ cup sugar
    4 egg yolks, beaten
    2 ounces Jamaica rum
    1 cup heavy cream, whipped

In a saucepan soak the gelatin in the water for 5 minutes. Stir in the hot milk and sugar, and stir over the fire until the mixture is very hot but not boiling. Pour very gradually over the egg yolks, stirring constantly. Add the rum and stir the mixture over cracked ice until it is cool and has begun to set. Fold in the whipped cream and pour over the cake, which is still in the pan. Chill in the refrigerator until ready to serve.

SOUR CREAM FROSTING

Cook 2 cups sugar with 1 cup sour cream very slowly for about 20 minutes, or until it forms a soft ball when a little of it is dropped into cold water. Cool. Stir in ½ teaspoon maple flavoring, beat until it is creamy, and spread it between the layers and cover top and sides of a cake. Decorate cake with walnut halves.

ORANGE FLUFF TOPPING

3 egg yolks
½ cup sugar
½ cup orange juice
1 tablespoon grated orange rind
1 cup heavy cream, whipped
½ cup grated fresh coconut

In the top of a double boiler combine the egg yolks and sugar. Stir in the orange juice and cook the mixture over hot water, stirring constantly, until it thickens (about 15 minutes). Remove from the heat and stir in the orange rind. Cool and then fold in the whipped cream and coconut.

MERINGUE FROSTINGS

MOUNTAIN CREAM, *Italian Meringue*

1 cup sugar
⅓ cup water
¼ teaspoon cream of tartar
4 egg whites
1 teaspoon vanilla

In a small saucepan combine the sugar, water, and cream of tartar and stir until the sugar is dissolved. Place on heat, cover the pan, and bring the syrup to a boil. Remove cover and boil rapidly until the syrup spins a long thread (6–8 inches), or to 242° F. on a candy thermometer. Beat the egg whites until stiff enough to hold a peak. Pour the hot syrup slowly, in a thin stream, into the egg whites, beating constantly with an electric or rotary beater until all the syrup has been added and the frosting stands in very stiff peaks. Stir in vanilla.

    CARAMEL   Use light brown sugar in place of white.
    COFFEE   Use strong black coffee in place of water.
    CHOCOLATE   When the frosting is ready to spread, add 3 ounces unsweetened chocolate which has been melted and cooled.
    FRUIT   When frosting is ready to spread, fold in 1 cup fruit purée.
    JAM   When frosting is ready to spread, fold in 1 cup strawberry jam.
    NUT   When frosting is ready to spread, fold in 1 cup chopped nuts.
    MARSHMALLOW   Make half the quantity of frosting and beat in 12 chopped marshmallows as soon as all the syrup has been added to the egg whites.
    PEPPERMINT   Blend into frosting ⅔ cup crushed peppermint candy.

7-MINUTE FROSTING

3 egg whites
¾ cup sugar
6 tablespoons light corn syrup
Pinch salt
1 teaspoon vanilla

In the top of a double boiler combine the egg whites, unbeaten, sugar, corn syrup, and salt. Place over rapidly boiling water and beat with a rotary beater for 7 minutes, or until the mixture stands in soft mounds. Remove from the heat, add the vanilla, and continue beating until the frosting stands in peaks.

7-MINUTE LEMON FROSTING

1 egg white
¾ cup sugar
1 tablespoon water
2 tablespoons lemon juice
1 teaspoon grated lemon rind

In the top of a double boiler combine the egg white, unbeaten, sugar, water, and lemon juice. Place over rapidly boiling water and beat with a rotary beater for 7 minutes, or until the mixture stands in soft mounds. Remove from the heat and continue beating until the frosting is thick enough to spread. Stir in the lemon rind and a little yellow vegetable coloring, if desired.

4-MINUTE STRAWBERRY FROSTING

1 egg white
½ cup sugar
Pinch salt
⅔ cup sliced strawberries

In the top of a double boiler combine the egg white, unbeaten, the sugar, salt, and half the sliced strawberries. Place over rapidly boiling water and beat with a rotary beater for 4 minutes. Remove from the heat and continue to beat until the frosting is cool. Fold in the remaining strawberries.

LEMON MERINGUE

Beat gradually ½ cup sifted confectioners' sugar into 1 stiffly beaten egg white. Add a dash salt and the juice and rind of ½ lemon.

FILLINGS

RUM OR VANILLA PASTRY CREAM

1 egg
1 egg yolk
3 tablespoons sugar
3 tablespoons flour
2 teaspoons gelatin
¾ cup hot milk
2 egg whites, stiffly beaten
½ cup heavy cream, whipped
Vanilla or rum

In a saucepan combine the egg, egg yolk, sugar, and flour and beat until it is smooth. Mix in the gelatin and then gradually stir in the hot milk. Stir the mixture over the fire until it becomes thick and then stir it over cracked ice until it is cool. Stir in the egg whites and whipped cream and flavor with either 2 teaspoons vanilla or 2 tablespoons Jamaica rum.

CHOCOLATE PASTRY CREAM

1 egg
1 egg yolk
3 tablespoons sugar
3 tablespoons flour

1 tablespoon gelatin
6 ounces semi-sweet chocolate
5 tablespoons strong coffee
¾ cup hot milk
2 egg whites, stiffly beaten
½ cup heavy cream, whipped
1 tablespoon rum

Put the egg, egg yolk, sugar, and flour into a saucepan and beat until light and fluffy. Mix in the gelatin. Break the chocolate into small pieces, add the coffee, and stir over a low flame until melted. Add the hot milk gradually, stirring constantly. Stir this chocolate milk into the egg mixture and stir over a low flame until thickened and very hot. Stir over cracked ice until cool. Fold in the egg whites, cream, and rum.

CHARLOTTE RUSSE CREAM

Dissolve 1 tablespoon (envelope) gelatin in ½ cup water. Stir in 2 tablespoons sugar. Whip 1 cup heavy cream until stiff, flavor it with vanilla, and then strain in the dissolved gelatin. Mix thoroughly, turn into cake shell, and chill until it is set.

CREME À L'ANGLAISE COLLEE

½ tablespoon (envelope) gelatin
2 tablespoons water
⅓ cup sugar
3 egg yolks
1 cup milk
1 piece vanilla bean

Soften the gelatin in the water and let it stand for 5 minutes. Combine the sugar and egg yolks and beat the mixture until it is thick and pale in color. Scald the milk and vanilla bean together and then stir it gradually into the egg-yolk mixture. Cook slowly, stirring constantly, over low heat until it comes to the boiling point. Do not let it boil. Remove the vanilla bean and stir in the softened gelatin. Cool over cracked ice, stirring vigorously at first and then from time to time to prevent a crust from forming on top.

BAVAROIS VANILLE, *Vanilla Bavarian Cream* As the mixture begins to set or starts to become thickened as it is stirred over the cracked ice, fold in ¾ cup heavy cream, whipped. Then stir occasionally to prevent a crust from forming on top.

CHOCOLATE BAVARIAN CREAM Follow the directions above for Vanilla Bavarian Cream, adding 2 squares (ounces) unsweetened chocolate, melted, along with the gelatin.

COFFEE BAVARIAN CREAM Follow the recipe for Vanilla Bavarian Cream above but omit the vanilla bean. Add 1½ tablespoons coffee extract along with the gelatin.

STRAWBERRY VANILLA CREAM

1 quart strawberries
1 tablespoon lemon juice
¾ cup sugar
2 tablespoons gelatin
¼ cup cold water
2 cups heavy cream, whipped

Wash and hull the berries; mash them and strain them through a fine sieve. To the resulting purée add the lemon juice and sugar and stir until the sugar is completely dissolved. Soften the gelatin in the cold water, place it over hot water, and stir until the gelatin is dissolved. Add the gelatin to the strawberries and stir the mixture over cracked ice until it begins to thicken. Then fold in the whipped cream.

STRAWBERRY CREAM

1 cup strawberry purée
Sugar to taste
½ tablespoon (envelope) gelatin
2 tablespoons cold water
1 cup heavy cream

Rub through a fine sieve enough fresh or frozen strawberries to make 1 cup purée and sweeten it to taste. Soak the gelatin in the cold water for 5 minutes and then dissolve it over boiling water. Strain this into the purée and mix thoroughly. Whip the cream, not too stiff, and fold into the purée.

CRÈME PATISSIERE I

2 cups milk
½ teaspoon vanilla
6 tablespoons flour
½ teaspoon cornstarch
½ cup sugar
4 egg yolks

Heat the milk with the vanilla until nearly boiling. Combine the flour, cornstarch, sugar, and egg yolks in a saucepan and beat well.

Add the hot milk gradually, place the saucepan over the fire, and cook until thickened, stirring rapidly. This cream should be the consistency of mayonnaise when finished and may be flavored with curaçao, Grand Marnier, chartreuse, or rum.

CRÈME PÂTISSIÈRE II

¾ cup sugar
6 egg yolks
⅓ cup flour
2 cups milk
1 piece vanilla bean

Mix together the sugar and egg yolks and beat the mixture until it is thick and pale in color. Add the flour and mix just enough to combine. Scald the milk with the vanilla bean and stir it gradually into the egg-yolk mixture. Then cook over a low flame, stirring vigorously, until it reaches the boiling point. Cook, stirring, for 2 minutes. Remove the vanilla bean. Strain and cool, stirring occasionally to prevent the formation of a crust on top.

CREME ST. HONORÉ

3 cups Crème Pâtissière
1 tablespoon (envelope) gelatin
2 tablespoons cold water
6 egg whites
3 tablespoons sugar

Soften the gelatin in the water and add it to the Crème Pâtissière while it is still hot, then cool. Combine thoroughly. Beat the egg whites until stiff, gradually beat in the sugar, and fold this meringue into the cool cream.

CUSTARD FILLING

3 egg yolks
½ cup sugar
2 tablespoons cornstarch
2 cups rich milk

Combine the egg yolks, sugar and cornstarch and add gradually, while stirring, the milk. Cook, stirring, over hot water until thickened, and allow to cool before using.

LEMON CUSTARD FILLING

1 cup sugar
2½ tablespoons flour
Grated rind of 2 lemons
¼ cup lemon juice
1 egg, slightly beaten
1 teaspoon butter

Combine the sugar and flour, add the lemon rind and juice and the egg. Cook over boiling water, stirring constantly, until thickened. Stir in the butter and cool.

ORANGE CUSTARD FILLING Reduce the amount of sugar to ½ cup and add the grated rind of ½ orange, ¼ cup orange juice, and 1 tablespoon lemon juice, in place of the lemon rind and juice.

ORANGE RAISIN FILLING

2 tablespoons brown sugar
2 tablespoons cake flour
¼ cup orange juice
¾ cup water
1 cup raisins
Grated rind of 1 orange

In a saucepan combine the sugar and flour. Gradually stir in the orange juice and water. Add the raisins. Cook over low heat for 10 minutes, or until thickened, stirring constantly. Remove from the heat, stir in the grated orange rind, and cool.

DATE FILLING

Boil 1 pound pitted dates, chopped, with 1 cup sugar and ½ cup water, stirring constantly until smooth (about 8 minutes), and then cool. Stir in 1 tablespoon lemon juice and 1 tablespoon butter and cool.

DATE AND NUT FILLING

Combine in a saucepan 1½ cups sliced dates, ½ cup sugar, and ½ cup water. Cook over direct heat, stirring constantly, until it becomes a thick paste. Cool and mix in ½ cup chopped nuts.

RAISIN, FIG, AND DATE FILLING

Mix together in a saucepan ½ cup finely cut raisins, ½ cup finely cut figs, ½ cup finely cut dates, ½ cup sugar, ½ cup water, and 2 tablespoons lemon juice. Cook slowly, stirring constantly, until thickened (about 8 minutes). Cool before using.

PINEAPPLE FILLING

Mix together in a saucepan 1 cup sugar and 4 tablespoons flour. Stir in 1½ cups crushed pineapple (No. 2 can), 4 tablespoons lemon juice, 3 tablespoons butter, and ¾ cup pineapple juice. Cook slowly, stirring constantly, until thickened (about 8 minutes). Cool.

PRUNE ORANGE FILLING

3 cups cut-up, cooked, drained prunes
½ cup sugar
½ cup orange juice
2 tablespoons lemon juice
2 tablespoons grated orange rind

Combine ingredients in a saucepan. Cook over low heat, stirring constantly, for 8 minutes, or until thickened. Cool before using.

DATE APRICOT FILLING

1 cup cut-up dates
2 cups mashed, cooked, drained, dried apricots
½ cup sugar
2 tablespoons apricot juice

Combine ingredients in a saucepan. Cook over low heat, stirring constantly, for 8 minutes, or until thickened. Cool before using.

SAUCES

THIN CHOCOLATE SAUCE

1 cup sugar
½ cup water or coffee
Pinch cream of tartar
1½ squares chocolate, melted
½ teaspoon vanilla

Combine the sugar, water, and cream of tartar. Stir over a low flame until the sugar is dissolved and then boil rapidly for 5 minutes. Pour slowly over the chocolate and mix thoroughly. Cool slightly and flavor with the vanilla. Serve hot or cold.

BUTTERSCOTCH SAUCE

1¼ cups brown sugar
⅔ cup corn syrup
4 tablespoons butter

⅜ cup heavy cream
⅜ cup milk

Place the brown sugar, corn syrup, and butter in a saucepan, bring to a boil, and cook until a soft ball may be formed when a small amount of the syrup is dropped into cold water, or to 230° F. on a candy thermometer. Add the cream and milk and stir until the ingredients are well combined.

JAM OR JELLY SAUCE

Put 1 cup well-flavored jam or jelly through a sieve. Stir in 3 tablespoons hot water and stir the mixture over a low flame until it is heated through.

APRICOT SAUCE

¾ cup apricot purée
Sugar to taste
¾ cup heavy cream, whipped

Drain canned or stewed apricots and rub enough through a sieve to make ¾ cup purée. Sweeten the purée to taste and then fold in the cream, which has been whipped, but not too stiff.

LEMON SAUCE

½ cup sugar
1 tablespoon cornstarch
1 cup water
2 tablespoons butter
1 teaspoon grated lemon rind
2 tablespoons lemon juice
Pinch salt

Combine the sugar, cornstarch, and water in a saucepan and stir the mixture over a low flame until it is thickened. Remove from the heat and stir in the butter, lemon rind and juice, and salt.

ORANGE SAUCE

Peel and dice 6 oranges, being careful to save all the juice. Add to the oranges and juice 2 tablespoons sugar and bring the mixture to the boiling point. Remove from the heat and stir in 2 tablespoons kirsch, rum, or brandy. Serve cold over hot pudding.

STRAWBERRY OR RASPBERRY SAUCE

Mash 2 cups strawberries or raspberries, fresh or frozen, and force them through a fine sieve. Sweeten to taste with sugar. A little whipped cream may be folded in if desired.

FRUIT SAUCE

Add a little lemon juice to 1 cup of any fruit juice. Add sugar to taste, bring to a boil, and stir in 1 teaspoon cornstarch mixed to a paste with a little of the cold fruit juice.

SABAYON SAUCE, *Wine Sauce*

4 egg yolks
½ cup sugar
1 cup white wine
½ cup heavy cream, if desired

Blend the ingredients and whip over boiling water until it becomes thick and fluffy. Remove from the heat but continue to stir for a few minutes. Cool and fold in, if desired, ½ cup heavy cream, whipped.

FOAMY BRANDY SAUCE

1 cup sugar
1 tablespoon quick-cooking tapioca
Pinch salt
1½ cups boiling water
1 egg
1½ tablespoons butter
¼ cup brandy, sherry, or fruit juice

Combine the sugar, tapioca, and salt in the upper part of a double boiler. Add the water gradually, stirring constantly. Beat the egg until light, blend it with a little of the hot sauce, and stir it into the sauce in the double boiler. Cook over hot water, stirring constantly, for 5 minutes, or until slightly thickened. Remove from the heat and stir in the butter and brandy or flavoring.

HARD SAUCE

Cream ½ cup sweet butter until it is very fluffy. Gradually add 1 cup confectioners' sugar, or enough to make a firm paste, and 1 tablespoon rum, brandy, or liqueur.

APRICOT GLAZE

Soak ¼ pound dried apricots overnight in 1 cup water. Cook them with ⅓ cup sugar until soft. Strain through a fine sieve, and pour, while hot, into a sterilized jar; seal. When ready to use, dilute the glaze with a little hot water to make the proper spreading consistency.

BAKED PRODUCTS IN YOUR HOME FREEZER

BREAD OR ROLLS, BAKED
TO FREEZE Cool, wrap in freezer paper, and freeze.
MAXIMUM STORAGE 12 months.
TO USE Thaw in unopened freezer wrapper in a 300° F. oven for 30 minutes.

BREAD, UNBAKED
TO FREEZE Let dough rise until doubled in bulk. Shape loaves and place in greased bread pans. Grease top of bread well, wrap and freeze.
MAXIMUM STORAGE 1 week.
TO USE Remove from freezer to warm place to rise until nearly doubled in bulk. Bake as freshly made bread or rolls.

ROLLS, UNBAKED
TO FREEZE   Let dough rise until doubled in bulk. Shape rolls of any desired shape and place on greased baking sheet. Grease surface of rolls and freeze. Package, wrap, and store.
MAXIMUM STORAGE   1 week.
TO USE   Remove from freezer to warm place to rise until nearly doubled in bulk. Bake as freshly made bread or rolls.

BAKING POWDER BISCUITS
TO FREEZE   Bake, cool, wrap in freezer paper, and freeze.
MAXIMUM STORAGE   4 weeks.
TO USE   Thaw in unopened freezer wrapper in a 300° F. oven for 20 minutes.

CAKES, BAKED, ICED
TO FREEZE   Frost cake and freeze. Then wrap in freezer paper and store.
MAXIMUM STORAGE   6 months (fruitcakes 1 year).
TO USE   Thaw at room temperature for 3 hours. Keep cake wrapped during thawing to prevent moisture collecting on the surface.

CAKES, BAKED, UNICED (Spongecakes, angel food, gingerbread, and pound cakes)
TO FREEZE   Wrap cooled layers or loaves and freeze.
MAXIMUM STORAGE   6 months (fruitcakes 1 year).
TO USE   Thaw at room temperature for 3 hours. Keep cake wrapped during thawing to prevent moisture collecting on the surface.

CAKE BATTERS, UNBAKED
TO FREEZE   Package and freeze.
MAXIMUM STORAGE   2 weeks.
TO USE   Thaw in package for 1½ hours at room temperature. Turn into greased cake pan or muffin cups and bake according to recipe.

COOKIES, BAKED
TO FREEZE   Cool, package, wrap in freezer paper, and freeze.
MAXIMUM STORAGE   6 months.
TO USE   Thaw at room temperature for 1 hour, or in a 350° F. oven for 8 minutes.

ROLLED COOKIES, UNBAKED
TO FREEZE   Cut dough into cooky shapes. Stack them with two pieces wax paper between each cooky and freeze.

MAXIMUM STORAGE   6 months.
TO USE   Place cookies a little apart on a greased baking sheet without thawing. Bake according to recipe. Baking time will be increased by about 3 minutes.

DROP COOKIES, UNBAKED
TO FREEZE   Drop dough on cooky sheet close together and freeze. Package in carton with two pieces wax paper between each layer. Wrap and store.
MAXIMUM STORAGE   3 months.
TO USE   Remove from carton, place 1 inch apart on greased baking sheet, and bake without thawing according to recipe, increasing baking time about 3 minutes.

REFRIGERATOR COOKIES, UNBAKED
TO FREEZE   Pack dough in cooky molds or shape into rolls, wrap, and freeze.
MAXIMUM STORAGE   6 months.
TO USE   Slice while frozen, place cookies a little apart on a greased baking sheet, and bake according to recipe, increasing baking time about 3 minutes.

MERINGUES, BAKED
TO FREEZE   Cool, package, and freeze.
MAXIMUM STORAGE   1 month.
TO USE   Thaw at room temperature for 10 minutes.

CREAM PUFFS, ÉCLAIRS, BAKED
TO FREEZE   Cool, package, and freeze. (May be filled with ice cream before packaging.)
MAXIMUM STORAGE   1 month.
TO USE   Thaw at room temperature for 10 minutes, fill, and serve.

PIES, BAKED
TO FREEZE   Cool, wrap, and freeze.
MAXIMUM STORAGE   4 months.
TO USE   Thaw in 350° F. oven for 30 minutes.

PIES, TWO-CRUST, UNBAKED
TO FREEZE   Make fruit pies according to recipe, but do not cut openings in the top crust. Wrap and freeze.
MAXIMUM STORAGE   4 months.

TO USE   Cut steam vents in the top crust and bake without thawing according to the recipe. Baking time will be increased about 15 minutes.

PIES, OPEN, UNBAKED

TO FREEZE   Make pie in pie plate according to recipe and freeze. If pie filling is heaped above the crust, protect it by placing a ring of cardboard, cut as high as the filling, around the pie before wrapping.
MAXIMUM STORAGE   4 months.

TO FREEZE LEFTOVER EGG WHITES

Simply package and freeze. 1½ tablespoons thawed egg whites=1 egg white.

TO FREEZE LEFTOVER EGG YOLKS

Add 1 tablespoon sugar or corn syrup to each cup egg yolks. Blend with a rotary beater thoroughly, but without whipping air into them. Strain into package, skim off any air bubbles from the surface, and freeze immediately. 1 tablespoon thawed yolk=1 egg yolk.

ICE CREAM CAKE FROM YOUR HOME FREEZER

Bake an angel food or spongecake in a loaf pan (10×5×3 inches). Cut the cake lengthwise into three layers. Spread a different flavored and colored ice cream between each layer and place the filled cake in the freezer. When it is frozen, frost the top and sides with sweetened whipped cream and sprinkle generously with shredded coconut. Return the cake to the freezer until the whipped cream is hard. Wrap and store in freezer until ready to serve, or for 1 month.

ICE CREAM PIE FROM YOUR FREEZER

Make a Graham Cracker Pastry Shell in a 9-inch pie plate and fill it with vanilla ice cream. Hull, sort, and slice ¼ inch thick enough firm strawberries to make 2 cups. Mix them with ½ cup sugar. Make a circle of the sliced and sugared berries around the pie and place a mound in the center. Wrap and freeze until ready to serve, or for 2 months. Other fruits or berries may be used in place of the strawberries.

TO USE FRUIT AND NUTS IN BAKING

SEEDED RAISINS are raisins from which the seeds were removed before they were dried. They are sweet and sticky.

SEEDLESS RAISINS are a small variety of seedless grapes which have been dried. Both light and dark are available. They should be cut or chopped to get the benefit of their full flavor.

TO PLUMP SEEDLESS RAISINS Wash them and spread them out in a flat pan. Cover the pan tightly and heat them in a 350° F. oven until they puff and lose their wrinkles.

TO CUT DATES AND OTHER STICKY FRUITS Use kitchen scissors and dip the scissors in water frequently as you work.

NUTS may be broken with the fingers into chunks or cut into coarse pieces with scissors. To chop nuts, place them on a chopping board. Use a long straight sharp knife. Hold the knife point against the board and chop through the nuts, swinging the handle around in a half circle and back again.

TO BLANCH NUTS Cover them with boiling water and let them steep for 3–5 minutes, or until the skins are loosened. Pour off the hot water, rinse in cold, and then pinch each nut between the thumb and finger. If the skins are still stubborn as in the case of brazil nuts, use a sharp knife to help remove them.

TO SLIVER NUTS Use a cutting board and a sharp knife and shred them after blanching while they are still warm and moist.

TO GRIND NUTS Nuts must be dried in a warm oven before grinding them or they will exude oil. Use the fine knife of a food chopper.

RULES FOR SUCCESSFUL BAKING

1. *Read the introduction to each chapter* before trying a recipe that is unfamiliar to you.
2. *Use Accurate Measurements in Standard Spoons and Cups.*
3. *Sift Flour Once Before Measuring It* and spoon it lightly into a measuring cup. One cup unsifted flour equals 1¼ cups sifted flour. All-purpose flour is used extensively throughout the book unless otherwise specified. Homemakers will find this type of flour suitable for most baking requirements.
4. *Milk Is Always Sweet Milk* unless otherwise indicated. Skim milk may be used, but whole milk will give added nourishment and richer flavor.
5. *Buttermilk or Sour Milk May Be Used Interchangeably.* To make sour milk from sweet, add 1 tablespoon vinegar to each cup of sweet milk.
6. *Sugar Is White Granulated* unless otherwise noted. Fine granulated sugar should always be kept on hand for use in fine cakes and cookies, when called for in recipes. Brown sugar should be firmly packed into the cup for accurate measurement.
7. *Use the Correct Type of Chocolate.* There are three types used in the recipes: unsweetened, bittersweet or semi-sweet, and sweet. Bittersweet, semi-sweet, or sweet may be used interchangeably.
8. *Margarine or Part Vegetable Fat May Be Substituted for Butter,* but butter is used extensively throughout the book for the simple reason that the author believes that butter results in a better-flavored, richer baked product.
9. *Eggs Vary in Size.* Use large fresh eggs (2 ounces) or an equivalent amount of smaller eggs. Use 4 medium-sized eggs for each 3 large eggs called for.

EQUIPMENT NECESSARY TO GOOD BAKING

Breadboard

Flour sifter

Rolling pin

Baking pans in assorted shapes and sizes
- SANDWICH TIN
- RING MOULD
- ROUND AND SQUARE CAKE PANS
- BREAD PANS (4×8 INCHES)
- PIE PLATES
- TART PANS, PLAIN OR FLUTED
- SMALL DARIOLE MOULDS FOR MUFFINS

Baking sheets (at least 2)

Rubber scraper

Flexible spatulas—1 broad, 1 thin

Mixing bowls of assorted sizes

Rotary egg beater

Wire whip

Pastry brush

Measuring cups and spoons (at least 2 of each)

Griddle

Cake racks for cooling

Biscuit, doughnut, and cooky cutters

Heavy skillet

Double boiler

Small saucepan

2-tined, long-handled fork

Wooden spoons

Scissors

Paring knife

Straight-edged knife for leveling off

Index

Almond: Bavarian Cream Pie, 282
  Bread (Yeast), 56
  Butter Frosting, 339
  Chocolate Chiffon Pie, 294
  Filling, 327
  Ginger Snaps, 226
  Paste, 200, 324
  Ring, Cherry, 98
  Shortbread, 238
  Sticks, 237
  Strudel, 333
  Tarts, 238, 304
  Torte, 186
  Wafers, 238
  Wreaths, Danish, 245
Altitude Baking, Recipe Adjustment Chart for, 194

Angel Food, 145
  Brown and White, 146
  Chocolate, 146
  Custard, 147
  Fruit and Nut, 146
  Gold and White, 147
  Lemon, 147
  Orange, 147
  Peppermint, 147
Anise Cookies, 230
Apfelstrudel, 331
Apple: Biscuits, 74
  Bread (Yeast), 45
  Brown Betty, 309
  Cake, 168
    Dutch (Yeast), 47
  Cobbler, 78

Apple—(Cont'd)
  Coffeecake, 96
    (Yeast), 46
  Dumplings, 77
  Filling, 34
  Fritters, 112
    à la Princesse, 113
  Muffins, 84
  Pandowdy, 80, 299
  Pie, 259
    Cream, 258
    Crumb, 259
    Custard, 267, 286
    Deep-dish, 298
    Honey, 259
    Pecan Raisin, 259
  Pudding, Dutch, 310
  Roll, 80
  Roly Poly, 79
  Strudel, 331
  Torte, 275
  Waffles, 125
Apples, Marzipan, 202
Applesauce: Cake, 92
  Pancakes, 116
  Spice Cake, 136
  Torte, 277
Apricot: Bran Bread, 91
  Breakfast Bread, 90
  Chiffon Pie, 292
  Circles, 156
  Cobbler, 79
  Date Filling, 353
  Filling, 33
  Fluff Pie, 290
  Glaze, 355
  Muffins, 84
  Prune: Cake (Yeast), 53
    Filling, 34
  Rum Tarts, 303
  Sandwiches, 321
  Sauce, 354
  Timbales, 157
  Upside-down Coffeecake, 96
Austrian Pastry Roll, 324
Autrichiennes, Tartes, 301

Baba au Rhum (Yeast), 65
Bacon: Biscuits, 74
  Rolls, 74

Baked Products in Your Home Freezer, 356
Baking: Temperatures for Yeast Doughs, 9
  Yeast Dough, 8
Baking Powder Biscuits. *See* Biscuits, Baking Powder
Baking Powder Breads and Coffeecakes. *See* Breads, Quick
Baklava, 328
Banana: Bran Bread, 95
  Cake, 137
  Cream Pie, 283
  Fritters, 113
  Jalousie, 318
  Muffins, 87
  Pancakes, 116
  Waffles, 125
Banbury Turnovers, 308
Bannocks, Rhode Island, 103
Basic: Baking Powder Biscuits, 73
  Beaten Batter, 24
  Drop Cookies, 205
  Fritter Batter, 110
  Pan Cookies, 209
  Pancake Batter, 115
  Recipe for Plain Bread Dough and method in detail, 10
    Sponge Method, 12
  Refrigerator Cookies, 207
  Rich Kuchen Dough, 53
  Rolled Cookies, 208
  rules for cake baking, 130
  Spongecake, 147
  Sweet Dough, 21
  Waffle Batter, 124
Baskets, 157
Bath Buns (Yeast), 62
Batter Bread, 101
  Southern, 101
Bavarian Cream: Chocolate, 350
  Coffee, 350
  Vanilla, 349
Bavarois Vanille, 349
Beaten Batter (Yeast), 24
Beaten Biscuits, 81
Beating yeast dough, 6
Beer Batter for Vegetable Fritters, 110
Berliner Kranzer, 247
Berry: Baskets, 319
  fillings for tart shells, 301

Pancakes, Hungarian, 120
Roll, 326
Birthday: Cake, 3-Layer, 177
  Cooky Place Cards, 251
Bischofsbrot, 163
Biscuit Bunnies. See List of Illustrations
Biscuits, Baking Powder, 73
  Apple, 74
  Bacon, 74
    Rolls, 74
  Basic Recipe for 1 Dozen, 73
  Beaten, 81
  Bran, 74
  Bunnies. See List of Illustrations
  Buttermilk, 74
  Butterscotch, 74
  Caraway Seed, 75
  Cheese, 75
  Corn Meal, 75
  Cream, 82
  Drop, 74
  to freeze, 357
  Fruit, 75
    Drops, 75
    Turnovers, 75
  Ginger, 75
  Honey Buns, 75
  Jam, 75
  Lemon, 75
  Maple, 76
  Orange, 76
  Peanut Butter, 76
  Pecan, 76
  Pineapple Rolls, 76
  Savory Teasers, 76
  Sour Cream, 76
  Strawberry Shortcake. See List of Illustrations
  Surprise, 76
  Sweet Potato, 76
  Thimble, 76
  Turnovers, 76
  Whole Wheat, 77
Bismarcks: Quick, 108
  Yeast, 66
Black Bottom Pie, 295
Blackberry: Cobbler, 79
  Pie, 263
  Roly Poly, 79

Blinis (Yeast), 69
Blintzes, 121
Blitz Torte, 180
Blueberry: Cobbler, 77
  Fritters, 112
  Kuchen, 278
  Muffins, 84
  Pancakes, 116
  Pie, 263
    Deep-dish, 298
  Roll, 81
  Roly Poly, 79
  Torte, 276
Bonnet Cake, 197
Borrachitos, 242
Boston Cream Cake, 156
Bowknots (Yeast), 27
Bran: Biscuits, 74
  Bread, 94
    Apricot, 91
    Banana, 95
    Cherry, 91
    Yeast, 15
  Muffins: Nut, 84
    Spiced, 85
Brandy: Batter for Fruit Fritters, 111
  Doughnuts, 108
  Rings, 214
  Sauce, Foamy, 355
Brazil Nut Pastry Shell, 279
Bread: to freeze, 356
  Pudding, Old-fashioned, 312
  Sticks, 14
  Yeast: to freshen, 10
    steps in making, 6
    storing, 9
    what constitutes a good loaf, 10
Breads, Quick:
  Apricot: Breakfast, 90
    Bran, 91
  Banana Bran, 95
  Bran, 94
  Cherry Bran, 91
  Chocolate, 92
  Date and Nut, 89
  Fruit, 94
  Ginger, 95
  Harvest, 92
  Orange Date Nut, 90
  Pain d'Épice, 93

Breads, Quick—(Cont'd)
  Pecan Nut, 88
  Whole Wheat Nut, 89
  See also Coffeecakes, Quick
Breads, Sweet Yeast: Almond, 56
  Braided Fruit, 42
  Bubble Loaf, 46
  Christmas Fruit, 44
  Coffee, Rich, 62
  Filled Egg, 61
  Moravian, 41
  Norwegian Jule Kage, 43
  Old-fashioned Dessert, 52
  Pan de Huevos (Mexican Egg), 58
  Panettone di Natale (Italian Christmas), 58
  Poppy Seed Braid, 42
  Spanish Sweet, 43
  Ukrainian Easter, 59
  See also Cakes and Kuchens, Yeast; Muffins, Rolls, Sweet Yeast
Breads, Yeast: Bran, 15
  Butter Braids, 14
  Buttermilk, 15
  Cracked Wheat, 15
  Date, 15
  Fruit and Nut, 15
  Garlic, 19
  Herb, 19
  Honey, 15
  Nut, 15
  Plain, 10
    Sponge Method, 12
  Raisin, 15
  Rye Molasses, 15
  Sally Lunn, 18
  Salt Rising, 16
  Sour Dough: French, 16
    Rye, 18
  Sticks, 14
  Swedish Rye, 18
  Vienna, 13
  Water Rolls (Vienna Type), 14
  Whole Wheat, 15
    100%, 19
Bride's Cake, 166
Brioches (Yeast), 63
Brown Beauty Icing, 340
Brown Betty: Apple, 309
  Rhubarb, 309

Brown Sugar: Drop Cookies, 206
  Macaroons, 241
  Muffins, 84
Brown and White Angel Food, 146
Browned Butter Frosting, 339
Brownies, 209
  Date, 210
  Thin, 210
Bubble Loaf (Yeast), 46
Buckwheat Pancakes, 117
  Yeast, 70
Butter: Balls, 215
  Braids (Yeast), 14
  Cake, Sour Milk, 142
  Cakes: with Beaten Whole Eggs, 131
    with Beaten Egg Whites Folded In, 138
  Cookies, 208
    Frosted, 214
  Cream Frosting: Chocolate, 343
    Mocha, 343
  Frostings: Almond, 339
    Browned, 339
    Chocolate, 339
    Cocoa, 340
    Vanilla, 338
  Horns (Yeast), 40
Butterfly: Frosting, 338
  Rolls (Yeast), 26
Buttermilk: Biscuits, 74
  Bread (Yeast), 15
  Pancakes, 116
  Rolls (Yeast), 37
  Waffles, 126
Butterscotch: Biscuits, 74
  Chiffon Pie, 292
  Cookies, 212
  Cream Pie, 285
  Pecan Pinwheels (Yeast), 31
  Pecan Roll (Yeast), 51
  Pecan Rolls (Yeast), 31
  Sauce, 353

Cakes: Almond Torte, 186
  Angel Food, 145–47
    Brown and White, 146
    Chocolate, 146
    Custard, 147
    Fruit and Nut, 146
    Gold and White, 147

Lemon, 147
Orange, 147
Peppermint, 147
Apple, 168
Applesauce Spice, 136
Basic Rules for, 130
Birthday, 3-Layer, 177
Bischofsbrot, 163
Blitz Torte, 180
Boston Cream, 156
Bride's, 166
Butter, with Beaten Whole Eggs, 131
  with Stiffly Beaten Egg Whites Folded In, 138
Cassata Palermitana, 173
Cheese, 170–73
  Cottage, 170
  Cream I, 171
  II, 172
  French, 172
  Strawberry, 173
Chiffon: Bit o' Walnut, 153
  Orange, 152
  Spice, 154
  Vanilla and Almond, 154
  Yellow, 153
Chocolate: Chip, 175
  Fudge, 174
  Layer, 134
  Nut, 139
  One-egg, 132
  Roll, 150
  Soufflé Torte, 184
  Sour Milk, 140
  Torte, 183
Coconut Fluff, 176
Crazy, 178
Cream, 132
Date and Walnut Torte, 185
Devil's Food: Chocolate Nut-filled, 135
  Coffee, 134
  Sour Milk, 133
  Sweet Milk, 133
Dobos Torte, 179
Easy-mix Cakes, 174
Fluffy, with Marshmallow Topping, 136
Four-egg, 139
to freeze, 357

Fruit, 159
  Bun, 167
  Christmas, 159
  Dark, 160
  Golden, 162
  Light, 161
Fudge Nut, 140
Génoise, 155
Gingerbread, 136
Gold, 148
Gumdrop, 142
Hazelnut Torte, 180
Hickory Nut Loaf, 143
How to: decorate, 195
  decorate with a pastry bag, 198
  frost, 194
Lazy Daisy, 174
Linzer Torte, 182
Maple Cream, 137
Maraschino Party, 177
Marble Swirl, 141
Mocha Torte, 184
Nut, 141
  Loaf, 178
Orange Layer, 142
Peach Upside-down, 168
Pear Upside-down, 169
Pecan: Bourbon, 143
  Southern, 154
Peppermint Chip, 153
Pineapple Upside-down, 169
Pound, 144
Recipe Adjustment Chart for High-altitude Baking, 194
Ribbon. *See* List of Illustrations
Rococo Torte, 185
Rum, 151
Russian Tea, 151
Sacher Torte, 181
Schaum Torte, 181
Simnel, 163
Sour Milk Butter, 142
Spice: with Brown Sugar Meringue, 135
  Applesauce, 136
Sponge: Basic, 147
  Easy, 149
  Jiffy, 149
Spring Bonnet, 197
Thousand Leaves Torte, 188
Two-egg, 139

Cakes—(Cont'd)
 Valentine, 196
 Vanilla Torte, 187
 Wedding, 163
  3-Tiered, 165
 Whipped Cream, 133
 White: Layer Using Only Egg Whites, 144
  One-egg, 132
 Woolly Lamb, 196
 Zwieback Torte, 186
 See also Cakes and Kuchens, Yeast; Cupcakes
Cakes and Kuchens, Yeast:
 Apple Coffeecake, 46
 Apricot Prune, 53
 Baba au Rhum, 65
 Brioches, 63
 Butterscotch Pecan Roll, 51
 Cinnamon, Plain, 48
 Coffeecake, 49
  Crumble, 47
  Dutch Apple, 47
 English Fruit Bun, 50
 Frosted Fruit Loaf, 52
 Golden Dukats, 51
 Honey Twist, 48
 Hornet's Nests, 57
 Hungarian Coffeecake, 56
 Jam Swirl Coffeecake, 46
 Kuchen: Chocolate-filled, 54
  Fruit- and Nut-filled, 54
  Layer, 55
  Marmalade, 54
  Open Fruit, 55
  Plain, 53
 Kugelhoff, 60
  with Chocolate, 60
  Filled, 61
 Lepeny, 63
 Norwegian Jule Kage, 43
 Orehnjaca, 49
 Putica, 50
 Savarin, 64
 Sour Cherry, 56
 Spaetzel, 57
 Stollen, 55
 Swedish Tea Ring, 45
 Whole Wheat with Dates, 48
Caramel: Glaze, 46
 Mountain Cream Frosting, 347

Caraway Seed Biscuits, 75
Cardamom Cookies, 229
Cassata Palermitana, 173
Charlotte Russe Cream, 349
Chartreuse Custard Pie, 286
Cheese: Biscuits, 75
 Cake: Cottage, 170
  Cream I, 171
   II, 172
  French, 172
  Strawberry, 173
 Filling, 36, 327
 Pastry, 256
  Cream, 257
  Pot, 256
 Pie: Cottage, 272
  Pineapple, 273
  Switzerland Swiss, 273
 Strudel: Cottage, 332
  Cream, 332
Cherry: Almond Ring, 98
 Bran Bread, 91
 Cobbler, Fresh, 78
 Kuchen, 277
 and Peach Dessert, 156
 Pie, Fresh, 260
 Pudding, Black, 310
 Roll: Sour, 81
  Sweet, 81
 Strudel: Sour, 331
  Sweet, 331
 Tarts, Black, 302
 Torte, Country Style, 276
Chess: Pie, Kentucky, 269
 Tarts, 306
Chiffon Cakes: Bit o' Walnut, 153
 Orange, 152
 Spice, 154
 Vanilla and Almond, 154
 Yellow, 153
Chocolate: Almond Chiffon Pie, 294
 Angel Food, 146
 Angel Pie, 284
 Bavarian Cream, 350
 Bread, 92
 Butter Cream, 343
 Butter Frosting, 339
 Cake: Chip, 175
  Devil's Food: Coffee, 134
   Nut-filled, 135

Sour Milk, 133
Sweet Milk, 133
Fudge, 174
Nut, 140
Layer, 134
Nut, 139
One-egg, 132
Sour Milk, 140
Cake Pie, 274
Cookies, 209
   Almond, 218
   Chip, 217
   Crisp, 217
   Refrigerator, 207
   Walnut, 218
Cream for Dobos Torte, 344
Cream Pie, 285
Cupcakes, 189
Doughnuts, 106
Drops, 206, 216
Filled Kuchen (Yeast), 54
Fondant, 341
Frosting: Betty Crocker, 344
   Mountain Cream, 347
Kisses, 240
Macaroons, 241
Muffins, 84
Nut-filled Devil's Food, 135
Pastry Cream, 348
Pie, Cake, 274
Pretzels, 220
Roll, 150
Sauce, Thin, 353
Sticks, 219
Strudel, 334
Torte, 183
   Soufflé, 184
   and Vanilla Pinwheels, 219
Waffles, 127
   Spiced, 127
Christmas: Bread, Italian (Yeast), 58
   Fruit Bread (Yeast), 44
   Fruitcake, 159
   Ginger Snaps, 226
   Spice Cookies, 228
Chunk Bread (Yeast), 68
Cinnamon: Buns (Yeast), 57
   Cake, Plain (Yeast), 48
   Pinwheels (Yeast), 31
   Refrigerator Cookies, 208
   Twists (Yeast), 30

Cloverleaf: Cookies, 236
   Rolls (Yeast), 26
Cobblers: Apple, 78
   Apricot, 79
   Blackberry, 79
   Cherry, Fresh, 78
   Fruit, 77
   Peach, 77, 79
Cockscombs, Danish (Yeast), 324
Cocoa: Butter Frosting, 340
   Cupcakes, 190
   Icing, Cooked, 344
   Kisses, 240
   Muffins, 84
   Pudding, Hot, 311
   Waffles, 125
Coconut: and Black Walnut Bars, 235
   Buns (Yeast), 28
   Cake, 154
   Cream Pie, 281
      Toasted, 281
   Curls (Yeast), 32
   Custard Pie, 266, 287
   Drops, 206
   Fluff Cake, 175
   Icebox Cookies, 237
   Jam Rounds, 156
   Kisses, 240
   Pinwheels (Yeast), 32
   Tarts, 304
   to tint, 196
   to toast, 196
Coffee: Bread, Rich (Yeast), 62
   Chiffon Pie, 292
   Custard Pie, 287
   Mountain Cream Frosting, 347
   Ring, 96
      to make from Plain Bread Dough, 13
   Spice Drops, 206
   Twists (Yeast), 57
Coffeecakes, Quick: Apple, 96
   Applesauce, 92
   Apricot Upside-down, 96
   Cherry Almond, 97
   Jam-filled, 97
   Orange-filled, 95
   Quick, 93
   Ring, 96
Coffeecakes, Yeast. *See* Cakes and Kuchens, Yeast

Confectioners' Sugar Icing, 338
Cookies:
  Almond: Ginger Snaps, 226
    Shortbread, 238
    Sticks, 237
    Tarts, 238
    Wafers, 238
    Wreaths, Danish, 245
  Anise, 230
  Basic: Drop, 206
    Pan, 209
    Refrigerator, 207
    Rolled, 208
  Berliner Kranzer, 247
  Birthday Place Cards, 251
  Black Walnut and Coconut Bars, 235
  Borrachitos, 242
  Brandy Rings, 214
  Brownies, 209
    Date, 210
    Thin, 210
  Brown Sugar: Drops, 206
    Macaroons, 241
  Butter, 208
    Balls, 215
  Butterscotch, 212
  Cardamom, 229
  Chocolate, 207, 209
    Almond, 218
    Chip, 217
    Crisp, 217
    Drop, 206, 216
    Kisses, 240
    Macaroons, 241
    Pinwheels, Vanilla, 219
    Pretzels, 220
    Sticks, 219
    Walnut, 218
  Christmas, 249–51
    Ginger Snaps, 226
    Spice, 228
  Cinnamon, 208
  Cloverleaf, 236
  Cocoa Kisses, 240
  Coconut: Drops, 206
    Icebox, 237
    Kisses, 240
  Coffee Spice Drops, 206
  Cornflake Macaroons, 241
  Crisp: Ginger, 224
    Sugar, 210
  Date and Nut: Kisses, 241
    Rolled, 232
    Sticks, 231
  Date-filled Oat Squares, 223
  Diagonals, 213
  Dream Drops, 216
  Dutch Squares, 244
  Egg, 213
  Fig, 232
    and Date Kisses, 241
  Filled, 209, 232
  Finnska Kabor, 242
  Flower, 251
  to freeze, 359
  Frosted Butter, 214
  Fruit: and Nut, 207
    Drop, 230, 260
  Fudge Fingers, 220
  George Washington's Birthday, 251
  Ginger: Creams, 227
    Crisp, 224
    Snaps, 225
    Wafers, 224
  Gingerbread: House, 227
    Man, 250
  Goosnargh, 249
  Grandmother's Sugar, 210
  Hermits, 206, 231
  Holiday, 249–51
  Honey: Bars, 235
    Nut Tarts, 236
    and Spice, 229
  how to make, 205
  Indians, 221
  Krom Cakes, 246
  Lebkuchen, 245
  Lemon, 209
  Mandelchen, 244
  Marguerites, 239
  Marzipan, 249
  Meringue: Drops, 239
    Kisses, 239
  Molasses, Thick, 225
  Monkey Faces, 251
  Norwegian Mandelkaker, 248
  Nut, 207, 209
    Drops, 206
    Kisses, 240
  Oat, Simple, 222

Oatmeal: Crispy, 221
   Date, 224
   Drops, 223
   Molasses, 222
Orange, 214
   Almond, 208
to pack for gifts, 251
Peanut Butter, 233
Pecan: Kisses, 239
   Wafers, 239
Petits Gâteaux Tailles, 243
Pfeffernuesse, 247
Pineapple Drops, 233
Pistachio Kisses, 241
Pumpkin, 234
Quick Nut, 233
Raisin, 230
Rocks, 236
Rosettes, 215
Russian Nut Balls, 242
Sandwiches, 208
Scotch: Shortbread, 243
   Wafers, 243
Scottish Fancies, 222
Sour Cream, 211
Sour Milk, 212
Spice, 228
   Raisin, 228
Springerle, 244
Spritz, 246
Stars, 250
Sugar: Crisps, 210
   Grandmother's, 210
Swedish: Macaroons, 246
   Sand Tarts, 248
Tree Ornaments, 251
Trilbies, 221
Turnovers, 209
Valentine, 251
Vanilla, 207, 212
   Drops, 211
   Rocks, 213
Walnut: Squares, 234
   Sticks, 234
Wreaths, 250
Zucker Hütchen, 248
Cooling yeast bread, 9
Corbeille de Fruits, 159
Corn: Bread Waffles, 126
   Dodger, 104

Fritters, 111
Lace Puffs, 102
Muffins: Kernel, 84
   Northern, 86
   Southern, 85
   Yeast, 29
Pones, 103
Sticks, 105
Corn Breads: Bannocks, 103
   Batter, 101
   Southern, 101
   Dodger, 104
   Johnnycake, Pan-baked, 99
     Rhode Island, 119
   Yogurt, 102
   Kentucky, 100
   Kernel, 102
   Lace Puffs, 102
   Old-fashioned, 99
   Pones, 103
   Sour Milk, 99
   Southern, 100
   Spider, 100
   Spoon, 104
     Virginia, 104
   Sticks, 105
   Yogurt Squares, 101
Corn Meal: Biscuits, 75
   Fruit Gems, 86
   Griddlecakes, 69
   Squares, 101
Corncake: Kentucky, 100
   Spider, 100
Cornflake: Macaroons, 241
   Shell, 280
Cottage Cheese: Cake, 170
   Pie, 272
   Strudel, 332
Cottage Pudding, Old-fashioned, 312
Cracked Wheat Bread (Yeast), 15
Cranberry: Muffins, 84
   Pie, 263
Crazy Cake, 178
Cream: Biscuits, 82
   Cake, 132
     Whipped, 133
   fillings for tart shells, 301
   to freeze, 359
   Muffins, 84
   Pancakes, Rolled, 120

Cream—(Cont'd)
    Puff Paste (Pâte à Choux), 313
    Puff Triplets, 314
    Puffs, 314
Cream Cheese: Cake I, 171
    Cake II, 172
    Cookies, 258
    Pastry, 257
    Strudel, 332
Creams: à l'Anglaise Collée, 349
    Bavarian, 349
        Chocolate, 350
        Coffee, 350
        Vanilla, 349
    Charlotte Russe, 349
    Chocolate Pastry, 348
    Pastry I, 350
        II, 351
    Rum or Vanilla Pastry, 348
    St. Honoré, 351
    Strawberry, 350
    Vanilla, 350
    Vanilla, 324
Crème: à l'Anglaise Collée, 349
    Bavarois. See Vanilla Bavarian Cream
    Patissière I, 350
        II, 351
    St. Honoré, 351
Crêpes. See Pancakes
Crescents, Danish (Yeast), 324
    (Yeast), 26
Croissants, 322
Croquembouche, 315
Crossettes (Yeast), 27
Croûtes de Prunes, 159
Crown of Puff Paste, 314
Crullers: Plain, 107
    Rich, 107
    Yeast, 66
Crumb: Cake Pudding, 312
    Cakes, 191
Crumble: Coffeecake (Yeast), 47
    Topping, 47
Crumpets (Yeast), 41
Crystallized Violets, 200
Cupcakes: Chocolate, 189
    Cocoa, 190
    Fruit or Nut, 189
    Vanilla, 189

Currant: and Honey Turnovers, 308
    Filling, 318
    Muffins, 84
Cushions (Yeast), 27
Custard: Angel Cake, 147
    Filling, 351
    Lemon, 352
    Orange, 352
    Pies, 266
        Apple, 267
        Chartreuse, 286
        Coconut, 266
        Coffee, 287
        Peach, 267
        Pineapple, 287
        Raspberry, 267
        Rich, 266
        Wine, 268
    Pudding, Lemon, 311

Daisies, Marzipan, 202
Danish: Almond Wreaths, 245
    Ebelskiver (Yeast), 34
    Pastry, 323
Date: Apricot Filling, 353
    Bread (Yeast), 15
    Brownies, 210
    and Butter Filling, 34
    Cookies, Rolled, 232
    Filled Oat Squares, 223
    Filling, 352
    Kisses, 240
    Muffins, 84
    Oatmeal Cookies, 224
    Raisin and Fig Filling, 352
    Rolled Cookies, 232
    and Walnut Torte, 185
Date and Nut: Bread, 89
    (Yeast), 15
    Filling, 34, 352
    Kisses, 241
    Sticks, 231
Dates, to cut, 360
Decorating, cake, 195, 198
Decorative Frosting, Colored, 339
Deep-dish Pies: Apple, 298
    Blueberry, 298
    Fruit, 297
    Rhubarb, 299
Deer Horns, 110
Dessert Waffles, Rich, 126

Desserts from Génoise or Génoise-
    type Cake, 155
  Apricot: Circles, 156
    Timbales, 157
  Baskets, 157
  Boston Cream Cake, 156
  Coconut Jam Rounds, 156
  Corbeille de Fruits, 159
  Cream-filled Strawberry Cake, 159
  Croûtes de Prunes, 159
  Fried Cake, 157
  Fruit Loaf, 158
  Hot Peach Rounds, 156
  Ice Cream Rolls, 156
  Icecapade, 158
  Nut Fingers, 156
  Oeufs en Surprise, 158
  Orange: Delight, 155
    Ice Bombe, 158
  Peach: and Cherry Dessert, 156
    Pyramid, 158
    Surprise, 157
  Rum Cake Dessert, 156
Diagonals, 213
Dinner Rolls (Yeast), 26
Dobos Torte, 179
Dough, Yeast: Basic: Sweet, 21
  food for, 4
  Hungarian Egg, 56
  Kuchen: Basic Rich, 53
    Sour Cream, 54
  to make a dough that is 80° F., 4
  methods of mixing and raising, 5
  Plain, 10
    Sponge Method, 12
  Plain Bread: Basic Method, 10
    Sponge or Long Method, 12
  Refrigerator: Basic, 23
    how to store, 22
    Potato, 23
    Rich Potato, Sponge Method, 24
  steps in making, 6
  Sweet, how to make from Plain
    Bread Dough, 13
Doughnuts, Quick: Bismarcks, 108
  Brandy, 108
  Chocolate, 106
  Crullers: Plain, 107
    Rich, 107
  Deer Horns, 110
  Drop, 106
  Fruit, 106
  Hush Puppies, 109
  Molasses, 107
  Orange, 106
  Plain, Recipe for 3 Dozen, 105
  Potato, 108
  Rice, 109
  Sour Milk, 107
  Spice, 107
  Sugar, 106
  Swiss Fried Cakes, 109
  See also Fritters
Doughnuts, Yeast, 65
  Bismarcks, 66
  Chunk Bread, 68
  Crullers, 66
  Fastnachts Kuchen, 67
  Krapfen, 67
  Munker, 34
  Olykoek, 67
  Refrigerator, 66
  Spiced, 66
  Sugar, 66
Dream Drops, 216
Drop: Biscuits, 74
  Cookies, Basic, 206
  Doughnuts, 106
Dumplings, 77
  Apple, 77
    Roll, 80
  Blueberry Roll, 81
  Cherry Roll, Sour, 81
    Sweet, 81
  Fruit, Rolled, 80
    Canned, 81
  in Nectar, 77
  Peach, 81
  Rhubarb, 77
    and Strawberry Roll, 80
Dutch: Apple Pudding, 310
  Babies, 87
  Squares, 244

Easter Bread, Ukrainian (Yeast), 59
Easy-mix Cakes, 174
Ebelskiver, Danish (Yeast), 34
Éclairs, 314
  to freeze, 359
Egg: Bread, Filled (Yeast), 61
  Cookies, 213
Eggnog Cream Pie, 284

Eggs, to freeze, 359
English Muffins (Yeast), 41
Envelopes, Danish (Yeast), 324
Equipment: Necessary to Good Baking, 362

Fan Tans (Yeast), 26
Fastnachts Kuchen (Yeast), 67
Fig: Cookies, 232
  Date, and Raisin Filling, 352
  Kisses, 240
  and Nut Filling, 34
Figure 8 Rolls (Yeast), 28
Filled: Cookies, 209, 232
  Egg Bread (Yeast), 61
  Horns (Yeast), 39
  Kugelhoff, 61
Fillings:
  Bavarian Cream, Chocolate, 350
    Coffee, 350
    Vanilla, 349
  Charlotte Russe Cream, 349
  Crème: à l'Anglaise Collée, 349
    Patissière I, 350
    II, 351
    St. Honoré, 351
  Custard, 351
    Lemon, 352
    Orange, 352
  Date, 352
    Apricot, 353
    and nut, 352
  Orange Raisin, 352
  Pastry Cream: Chocolate, 348
    Rum, 348
    Vanilla, 348
  Pineapple, 353
  Prune Orange, 353
  Raisin, Fig, and Date, 352
  Strawberry Vanilla, 350
Fillings for Sweet Breads and Rolls, 21
  Apple, 34
  Apricot, 33
    Prune, 34
  Cheese, 36, 121
  Currant, 318
  Date: and Butter, 34
    and Nut, 32, 34

Fig and Nut, 34
Fruit and Nut, 32
Orange, 96
Poppy Seed, 34, 40
  Fruit and Nut, 61
Prune, 33, 36
Raisin, 36
Walnut, 40, 50
Finnska Kabor, 242
Flapjacks. *See* Pancakes
Flower Cookies, 251
Fondant, dipping with, 341
Fondant Frostings: Chocolate, 341
  Maple, 342
  Plain, 341
Freezing baked products, 356
Freshening yeast bread and rolls, 10
Fried: Cake, 157
  Pies, Little, 326
Fritter Batter: Basic, 110
  Beer, for Vegetables, 110
  Brandy, for Fruits, 111
  Wine, 111
Fritters, 110
  Apple, 112
    à la Princesse, 113
  Banana, 113
  Basic Batter for, 110
  Beer Batter for, 110
  Blueberry, 112
  Brandy Batter for, 111
  Corn, 111
  Fruit: Fresh, 112
    Large Canned, 112
    Small, and Berries, 112
  Orange, 113
  Pâte à Frire à la Carême, 114
  Peach, 112
  Pets de Nonne, 114
  Pineapple, 113
  Vegetable, 110
  Wine Batter, 111
  Zuckersträuben, 115
Frosted Fruit Loaf (Yeast), 52
Frosting: simple decorative touches, 195
  Sweet Bread and Rolls, 21
Frostings: Almond Butter, 339
  Brown Beauty, 340
  Browned Butter, 339
  Butterfly, 338

Chocolate: Betty Crocker, 344
  Butter, 339
  Cream, 343
  Cream for Dobos Torte, 344
Cocoa: Butter, 340
  Cooked, 344
Colored Decorative, 339
Confectioners' Sugar, 338
Fondant: Chocolate, 341
  Maple, 342
  Plain, 341
Lemon Meringue, 348
Mocha, 340, 345
  Butter Cream, 343
Mountain Cream (Italian Meringue), 346
  Caramel, 347
  Chocolate, 347
  Coffee, 347
  Fruit, 347
  Jam, 347
  Marshmallow, 347
  Nut, 347
  Peppermint, 347
Orange: Cream, 342
  Fluff, 346
  Sugar, 338
Royal, 337
Rum Cream, 345
Russian Tea Cake, 345
7-Minute, 347
  Lemon, 347
Sour Cream, 346
Strawberry, 4-Minute, 348
Vanilla: Butter, 338
  Cream, 342
Fruit: and Nut Bread, 15
  Biscuits, 75
  Bread (Yeast), 94
  Braided (Yeast), 42
  Christmas (Yeast), 44
  Bun, 167
  English (Yeast), 50
  Cake: Christmas, 159
    Dark, 160
    Golden, 162
    Light, 161
  Cobbler, 77
  Cupcakes, 189
  Doughnuts, 106
  Drops, 75, 206, 230

Dumplings, Rolled, 80
Fritters: Fresh, 112
  Large Canned, 112
  Small, and Berries, 112
Kuchens, Open (Yeast), 55
Loaf, 158
  Frosted (Yeast), 52
Marzipan, 202
Mountain Cream Frosting, 347
Pies, Deep-dish, 297
Roll, Canned, 81
Roly Poly, 79
Preserved, 79
Sauce, 355
Turnovers: Mixed, 306
  Preserved, 306
Waffles, 125
Fruit and Nut: Angel Food, 146
  Bread (Yeast), 44
  Cookies, 207
  Kuchen, 54
  Pinwheels (Yeast), 32
  Refrigerator Cookies, 207
Fruited Cakes, Little, 193
Fruits: and Nuts in Baking, 360
  Marzipan, 202
Fudge: Fingers, 220
  Nut Cake, 140
  Pie, 272

Garlic Bread, 19
Garnishes for sweet breads and rolls, 21
Gâteaux: d'Amande, 320
  St. Honoré, 320
Gaufres Parisiennes, 128
Génoise, 155
George Washington's Birthday Cookies, 251
German Skillet Cake, 119
Ginger: Biscuits, 75
  Cookies: Almond, 226
    Crisp, 224
  Creams, 227
  Snaps, 225
    Christmas, 226
  Wafers, 224
Gingerbread, 95
  Cake, 136
  House, 227

Gingerbread—(Cont'd)
 Man, 250
 Waffles, 127
Glazing and decorating sweet breads and rolls, 21
Godcakes, 318
Gold: Cake, 148
 and White Angel Food, 147
Golden Dukats (Yeast), 51
Gooseberry: Roly Poly, 79
 Torte, 276
Goosnargh, 249
Graham Cracker Pastry Shell, 280
Grape Pie, 264
Greek Sandwiches, 319
Griddle Scones, 82
 Drop, 83
Griddlecakes. See Pancakes
Gumdrop Cake, 142

Hard Sauce, 355
Harvest Bread, 92
Hazelnut Torte, 180
Herb Bread, 19
Hermits, 206, 231
Hickory Nut Cake, 143
High-altitude Baking, Recipe Adjustment Chart, 194
Hoecakes, 119
Hominy: to cook, 104
 Spoon Bread, 103
Honey: Apple Pie, 259
 Bars, 235
 Bran Muffins, 87
 Bread (Yeast), 15
 Buns, 75
 Fingers (Yeast), 30
 Nut Tarts, 236
 Snails (Yeast), 30
 and Spice Cookies, 229
 Topping, 48
 Twist (Yeast), 48
Hornet's Nests (Yeast), 57
Hot Cross Buns: Old English, 37
 Quick, 81
 from Sweet Dough (Yeast), 36
How to: decorate with a pastry bag, 198
 frost a cake, 194
 make cookies, 205
 store refrigerator yeast doughs, 22

Hungarian: Coffeecake (Yeast), 49, 56
 Egg Dough, 56
 Filled Buns (Yeast), 35
 Pancakes, Berry, 120
 Pité, 326
 Plum Pité, 278
 Puff Pastry, 321
Hush Puppies, 109

Ice Cream: Cake, 359
 Pie, 359
 Rolls, 156
Icecapade, 158
Icings. See Frostings
Indians, 192, 221
Italian: Christmas Bread, 58
 Meringue, 346

Jam: Biscuits, 75
 Filled Breakfast Cake, 97
 Muffins, 85
 Mountain Cream Frosting, 347
 Sauce, 354
 Swirl Coffeecake (Yeast), 46
Jelly: Roll, 150
 Sauce, 354
Johnnycake: Pan-baked, 99
 Yogurt, 102
Johnnycakes, Rhode Island, 119
Jule Kage, Norwegian (Yeast), 43

Kentucky: Chess Pie, 269
 Corncake, 100
Kernel: Corn Bread, 102
 Corn Muffins, 84
Kipfels, 321
Kisses: Chocolate, 240
 Cocoa, 240
 Coconut, 240
 Date and Nut, 241
 Fig or Date, 240
 Meringue, 239
 Nut, 240
 Pecan, 239
 Pistachio, 241
Kneading yeast dough, 6
Kolacky (Yeast), 33
Krapfen (Yeast), 67
Krom Cakes, 246

Kuchen: Basic Rich Dough, 53
 Chocolate-filled, 54
 Fruit- and Nut-filled, 54
 Layer, 55
 Marmalade, 54
 Open Fruit, 54
 Plain, 53
 Sour Cream Dough, 54
Kugelhoff, 60
 with Chocolate, 60
 Filled, 61

Lacy Pantycakes, 118
Lady Fingers, 191
Lady Locks, 321
Lamb Cake, 196
Lattice-top Pies, 255
Layer: Kuchen (Yeast), 55
 Strudel, 335
Lazy Daisy Cake, 174
Leaves, Marzipan, 203
Lebkuchen, 245
Lemon: Angel Food, 147
 Biscuits, 75
 Cake Pie, 274
 Chiffon Pie, 290
 Cookies, 209
 Custard: Filling, 351
  Pudding, 311
 Drops (Yeast), 36
 Fluff Pie, 289
 Frosting, 7-Minute, 347
 Meringue, 348
  Pie, 288
 Sauce, 354
 Strudel, 334
 Sugar, 36
Lemons, Marzipan, 203
Lepeny (Yeast), 63
Lime: Chiffon Pie, 291
 Fluff Pie, 290
 Meringue Pie, 289
Linzer Torte, 182
Little Fried Pies, 326
Long Johns (Yeast), 27
Love Letters, 325
Lucky Clovers (Yeast), 26

Macaroons: Brown Sugar, 241
 Chocolate, 241

Cornflake, 241
 Swedish, 246
Madeleines, 192
Magdalena Pie, 278
Mandelchen, 244
Mandelkaker, 248
Maple: Biscuits, 76
 Chiffon Pie, 293
 Cream Cake, 137
 Fondant Frosting, 342
Maraschino Party Cake, 177
Marble Swirl Cake, 141
Marguerites, 239
Mark Smith's Flapjacks, 118
Marmalade: Kuchen (Yeast), 54
 Squares, 319
 Turnovers, 308
Marron Stars, 319
Marshmallow: Cakes, 191
 Mountain Cream Frosting, 347
Marzipan, 201
 Base No. I, 201
  II, 201
 Cookies, 249
 Flowers, 202
 Fruit, 202–3
Meringue: Drops, 239
 Kisses, 239
 Pastry Shell, 280
 Pie: Lemon, 288
  Lime, 289
 Topping, 279
Meringue Frostings: 4-Minute Strawberry, 348
 Italian (Mountain Cream), 346
 Caramel, 347
 Chocolate, 347
 Coffee, 347
 Fruit, 347
 Jam, 347
 Marshmallow, 347
 Nut, 347
 Peppermint, 347
 Lemon, 348
 7-Minute, 347
 Lemon, 347
Meringues, to freeze, 359
Methods of mixing and raising dough, 5
Mexican Egg Bread (Yeast), 58
Millefeuilles, 317

Mincemeat, 260
  Pie, 261
Mixing yeast dough, 6
Mocha: Butter Cream Frosting, 343
  Filling and Frosting, 345
  Frosting, 340
  Torte, 184
Molasses: Cookies, Thick, 225
  Doughnuts, 107
  Pie, 270
  Puffs, 88
Monkey Faces, 251
Moravian Bread (Yeast), 41
Mountain Cream Frosting, 346
  Caramel, 347
  Chocolate, 347
  Coffee, 347
  Fruit, 347
  Jam, 347
  Marshmallow, 347
  Nut, 347
  Peppermint, 347
Muffins: Apple, 84
  Apricot, 84
  Banana, 87
  Basic Recipe for 1 Dozen, 83
  Blueberry, 84
  Bran Nut, 84
  Brown Sugar, 84
  Chocolate, 84
  Cocoa, 84
  Corn: Kernel, 84
    Northern, 86
    Southern, 85
    Yeast, 29
  Corn Meal Fruit, 86
  Cranberry, 84
  Cream, 84
  Currant, 84
  Date, 84
  Dutch Babies, 87
  English (Yeast), 41
  Honey Bran, 87
  Jam, 85
  Molasses Puffs, 88
  Nut, 85
  Peanut Butter, 85
  Pecan, 85
  Popovers, 88
  Sour Cream, 85
  Sour Milk, 85
  Spiced, 85
  Prune, 85
  Surprise, 85
  Whole Wheat Fruit, 85
Munker (Yeast), 34
Mürbe Teig, 275

Napoleons, 317
Nesselrode Pie, 296
Norwegian: Jule Kage, 43
  Mandelkaker, 248
Nut: Balls, Russian, 242
  Bread (Yeast), 15
  Cake, 141
    Fudge, 140
    Hickory, 143
    Pecan Bourbon, 143
  Cookies, 209
  Cupcakes, 189
  and Date Kisses, 241
  Doughnuts, 106
  Drops, 206
  Fingers, 156
  Kisses, 240
  Loaf, 178
  Mountain Cream Frosting, 347
  Muffins, 85
  Patties, Quick, 233
  Refrigerator Cookies, 207
  Tarts, Honey, 236
  Waffles, 125
Nuts: to blanch, 360
  to grind, 360
  to sliver, 360

Oat: Cakes, 116
  Cookies, Simple, 222
  Squares, Date-filled, 223
Oatmeal Cookies: Crispy, 221
  Date, 224
  Filled Squares, 223
  Drop, 223
  Molasses, 222
  Scottish Fancies, 222
  Simple, 222
  Trilbies, 221
Oatmeal Griddlecakes, 117
Oeufs en Surprise, 158
Old-fashioned: Buckwheat Cakes (Yeast), 70

Corn Bread, 99
Dessert Bread (Yeast), 52
Olykoek (Yeast), 67
Orange: Almond Refrigerator Cookies, 208
  Angel Food, 147
  Biscuits, 76
  Chiffon Cake, 152
  Cookies, 214
  Cream Frosting, 342
  Custard Filling, 352
  Date Nut Loaf, 90
  Delight, 155
  Doughnuts, 106
  Filled Coffeecake, 95
  Filling, 96
  Fluff Topping, 346
  Fritters, 113
  Ice Bombe, 158
  Layer Cake, 142
  Pinwheels (Yeast), 31
  Prune Filling, 353
  Raisin Filling, 352
  Rolls (Yeast), 30
  Sauce, 354
  Sugar Frosting, 338
  Topping, 30
  Walnut Torte, 186
Oranges, Marzipan, 203
Orehnjaca (Yeast), 49

Pain d'Épice, 93
Palets de Dames, 193
Pan: Cookies, Basic, 209
  Rolls (Yeast), 25
Pan de Huevos (Mexican Egg Bread), (Yeast), 58
Pan Dulce (Sweet Egg Buns), (Yeast), 59
Pancakes: Applesauce, 116
  to bake, 116
  Banana, 116
  Basic Batter, 115
  Blinis (Yeast), 69
  Blintzes, 121
  Blueberry, 116
  Buckwheat, 117
    Old-fashioned (Yeast), 70
  Buttermilk, 116
  Corn Meal, 69

Crêpes, 122
  Ménagère, 122
  with Kirsch, 123
  with Pineapple, 124
  Suzette, 123
  Suzette, Easy, 124
German Skillet, 119
Hungarian Berry, 120
Lacy Pantycakes, 118
Mark Smith's Flapjacks, 118
Oat, 116
Plättar, 122
Potato, 117
Raw, 119
Rhode Island Johnnycakes, 119
Rolled Cream, 120
Swedish, 121
Whole Wheat, 116
Yeast, French, 68
Yogurt Oatmeal, 117
Panettone di Natale (Yeast), 58
Parker House Rolls (Yeast), 25
Pastry, 252
  Cheese, 256
  Cream Cheese, 257
  Cream Puff, 313
  Danish, 323
  Filling I, 350
    II, 351
  Flaky, 256
  Flan, 275
  Hungarian Puff, 321
  Plain, 254
  Pot Cheese, 256
  Puff, 315
  Rich Flaky, 256
  Roll: Austrian, 324
    Berry, 326
  Sour Cream, 257, 275
  Swedish, 323
  Sweet, 258
  Walnut, 257
Pastry shells, baked: Brazil Nut, 279
  Cornflake, 280
  Graham Cracker, 280
  Meringue, 280
  Wafer, 280
  Zwieback, 280
Pâte: Brisée, 275
  à Choux, 313
  Feuilletée, 315

Pâte—(Cont'd)
  à Foncer, 275
  à Frire à la Carême, 114
Peach: and Cherry Dessert, 156
  Cobbler, 77
  Fritters, 112
  Hearts, 318
  Pie: Custard, 267
    Fresh, 262
    Skillet, 299
  Pyramid, 158
  Roll, 81
  Roly Poly, 79
  Rounds, Hot, 156
  Strudel, 331
  Surprise, 157
  Tarts, Fresh, 302
  Torte, 275
  Turnovers, Poached, 307
  Upside-down Cake, 168
Peaches, Marzipan, 202
Peanut Butter: Biscuits, 76
  Cookies, 233
  Muffins, 85
Pear: Pie, Fresh, 261
  Upside-down Cake, 169
Pears, Marzipan, 202
Peas in the Pod, Marzipan, 203
Pecan: Biscuits, 76
  Cake: Bourbon, 143
    Southern, 154
  Kisses, 239
  Muffins, 85
  Nut Bread, 88
  Paste, 324
  Pie, 271
    Apple, 259
    Sour Cream, 271
  Wafers, 239
Peppermint: Angel Food, 147
  Chip Cake, 153
  Mountain Cream Frosting, 347
Petits Gâteaux Tailles, 243
Petits Fours, 190
  Filled, 191
Pets de Nonne, 114
Pfeffernuesse, 247
Pies:
  Almond: Bavarian Cream, 282
    Chocolate Chiffon, 294

Apple, 259
  Cream, 258
  Crumb, 259
  Custard, 267, 286
  Deep-dish, 298
  Honey, 259
  Pandowdy, 299
  Pecan Raisin, 259
Apricot: Chiffon, 292
  Fluff, 290
Banana Cream, 283
Black Bottom, 295
Blackberry, 263
Blueberry, 263
  Deep-dish, 298
  Kuchen, 278
Butterscotch: Chiffon, 292
  Cream, 285
Chartreuse Custard, 286
Cheese: Cottage, 272
  Pineapple, 273
  Switzerland Swiss, 273
Cherry: Fresh, 260
  Kuchen, 277
Chess, Kentucky, 269
Chocolate: Angel, 284
  Cake, 274
  Cream, 285
Coconut: Cream, 281
  Cream, Toasted, 281
  Custard, 287
Coffee: Chiffon, 292
  Custard, 287
Cranberry, 263
Custard, 266
  Coconut, 266
  Rich, 266
Eggnog Cream, 284
to freeze, 359
Fried, Little, 326
Fruit, Deep-dish, 297
Fudge, 272
Grape, 264
Lemon: Cake, 274
  Chiffon, 290
  Fluff, 289
  Meringue, 288
Lime: Chiffon, 291
  Fluff, 290
  Meringue, 289
Magdalena, 278

Maple Chiffon, 293
Mincemeat, 261
Molasses, 270
Nesselrode, 296
Peach: Custard, 267
    Fresh, 262
    Skillet, 299
Pear, Fresh, 261
Pecan, 271
    Sour Cream, 271
Pineapple: Cake, 274
    Chiffon, 296
    Custard, 287
    Fresh, 262
    and Strawberry, 262
Plum: Fresh, 262
    Pité, Hungarian, 278
Prune, 264
    Kuchen, 276
Pumpkin, 268
    Cream, 268
Raisin, 263
Raspberry: Custard, 267
    Fresh, 264
Rhubarb: Deep-dish, 299
    Fresh, 260
Rum: Chiffon, 293
    Cream, 284
Shoofly, 270
Spanish Cream, 283
Squash, New England, 269
Strawberry: Cake, 274
    Chiffon, 294
    Cream Custard, 286
    Fresh, 264
    Tart, 288
Sweet Potato, 270
Torta de Ricotta, 265
Vanilla Cream, 282
Vinegar, 265
Wine Custard, 268
See also Tortes; Turnovers
Pineapple: Cake, Upside-down, 169
    Drops, 233
    Filling, 353
    Fritters, 113
    Pie: Cake, 274
        Cheese, 273
        Chiffon, 296
            Canned, 292
        Custard, 287

    Fresh, 262
    and Strawberry, 262
    Rolls, 76
Pinwheels (Yeast), 31
    Butterscotch Pecan, 31
    Cinnamon, 31
    Coconut, 32
    Fruit and Nut, 32
    Orange, Sticky, 31
Pistachio Kisses, 241
Plättar, 122
Plum: Buns (Yeast), 35
    Pie, Fresh, 262
    Pité, Hungarian, 278
Popovers, 88
Poppy Seed: Braid (Yeast), 42
    Crescents (Yeast), 29
    Filling, 29, 34, 40, 61
    Strudel, 335
Pot Cheese Pastry, 256
Potato: Doughnuts, 108
    Pancakes, 117
    Raw, 119
    Refrigerator Doughs (Yeast), 22
        Basic, 23
        Rich Sponge Method (Yeast), 24
Pound Cake, 144
Pozsonyi Patko (Yeast), 39
Pozunski Roscici, 327
Prune: Apricot Cake (Yeast), 53
    and Apricot Filling, 34
    Filling, 33, 36
    Kuchen, 276
    Muffins, Spiced, 85
    Orange Filling, 353
    Pie, 264
    Turnovers, Fried, 308
Puddings, Baked: Apple, Dutch, 310
    Bread, Old-fashioned, 312
    Brown Betty: Apple, 309
        Rhubarb, 309
    Cherry, Black, 310
    Cocoa, Hot, 311
    Cottage, Old-fashioned, 312
    Crumb Cake, 312
    Lemon Custard, 311
Puff Pastry, 315
    Hungarian, 321
    Shells, 317
    Turnovers, 307
Puff Puffs, 319

Pumpkin: Cookies, 234
 Pie, 268
  Cream, 268
Punching down yeast dough, 7
Putica (Yeast), 50

Quick Breads. See Breads, Quick
Quick Coffeecake, 93

Raisin: Bread (Yeast), 15
 Cookies, 230
  Spice, 228
 Fig and Date Filling, 352
 Filling, 36
 Nut Buns (Yeast), 28
 Orange Filling, 352
 Pie, 263
 Tartlets, 304
Raising yeast dough, 6
Raisins: to plump, 360
 seeded, 360
 seedless, 360
Raspberry: Custard Pie, 267
 Pie, Fresh, 264
 Sauce, 354
Refrigerator: Cookies, Basic, 207
 Doughnuts (Yeast), 66
 Doughs (Yeast), 22
  Basic, 23
  how to store, 22
  Potato, 23
  Rich Potato, Sponge Method, 23
Religieuse, 316
Rhode Island Johnnycakes, 119
Rhubarb: Brown Betty, 309
 Dumplings, 77
 Pie, Fresh, 260
  Deep-dish, 299
 Roll, and Strawberry, 80
Ribbon Cake. See List of Illustrations
Rice Cakes, 109
Rings of Puff Paste, 314
Rocks, 236
Rococo Torte, 185
Rolled: Cookies, Basic, 208
 Cream Pancakes, 120
 Date Cookies, 232
 Fruit Dumplings, 80
 Wafers, 216
Rolls, Sweet, how to make from Plain Bread Dough, 13

Rolls and Breads, Sweet Yeast: fillings, 21
 to freshen, 10
 to freeze, 356
 frosting, 21
 garnishes, 21
 glazing, 21
Rolls and Muffins, Sweet Yeast:
 Bath Buns, 62
 Bowknots, 27
 Brioches, 63
 Butterflies, 26
 Buttermilk Rolls, 37
 Cinnamon: Buns, 57
  Twists, 30
 Cloverleaf Rolls, 26
 Coconut Buns, 28
 Coffee Twists, 57
 Corn Muffins, 29
 Crescents, 26
 Crossettes, 27
 Crumpets, 41
 Cushions, 27
 Dinner Rolls, 26
 English Muffins, 41
 Fan Tans, 26
 Figure 8 Rolls, 28
 Honey: Fingers, 30
  Snails, 30
 Horns: Butter, 40
  Filled, 39
 Hot Cross Buns: Old English, 37
  from Sweet Dough, 36
 Hungarian Filled, 35
 Kolacky, 33
 Lemon Drops, 36
 Long Johns, 27
 Lucky Clovers, 26
 Orange Rolls, 30
 Pan Dulce, 59
 Pan Rolls, 25
 Parker House Rolls, 25
 Pinwheels, 31
  Butterscotch Pecan, 31
  Cinnamon, 31
  Coconut, 32
  Fruit and Nut, 32
  Orange, Sticky, 31
 Plum Buns, 35
 Poppy Seed Crescents, 29
 Raisin Nut Buns, 28

Rosettes, 28
Saffron Buns, 38
Schnecken, 39
Snails, 28
Sour Cream Twists, 40
Surprise Rolls, 32
    Almond, 33
    Apricot, 33
    Date, 33
    Orange, 33
    Marshmallow, 33
    Pecan, 33
Tea Puffs, 25
Triple Deckers, 27
Two-in-One Twists, 28
Roly Poly, Fruit, 79
    Suet, 79
Rosettes, 215
    (Yeast), 28
Royal Icing, 337
Rum: Cake, 151
    Cake Dessert, 156
    Cream Topping, 347
    Pastry Cream, 348
    Pie: Chiffon, 293
        Cream, 284
Rusks (Yeast), 70
Russian: Nut Balls, 242
    Tea Cake, 151
    Icing, 345
Rye Bread: Molasses (Yeast), 15
    Sour Dough (Yeast), 18
    Swedish (Yeast), 18

Sabayon Sauce, 355
Sacher Torte, 183
Saffron Buns (Yeast), 38
Sally Lunn (Yeast), 18
Salt Rising Bread, 16
Sauces: Apricot, 354
    Brandy, Foamy, 355
    Butterscotch, 353
    Chocolate, Thin, 353
    Fruit, 355
    Hard, 355
    Jam or Jelly, 354
    Lemon, 354
    Orange, 354
    Raspberry, 354
    Sabayon, 355
    Strawberry, 354

Savarin (Yeast), 64
Savory Teasers, 76
Schaum Torte, 181
Schnecken (Yeast), 39
    Danish, 323
Scones: Drop Griddle, 83
    Griddle, 82
    Oven, 82
Scotch: Shortbread, 243
    Wafers, 243
Scottish Fancies, 222
7-Minute Frosting, 347
    Lemon, 347
Shaping yeast dough into loaves, 8
Shoofly Pie, 270
Shortbread: Almond, 238
    Scotch, 243
Simnel Cake, 163
Skillet: Cake, German, 119
    Pie, Peach, 299
Snails (Yeast), 28
Sour Cherry Cake (Yeast), 56
Sour Cream: Biscuits, 76
    Cookies, 211
    Frosting, 346
    Kuchen Dough (Yeast), 54
    Muffins, 85
    Pastry, 257, 275
    Pecan Pie, 271
    Snails (Yeast), 28
    Strudel, 335
    Twists (Yeast), 40
    Waffles, 126
Sour Dough: French Bread (Yeast), 16
    Rye Bread (Yeast), 18
Sour Milk: Butter Cake, 142
    Chocolate Cake, 140
    Cookies, 212
    Corn Bread, 99
    Doughnuts, 107
    Muffins, 85
Spaetzel (Yeast), 57
Spanish: Cream Pie, 283
    Sweet Bread (Yeast), 43
Spice: Cake with Brown Sugar Meringue, 135
    Cookies, 228
        Christmas, 228
        Raisin, 228

Spice—(*Cont'd*)
 Doughnuts, 107
 and Honey Cookies, 229
Spicecake Tarts, 305
Spiced: Doughnuts (Yeast), 66
 Muffins, 85
 Prune Muffins, 85
Spider Corncake, 100
Spongecake: Basic, 147
 Easy, 149
 Jiffy, 149
 Waffles, 127
Spoon Bread, 104
 Hominy, 103
 Virginia, 104
Spring Bonnet, 197
Springerle, 244
Spritz, 246
Spun Sugar, 200
Squash Pie, New England, 269
Stars, 250
Steps in making yeast bread, 6
Stollen (Yeast), 55
Storing yeast bread, 9
Strawberries, Marzipan, 202
Strawberry: Cake, 176
  Cream-filled, 159
 Cheese Flan, 173
 Cream, 350
 Frosting, 4-Minute, 348
 Glaze, 173
 Pie: Cake, 274
   Chiffon, 294
   Cream Custard, 286
   Fresh, 264
 and Pineapple Pie, 262
 and Rhubarb Roll, 80
 Roll, 150
 Sauce, 354
 Shortcake. *See* List of Illustrations
 Tart, 258, 288
 Tarts, 303
 Vanilla Cream, 350
Strudels: Almond, 333
 Apple, 331
 Cherry: Sour, 331
   Sweet, 331
 Chocolate, 334
 Cottage Cheese, 332
 Cream Cheese, 332
 Dough for, 330

 Layer, 335
 Lemon, 334
 Peach, 331
 Poppy Seed, 335
 Sour Cream, 335
 Tyrolese, 333
Suet Roly Poly, 79
Sugar: Colored, 250
 Pulled, 199
 Spun, 200
Surprise: Biscuits, 76
 Muffins, 85
 Rolls (Yeast), 32, 33
Swedish: Macaroons, 246
 Pancakes, 121
 Pastry, 323
 Rye Bread (Yeast), 18
 Sand Tarts, 248
 Struvor, 215
 Tea Ring (Yeast), 45
Sweet: Bread and Rolls (Yeast), 20
 Dough: Basic (Yeast), 21
   to make from Plain Bread Dough, 13
   Whole Wheat (Yeast), 22
 Pastry, 258
Sweet Potato: Biscuits, 76
 Pie, 270
Swiss Fried Cakes, 109
Switzerland Swiss Cheese Pie, 273

Tart Shells: to bake, 300
 Cream Fillings for, 301
 Fresh Fruit or Berry Fillings for, 301
 Fruit and Cream Fillings for, 301
Tarts: Almond, 304
 Apricot Rum, 303
 Autrichiennes, 301
 Black Cherry, 302
 Chess, 306
 Coconut, 304
 Peach, Fresh, 302
 Raisin, 304
 Spicecake, 305
 Strawberry, 258, 303
 Transparent, 305
Tea Puffs (Yeast), 25
Tea Rings. *See* Cakes and Kuchens, Yeast

Ten Commandments for Successful Baking, 361
Thimble Biscuits, 76
Thousand Leaves Torte, 188
Tiroler, 322
Torta de Ricotta, 265
Tortes: Almond, 186
  Apple, 275
  Applesauce, 277
  Blitz, 180
  Blueberry, 276
  Cherry, Country Style, 276
  Chocolate, 183
    Soufflé, 184
  Date and Walnut, 185
  Dobos, 179
  Gooseberry, 276
  Hazelnut, 180
  Linzer, 182
  Mocha, 184
  Orange Walnut, 186
  Peach, 275
  Rococo, 185
  Sacher, 183
  Schaum, 181
  Thousand Leaves, 188
  Vanilla, 187
  Walnut, 187
  Zwieback, 186
Transparent Tarts, 305
Trilbies, 221
Turnovers, 209
  Baking Powder, 76
  Banbury, 308
  Cherry, 307
  Currant and Honey, 30
  Fruit: Mixed, 306
    Preserved, 306
  Marmalade, 308
  Peach, Poached, 307
  Prune, Fried, 308
  Puff Pastry, 307
Twisted Rolls (Yeast), 27
  Bowknots, 27
  Figure 8, 28
  Rosettes, 28
  Snails, 28
Two-in-One Twists (Yeast), 28
Tyrolese Strudel, 333

Ukrainian Easter Bread (Yeast), 59

Valentine: Cake, 196
  Cookies, 251
Vegetable Fritters, 110
Vienna Bread (Yeast), 13
Vinegar Pie, 265
Violets: Crystallized, 200
  Marzipan, 202

Wafer Pastry Shell, 280
Waffles, 124
  Apple, 125
  Banana, 125
  Buttermilk, 126
  Chocolate, 127
  Cocoa, 125
  Corn Bread, 126
  Dessert, Rich, 126
  Fruit, 125
  Gaufres Parisiennes, 128
  Gingerbread, 127
  Nut, 125
  Sour Cream, 126
  Spongecake, 127
  Yeast, 68
  Yogurt, 126
Walnut: and Coconut Bars, 235
  Chiffon Cake, Bit o', 153
  and Date Torte, 185
  Filling, 40, 50
  Orange Torte, 186
  Paste, 324
  Pastry, 257
  Squares, 234
  Sticks, 234
  Torte, 187
Water Rolls, Plain Crusty, Vienna Type (Yeast), 14
Wedding Cake, 163
  3-Tiered, 165
What constitutes a good loaf of bread, 10
White Cake: Layer, 144
  One-egg, 132
Whole Wheat: Biscuits, 77
  Bread (Yeast), 15
  100%, 19
  Coffeecake with Dates (Yeast), 48
  Muffins, 85
  Nut Bread, 89
  Pancakes, 116
  Sweet Dough, Basic (Yeast), 22

Wild Roses, Marzipan, 202
Wine: Batter for Fritters, 111
    Custard Pie, 268
Woolly Lamb, 197
Wreaths, 250

Yeast, 2
    amount of, 3
    compressed, 3
    dry, 3
    heat, 3
    moisture, 3
Yeast Breads. *See* Breads, Yeast
Yeast Corn Muffins, 29
Yeast Doughs: food for, 4
    to make a dough that is 80° F., 4
    to make Sweet Dough from Plain Bread Dough, 13

Plain Bread Dough, 10
    Sponge Method, 12
Yeast Pancakes: Blinis, 69
    Buckwheat, 70
    Corn Meal, 69
    French, 68
Yeast Rolls. *See* Rolls, Sweet Yeast
Yogurt: Corn Meal Squares, 101
    Johnnycake, 102
    Oatmeal Griddlecakes, 117
    Waffles, 126
Yorkshire Pudding, 83

Zucker Hütchen, 248
Zuckersträuben, 115
Zwieback (Yeast), 71
    Pastry Shell, 280
    Torte, 186